Everyday Islamic Law and the Making of Modern South Asia

Islamic Civilization and Muslim Networks

Carl W. Ernst and Bruce B. Lawrence, *editors*

Highlighting themes with historical as well as contemporary significance, Islamic Civilization and Muslim Networks features works that explore Islamic societies and Muslim peoples from a fresh perspective, drawing on new interpretive frameworks or theoretical strategies in a variety of disciplines. Special emphasis is given to systems of exchange that have promoted the creation and development of Islamic identities—cultural, religious, or geopolitical. The series spans all periods and regions of Islamic civilization.

A complete list of titles published in this series appears at the end of the book.

Everyday Islamic Law and the Making of Modern South Asia

ELIZABETH LHOST

The University of North Carolina Press Chapel Hill

This book was published with the assistance of Dartmouth College.

Set in Charis by Westchester Publishing Services
Manufactured in the United States of America

The University of North Carolina Press has been a member
of the Green Press Initiative since 2003.

Complete Cataloging-in-Publication information for this title
is available through the Library of Congress.

ISBN 978-1-4696-6811-6 (cloth: alk. paper)
ISBN 978-1-4696-6812-3 (pbk.: alk. paper)
ISBN 978-1-4696-6813-0 (ebook)

Cover illustrations: Photo of the mufti's library at the Madrasa Aminiya in
Delhi, with photos of fatwa files (upper left corner) and postcard stamps
(background, center blue title square).

To everyone who has tried to make sense of the law

Contents

Figures, Maps, and Table

Figures

Maps

Table

Note on Translation and Transliteration

Transliteration follows Francis Joseph Steingass's *Comprehensive Persian-English Dictionary.*[1] For the sake of clarity, I have omitted the final hamza on many words that appear throughout the text (e.g., *iftā'*, *istiftā'*). When possible, I retain the original, archival spellings of names (e.g., Hyatoolakhan vs. Ḥayāt Allāh Ḵẖān) to reflect (and respect) orthographical difference across South Asia.[2] To aid the reader, I supplement these original spellings with full transliteration in brackets, acknowledging that access to multiple spellings can be beneficial for some readers. For place-names, I retain the historical spellings (e.g., Bombay vs. Mumbai) but have noted current or conventional spellings in brackets for clarity (e.g., Broach [Bharuch]). Other terms (e.g., *kazi, kadi, cazy, cauzy, cazee, qazee, qadi*, etc.) appear as written when taken from archival sources but otherwise appear according to Persian/Urdu pronunciation (e.g., *qazi* vs. *qadi*) in the main text. For terms that have entered the English language (e.g., mufti, begum), I follow Merriam-Webster. All translations from Persian, Urdu, Arabic, and other languages are my own, unless otherwise noted.

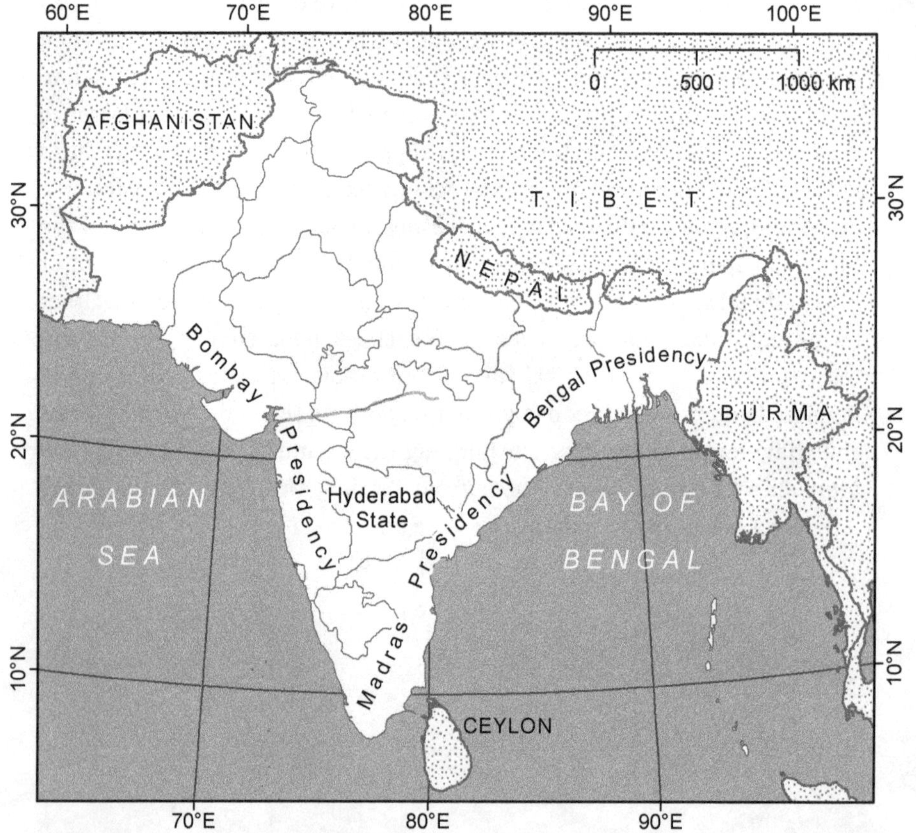

British India, showing the presidencies of Bombay, Bengal, and Madras. Created by Jonathan W. Chipman, Dartmouth College.

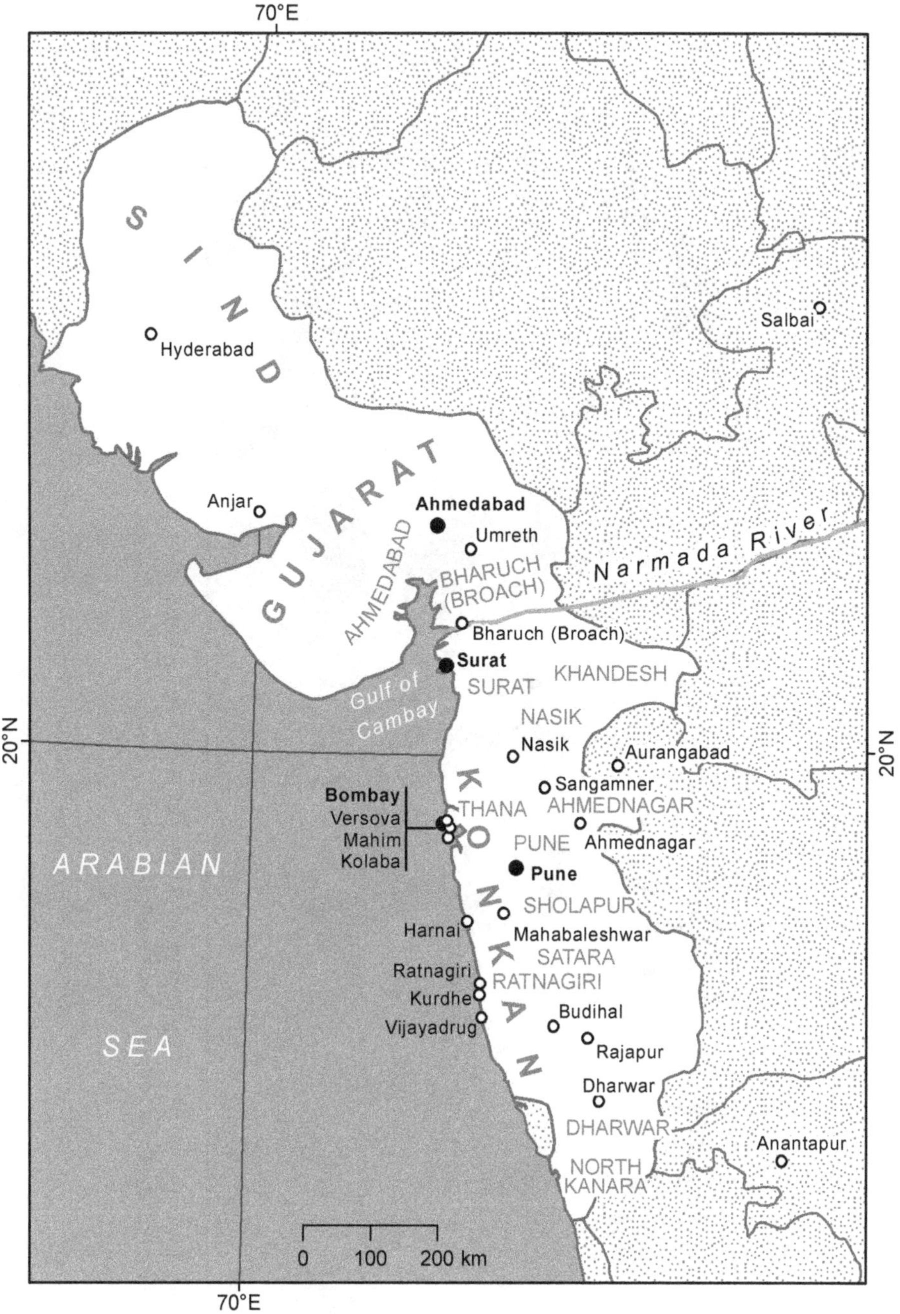

The Bombay Presidency, showing regions and places of interest.
Created by Jonathan W. Chipman, Dartmouth College.

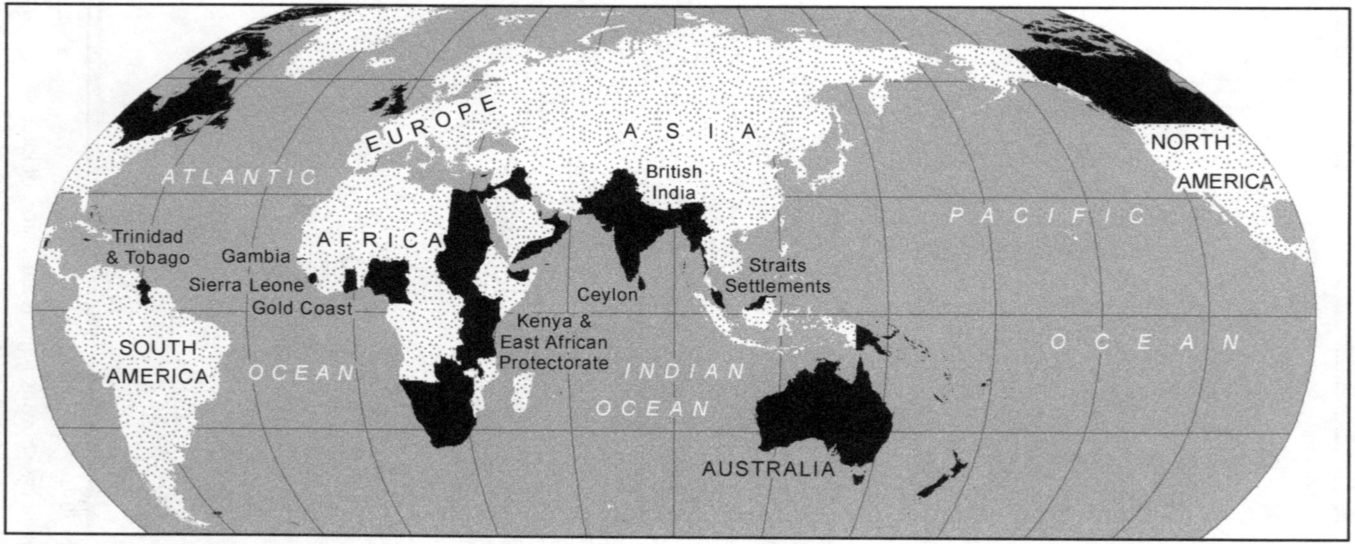

The British Empire, showing the places where laws relating to Muslim marriages were enacted.
Created by Jonathan W. Chipman, Dartmouth College.

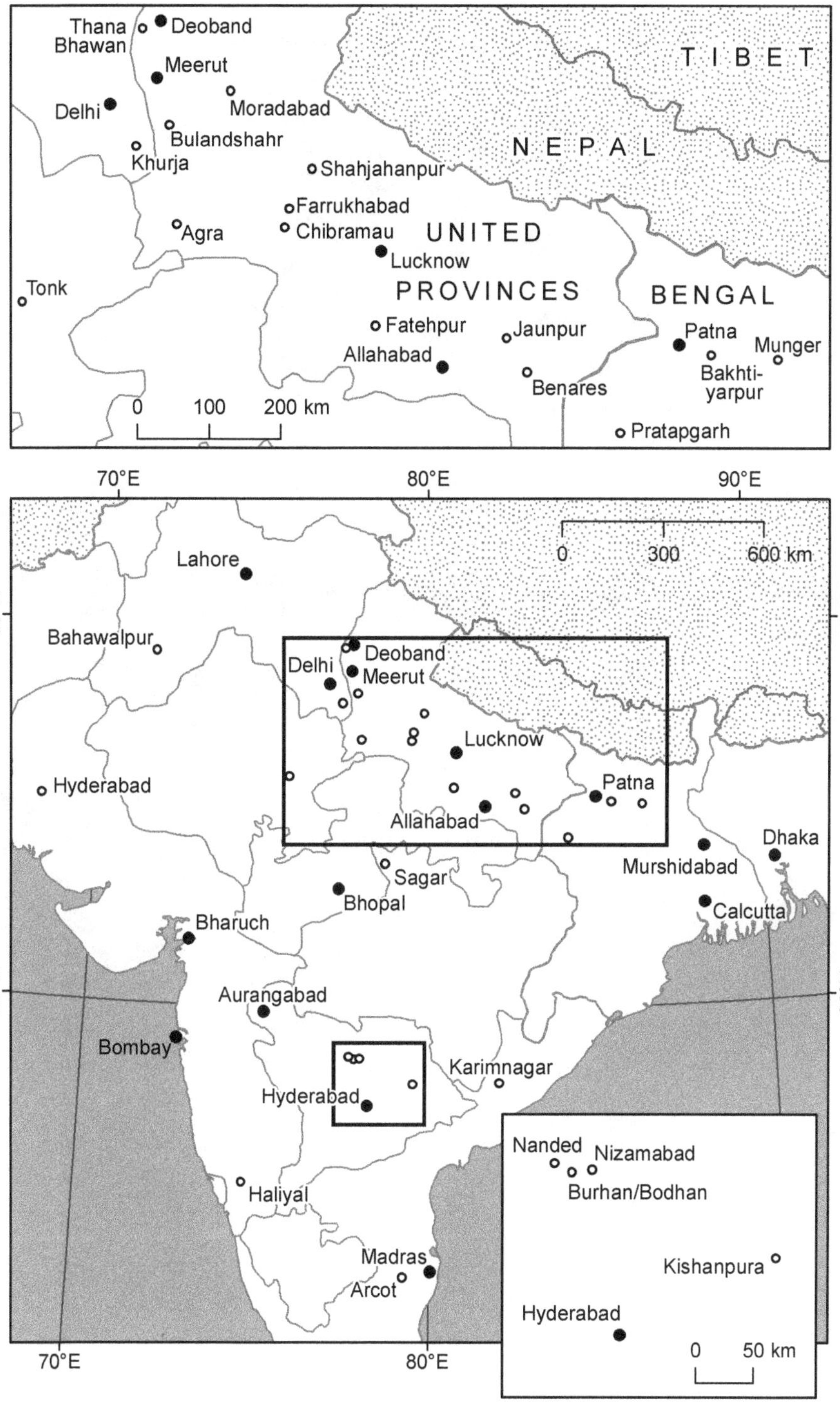

British India, marking places of interest.
Created by Jonathan W. Chipman, Dartmouth College.

Everyday Islamic Law and the Making of Modern South Asia

SUNDAY EDITION

REGD. NO. B. 1065

The Bombay Chronicle

FOUNDED BY SIR PHEROZESHAH M. MEHTA IN 1913

VOL. XIX NO 32— BOMBAY SUNDAY, AUGUST 16, 1931 PRICE TWO ANNAS.

True To Islamic Traditions.

Moulana Mohamed Sajjad, Naib Amir Shariat, Bihar.

Moulana Ahmad Saeed, Secretary Jamiat-ul-Ulema-i-Hind.

Moulana Mufti Kifayatullah, President of the Jamiat-ul-Ulema-i-Hind, an institution which stands for Joint Electorates.

Moulana Hifzur Rahman, a member of the Working Committee of the Jamiat-ul-Ulema.

Mr. Rafi Ahmad Kidwai, Secretary All-India Nationalist Muslim Party.

FIGURE 0.1 Front page of the *Bombay Chronicle*, August 16, 1931, showing Mufti Muhammad Kifayatullah prominently featured in a photo array, along with several other leading members of the *ʿulama* (scholarly community).

Introduction

Life, Law, and Legal History

Picturing Law

In August 1931 the *Bombay Chronicle* published a picture of Muftī Muḥammad Kifāyatullāh (ca. 1875–1952) alongside coverage of the Indian National Congress Working Committee's recent meetings in Bombay (figure 0.1).[1] Shortly after its publication, a reader of the *Chronicle* asked Kifayatullah about the photograph.[2] The reader likely knew about Kifayatullah's work as an Islamic legal scholar and was perhaps also familiar with the Islamic legal opinions (fatwas; *fatāwá*) he had written—including fatwas against photography.[3] Was the mufti aware that his photograph had appeared in the Bombay newspaper, and did he consider its publication permissible (*jāʾiz*)? the reader inquired. Drawing attention to the photograph's unexpected publication, the *Chronicle*'s unnamed reader called on the mufti to account for his presence in the paper and to make sense of the rules he had seemingly broken.

Two months after the photograph appeared, in October 1931, Kifayatullah addressed the reader's concerns by writing a fatwa for his own periodical, the Urdu-language newspaper *Al-Jamʿīyat*, which was published by the organization he headed as president, the Jamʿiyat-ul-ʿUlama-yi Hind (Council of Indian Muslim Theologians): "I consider it impermissible [*nā-jāʾiz*] to take photos [*fōṭō lēnā*] or to have photos taken [*fōṭō banwānā*]," he began, before continuing, "I did not give anyone permission to take my photo . . . I also do not know who took this photo or when it was taken. . . . These days, anyone's photo might be taken with a hand[held] camera [*dastī-kaimrōn̲ sē*] without him even knowing. That is how my photo must have been taken."[4] More an explanation or justification than an edict or decree, the mufti explained that the publication of his photograph in the newspaper did not mean that he had granted the photographer permission, nor had he agreed to be photographed. Technology made it possible for the photographer to publish the photo without his permission.

Kifayatullah printed this fatwa in the "Ḥawādiṣ wa Aḥkām" (Incidents and injunctions) column of *Al-Jamʿīyat*.[5] It included the reader's greeting, "Honored and respected Mufti, Sir, may your shadow never vanish," and ended with the mufti's sign-off, "Muhammad Kifayatullah, may God forgive him, *Madrasa Amīnīya, Dihlī*." Sandwiched between these lines was a brief description of the incident, followed by the mufti's response to it, presented in the form of a fatwa—a legal question and answer. Rooted in communication networks tied to the vibrant English and Urdu public spheres, the entire exchange represented the new character and contours of Islamic legal discourse in twentieth-century South Asia. It was, in other words, an example of everyday Islamic law. The reader's question was simple, the mufti's response straightforward, yet the exchange participated in a wider world of Islamic legal activity in which ordinary individuals (newspaper readers) and legal experts (muftis) played important roles; in which postcards, letters, and telegrams carried their exchanges; and for which expert opinions were as dependent on religious fundamentals as they were on changing circumstances and diverse experiences. In the context of nationalist movements and political change, this exchange stands out not for being unique or extraordinary but for being routine and ordinary. It was, and is, one of thousands of possible examples of everyday Islamic law and legal practice from this period.

Traveling from Bombay, where the *Chronicle* was published, to the Jamʿiyat's headquarters in Delhi, the reader's question tied English-language reporting on political events in one region to a legal opinion published in an Urdu-language newspaper elsewhere. It tied the political activities of the Indian National Congress to the status and reputation of Indian Muslim leaders and the institutions they ran; and it linked Kifayatullah's writings on Islamic law, photography, and life in British India to the public sphere of English- and vernacular-language newspapers, periodicals, and the broader circulation of information on the subcontinent.[6] Everyday Islamic law bound together these (and other) activities in an evolving sense of being and belonging in the world—one that was tied up in law but framed by circumstance; that was constant and unrelenting yet commonplace and accommodating; and that drew from time-honored traditions yet was characterized by modern technology and tools. *Everyday Islamic Law and the Making of Modern South Asia* tells the story of how these practices came into being, how they contributed to the making of modern South Asia, and how they produced the plurality, multiplicity, and possibility that have defined it since then.

"Everyday Islamic law" refers to a cluster of overlapping and intersecting practices that developed across the nineteenth century in response to the challenges of foreign rule, in conjunction with the rise of technological modernity, and alongside the shrinking of time and space that accompanied the expansion of steam navigation and print communications. Focusing on the social history of law, I use the expression "everyday Islamic law" to describe the quotidian practices and banal encounters that came to define ordinary individuals' engagement with and understanding of law. By focusing on the "law" part of everyday Islamic law, I recognize a common distinction between *sharīʿa*—divine guidance for correct living—and Islamic law, the earthly and human-driven interpretation of that guidance. Yet the history of everyday Islamic law is about more than simply separating divine guidance from its earthly manifestations and its particular interpretations for a specific time and place. It is also about the rise of the modern, administrative state and its effects on ordinary individuals' understandings of what law is and the influence it has on their everyday affairs. Teasing apart the legacies of the colonial state, the modern state, and the postcolonial nation-state in South Asian society has been a principal preoccupation among historians of South Asia for decades.[7] This study builds on that robust literature but does so by shifting the focus away from nationalism and the nation-state to the procedural mechanisms of law and the process of legal change. In this book, then, law is not an object that can be picked up and analyzed outside the social context in which it originates. Rather, "law" is an amalgamation of strategies and tactics (to borrow from Michel de Certeau's discussion of the "everyday") that come into being when called on to solve problems, settle disputes, or define one's place in the world.[8]

Law and society scholars use the term "legal consciousness" to describe ordinary individuals' engagements with law. On one level, this term encapsulates and reflects lay persons' ideas about justice and equity—the higher aims and objects of "law" and the legal system. People go to court because they feel they have been wronged and want the courts to do something about it. They want their neighbor to pay and to prove that they are right and he is wrong.[9] On another level, "legal consciousness" refers to the knowledge and wherewithal that ordinary individuals possess about the law—what it means, what it does, and how it works.[10] Sometimes, this knowledge accurately reflects formal legal procedure: if I want to sue my neighbor, I must file this form; if I want to contest my tax bill, I must follow this process. Other times, it does not. In the words of socio-legal scholar Sally Merry, law is "a complex repertoire of meanings and categories understood differently by different people depending on their experience with and knowledge of the law."[11] The ordinary individuals who populate parts II and III of this book possess this type of knowledge to varying degrees. They (or their relatives, allies, supporters, and adversaries) have some knowledge of what the law is and how it works, but they have gaps, lapses, inconsistencies, and uncertainties in their knowledge.[12] In most cases, they enter the archive—and their experience with legal expertise begins—where their informal knowledge ends.[13] They also carry with them an interest in doing what is "right" or "just" in relation to their circumstances and in relation to what it means to be a good Muslim. Their legal consciousness is not only patchy but also layered.

Along with the story of everyday legal consciousness, this book also tells the story of a rising *Islamic* legal consciousness in the context of colonial legal pluralism. Legal pluralism—with different laws applied to different groups (citizens/foreigners; adults/children)—has always been a feature of human societies, but beginning in the sixteenth century, European imperial expansion created unique flavors of legal pluralism that have had lasting effects on postcolonial societies.[14] British India's brand of legal pluralism separated personal, family law from public law (making areas of family law the exception to the general rule of law) and made religion (and religious identity) the basis for legal distinction, beginning with distinctions between Hindus and Muslims but eventually expanding to other communities and becoming a defining feature of South Asian secularism.[15] If "everyday law" refers to rising legal consciousness in response to the expansion of the modern state, then "everyday Islamic law" refers to Muslims' experiences navigating and negotiating British India's variegated legal terrain as Muslims and in conjunction with Islam.[16]

As with the troubles that arise from efforts to disentangle modernity from colonial modernity, the emergence of everyday Islamic law is also bound up in changing definitions of law. Wedded to the idea of the nation and trapped in the framework of written legislation, most efforts to implement Islamic governance today embrace the project of "legislating shariʿa."[17] This approach assumes different forms in different contexts, but as critics contend, moving from shariʿa to statute either misses the point of divine guidance entirely or obscures the forest for the sake of the trees.[18] My approach to everyday Islamic law departs from these didactic, prescriptive approaches to focus less on what Islamic law should be and more on how ordinary individuals made sense of what the law was or could be. Each part of the expression thus works in tandem to form everyday Islamic law.

The idea of the "everyday" gestures toward the quotidian contexts and banal practices that constitute ordinary individuals' engagements with law.[19] Law, in this framework, is not separate from everyday life. Rather, law and everyday life are "mutually constitutive."[20] Much the same way Certeau describes the subconscious or semiconscious strategies of planning, preparing, and executing an evening meal, the people who occupy the social history outlined in this book draw on tools that are available to them and knowledge they have accumulated (sometimes formally but often informally) to work toward the aims and objectives they hope to fulfill (defined in part by their needs and also by social context).[21] In reflecting on Islam in the context of the everyday, Islamic law's consumers, then, also contribute to the history of secularism and the secularization of British India, recognizing (but not always accepting) the separation of law and politics from religion and family.[22] If "the everyday" refers to practices that are at once conscious and unconscious, prescribed and implied, quotidian and mundane, then the choice to engage with specific legal genres, experts, and fora makes those practices "Islamic."[23]

While the making of everyday law is tied to the evolution of the modern state more broadly, the specific forms interrogated here reflect the process of making that law distinctly Islamic, as it became part of what defined one's life in relation to Islam; gave shape to one's familial, interpersonal, and economic relations; and defined those relationships in terms of being Muslim. It determined how one would live, work, and play in the world. Yet in so doing, everyday Islamic law operated not at the level of diktats or decrees but at the level of conversations, inquiries, dialogues, and debates. Today, with much of the popular discourse portraying Islamic law negatively, newcomers to the field of Islamic legal studies expect to encounter something baffling, terrifying, or even awe-inspiring. Few expect to encounter the quotidian inquiries that ordinary Muslims made or the banal issues that they brought to legal experts, and fewer still expect to find Islamic law expressed in generic forms like letters and newspaper columns. Whereas postcards, telegrams, pamphlets, and printed stationery defined everyday Islamic law in the nineteenth and early twentieth centuries, today one might instead locate it in text messages, email inboxes, YouTube videos, and television programs.[24] The modalities change with each generation, but the patterns of ordinary inquiry and quotidian interpretation that characterized Islamic legal practice in the nineteenth century still resonate today, as debates continue over who defines, interprets, and controls Islamic law across parliamentary, political, and institutional forms.[25] The *Chronicle* reader's inquiry, one of thousands of inquiries that ordinary individuals transmitted in the first half of the twentieth century, was part of this larger process.

Like the *Chronicle* reader's exchange with Kifayatullah, everyday Islamic law depended as much on material forms as it did on ideological commitments. Trading in documents, registers, files, and forms, the British East India Company (EIC) bred a fetishization of documentary forms that drew from earlier, precolonial interests in writing, reading, and recording but accelerated under British rule.[26] Not only did the Company and Crown governments introduce innumerable laws pertaining to documentation, but they also engaged in acts of reviewing, authenticating, and validating precolonial documents. Colonial law's emphasis on material forms undergirded and propelled a corresponding turn toward written documents among Islamic legal practitioners, who not only commented on the meanings and implications of the Anglo-Indian legal system's documentary requirements but also worked to make Islamic legal practice compatible with those demands. The result was a hybrid system of legal activity that adopted the material forms of the colonial state but simultaneously pushed back against that state's authority.

By this token, technology and materiality are necessarily part of the story here, but they are not its sole point of origin. It would be difficult to imagine everyday Islamic law emerging as it did without the availability or accessibility of increasingly complex documentary forms and the technologies that enabled their production, but the networks of exchange from which they grew and the patterns of migration and mobility on which they relied had antecedents in the precolonial period as well.[27] Communications technologies facilitated the exchange of ideas from South India to the north, from East Africa to North India, from Mecca to Meerut, but these exchanges could not have flourished without the broader interest that Muslims took in what their coreligionists over there, in that place, or halfway around the world were doing.[28] Likewise, print culture enabled the publication and dissemination of new ideas, but its arrival and availability played only a small role in promoting the cultures of citation, quotation, and accountability that accelerated with its arrival. Scholasticism and an investment in textuality had deep roots in Islamic learning before the arrival of these technologies, though new modalities certainly extended and expanded their reach.[29]

In addition to drawing on new technologies, everyday Islamic law also emerged from new institutions. These institutions included the ones where students studied and scholars trained, where books were authored and periodicals published, where debates were held and divergent opinions addressed. They were the places where scholars of Islamic law set up offices specifically for the purposes of receiving and responding to legal questions (the *dār-ul-iftā᾽*, fatwa institute), including the government-sponsored dar-ul-ifta in Hyderabad and the Madrasa Aminiya in Delhi, where Kifayatullah worked. They were newly formed institutes like the Dar-ul-ʿUlum at Deoband (est. 1866), Nadwat-ul-ʿUlama in Lucknow (est. 1891–94), and the Muhammadan Anglo-Oriental College in Aligarh (est. 1875)—all of which borrowed from British models, built on existing Islamic foundations, and grew from established centers of learning like those of the famed Farangi Mahall family.[30] They were civic societies and social organizations like the Anjuman-i Islam (Islamic Society) in Mumbai, whose president consulted the government on judicial appointments in 1879; the Anjuman-i Panjab (Punjab Society), which compiled a multipage report in 1880 outlining the status of Islamic judges (*qāẓīs*) in response to proposed legislation relating to them; and the Anjuman-i Mustashar-ul-ʿUlama (Society of Consulted Scholars) in Lahore, which published a collection of *fatāwá* using consensus and collective authorship in 1907.[31] Printing presses and publishers, which Islamic legal practitioners like the qazis in Meerut commissioned to print their marriage registers and like the dar-ul-ifta in Hyderabad hired to print its innovative fatwa forms, were also part of this institutional landscape.[32] These institutions gave shape to and made accessible the practice of everyday Islamic law, through the physical offices (*daftars*, *dafātir*) they occupied, the written records and registers (*daftars*, *dafātir*) they introduced, the routine procedures they employed, and the spaces they created for conversation, discussion, and exchange.[33]

By participating in this wider world of everyday Islamic law, the unnamed *Chronicle* reader was doing more than verifying the substance of the legal question on the permissibility of representing human figures in photographs. He was also thinking about Islamic law in action. Assuming that he was already aware of the mufti's stance against photography (as the question's phrasing seems to imply), then he was also checking the general rule's application to this specific context. In response, the mufti's reference to "these days" (*āj-kal*) was an acknowledgment that context mattered: the rules were not timeless, their application not blind, nor their interpretation eternal. Authoring an answer that reflected the contingency of the moment, Kifayatullah acknowledged the photo's presence, denied his acquiescence to its publication, and reiterated his general stance against photography. Using the newspaper, printing press, and fatwa form, he, too, contributed to the making of everyday Islamic law.

Legal Practitioners and the Making of Everyday Islamic Law

The everyday Islamic law that developed across the nineteenth century was orchestrated by Islamic legal practitioners and motivated by ordinary individuals. Qazis and muftis, the two groups of professionals under consideration here, each traced their origins back to the time of the Prophet. In their earlier iterations, qazis (*qāḍī/qāẓī*), a title conventionally translated as "judge," "Islamic judge," or "shariʿa-court judge," supervised the day-to-day administration of justice.[34] They were typically appointed by rulers (emperors, sultans, or governors) and were responsible for executing imperial orders and upholding God's commands on earth. From the outset, however, the qazi's commitments to interpreting divine will, on the one hand, and to representing the state, on the other, complicated his position.[35] Moral duty made it incumbent on appointees to accept their nominations, but everyone recognized the moral hazards of holding a judgeship, owing to the corrupting influence of earthly temptations and rewards.[36] Evidence of the judgeship's putative irreverence is available in sources ranging from Arabic maxims, to the Eurasian folktales that influenced William Shakespeare's plays, to Max Weber's critical writings on the despotism of arbitrary *kadijustiz* (qadi-justice), to the judicial opinions of American jurist Felix Frankfurter (1882–1965).[37] Undoubtedly, some assessments of the qazi's baseness and corruption were true. After all, despite their assignment to uphold God's will on earth, qazis were human and therefore susceptible to the temptations and pleasures of bodily existence. At the same time, however, many also had long (and successful) careers as ordinary, run-of-the-mill bureaucrats and administrators in Islamic states from Sumatra to sub-Saharan Africa and from Turkey to Tunisia.[38] While much work still remains to uncover the granular details of the lives and careers of these imperial agents, studies looking at qazis across the Islamic world have provided historians with a rich picture of what it was like to serve as an "Islamic judge."[39] For some cases, first-person narratives and the diaries of prominent jurists can supplement the details historians have painstakingly gleaned from the court records (*sijills*) that imperial qazis left behind.[40] Yet despite their richness, most of these studies examine the qazi's role in Muslim states, for the premodern period, or in Muslim-majority states, for the modern period.[41] The history outlined here departs from that scholarship first by looking at qazis in a colonial context and second by looking at the history of the qazi's office in a Muslim-minority setting.

The qazi, the Islamic state's judge-administrator, was accompanied by the mufti, its scholar-jurist. Muftis, who qualify for office through their training and expertise in *futyā* or *iftāʾ* (resolving legal questions), also have their origins in practices of inquiry and analysis that first emerged during the Prophet's lifetime and subsequently expanded into a robust practice of legal inquiry, evaluation, and opinion writing.[42] Where qazis sat in court and heard cases, often involving disputes between two or more parties, muftis occupied more scholastic spaces—schools (*madrasas*), libraries (*kutb-k̲h̲ānas*), and universities. There, they engaged in deep study and intellectual inquiry, plumbing the revealed sources—the Qurʾan (revealed text) and Hadith (recorded sayings of the Prophet)—for insights and employing analytical methods, drawn from logic and philosophy, to determine the application of divine principles to real-world scenarios. They developed systematic means for creating analogies to extend existing principles to new cases and precise methods for evaluating and ranking possible interpretations. They produced scholarly lineages that guided these approaches and facilitated their opinion writing. These lineages eventually became recognized as "schools" of jurisprudence (*maz̲hab*, pl. *maz̲āhib*). Adherence to or departure from one's school varies by jurists over time, but in South Asia, the Ḥanafī school has been dominant among the subcontinent's inland and northern Muslims, while the Shāfiʿī school maintains a robust presence along the southwest coast. Following the traditions of his school shaped a mufti's approach to legal questions and the sources he might consult to support his answer but did not necessarily dictate it. The making of everyday Islamic law called on muftis to offer shariʿa-minded guidance on a range of new issues and ideas, many of which became "legal" ideas (as opposed to moral or ethical concerns) in response to colonial legal change.

From the formative period onward, whenever new technologies came into existence, muftis would reason on the basis of their similarity to or difference from existing technologies to determine whether their use was acceptable or unacceptable, laudable or condemnable, or perhaps simply neutral.[43] When new crops, foodstuffs, stimulants, social structures, environments, or peoples entered Islamic states, muftis addressed questions of assimilating, tolerating, differentiating, or accepting new goods and peoples in those contexts.[44] From then until now, muftis have continued to engage with questions of novelty in light of principles and precepts passed down from the Prophet and in line with their own abilities to rationalize, comprehend, engage with, or accept those innovations. Today, with countless online fora and digital media dedicated to interpreting legal issues and offering religio-legal advice in the form of fatwas, it is hard to imagine everyday life unfolding for ordinary Muslims without constant input and guidance from these legal experts.[45] Thus muftis, who write legal opinions in response to the questions (*istiftāʾ*s) they receive, connect changing contexts and technological innovations to enduring principles of law, morality, ethics, and comportment.

Developments in the nineteenth and twentieth centuries, which form the core focus of this book, not only drove legal change during this period but also made law an everyday object for ordinary Muslims around the world. British India was not the only place in which these changes occurred, but the status of Muslims as a minority made the development of everyday Islamic law on the subcontinent a template for its expression in postimperial, postcolonial, and diasporic contexts today.[46] Continuity between the responses of Indian Muslims living under British rule and the practice of Islamic law around the world today makes South Asia especially relevant for the study of Islamic legal history—not to mention the fact that India is home to the world's third-largest Muslim population, even though Muslims constitute only 10 to 15 percent of the country's total population.[47] To understand Muslim life in North America and Europe today, one needs to understand the history of Islamic law and legal practice during British rule in India. Indeed, many of the institutions that developed and the debates that played out in that context not only resonate in South Asia today but also reverberate around the world.

The history of Islamic law and legal practice in the colonial period, as in any period, necessitates thinking about qazis and muftis—judges and jurists, practitioners and scholars—together. While one was engaged in adjudication and enforcement, the other dealt with interpretation and ideology. While one evaluated conflicts and disputes, the other considered questions and authored answers. In the simplest setup, qazis would hear testimony and decide cases, while muftis would evaluate points of law and offer legal interpretations. Ideally, the two worked together, with qazis referring legal questions to muftis and muftis offering their answers to aid the qazis' decision-making, but much of the qazis' work was likely rote and routine—hearing cases, questioning witnesses, and applying laws—and much of the muftis' work was highly specialized and sometimes detached from the qazis' day-to-day activities.[48]

Professionals employed in any legal system today will likely find familiar parallels with the broader patterns of judicial administration and legal inquiry that defined qazis' and muftis' everyday activities: While the majority of cases fit routine patterns, giving lawyers and judges little room to experiment with novel arguments or unconventional interpretations, cases that require new approaches or novel arguments are few and far between. Islamic legal practice was (and is) no different. Day-to-day practices are run of the mill; drastic, game-changing developments are rare. What differentiates everyday Islamic law in this analogy, however, is the way that it has been displaced as *the* legal system for the state and has accordingly had to adjust, to recognize—and to redefine—itself as separate, not as the law of the land but as the law of a particular religious community. In some places, perhaps, this accommodation has been more successful than in others.[49] In modern South Asia (particularly in India but also in Pakistan, Bangladesh, and Sri Lanka), the process of adjustment and negotiation has been fraught, to say the least. While it is still possible to find qazis and muftis working across the subcontinent, the way they operate and the authority, respect, and recognition they receive change depending not only on the legal issue involved but also on whom one asks. *Everyday Islamic Law* thus follows the evolution of these individuals' careers—as private practitioners and as a community of experts—to understand why and how they operate today.

To uncover this history, I draw from material written and produced by qazis and muftis and move away from official colonial narratives. Looking beyond the imperial archive, my analysis draws from two extraordinary collections of records from the nineteenth and twentieth centuries. These collections come from Bharuch (Gujarat) and Meerut (near Delhi) and consist of the unpublished notebooks, registers, and papers from two families of qazis whose lives and work span the precolonial, colonial, and postcolonial periods. Written in Persian and Urdu, and authored and recorded by the chief qazi and his assistants, these records showcase everyday Islamic law in action, and their preservation on microfilm has made them accessible to researchers.[50] In addition to these unpublished qazi collections, I also draw from the published and unpublished records of South Asia's most prominent and less well-known muftis. While published, multivolume fatwa collections speak to the breadth and depth of a mufti's engagement with questions of life and law, unpublished fatwa files, like those from the dar-ul-ifta of the princely state of Hyderabad, complement these publications to provide a detailed picture of Islamic law on the ground.[51] As the files accumulated papers and moved from initial inquiry to final answer, they not only engaged with personnel across the dar-ul-ifta but also moved between offices and through various genres of paperwork and writing. Money orders, memos, certified mail receipts, postcards, and telegraphs came into and were sent from the dar-ul-ifta as its employees worked to solve fatwa seekers' problems. To understand what law means also requires looking at how law works, and these archives provide that perspective.

These sources, complementary in some places and contradictory in others, paint a picture of law and legal life that often escapes traditional legal histories.[52] They show how legislation peppered ordinary individuals' understandings of how they should live and the countless ways in which new acts and regulations created, added to, and augmented their confusion about what the law was and how it applied to them. They reveal in great detail how individuals, and the legal experts they consulted, took the messiness of everyday life—the petty squabbles of rural life, the domestic spats of reluctant couples, and the complaints of ordinary people going about their everyday business under colonial rule—and turned their problems, disputes, and disagreements into written records, legal deeds, authoritative documents, and formal complaints.[53] They show that in many cases, different ideas and definitions of law were operating at different levels, that there was often more than one way to solve a legal problem, and that experts frequently contributed different opinions and different types of advice at various stages. To call the whole process "messy" would be one way to put it, but to think instead about law and legal dispute resolution as framed by diversity and multiplicity offers a more productive framework.

In highlighting the multiplicity that emerges from these records, my discussion untangles these component pieces to distill the main ingredients that went into the making of legal life not for lawmakers, legislators, and colonial officers in London but for railway clerks in Lahore, students in Surat, and traders in Calcutta. At the same time, it draws attention to the fact that there were multiple ideas about Muslim personal law in circulation and multiple understandings of the elements of Islamic jurisprudence (*fiqh*) that went into its making. Within the formal legal system, legislation provided one means for capturing the spirit of Islamic law in legible rules that everyone could follow, interpret, and apply; this approach was grounded in ideas of legal codification and produced a stultifying, if not inaccurate, portrait of Islam. By contrast, Indian Muslim judges, a cadre of primarily English-educated elites, thought they could open new doorways to "authentic" interpretation by accessing the untranslated texts of prominent Islamic jurists.[54] In turn, they would author many of the concurring and dissenting opinions that further defined the limits and reach of Anglo-Muslim jurisprudence.[55] Outside the formal legal system, an array of Muslims occupied other institutions, engaged in formal and informal legal debate, and worked alongside and against the colonial legal system to resolve their disputes. They petitioned for and promoted new laws and legislative interventions to rectify the colonial state's construction of Muslim personal law, while at the same time protesting the state's intervention into religious personal law and criticizing its failure to uphold the principles of religious noninterference. Nonstate legal actors—such as muftis employed in private institutions and community qazis who retained authority in some areas but not in others—also weighed in on how "law" (sometimes meaning statutes and legislation, sometimes meaning the Qurʾan) should be interpreted. Adjudication under Anglo-Muslim law was thus one of several possible approaches to Islamic adjudication at the time, and even within the framework of Muslim personal law, there were multiple modes and methods for its interpretation and application.[56] Decentering the role of state law from the narrative of Islamic legal practice and its evolution in British India is one of this book's main aims.

To complement existing histories of legal pluralism and religious personal law, the narrative I offer creates and excavates an alternative archive of legal information. If law on the books is the companion to law in action, then focusing on law in action requires moving away from the archive of law on the books. Colonial legislation appears in several chapters but is not the primary focus of any of them (with the exception, perhaps, of chapter 3). What the book draws from instead is a library of legal sources that in many cases evaded or stayed below the radar of the formal legal system. For instance, petitions from qazis that never made it to imperial offices in Calcutta or Delhi, let alone to London, offer a unique perspective on who these legal practitioners were and how they viewed the work they performed (see chapters 1–3). They also reveal how real-time decisions contradicted and obscured the larger aims and objectives of British policy. Likewise, fatwa questions and their answers—whether formally published or left unpublished—provide another set of sources for this study. These materials cover much of the "substance" that made up everyday Islamic law outside and beyond the ambit of colonial legislation and reported cases, but as a body of evidence, they lack the sense of definitiveness that discussions of the law tend to demand. As the discussion in chapter 4 reveals, fatwas contributed to the making of law but did so through collaborative and cumulative processes of affirmation, repetition, and accretion. In histories of lawmaking, such sources provide messy narratives at best and obfuscate any effort to find a clear narrative at their worst. *Everyday Islamic Law* thus provides a social history of law in society that focuses less on what the law was and more on how ordinary individuals thought the law should work.

Looking at legal history from this perspective forces law as *product* to fall away and law as *process* to take over, as divergent voices step in to grapple with what a guideline means or an institution might be authorized to do. It is my hope that the reader will continue to learn about Islam and law and how they shape everyday Muslim life but will also enjoy having the opportunity to peer into the experiences of a family, a community, or a specific jurist to learn not about what Islamic law is or says but about how people called on its practices and principles at specific moments in their lives when looking for an equitable solution or meaningful resolution to the problems they faced. Legal practitioners, the institutions they inhabited, and the people they encountered are the substance of this history, but the ideas they conjure are ones that not only resonated in the past but also continue into the present.

Capturing Change over Time amid Pluralism and Multiplicity

On the surface, the basic contours of Islamic legal practice have remained constant across centuries and wide swaths of the world, but change and differentiation are also evident at multiple levels. While the titles of the qazi and the mufti may have historical connections to precolonial practices and resonances with legal institutions that still exist today (e.g., qazi courts, shariʿa courts, shariʿa councils), shared terminology should neither stand in for shared practices nor signal static, unchanging approaches. The process of approaching a qazi in 1947, when British rule came to an end on the subcontinent, was quite different from what it was in 1847, which again was quite different from what that process was in 1747. Similarly, not only was the process of approaching the mufti, registering a fatwa request, and receiving an answer in 1947 different from what one would have encountered in 1847, but the process was also quite different from what one might expect in 2047. In other words, there may be similarities in abstract terms, but the day-to-day practicalities of calling on legal experts have changed considerably over the past several centuries and continue to evolve. For that reason, the narrative that unfolds here is one that remains aware of history's dramatic breaks and ruptures while at the same time offering a narrative that allows change to unfold gradually over time. Emphasizing law as process also lends itself to fuzzy chronologies, as processes from earlier periods carried over into later ones, as shifts in interpretation preceded changes in legislation, and as formal breaks in government and politics ignored the continuity of practices on the ground.

A political history of this period might chart a path through the defining moments of British rule, beginning with the EIC's victory in the Battle of Plassey in 1757 and receipt of the *dīwānī* rights (right to collect revenue) from the Mughal emperor Shah ʿAlam II in 1765 after the Battle of Buxar and the signing of the Treaty of Allahabad.[57] The Uprising of 1857 and the Government of India Act of 1858 brought Company rule to an end and ushered in the next phase of political history: Crown rule. Independence in 1947 brought Crown rule to a close, though earlier acts promulgated in the first half of the twentieth century (specifically the 1919 and 1935 Government of India Acts) paved the way for decolonization—a process that for many still continues today. Political history thus provides one way to navigate this period, but the history of everyday Islamic law tends to take place below the momentous frames of political history. That history requires another chronology.

For Islamic legal practitioners—the qazis and muftis who populate the story that follows—a simple chronology might start in 1793, with the introduction of Bengal Regulation XXXIX of 1793, "A regulation for the appointment of the Cauzy-ul-Cozaat." From there, it might travel to the Madras Presidency for Regulation III of 1808, and then to the Bombay Presidency for Regulation XXVI of 1827, which provided similar structures for the appointment of qazis under the EIC. In this chronology, Act XI of 1864 might come next, repealing the earlier regulations for appointing qazis, followed by Act XII of 1880, the Kazis' Act, which then reintroduced qazi appointments. The story might end in 1945 with M. A. Kazmi's legislative council proposals to amend the existing Kazis' Act to strengthen its application and improve its utility, but his proposal failed, and instead the 1880 act remains on the books in India today.[58] Official regulations and legislation relating to the appointment of qazis and Muslim law officers thus provide another way to mark time, but again, this approach misses the operation of law on the ground, before, during, and after these legislative interventions. The social life of everyday Islamic law instead takes place on top of, across, and in addition to these formal regulations.

The "interludes" framing parts I, II, and III offer yet another way to mark time, one that has been widely adopted in South Asian legal history.[59] The Hastings Plan of 1772, the Queen's Proclamation of 1858, and the Muslim Personal Law (Shariat) Application Act of 1937 are strong chronological markers that reflected prevalent attitudes toward religious difference and religious law across this period. The Hastings Plan laid the foundation for religious legal pluralism when the EIC's government began in Bengal in the late eighteenth century. The shift following the Queen's Proclamation, as Karuna Mantena and others have noted, made irreconcilable religious differences the basis for colonial policy-making, respecting religious difference while at the same time essentializing and solidifying religious categories.[60] Less remarked on, the Muslim Personal Law (Shariat) Application Act differs from these other moments in its specific attention to Muslim personal law, yet it, too, represents a particular shift in outlooks and ideas.[61] If the former two moments marked imperial attitudes toward religious law, then the latter marks both a rejection and an embrace of the particularities the former moments enshrined. It stands out as a moment of self-definition and self-declaration in which Muslim intellectuals and lobbyists asserted their commitment and dedication not to colonial law or to Anglo-Indian legal precedent but to the laws of Islam and to shariʿa, while at the same time paradoxically calling on the colonial state to enshrine that law as law for Muslims.

One could write—and indeed, scholars have written—compelling narratives following this chronology. But in the chapters that follow, these moments serve not as decisive breaks or chronological divisions but as touchstones—interludes that provide the reader with a wider frame and theoretical vantage from which to examine the examples presented in the main chapters. Indeed, 1772 might be the initial point of departure for the EIC's approach to legal administration on the subcontinent, but legal pluralism was not the Company's invention; Company policy drew from earlier practices.[62] Furthermore, the 1772 plan did not introduce a new legal system wholesale. As early regulations pertaining to qazis demonstrate, judicial regulations in this period recognized and drew from existing personnel and established procedures, and these regulations also changed over time. Chapter 1, for instance, outlines how the 1772 plan (as well as its expansion in 1793 and its replication in other presidencies) kept what already existed in place. For that reason, the plan provides a good theoretical framework for evaluating early approaches to law and order but should not be taken as the ultimate origin of religious legal pluralism in South Asia.[63] Part I engages with this chronology up to a point, but it also moves beyond the transition to Crown rule by carrying the history of legislation pertaining to qazis beyond 1858. Despite the symbolic significance of 1858, many of the players from the Company period (Indian and British) continued after the transition to Crown rule with similar (or slightly revised) roles in the administration of law. For these reasons, just as the Hastings Plan of 1772 does not mark the definitive point of origin for legal pluralism, the Queen's Proclamation does not signal a total transformation in attitudes toward religious law following the Uprising of 1857.

As with the interlude on the Queen's Proclamation, the final interlude, featuring the Muslim Personal Law (Shariat) Application Act of 1937, arrives not to mark a chronological break but to represent an emergent perspective and to provoke specific questions about who or what would define Muslim personal law. The courts' willingness to accept custom as a source for personal law not only challenged the authority of the *ʿulamāʾ* (community of Islamic scholars) but also threatened Muslim solidarity.[64] By placing "shariʿa" at the center of Muslim personal law, the legislators, politicians, and lobbyists who supported the act rejected earlier interventions into the substance and interpretation of the personal laws applied to Muslims. Recourse to shariʿa—through legislation—was meant to unite and redefine the Muslim community. On the one hand, these changes were already under way in the proliferation of Islamic legal discourses, experts, and institutes. On the other hand, the 1937 act paved the way for subsequent legislative interventions into Muslim personal law like the Dissolution of Muslim Marriages Act of 1939, which was itself as much a reactive measure as it was a progressive one. As with the other moments, the Shariat Application Act reflected patterns, practices, and perspectives that were in circulation before and remained contested after the act's adoption. And despite its seemingly transformative potential, it left many practical questions about jurisdiction, interpretation, and authority unanswered.

Moving away from a chronology defined by breaks and ruptures, the history of Islamic legal practice outlined here does not ignore the fact that tensions boiled over and ruptures occurred. Instead, by focusing on everyday encounters with law and the social histories they frame, it challenges the extent to which legislative enactments marked moments of clear and decisive break. At the same time, and especially within the context of Islamic juridical discourse, it also challenges the idea that answering a legal question once is enough. As the plurality, multiplicity, and repetition of these discourses demonstrate, a definitive answer to a legal question at one moment, or with respect to a specific case, did not mean that the question never arose again, that competing or contradictory answers never surfaced, or that the practices or behaviors already expressly discouraged or forbidden did not later reappear in similar or different forms. At the levels of legislation and legal practice, law makes slow, incremental, and not always linear movements.

Yet changes certainly did appear over time. With the rise of different legal categories for Hindus and Muslims, communities with composite or unsure statuses had to choose one side or the other, making the lines separating "Hindu" and "Muslim" clearer and sharper in the process. At the same time, practices among Muslims became standardized and more uniform as discourses, decisions, and debates spread from one locale to another with increasing frequency. The forces behind this standardization were manifold, and their influences arose across diverse arenas, including in scholarship and scholarly publishing; in education and educational institutions; in family and domestic life; in political organizations, attachments, and affiliations; and through law's many faces and forms. Some of these changes came from the outside, and others were initiated from within. Some emerged in response to changes happening in South Asia or across the world; others came about in opposition to, or as a way of rejecting, the encroachment of the changing world on traditional ways of living and being. Most, if not all, of these changes touched on aspects of law in one way or another.

Outlines of Legal History in Everyday Life

The story narrated here unfolds across eight chapters. Parts I and II focus on the legal practitioners at the heart of the story, how they negotiated with the judicial department of the EIC in the first half of the nineteenth century, how they contributed to the passage of new legislation in the second half of the century, and how they developed new institutions and new approaches to their work in response to government interventions throughout this period. Part III focuses on what these changes meant for the ordinary individuals who called on Islamic law to resolve their everyday disputes. Beginning in the late eighteenth century, chapter 1 looks at how Company policies attempted to co-opt and to reengineer precolonial systems and personnel to suit their purposes, allowing many local leaders, administrators, and titleholders to stay in office but only by dint of British authority and authorization. It focuses on government-appointed community qazis in western India, in the expanding territory that formed the Bombay Presidency, as Company authority spread from coastal ports and trading entrepôts to the interior, encountering willing collaborators and recalcitrant resistors along the way. It offers some suggestions for why the Company invested in qazi appointments and why qazis invested in Company recognition. Chapter 2 builds on this discussion to outline patterns of intervention, professionalization, and bureaucratization that would come to characterize Islamic legal practice throughout this period. Moving between the objectives of Company policy and the obstacles to its straightforward implementation, this chapter introduces the expectations and practical considerations that shaped later negotiations over Islamic law in later decades. While some agents argued for merit-based appointments, others argued for upholding hereditary statuses and social structures. The contradictions in these outlooks—and the failure to resolve them—played out in debates over authority, autonomy, and authenticity that continued into the twentieth century. Chapter 3 continues this line of analysis to consider how specific arguments for government involvement in the appointment and recognition of qazis contributed to a system of mutual dependence in which neither Islamic legal practitioners nor the state could operate without reference to or dependence on the other. These entanglements continue to plague the personal law system in India today.

Part II shifts away from the state administration of Islamic law and legal personnel toward the dozens, if not hundreds, of muftis who lived and worked in British India. Unlike qazis who received nominal appointments from the colonial state, muftis did not receive formal appointments from the British and instead depended on their own status, ability, and reputation to influence Islamic legal practice.[65] Looking at how law operated beyond the realm of legislation and courtroom adjudication, chapter 4 explores the production and circulation of fatwas as a form of substantive legal change, one that relied on diffuse networks of authority and disaggregated mechanisms of implementation. Here, legal scholarship and community enforcement came together not only to give ordinary Muslims a better understanding of Islamic law as it applied to them but also to make following that law a more central part of being Muslim. Chapter 5 then examines how institutional mechanisms gave status and structure to the determination and implementation of the legal norms and ideas disseminated in fatwa literature. It focuses on the government institute for issuing fatwas (dar-ul-ifta) in the princely state of Hyderabad to outline how fatwas, as unenforceable legal opinions, operated alongside other legal institutions to shape individual lives and to resolve interpersonal legal disputes. In a similar vein, chapter 6 follows the operation of law not from the level of legislative enactments or courtroom decrees but from the perspective of registering a marriage, dividing family property, or documenting divorce, marital dissolution, or death. In each of these chapters, the mechanisms for registering complaints, recording legal acts, and resolving legal disputes parallel formal state legal institutions but take place outside the formal colonial legal system. Everyday Islamic law intersected with the courts and their formal legal procedures but was most often called on, talked about, applied in addition to, or designed for situations not adequately addressed by colonial legal institutions.

The final part of the book, part III, brings these ideas together to understand how ordinary individuals made sense of the substance and procedure of everyday Islamic law in the context of colonial legal change. Chapter 7 looks specifically at questions of jurisdiction and authority by examining how the colonial courts attempted to replace or to displace Islamic legal practitioners (qazis, specifically, but also muftis) and how ordinary individuals pushed back against the hegemony of the colonial legal system by identifying the inadequacies and inaccuracies of that system. Here I focus on two figures—one a high court judge, the other a prominent mufti—to outline how they imagined and challenged the role of the courts in resolving questions of Muslim personal law. The discussion considers what individuals did when they were dissatisfied with the court's ruling and how they checked the outcomes of those disputes against the "right" interpretation of Islamic law by calling on nonstate legal experts. The final chapter, chapter 8, pushes this analysis one step further to look not only at how legal disputes traveled between and across different legal fora but also at how legal processes and procedures transcended the traditional chronologies of political history. Many of the institutions that developed in British India still exist today, and many of the obstacles individuals face when resolving legal issues still permeate everyday life across the subcontinent. Carrying this narrative beyond the chronological divider that separates colonial and postcolonial South Asia, into and out of legislative histories, and back and forth across different territories and legal institutions, chapter 8 identifies the legal paths that individuals followed not only to resolve legal disputes but also to make sense of their place in the world. The conclusion then carries these practices into the present. Across its eight chapters and three parts, *Everyday Islamic Law* gives voice to ordinary individuals with routine, run-of-the-mill problems who were not always looking for the most accurate answer to their queries but were often looking for the answer that would work for them. Understanding these contingencies and necessities is also part of recognizing the making of everyday Islamic law. Acknowledging such contingencies, Kifayatullah may not have agreed with the publication of his photograph in the *Bombay Chronicle* in August 1931, but he was also to be forgiven for its unauthorized appearance.

Part I Professionals

Interlude I

Rethinking Law, Religion, and the State

That in all Suits regarding Inheritance, Marriage, Caste, and all other religious Usages or Institutions, the Laws of the Koran with respect to *Mahometans*, and those of the Shaster with respect to *Gentoos*, shall be invariably adhered to: On all such Occasions, the Moulavies or Brahmins shall respectively attend and expound the Law, and they shall sign the Report, and assist in passing the Decree.

—Clause XXIII, "A Plan for the Administration of Justice," 1772

Text and Context: The Judicial Plan of 1772

Following military victories (the Battles of Plassey and Buxar), diplomatic successes (the signing of the Treaty of Allahabad and receipt of the *dīwānī*—revenue collecting—rights), and protracted debates over the British East India Company's status, the 1772 "Plan for the Administration of Justice" was the founding document for the British East India Company's judicial system on the subcontinent.[1] Crafted in consultation with the nawab, still the reigning sovereign in Bengal, the plan brought existing institutions under British authority, dispatched with other offices, and laid the foundation for the Company's transition from trading outfit to governing body, at least insofar as Bengal was concerned.[2] In addition to the passage just excerpted (Clause XXIII), the plan included thirty additional rules relating to judicial affairs.[3] A symbolic and pragmatic response to the Company's decision to "stand forth" as *dīwān*, the 1772 plan presupposed radical change, while largely maintaining the status quo.[4]

The multipart plan began by outlining a hierarchy of courts for civil and criminal cases. It summarized procedures, named and appointed personnel, and even indicated when each would be open to hear which types of cases. The Provincial Court of Dewanee (Mufaṣṣal Dīwānī ʿAdālat) would oversee matters related to property, inheritance, marriage, caste, debts, accounts, contracts, partnerships, and rent, while the Provincial Criminal Court (Mufaṣṣal Faujdārī ʿAdālat) would hear all cases of murder, robbery, theft, "and all other Felonies," forgery, perjury, "and all sorts of Frauds and Misdemeanors, assaults, frays, quarrels, adultery, and every other Breach of the Peace, or violent Invasions of Property."[5] The plan recommended employing councils of judges and using local legal personnel—including "the Chief Câzee, the Chief Muftee, and Three capable Moulavies" in the apex court (the Niẓāmat ʿAdālat) (VII) and "the Câzee and Muftee of the District, and Two Moulavies . . . to expound the Law" in the criminal courts (IV)—to aid councils of (European) judges.[6] The plan thus drew on existing practices, personnel, and institutions to build the new judicial infrastructure of the Company-state.

The plan also included guidelines for making local justice accessible and equitable. It established procedures for receiving complaints and hearing petitions with the placement of a "Box" at the "Door of the Cutcherry [court]" to receive those complaints from the public at all hours of the day and night (IX).[7] It granted the "Head Farmer" in the district ("Purgunnah") permission to hear cases "not exceeding Ten Rupees" to make justice accessible locally (XI).[8]

It instituted uniform procedures for hearing cases and evaluating evidence (XII) and offered additional measures to guard against excessive litigiousness by implementing time limits (XV).[9] In other words, the plan imbued the judicial system not only with symbolic content but also with practical measures to ensure open access and fair treatment.

Focusing on revenue collection and extraction as much as on facilitating just and equitable governance, the plan also altered practices related to the receipt of payments and collection of fees. It prohibited the collector from summoning "any Persons . . . who are in any ways connected with the Revenue" during the months of harvest, so as not to interfere with agricultural work (X).[10] The plan further adjusted the interest rates for moneylending (noting that the current rates were "exorbitant"), demanded that all bonds be "executed in the Presence of Two Witnesses," and limited the extent to which debtors were beholden to their bondsmen (XVIII–XX).[11] It curtailed the practice of charging commissions and allowing arbitrators to take a cut from the suits they settled (XVI).[12] It also abolished the practice of paying fees to qazis and muftis as annual tributes ("Rassooms," *rusūms*) or for performing certain ceremonies and recommended replacing those fees with a "Monthly Salary" (XXXIII).[13] In short, the plan introduced lasting changes while leaving preexisting local hierarchies and administrative structures in place. It was a founding document that also invited future interventions.

Rereading the Hastings Plan in the Context of Religious Freedom

In scholarship on South Asia, the 1772 "Plan for the Administration of Justice"—colloquially referred to as the Hastings Plan, in recognition of Warren Hastings's role in its design—marks many beginnings for British rule on the subcontinent. Read for its symbolism as much as its substance, the plan tends to stand in for everything that was wrong—and for everything that went wrong—with British rule on the subcontinent, particularly in relation to religious law. Even without overstating its accomplishments, the plan signals a transition in the Company's history and offers insights into the ideologies of British imperialism.[14] The plan, for instance, gestures toward Britain's divide-and-rule philosophy—that is, to divide local inhabitants into distinct and competing factions (with perquisites, emoluments, and entitlements distributed unevenly among them)—while also signaling the recognition of communal difference as a sign of cultural deference.[15]

Naming two distinct communities (here "Mahometans" and "Gentoos," or "Muslims" and "Hindus"), the plan established Company rule through favors and special interests.[16] It also demarcated the boundaries of religious legal pluralism on the subcontinent—even though those terms do not appear here and their broader implications would take decades to develop.[17] Most notably, the plan announced that suits related to "Inheritance, Marriage, Caste, and all other religious Usages or Institutions" would be adjudicated according to two texts—the "Koran" [*Qur'ān*] and the "Shaster"—as "expound[ed]" by two groups of interpreters, "Moulavies or Brahmins," thereby planting the seeds for future visions of legal pluralism to grow.

In and of itself, this statement of legal pluralism was odd and exceptionally narrow, compared with contemporaneous descriptions of justice on the subcontinent.[18] Yet directing their attention to this moment, scholars have ascribed great importance to this statement and to the misinterpretation, misapplication, and "invention of tradition" that followed it.[19] The plan provided a road map for the administration of justice but left many questions unanswered and was subject to revision, rethinking, and modification throughout the late eighteenth century and into the nineteenth. At the same time, the plan reflected specific assumptions about South Asian society and turned those observations into policy prescriptions. The plan recognized two communities (Hindus and Muslims) belonging to distinct (religious) traditions, with unique laws for settling private disputes. Accordingly, the plan dictated that within areas of private or personal law, each community's scriptures (the "Koran" and "Shasters"), as interpreted by recognized religious leaders ("Maulvis" and "Brahmins"), would "invariably" apply to those categories of disputes for those groups of disputants.

There is much to critique here. To begin with, the formulation made the two groups it named, whitewashing local difference and diversity for the sake of simplifying judicial practice.[20] It also located legal practice (qua dispute resolution) within textual sources and dictated who would interpret those texts. The plan amalgamated and simplified a diverse array of local practices, customary observances, and legal traditions under the "Gentoo" and "Mahometan" umbrellas, and ushered in new projects to know, learn, fix, and reform those categories. The legacies of these invented religio-legal traditions haunt scholars of law and religion today. For scholars of Hinduism and Hindu law, the plan's simplistic formulations create a double bind.[21] To argue that "Hinduism" as a "Hindu religion" did not exist before British rule undermines the validity of practices and precedents that defined precolonial socioreligious life, yet to challenge colonialism's—and orientalist scholarship's—role in making Hindu religion overlooks the changes that took place under British rule (in the consolidation of Brahmanical authority, the reification of caste hierarchies, and the denial of legitimacy for nondominant or heterodox practices).[22] Likewise, for the study of legal history, denying the precolonial existence of "Hindu law" undermines and devalues the normative, moral, ethical, and legal systems that operated in precolonial South Asia and furthermore plays into imperial narratives of "backwardness" and "progress." Yet by naming a community "Gentoos" and ascribing to them a legal tradition rooted in the text of the "Shasters," the plan demanded an approach to law that was unlike what had existed before.[23]

Reference to the "Laws of the Koran" produces a similar conundrum. Here, arguments about colonial change take two forms. The first suggests that Islamic governance in precolonial South Asia (particularly with respect to the judicial institutionalization and application of Islamic legal norms) was absent or deficient. If the Mughal empire and its successor states were "Indo-Islamic" (i.e., only partially, syncretically, compositely, or "culturally" Islamic), then the plan's emphasis on the Qurʾan—and textual understandings of Islam drawn from it—necessarily introduced (and inscribed as law) an Islamic legal ethos that was dogmatically textual.[24] When nineteenth-century Islamic reform movements picked up this approach by advocating a return to the Qurʾan and Hadith to renew and revitalize Islamic life from within, they reinforced the idea that the "law" of Islam lay in the textbooks of orientalist inquiry.[25] But limiting law to "the Koran" displaced other sources of law (*ʿurf* [custom], *ʿādat* [customary practice], *ijmāʿ* [consensus], *ijtihād* [reasoning], *qiyās* [analogy], etc.) and sidestepped the possibility for more inclusive definitions of Islam (like the one Shahab Ahmed offers).[26] Put simply, the plan's textual essentialism excised Islam's lived and discursive traditions from religio-legal life.

Alongside this argument, the second critique focuses on the plan's reduction of Islamic legal substance to areas of personal, family law. The "jural colonization," to use Wael Hallaq's expression, of Islamic jurisprudence reduced the richness of shariʿa—the divine guidance for how one is to live in the world—to a small subset of legal issues: inheritance, marriage, caste, and religious usages.[27] Not only does *fiqh* (jurisprudence) extend beyond these areas (to economic relations, public life, political structures, commercial affairs, etc.), but it also draws from a wider body of sources and methods.[28] The Qurʾan is paramount, but (Sunni) jurisprudence also looks to (1) the Sunna (the example of the Prophet Muhammad, recorded in a series of sayings and reports known as the *ḥadīth*), (2) *ijmāʿ* (consensus of the community or consensus of scholars),[29] and (3) *qiyās* and *ijtihād* (analogy and reasoning), consensus and reasoning being methods for determining new "law" on the basis of existing material contained in the Qurʾan and Hadith.[30] In other words, the plan removed Islamic influences from social, political, and economic life at the same time that it reduced the source base from which Muslim personal law drew legal content. Tying religious law to texts and winnowing its application to personal, family law, the Hastings Plan thus produced a definition of "religious law" that came from outside (through textual adherence) and represented something entirely new (through its application to a subset of issues).

Litigating the Legacies of the Hastings Plan

For all its faults, the Hastings Plan provided parameters for religious adjudication in British India but did not create religious legal pluralism de novo. Expansive early modern empires like those of the Ottomans or Mughals allowed communities to settle some disputes locally, privately—much the same way that European guilds had the freedom to adjudicate disputes internally. Early modern legal pluralism differed from the plan's version, however, in that it granted separate communities autonomy in the adjudication of their disputes. The Hastings Plan instead brought the adjudication of different types of disputes for different communities under the umbrella of a (state-administered) legal system, undermining earlier flexibilities in choice of law or choice of forum.[31] Thus, to read the Hastings Plan as a written version of prevailing practices misses the extent to which bringing those practices under the aegis of the Company's judicial system remade those practices.

Two legacies emerge from the plan's interventions. The first is that it brought dispute resolution to the Company's (and later Crown's) courts. The transition was subtle. Initially, local legal practitioners (like the qazis and muftis mentioned in the plan) retained some authority and autonomy, but their autonomy dissipated as the Company became paramount. In subsequent decades, these figures would learn to invoke "religion" and the principle of religious noninterference to reclaim some of their rights (see interlude II), but their dependence on the British government persisted. The second legacy involves communalism. By recognizing two distinct communities—Hindus and Muslims—the plan shored up those categories while overlooking other religious and ethnic communities, each of which (theoretically) had the right to its laws, customs, and practices. Legal and legislative battles played out over the course of the nineteenth century to exclude certain groups from Hindu and Muslim law, to create separate religious laws or legal institutions for others, and to formulate a "civil law" category for the rest.[32] Those groups' paths to legal reform lay in claims to religious difference or distinction, skillfully deploying the colonial legal system's own understanding of religion and identity while pointing to flaws and shortcomings in the framing of legal pluralism as articulated in the 1772 plan.

In part I, these legacies play out in the context of everyday Islamic law through negotiations over the qazi's title, his status, and his position in the community, focusing on western India, where plentiful archival evidence provides a detailed picture of the conflicts, controversies, and competing aims that clouded the Company's expansion. Chapters 1–3 show how successive phases of administration co-opted the qazi's authority, reframed his responsibilities, and placed the rules of religious adjudication beyond his reach. As these negotiations remade the qazi's office, they drew on normative understandings of the qazi's title and definitions of religion and religious law tied to the 1772 plan. This transformative document thus laid the foundation for policies and practices that have had lasting effects on the everyday life of Islamic law and legal practice.

1 Becoming Qazi in British Bombay

Imperial Expansion, Legal Administration, and Everyday Negotiation

> The Câzee [*qāẓī*] is assisted by the Muftee [*muftī*] and Mohtesib [*muḥtasib*] in his Court: After hearing the Parties and Evidences, the Muftee writes the Fettwa [*fatwā*], or the Law applicable to the Case in Question, and the Câzee pronounces Judgment accordingly. If either the Câzee or Mohtesib disapprove of the Fettwa, the Cause is referred to the Nazim [*nāẓim*], who summons the Ijlas [*ijlās*], or General Assembly, consisting of the Câzee, Muftee, Mohtesib, the Darogos [*dārog̱has*; prefects] of the Adawlut [*ʿadālat*; court], the Moulavies [*maulvīs*; scholars], and all the learned in the Law, to meet and decide upon it. Their decision is final.
>
> —"Letter from the Committee of Circuit to the Council at Fort William," in Forrest, *Selections from the State Papers*, 283

Community Qazis and Early Colonial Legal Landscapes

By all accounts, Nūr-ud-Dīn Ḥusain was an exemplary qazi.[1] Although little remembered today, he had an illustrious career for much of the nineteenth century, working with the British East India Company (EIC) and serving the Muslim community in his hometown of Bharuch, a once-prominent but dwindling port city up the Narmada River from the Gulf of Khambay in Gujarat.[2] Following in the footsteps of his father, Nur-ud-Din received a certificate of appointment (*sanad*) from the Company in 1848, and when Company rule ended a decade later, he remained one of the most prominent and well-paid qazis in the Bombay Presidency.[3] Throughout his career, he employed an assistant to perform day-to-day tasks and to keep the qazi's records while Nur-ud-Din, as head qazi, conducted personal and professional business elsewhere in Bharuch and Bombay. If Nur-ud-Din was exemplary not only for his work as qazi but also in his relations with British officials (who increasingly viewed positions like his as superfluous, if not bothersome), then the legacy of his contemporary, Qazi Shaik̲h̲ Aḥmad, was quite the opposite. Although Shaikh Ahmad also inherited the office from his father, he was not nearly as successful as Nur-ud-Din when it came to maintaining the integrity of his position in the military cantonment at Pune where he was stationed, roughly five hundred kilometers south of Bharuch.

Qazi Shaikh Ahmad was a rabble-rouser who got into trouble with his peers and with British authorities on more than one occasion. When Nur-ud-Din was successfully promoting his position and reputation in Gujarat, Shaikh Ahmad was demoted (from qazi to assistant qazi), temporarily suspended, and eventually dismissed from office. Yet for all the criticism Shaikh Ahmad attracted, he was not the only officeholder to complicate, if not to obfuscate, the Company's efforts to manage native qazis across its growing territorial empire. Dozens of individuals—sometimes prominent figures with long-standing connections to the qazi's office and sometimes no more than names briefly mentioned in the Company's records—contributed to the entanglements between Company (and later Crown) policies and local legal practices, entanglements that became knottier as Company officials tried to govern, administer, manage, and master local qazis as the empire expanded. Formal regulations, written policies, and legislative enactments shaped these engagements, but as the lives of the Bombay Presidency's qazis make clear, policies on paper rarely reflected the intricacies, hypocrisies, and complexities of how British rule played out in practice. The (attempted) management of qazis is no exception to this pattern, yet their history remains largely untold.

Along with Nur-ud-Din in Bharuch and Shaikh Ahmad in Pune, there were others. While the former was notable for his success and the latter notorious for his failings, another contemporary of the two, Qazi Maḥomed Yūsuf Moorghay [Murghē], qazi for the city of Bombay between 1837 and 1866, was noteworthy for another set of reasons. Unlike the others, Yusuf Moorghay did not inherit the office of qazi from his father. Instead, he received it in retirement at the recommendation of prominent Bombay Muslims and in recognition of his prior service to the Company. While Nur-ud-Din and Shaikh Ahmad learned the qazi's craft from family members, Yusuf Moorghay worked as translator and scribe (*munshī*) during the Company's campaigns in Sind. Like many of the intermediaries who contributed to but also complicated Britain's territorial expansion across the subcontinent, the retired munshi's record of service and dedication to the Company—paired with recommendations from his supervisors—helped him secure the position when the opening arose. Yet despite his singular background and unconventional appointment, Yusuf Moorghay was not detached from the duties of his office. Even after allegations of improper conduct resulted in a formal disciplinary inquiry (see chapter 2), he bounced back to bring a successful civil suit against his rivals and detractors. By this point, Yusuf Moorghay was nearing the end of his second career—and nearing the end of his life—but he still fought, using the full power of the civil courts to defend himself and his position (see chapter 3). His life was singular but his story was not wholly unique.

From the notable, to the notorious, to the noteworthy, the individuals appointed to, employed in, and dedicated to maintaining the office of the qazi were a motley crew. And while the three figures mentioned here fit the pattern, not all who claimed the title did. As Company officials learned, women and Hindus also made claims to the office, which was defined historically by being male and being Muslim.[4] Dispensing with these claims troubled British officials, who wanted fitness and merit to define appointees, and cast doubt on the mechanisms that officials used to assess officeholders. What is more, as Company policies changed, British territory expanded, and personnel circulated through the empire, new perspectives on, attitudes toward, and inconsistencies with respect to these issues surfaced time and again. Rather than mapping the career of India's qazis as one of marginalization and decline, the following account shows that qazis continued to challenge the core principles of British rule on the subcontinent, to advocate for continuities with the past over the abrupt disruptions of foreign rule, and to represent forcefully and persistently the voices and interests of the communities they served.[5] Their stories may not explain all there is to know about the history and legacies of British rule in South Asia, but the perspectives, voices, and interests they represent tie their negotiations over legal authority and legal practice to broader histories of imperial expansion and colonial rule.[6]

Following the lives and careers of qazis across successive phases of British rule, from the expanding Company-state in the first half of the nineteenth century; through the explosion of legislative interventions in the second half; into the befuddlement, frustration, and agitation that began to crescendo in the twentieth century, Islamic legal practitioners like those introduced here chart a tangled path through the multiple, layered, and overlapping legal landscapes that characterized British India. Their careers show how and why colonial efforts to rationalize the judicial administration routinely failed. Their experiences expose the ironies and mutual dependencies that made colonial officials and nonstate legal actors quarrelsome bedfellows, and their uncertain legacies underscore the nonlinear progression of legal change from the precolonial past to the postcolonial future. Qazis were not the only officeholders to complicate the trajectory of British rule, to expose the hypocrisies of colonial governance and its rule-of-law discourse, or to draw attention to the inconsistent invocations of religious difference and secular universality, but they stand out for their ubiquity from the eighteenth, through the nineteenth, and into the twentieth (and now twenty-first) century. Their presence thus provides an unrivaled view of colonial legal change not from the vantage of lawmakers and legislators but from the perspective of legal experts and the ordinary individuals they served.

As this chapter and the ones that follow will show, qazis remained relevant, amid successive attempts to supplant their judicial authority and to render their administrative functions redundant, by leveraging public support, demonstrating their ability to serve underserved communities, and deploying the language of religious difference to their advantage. Their protestations kept the qazi's office alive under the Company and transformed it into one of community service and colonial necessity under the Crown. This chapter traces the first phase of that process, focusing on three individuals who defined the qazi's office in the Bombay Presidency. The following two expand on this discussion: chapter 2 shows how Company efforts to manage qazis ultimately failed, and chapter 3 demonstrates how community agitation kept the office alive. Together, the three chapters in part I explain how and why local legal practice, rooted in Islamic norms and inflected by local experiences, became wedded to an expanding territorial empire, an invasive colonial project, and a burgeoning state legal system.

Definitional Dances: Pinning the Tail on the Qazi's Title

At the beginning of the nineteenth century, the term "qazi" encompassed a range of individuals. Some matched the term's formal definition as an Islamic judge; others departed from it. The EIC recognized some qazis through successive, overlapping, and contingent regulations, but there were others claiming the title who diverged from the qazi's traditional or conventional duties. These are the figures who challenged Shaikh Ahmad's suitability in Pune, gave Yusuf Moorghay a run for his money in Bombay, voiced a host of expectations for qazis elsewhere in the region, and stood in stark relief to the respectability (and special treatment) that Nur-ud-Din commanded in Bharuch. At the same time, even as imperial legislation struggled to define the office, title-bearers and officeholders pushed back (individually *and* collectively) against the expectations, limitations, and restrictions that Company regulations imposed. While some regulations drew on classical models of the qazi as judge, appointed by royal *sanad* (certificate of appointment) or *farmān* (decree) to hear cases and resolve disputes, others leveraged the qazi's local connections to advance the authority of the Company-state.[7] In other words, Company officials wanted to benefit from existing connections without giving away too much control, and these competing intentions made the early colonial history of qazis messy.[8]

The qazis I introduce here were similar to but separate from the "Native Law Officers" who worked in the courts of law.[9] Native law officers (variously labeled "qazi," "mufti," and "maulvi") answered questions and explained points of law for cases related to Muslim personal law, following the Hastings Plan of 1772 and its subsequent rearticulations (see interlude I). In addition to working in the *ṣadr dīwānī* and *faujdārī ʿadālats* (chief civil and criminal courts) in the presidency capitals of Calcutta (Kolkata), Madras (Chennai), and Bombay (Mumbai), native law officers also worked in *ẓilaʿ* (district) courts and accompanied district judges when they went "on circuit."[10] Lower-ranking positions were less lucrative than those in the chief (*ṣadr*) courts, but these officers still contributed to the definition and interpretation of law. Owing to their meager monthly salaries, native law officers who lacked outside income (from land or other entitlements) routinely lobbied Company officials for better postings and higher pay. When the Company could not provide, they took on other work.[11] In addition to court "qazis," "muftis" and "maulvis" (sometimes referred to as "moolnas") also worked as native law officers, blurring the classical distinction between the qazi, who would attend to the facts of the case, and the mufti, who would address points of law.[12] A parallel contingent of officials, labeled *paṇḍits* and *shāstrīs*, performed the same work for disputes among Hindus. The native law officer position thus employed old titles for new offices, making it difficult to discern how legal interpretation changed under the Company's configuration.

To complicate matters more, courtroom qazis who worked as native law officers also resembled community qazis who worked outside the courts, and their appointments, family backgrounds, and responsibilities overlapped. Community qazis and courtroom qazis came from scholarly families with extensive lineages and long histories serving Muslim (and non-Muslim) rulers.[13] Many of them were well versed in classical legal texts and familiar with local laws and customs; they could "translate" the rites, rituals, and common practices of their local communities into legal precepts and norms and could advise British judges and magistrates on specific cases. When judges struggled to fill vacancies, they called on community qazis to fill the gaps. Sometimes these qazis stepped in temporarily.[14] In other instances, they surrendered the inconsistent employment of a community qazi to accept a salaried position as a native law officer.[15] (In subsequent generations, they would become lawyers, judges, and legislators.)[16] Occasionally, qazis kept both titles, working as a native law officer in court and performing other types of work in the community. As salaried employees, native law officers generally ranked higher than community qazis, but the two categories often intersected: appointees for each office came from similar stock and shared comparable backgrounds.[17]

Native law officers oversaw disputes on topics outlined in the "Plan for the Judicial Administration" that were connected to personal law, religious customs, and usages. From 1772 to 1864, native law officers and courtroom qazis supported British efforts to administer justice, interpreting the texts, law books, and "codes" that British officials identified as legal sources, and unwittingly transforming their own perspectives and local insights into "law."[18] Alongside these courtroom qazis, community qazis performed a range of roles beyond the courts. While not employed to decide suits or to hear cases, these community qazis nonetheless remained involved in the administration of justice: They drafted legal documents and notarized them with seals and signatures.[19] They kept registers and records of the documents they drafted and notarized, doing the work of a town clerk or registrar.[20] Some of them performed religious functions, such as reading the congregational prayers at ʿEid or giving sermons on Fridays.[21] Others performed civil functions by reading marriages, granting divorces, looking after minors, and appointing trustees to oversee endowments (*waqfs*, pl. *auqāf*).[22] There were also individuals who claimed the title of qazi but did none of this work, revealing the term's slipperiness.

Without salaries, community qazis earned their livings in other ways. As landlords they made money by renting the tax-free lands they held under subsistence (*madad-i maʿāsh*) grants from previous rulers or leveraged this land to amass capital and earn even more as moneylenders.[23] Over time, access to unencumbered, tax-free wealth exacerbated the ridicule that titular qazis faced as agents of imperial power, turning the office into an object of scrutiny, rather than one of respect.[24] When many *madad-i maʿāsh* grants became hereditary during the reign of the Mughal emperor Aurangzeb (r. 1658–1707), the connection between land grant and professional service evaporated, making concerns about unscrupulous qazis particularly acute in late eighteenth- and early nineteenth-century South Asia.[25] Furthermore, because the "office" of the qazi was attached to landed property and because, in the absence of primogeniture, the officeholder's heirs would divide the property among themselves after the incumbent's death, the office also became divisible, further eroding the connection between the position and its perquisites.[26] In some districts, heirs continued to do the qazi's work; in others, they dropped their responsibilities.[27] Additionally, as landlords and moneylenders, some officeholders became de facto village headmen who arbitrated disputes and maintained law and order. Thus, by the time the EIC began to appoint qazis across its territories, the occupations of the claimants it encountered already deviated from the traditional translation of the qazi as "judge," even if the break between past expectations and current functions was not always clean.

Had the Company made a clean break with the past as its judicial establishment expanded, the history of qazis in British India would have been simpler.[28] Instead, by drawing on existing administrative structures and judicial personnel, the EIC employed a ragtag gang of officeholders and claimants who readily exchanged their existing titles for new certificates, perquisites, and emoluments.[29] Rather than creating its own qazi corps de novo, the judicial department employed a ramshackle cohort of inherited officeholders—improperly identified, inadequately trained, inadvertently misassigned, and incoherently managed. Recognizing them extended the Company's reach into the countryside, giving its nascent judicial department on-the-ground representatives in hard-to-reach places, but local ties and entrenched expectations also hurt efforts to build a rational, judicial infrastructure.[30] If the salaried employment of properly trained individuals is the metric for measuring qazis in the Bombay Presidency, then only a handful measured up. The rest presented a messier vision that reflected the competing impulses of Company rule.

Despite their overlaps, the history of the courtroom qazis and muftis, who worked as native law officers in the Company's courts, awaits a complete telling elsewhere.[31] The discussion here instead narrates the uneven, incomplete, incompetent, and at times contentious history of Company efforts simultaneously to benefit from and to reform the panoply of community qazis dotting the landscape of early colonial India. Although this chapter and chapter 2 focus on the Bombay Presidency, similar histories show up in other territories, and later chapters travel there—to the North-Western Provinces, to the Deccan, to judicial establishments in Madras and Bengal—to highlight these similarities. Qazis played a pivotal role in the expansion of British power on the subcontinent, but they also challenged Company hegemony and autonomy. Like other commercial, landholding, and ruling elites, qazis provide a test case for measuring the principles of utilitarian governance and rational legal reform that undergirded British rule on the subcontinent and for outlining the tensions that erupted when legal ideals (be they British or Islamic) met the realities of everyday life in nineteenth-century South Asia.[32]

Written regulations set the stage for the battles that would unfold between law and religion, state and society. The 1772 plan, for instance, expressed deference toward and respect for religious difference at the same time that it opened the door for subsequent interventions.[33] It referred to the qazi as "the Judge of all Claims of Inheritance or Succession; [who] also performs the Ceremonies of Weddings, Circumcision, and Funerals," and outlined his judicial functions as quoted in this chapter's epigraph.[34] Descriptive as much as it was prescriptive, the section on qazis also outlined precolonial judicial practice: qazis heard cases in their courts and referred matters to the mufti, who responded to points of law with a written opinion, a fatwa. The mufti's opinion would then aid the qazi's decision, but if court officials (the qazi and his comptroller, the *muḥtasib*) disagreed with the mufti, they would come together collectively, as an *ijlās*, or council, to decide the case.[35] Yet such summaries did more than simply describe the roles of qazis, muftis, and other officers; they also provided a template to follow. If Company appointees took the qazi's place as "judge," then "native law officers" could stand in for the mufti (for Muslim personal law cases) or the Brahmin pandit or shastri (for Hindu personal law cases) to interpret the legal substance.[36] On paper, the difference was subtle, but in practice it shifted legal authority away from local venues toward Company courts. Thus, when Company officials went on circuit, they not only expanded the EIC's judicial authority into rural hinterlands but also curtailed the rights and responsibilities of local officers. For qazis, the transition resulted in the separation of their legal-administrative work from their religio-communal functions.

Subsequent regulations reveal the effects of this transition more clearly. In Bengal, Regulation XXXIX of 1793 recognized the appointment of qazis "stationed at the cities of Patna, Dacca, and Moorshedabad . . . for the purpose of preparing and attesting deeds of transfer and other law papers, celebrating marriages, and performing such religious duties or ceremonies prescribed by the Mahomedan law." The regulation made qazis dependent on "the British Government" but essentially allowed them to continue performing the duties "as have hitherto been discharged by them." Owing to the qazi's involvement in "preparing and attesting deeds . . . and other law papers," the regulation also stipulated that officeholders should be "persons of character, and duly qualified with respect to legal knowledge."[37] References to "character" reflected Company anxieties about morality and merit in appointments and promotions and wed intangible character traits to tangible aspects of work performance.[38] A good person was one who did good work (and vice versa). Markers of merit (e.g., passing exams, holding degrees) later helped to fill administrative appointments, but character assumed greater importance as qazis' ties to religion and community became more entrenched.

If Regulation XXXIX of 1793 reduced the qazi's judicial responsibilities to notarial work, Regulation XL of that same year muddied the waters by undercutting the simple division between judicial and nonjudicial activities.[39] Regulation XL ("A regulation for granting Commissions to Natives to hear and decide Civil Suits . . .") required qazis in cities like Patna, Dhaka, and Murshidabad to "attend at the *cutcherree* or court-house . . . three days in each week, or as often as the Judge may direct," to aid in "the trial and decision of suits."[40] The regulation also required qazis to work as district commissioners. The qazi for Calcutta became the "Commissioner for the zillah [district] of the twenty-four pergunnahs [territory ceded to the Company in 1757]"; a qazi located near a district court became "commissioner for the zillah [district] by virtue of his office [as qazi]"; and those "in the large towns, bazars [*bāzārs*; markets], gunges [*ganjs*; commercial towns], hauts [*haṭṭas*; rural markets], or aurungs [*aurangs*; manufacturing villages]" could settle disputes as "referees and arbitrators only," unless the chief court should "empower" them to "act as munsiffs [*munṣifs*; subordinate judges]."[41] Although qazis were no longer "judges," Regulation XL granted them a number of judge-like powers, either owing to or in addition to their status as qazis. Regulations like these thus replaced qazis as judges with arbitrators, commissioners, and subordinate justices who just happened also to be qazis.

Titles and appointments were no more straightforward on the other side of the subcontinent. Even before the formal introduction of Regulation XXVI of 1827 (relating to qazis), Company officials received requests connected to the office.[42] In 1816 Qazi Ghulam Husain petitioned the government to widen a busy thoroughfare in the city of Bombay, harking back to the qazi's former role maintaining public roadways.[43] In 1818 the judge and magistrate at Ahmedabad requested permission to provide the local qazi with a pair of shawls, his honorary perquisite.[44] Later that year, the judge and magistrate for the Northern Konkan urged the government to provide guidelines for filling vacancies in the qazi's office. Then, in 1821, the magistrate in Anjar (Gujarat) wrote to Bombay to request a delay in the transfer of his *nāẓir* (court official, sheriff), who was scheduled to become qazi in the office of the political agent for Khandesh. The magistrate needed time to find a suitable replacement for this upwardly mobile junior official.[45] Company officials also received petitions from widows requesting their deceased husbands' pensions; from hereditary officeholders claiming positions they had been denied; and from incumbents wishing to pass appointments to their sons.[46] As the number of requests mounted, Company officials began to question their involvement with appointments, owing to the traditionally hereditary status of the qazis' office.[47] From titular qazis employed in other offices (judicial or otherwise), to hereditary qazis looking to maintain their (nonjudicial, community) offices, to those employed as native law officers in courts of law, early references to Company involvement with qazis in Bombay reflect the competing aims and overlapping definitions found in the Bengal regulations. Yet these snippets also make clear that qazis were highly mobile within the world of Company employment and were also highly invested in the compensation (monetary and symbolic) they received from these titles and appointments.

Clearer patterns for appointment begin to emerge after "Cazee" becomes a separate heading in the judicial department's proceedings in 1831, following the introduction of Regulation XXVI of 1827 ("A Regulation for the Appointment and Removal of Kazees, and for ensuring an efficient and regular discharge of their duties"). The other twenty-five of the first twenty-six regulations of 1827, known collectively as the Bombay Code, covered a range of topics tied to law, order, and good governance. These included civil and criminal law (Regulations II–X and XI–XV), revenue (Regulations XVI– XXI), the military (Regulation XXII), and miscellaneous affairs (Regulations XXIII–XXVI). The regulations addressed judicial procedure (Regulation IV), jurisdiction (Regulations V and XI), and substantive law (Regulations VI and X). They covered the appointment of officers (Regulations XVI and XV) and questions of proper conduct in office (Regulation XXIII). Organized under headings and subheadings, the regulations categorized the appointment of Hindu and Muslim law officers under the section on civil justice and placed the final regulation, relating to qazis, under the "Miscellaneous" heading.[48]

If placing the "Kazees" regulation at the end of the code, under the "Miscellaneous" heading, was not enough to signal the desire to separate the native law officer's courtroom responsibilities from the community qazi's nonjudicial role, then the regulation's wording supports this characterization. Replicating the descriptive and prescriptive elements found in the Bengal regulations, the preamble explained that throughout the presidency, "the office of kazee [*qāẓī*] exists, and is necessary for the purpose of authenticating and recording marriages, attesting divorces, and assisting in various other religious rites and ceremonies amongst Mahomedans [Muslims]"; that the office has "important uses . . . in furnishing the means of settling questions of inheritance and succession between Mahomedans"; and therefore that rules "for the appointment and removal of kazees, as for ensuring an efficient and regular discharge of the functions of their office, should be established and promulgated."[49] Like its predecessors in Bengal, the Bombay regulation asserted that the qazi's "purpose" was for record-keeping ("authenticating," "recording," "attesting") and for "settling questions" in relation to the "religious rites and ceremonies amongst Mahomedans." It built on the 1772 judicial plan by defining the qazi's expertise in terms of marriage, divorce, and inheritance but allowed the duties of community qazis to overlap with the work of native law officers.[50] At the same time, by linking community qazis to Muslims and categorizing the position as miscellaneous (not judicial), the regulation reframed their authority.[51] While continuing to blend "civil" and "religious" functions, Regulation XXVI envisioned a new relationship between qazis, the company state, and the local community, but weaving government management, community recognition, civic responsibility, and religious identity together in a single office created a tangled mess of rights and obligations that complicates legal pluralism to this day.[52]

Being Qazi in Bombay: A History in Three Lives

Appointing and managing qazis called on the full strength of the Company's administrative apparatus. Clearer processes and procedures emerged as Company rule expanded during the first half of the nineteenth century, but the colonial government's command over its qazis was only marginally better in 1864 (when Act XI of that year suspended the government's involvement in qazi appointments) than it had been in 1834, when systematic efforts to survey officeholders collided with the messy realities of existing appointments.[53] Qazis who mastered administrative protocols, deployed key terms, and remained persistent in their petitions were rewarded with lengthy careers and material benefits. Those who failed to master these protocols, however, found themselves sidelined. The success of some qazis marked failure for others, but the ultimate victors were not the qazis themselves but the communities they served. After nearly a century of engagement with government officials, qazis secured their place as meaningful intermediaries who served local constituencies and the colonial state. Excavating this earlier history, before legislative lobbying and civic associations redefined public politics in the latter half of the nineteenth century, thus helps to explain how transformations across the nineteenth century made everyday Islamic law and shaped subsequent interactions between nonstate Islamic legal practitioners and the state legal system into the postcolonial period.[54]

Nur-ud-Din Husain, Qazi for the City and Pargana of Bharuch (1848–1864)

For Nur-ud-Din Husain, it was easy to become a qazi under the Company. After arriving from Arabia, Nur-ud-Din's ancestors rose in rank, first under the Mughals and then under Bharuch's independent nawabs.[55] The family's relationship with the Company began in the final quarter of the eighteenth century when Nur-ud-Din's great-grandfather Zain-ul-ʿĀbidīn worked as qazi while the Company held Bharuch from 1772 to 1783. At that time, Zain-ul-ʿAbidin received a salary of forty rupees per month and a separate allowance of seventy-five rupees per month from the court (*ʿadālat*), a sum he shared with his assistant. When the Company handed Bharuch to the Marathas following the Treaty of Salbai in 1782, Zain-ul-ʿAbidin "continually offered up [his] prayers to the almighty," and they were later "realized" when a Company regiment reclaimed Bharuch in late August 1803.[56] The qazi longed to see the British return to power, and after British troops reclaimed the city, Zain-ul-ʿAbidin "strove in the best manner he could and assisted the British authorities in . . . establishing the Rules and Regulations of the British Government."[57] His assistance earned the qazi a monthly stipend of one hundred rupees, to supplement the small fees he collected for performing marriages and other ceremonies and also to persuade him to become a native law officer in the city's court, owing to "difficulty . . . in procuring Native Law Officers possessing the necessary qualifications."[58] Zain-ul-ʿAbidin also convinced the Company to continue his perquisites (*lawāzim*), which included the annual gift of a pair of shawls, valued between Rs. 100 and Rs. 120, on the occasion of the two ʿEids (ʿEid al-Aẓḥa and ʿEid al-Fiṭr). Additionally, the Company provided him an honorary guard of fifty to sixty garrison sepoys (*sipāhīs*; soldiers) to accompany him to the ʿEidgāh (the place outside town where he would lead the ʿEid prayers).[59] Salaries, perquisites, and honors reflected Zain-ul-ʿAbidin's status in Bharuch and among Company officials.

When Zain-ul-ʿAbidin passed way, his son and heir, Sayyid Murtaẓá, followed him as qazi and received a sanad from the Company on January 26, 1822.[60] After successfully petitioning the Company, Zain-ul-ʿAbidin's descendants also secured the continuation of their father's monthly allowance. Sayyid Murtaza received half of the one-hundred-rupee stipend; another son, ʿAbbās ʿAlī, and their mother received the other half.[61] Once in office, Sayyid Murtaza pursued his father's legacy. In 1831 he persuaded the judicial commissioner for Gujarat to convince Bombay to extend the qazi's territory to include the town and the *pargana* (district) of Bharuch. "Incompetent persons," the qazi related, caused him to be "molested and obstructed in the discharge of his duties."[62] After he paid the ten-rupee stamp fee for a new sanad, Sayyid Murtaza received an updated certificate, now issued under Regulation XXVI of 1827, that expanded his jurisdiction to include the town and district of Bharuch.[63] When he passed away in December of that year, his nephew Sayyid Aḥmad Ḥusain took over.

Like his predecessor, Qazi Ahmad Husain also petitioned the Company for increased compensation and perquisites. In March 1832 he asked the Company to continue paying him the monthly stipend that his uncle had received. Company officials were hesitant to continue the payment as a hereditary entitlement, so they converted it to a salary and, in April 1833, granted a monthly allowance of fifty rupees "to all future Qazees of that City."[64] Ahmad Husain was successful here, but his tenure as qazi also overlapped with a period of transition during which regular salaries and fee-based incomes gradually replaced stipendiary payments, honorary guards, and tributary gifts. As a result, Ahmad Husain's subsequent requests met with rejection. When, in 1835, the Company failed to provide him with the honorary guard that customarily accompanied the qazi to the ʿEidgah, he complained. The complaint he filed in 1836 received no response, so the following year, Ahmad Husain sent his assistant (*nāʾib*) to Surat (seventy kilometers to the south) with another petition: "The Eedool Fitr is fast approaching, and I am therefore compelled to trouble you with this [matter]," the qazi explained.[65] The session judge at Surat, James Sutherland, validated the qazi's complaint, noting that "a military party has accompanied the Kazee on these occasions, ever since the introduction of our judicial administration." He further added that "unless forbidden by Government, [he did] not think it in the Province of a commanding officer to discontinue [the practice], for in doing so embarrassment might be felt."[66] The government at Bombay confirmed that "a denial of customary observances on the occasion of religious ceremonies . . . should be avoided," but despite two rounds of inquiry, there is no indication that the qazi received his guard the following year.[67]

Two years later, Ahmad Husain filed another complaint addressed to the governor in council for the Bombay Presidency, objecting to the loss of income he faced owing to new regulations regarding court business. A recent order from the sadr court in Bombay had removed signing and validating *mukẖtār-* and *wakālat-nāmas* (deeds relating to power of attorney and representation) from the qazi's portfolio. Previously, qazis added their seals and signatures to these documents to verify their legitimacy and accuracy and recorded their details in registers "with the names of the parties to produce [as] proof in case of any other papers being lost or forged."[68] The qazi's seal and signature not only prevented forged documents from appearing in court, assuring that "the sirkar [*sarkār*; government] had nothing to fear of the peoples committing any fraud whatever," but also ensured that their contents were accurate and that family members did not misrepresent the wishes of their (female) relatives.[69] Ahmad Hussain's complaint was personal, but it spoke to larger transformations.

Mahomed Hossein, qazi of nearby Ahmedabad, voiced a similar complaint, arguing that not being able to seal and record *mukẖtār-* and *wakālat-nāmas* deprived him of valuable income. He "pray[ed] that adequate compensation may be granted in lieu" of the fees he received.[70] The naʾib qazi at Bharuch also argued that a substantial proportion of his annual earnings came from fees collected for these documents.[71] Unfortunately, Bombay Judicial Department register Henry [?] Young felt neither pity nor remorse about the policy change: "It is not within the competence of any Civil Court to compel all classes of person indiscriminately to authenticate their documents in the manner prescribed, which is rendered more objectionable from its subjecting parties to a tax in the shape of a fee," he explained.[72] Not only did it bother Young that the former practice required all parties, regardless of religion, to have documents authenticated "by Kazees" who, under Regulation XXVI of 1827, "affect only persons of Mahommedan Persuasion," but it also bothered him that the qazi's fees amounted to a "tax."[73] What Young failed to mention is that the "tax in the shape of a fee" did not disappear when qazis stopped adding their seals; the Company replaced them with stamp fees, the very fee-based tax that had, fifty years earlier, sparked an uprising in Britain's American colonies.[74] Young's rebuttal gave the qazis little relief.

Already, a few years into his tenure and a decade into the Company's management of qazis under Regulation XXVI of 1827, the rules relating to what they could do and where they could receive income had started to shift. Fortunately, the shift was not complete when, in 1848, Ahmad Husain petitioned the Company to recognize his son Sayyid Nūr-ud-Dīn Ḥusain Ḵẖān Shirāzī as his successor. Given the Company's ambiguous stance toward hereditary appointments (see chapter 2), Ahmad Husain made a strong case for his son. Nur-ud-Din was approaching middle age, his father was reaching old age, and the moment of transition had arrived.[75] Nur-ud-Din was "well versed in the Persian and Arabic languages and can write Persian exceedingly well."[76] The assistant judge at Bharuch also "found [him] quite competent."[77] Less than two months after Ahmad Husain's original petition, the government agreed to recognize Nur-ud-Din as qazi, and following the return and cancellation of his father's sanad, the government delivered a certificate of appointment to the new qazi in May of the following year.[78]

Nur-ud-Din was an exemplary qazi. Until the 1860s, he and his na'ib executed the qazi's work dutifully and diligently (to the extent that the government allowed it).[79] They performed and recorded marriages; maintained an archive of legal documents related to sales, land transfers, and other transactions; and carefully guarded the prestige of the office—and the reputation of the qazi's family—into the next phase of British rule.[80] Even after the government's relationship to qazis changed under Crown rule (see chapter 3), Nur-ud-Din's successors remained engaged in government and politics. His descendants were active participants in civic organizations and on committees dedicated to Muslim educational and political campaigns.[81] Furthermore, his grandson, who also bore the name Nur-ud-Din, facilitated the publication of the then-deceased qazi's *Treasury of Poets* (*Maḵẖzan-ush-Shuʿarā*), in partnership with the Anjuman-i Taraqqi-yi Urdu Press at Aurangabad in 1933.[82] None of these later accomplishments would have been possible had the qazis of Bharuch not been able to maintain their status under Company rule. For them, being qazi meant more than performing and recording routine transactions; it meant serving as community leaders and liaisons throughout the transition to British rule. Their engagement with Company officials in the early nineteenth century thus paved the way for future negotiations between Islamic legal practitioners and government agents in the decades that would follow.

Shaikh Ahmad, Qazi for the Military Cantonment at Pune (ca. 1847–1855)

For other qazis, the road to success was less clear. Qazi Shaikh Ahmad, qazi for the military cantonment at Pune, was one of these figures. Scattered across the archive, his life appears in fragments, popping up whenever his rival Qazi Hyatoolakhan [Ḥayāt Allāh Ḵẖān] submitted a complaint. For years, Hyatoolakhan worked to oust his competitors from Pune and its cantonment. Shaikh Ahmad was only one of Hyatoolakhan's opponents (he also fought his co-qazi, Muhammad Safdar), but the dispute with Shaikh Ahmad—and the Company's response to it—provides a useful counterpoint to Nur-ud-Din's story of success. On the surface, the dispute was one of territory and authority, but questions of reputation, respectability, and character lay beneath the surface. By the time Company officials removed Shaikh Ahmad from office, they had decided which rules were flexible and which were set in stone.

The dispute began in 1847, when Hyatoolakhan requested the extension of his jurisdiction from the town of Pune to the military cantonment on its outskirts. Writing to district court judge Henry Brown, Hyatoolakhan alleged that Shaikh Ahmad "has no Sunnud of Cauzee but officiates as such in the Cantonment." Hyatoolakhan, who received a sanad in 1846, thought Brown should stop the unlicensed qazi from working.[83] Cantonment officials did not agree. Captain J. R. Morse asserted that Shaikh Ahmad "ha[d] no regular sanad according to the Government's Regulations" but was instead "permitted to exercise those functions in succession to his father." In support, Morse cited a certificate granted by Thomas Ellis, the former superintendent of bazars, to Shaikh Ahmad's father, Shaiḵẖ Yūsuf, on July 10, 1818, and a "hookoom nama" (*ḥukm-nāma*; order) from General Lionel Smith, reconfirming the appointment in July 1828.[84] The order from Smith further indicated that Muslims in the camp "should consider Cazee Yoosoof their Cazee and spiritual guide, and [show] reverence by him."[85] Hyatoolakhan's accusations were accurate, but Smith's order made it clear that sanad or no, Shaikh Ahmad's father was qazi for the cantonment and had "performed his duties honorably" until death.[86] Shaikh Ahmad's inherited appointment was undocumented, but it was not entirely illegitimate.

The government offered a compromise. To avoid "the inconvenience of not having the Cazee resident in the Cantonment," the adjutant general of the army for Bombay recommended the "appointment of a fresh Cazee for the cantonment," and the judges of the sadr diwani ʿadalat agreed, adding that "the Cazy of the City of Poona should be directed to appoint a Naib [*nāʾib*] for the Cantonment."[87] Shaikh Ahmad would remain in office, but he would be demoted to the position of assistant qazi for the cantonment, subordinate to Hyatoolakhan's authority as chief qazi. The reconfiguration became a short-term solution when new complaints against Shaikh Ahmad arose the following year. In 1848 Sakīna, the wife of a man stationed in the cantonment, refused to live with her husband. After a community-led inquest, she was sentenced to the horrific and humiliating punishment of having her head shaved, her face painted black, and her body stripped and paraded naked through the cantonment seated backward on a donkey.[88] Shaikh Ahmad was implicated, and as a Company servant, his involvement in this savage miscarriage of justice was grounds for dismissal.

From Pune, Judge Brown launched an investigation. Seven witnesses gave testimony, revealing the naʾib qazi's partial participation: he was present at the meeting in which Sakina's husband (Karīm Bak̲h̲sh) brought charges against her, but he did not participate in the punishment that followed.[89] Speaking in his own defense, the assistant qazi explained, "I never gave orders that her head should be shaved and that she should be mounted on an ass . . . I was not present when they punished the woman and I never authorised them to do so."[90] By confirming that he did not participate in Sakina's violent humiliation, Shaikh Ahmad avoided a more serious punishment, but participating in the unauthorized inquest, failing to report the gathering, and not stopping the abuse that followed tarnished his reputation. He almost certainly would have been dismissed from office were it not for the numerous reports that *ṣūbadārs* (officers, captains), sepoys, *ḥawāldārs* (inferior officers), and others sent to the government supporting him. Instead of removal, Shaikh Ahmad received a six-month suspension and a strict warning that "in the event of any similar charge, being hereafter proved against him, he will be dismissed with disgrace from the service of Government." His commanding officer did not fare so well and was summarily dismissed.[91]

With his reputation tarnished but his position intact, Shaikh Ahmad continued to work as naʾib qazi for the camp at Pune for the next two years. Then, in 1850, Hyatoolakhan initiated another round of accusations, claiming the camp qazi refused to follow orders. Shaikh Ahmad rebutted Hyatoolakhan's complaints by making his own accusations regarding the "tyrannical" and "unjust" treatment he received from the city qazi. The government declined to intervene, but Shaikh Ahmad had to sit for an examination to prove his competence. The rivalry continued for the next few years while Hyatoolakhan gathered additional evidence. Finally, in 1854, he reported to the judge at Pune "that the register of marriages kept by Shaik Ahmed his Camp Naib was not formal and contained a number of errors." Shaikh Ahmad submitted his "Register Book . . . to the Mahomedan Law officer for enquiry and report," and upon inspection, the judges learned that "the irregularities complained of did exist and [much] want of care in keeping the register was apparent." The judicial establishment at Pune warned Shaikh Ahmad that further failure to perform his duties would lead to removal, and the following year, when Shaikh Ahmad failed to submit his registers for review, Judge Robert Keays had no choice but to assert that "the behavior of Shaik Ahmed [could] be tolerated no longer." He recommended Shaikh Ahmad's immediate dismissal, explaining that, already, the camp qazi "was allowed every possible opportunity for mending his conduct, and was fully apprised . . . that dismissal would inevitably follow the repetition of such contumacious behavior."[92] At the end of this long battle, the city qazi finally won. The government's resolution confirmed "that the Cazee misbehaved or is at least not good at his job and therefore should be dismissed."[93] Ultimately, being "not good at his job" lost Shaikh Ahmad his title. Rivalries not only interfered with the Company's administration but also ended some qazis' careers.

Despite his dismissal, Shaikh Ahmad did not give up. When Hyatoolakhan died in June 1859, he tried to reclaim his title. Reinvigorating the government's promise to separate the offices of city and cantonment qazi after the city qazi's death, Shaikh Ahmad gathered his supporters and began a vigorous campaign to get back into office. In July cantonment officials forwarded petitions from two factions—one supporting Shaikh Ahmad and the other supporting his replacement, Shaikh Allee [Shaik̲h̲ ʿAlī]. Roughly two hundred signatories favored Shaikh Allee (who had replaced Shaikh Ahmad as naʾib in 1855), but "a great portion of the community[,] about 1200 in number[,] presented a memorial" refuting Shaikh Allee's authority. The new qazi was "utterly ignorant of the religious law," and cantonment residents "were not willing to accept him." Furthermore, failing to consider what the petitioners believed was their long-standing right to elect their preferred qazi (a practice with little basis in Islamic jurisprudence but one that became increasingly favored among the British), the brigadier had put forth both names, "without seeing on which side was the majority, and on which the minority . . . and without paying any regard to the rule which prohibits the interference of the authorities in religious matters, or to the rule laid down in our religious law providing that a person voted for by the majority of the community should be appointed Kazee."[94] By ignoring their votes, he had trampled their religious rights.

Sending petitions directly to Bombay, Shaikh Ahmad made a valiant case for his reinstatement. He claimed Hyatoolakhan's earlier complaints against him were false, criticized his replacement for "understand[ing] very little of Mahamedanism," and cited the vote tallies favoring him.[95] Nearly 1,200 signatories supported Shaikh Ahmad's return to office, a figure representing "9/10 of the Mohamedan Population" in the area.[96] Furthermore, "the old community" of the Poona Cantonment not only supported Shaikh Ahmad's candidacy but also questioned Shaikh Allee's competence.[97] They warned that "should Government appoint Shaikh Ali, we will not have Nika (marriage) or any other rites whatever performed by him, as we do not consent to his appointment, we will have these ceremonies performed by anyone we like; and this measure will give rise to continual quarrels, and occasion trouble to Government."[98] Other supporters proclaimed it their right "according to our religion and also according to the law of England [that] we must have a man for our Cazee, who is ellected [*sic*] by majority and not by minority," adding that if "Shaik Alee be appointed as Cazee, we shall not allow him to interfere in the least in any of our ceremonies and not acknowledge his Cazeeship and authority against our conscience and religion."[99] Shaikh Ahmad's supporters were clear: if Shaikh Allee remained qazi, they would refuse to recognize or to patronize him, and the government would remain embroiled in disputes.

Despite these threats, the government could not overlook Shaikh Ahmed's prior record. Acting Registrar White stressed that "Shaikh Ahmed's general conduct appears to have been so bad that the Judges do not think he could be appointed."[100] Even if the judge at Pune could certify that Shaikh Ahmad had more supporters, the government could not put him back in office. In the end, the government gave cantonment inhabitants a choice: they could stick with Shaikh Allee, the current naʾib, or pick ʿAbd-ul-ʿAli, a second candidate the Company offered, instead.[101] When most inhabitants refused to vote for either candidate—owing to their assertion that both candidates belonged to a mutinous faction led by Nur-ul-Huda—the government had no option but to keep Shaikh Allee. Shaikh Ahmad's run for office had finally ended in defeat.

Shaikh Ahmad's history as qazi for the military camp at Pune offers several lessons about the history of the EIC's management of qazis in the first half of the nineteenth century. Although the entangled histories of qazi appointments, religious factions, and sectarian differences still requires additional consideration, Shaikh Ahmad's experiences at Pune make clear that government officials constantly weighed the exigencies of on-the-spot decision-making with the administrative rationales and bureaucratic expectations that shaped Company rule more broadly. From the beginning, Shaikh Ahmad's status was suspicious. After inheriting the office of cantonment qazi from his father, Shaikh Ahmad struggled to legitimate his position. When he failed to prove his legitimacy, the government demoted him to assistant. When he became implicated in an act of vigilante justice against an innocent woman, he received a six-month suspension, and finally, when he failed to complete the main task assigned to him (i.e., keeping accurate records of marriages and other transactions), he was dismissed. His quest for reappointment in 1859 followed these patterns, highlighting the government's inconsistencies when it came to relying on hereditary ties, public support, and fitness for office. Shaikh Ahmad may have been the better candidate because the community favored him, but misconduct and failure to keep his registers accurate and up-to-date put him on the fast track for dismissal. Yet what the petitioners' continued and repeated interactions with the Pune and Bombay governments make clear is that despite their threats to ignore the government's appointee, who the government appointed mattered, and refusing to acknowledge the government qazi was easier said than done. Even failed petitions express an investment in the government's authority.[102]

Muhammad Yusuf Moorghay, Qazi for the City of Bombay (1837–1866)

While Nur-ud-Din Husain and Shaikh Ahmad inherited their positions, Mahomed Yusuf Moorghay's path to the office of qazi for the city of Bombay was less conventional. Born around 1775 (1189 AH), Yusuf Moorghay spent much of his childhood under the care of his brother, Shaikẖ Muḥammad ʿAṭāʾ-ud-Dīn, following their father's premature death.[103] When his brother passed away, Yusuf Moorghay joined the EIC, starting as head munshi (secretary) for the military seminary at Versova.[104] In 1809 he joined Nicholas Hankey Smith's expedition to Hyderabad, Sind, working as a secretary and translator for the Company, before rising to the position of native agent. Yusuf Moorghay's scribal skills made him valuable as the Company struggled to control the northwestern frontier: "The Moonshee was especially useful in gaining intelligence . . . and being able to write Hindoostanee, in the Roman Character, even if his dispatches were intercepted, by the Meers of

Sindh . . . they could learn nothing from them."[105] His faithful and attentive work earned him generous compensation from the Company: in 1823 he successfully petitioned for an increase in his monthly salary from Rs. 200 to Rs. 425, placing him toward the top of the Company's pay scale.[106] He remained in Sind "at the constant peril of his life" after Smith's mission returned to Bombay, and he continued to supply the EIC with useful information about various plots and schemes: "The Political records of Government teem with useful information collected by this person . . . when it was difficult to be acquired."[107] Then, after two decades working in Sind, he retired in 1830 and returned to Bombay, receiving a Company pension of Rs. 150 per month for the remainder of his life.[108] Back in his hometown at the age of fifty-five, Yusuf Moorghay was ready to relax, yet rather than slide into old age, he took on new responsibilities managing family affairs.

For the next several years, Yusuf Moorghay acted as *wakīl* (lawyer, agent) for two of his female relatives—his brother Yūnas's wife, Rabia Beebee [Rābiʿa Bībī], and her sister Khadija [Ḵẖadīja]—while the two sisters were embroiled in a dispute over their father's estate with their brother, ʿAbd-ur-Raḥmān Nalkhanday. Rabia Beebee selected Yusuf Moorghay to represent them because he was "a simple honest person" and being her brother-in-law meant that he would "act for the benefit of [her]self and [her] children." She naturally believed he could be trusted and would "not act deceitfully or fraudulently towards" her.[109] The case dragged on for nearly a decade, from 1826 to 1835, during which "costs were incurred to a considerable amount," and Yusuf Moorghay took "various sums on loan at interest[,] and as collateral . . . he found it necessary to mortgage the family property."[110] When the suit ended in a compromise, there was little profit to split between the two sisters. Yusuf Moorghay's accounts from the case revealed that he overspent the amount he charged the two for representing their case. Furthermore, although he recommended that the two sisters split their award, Rabia Beebee instead allowed her sister to collect the six-thousand-rupee settlement while she alone accepted the debts of their legal fees.[111] Not all disputes receive such robust representation in the archives, but Rabia Beebee's complaints against her brother-in-law became part of the judicial department's records when Yusuf Moorghay became the Company's preferred candidate for a vacancy in the office of qazi for Bombay city.

In 1836, toward the end the inheritance dispute, Bombay's Qazi Kootbudeen [Quṯb-ud-Dīn] passed away. Immediately, petitions appeared, advocating for one candidate or another. Yusuf Moorghay's name rose to the top almost immediately. The brother of the deceased qazi, Moohumud Syeed

Mahimkur [Muḥammad Sayyid Mahīmkar], was only twenty-two years old at the time and was engaged in the study of "Mohomedan law," but he "had not yet gained such a proficiency as to enable him to conduct the duties of the high office." The petitioners, led by Ibrahim Jeeteykur [Jītaykar], thought Yusuf Moorghay could fill in: "Considering however that the Cazeeship has been held by his [Mahimkur's] family for a period of about 150 years, we request that, until . . . the deceased's brother qualifies himself to carry on the duties of the office, Your Excellency in Council will have the kindness to appoint Moohummud Yoosoof Saheb bin Moohummud Hussun Moorgey" in his stead.[112]

Support for Mahimkur was nearly unanimous, but not everyone agreed with Yusuf Moorghay's interim appointment. "Some people have given a petition in favor of Moohumud Yoosuf (Moorgey) but most people are not satisfied with him," a group led by Gyasoodeen Ahmud Moorad [Ġhiyāṣ-ud-Dīn Aḥmad Murād] explained. They acknowledged that Mahimkur was not ready to take over, but they wanted a better representative to fill in: "There are now at Bombay 50,000 Mussulmans of the 4 Sects (Hanifee, Shafiee, Hanbilee, Malikee). Should Government wish to gratify their wishes[,] then it is necessary that all[,] great and small[,] should be asked about their choice." Instead of Yusuf Mooghay, Gyasoodeen's faction suggested that the current assistant take over until the brother was ready. If that would not work, the petitioners named two additional candidates—"Moolvee Mahomed Tahir, and Mahomed Yoonus Hafiz (who has the Koran by heart)"—each of whom had already "passed an examination before the Sudder Adawlut, and who possess the requisite fitness and qualifications for this high office." Another group, led by Hussainoodeen [Ḥusain-ud-Dīn], also petitioned the government to reject Yusuf Moorghay. They drew attention to the high status of the office and, by implication, to Yusuf Moorghay's failure to measure up: "The Cazee for the Island of Bombay should be most learned and master of the principles of the Mahomedan law and of equity and who for the sake of God alone, would do what may be proper, without showing favor or regard to anyone." Yusuf Moorghay was not a suitable replacement because his appointment "would be right only if all the Mussulmans were unanimously in his favor." They urged the government to hold off "until a person of such description is found."[113]

By naming the four schools of Sunni jurisprudence, referring to the size and diversity of Bombay's Muslim population, and presenting additional candidates, the petitioners challenged Yusuf Moorghay's viability and questioned his fitness for office, but their complaints gained little traction. They failed to provide the government with any substantive arguments against his nomination. Yusuf Moorghay's status as a prominent and distinguished Sunni Muslim was well supported: government records not only described him as "a person much respected by his own Sect and considered as a strict Soonee Moosulman" but also recognized him as "one of those distinguished Natives, who ought to be honored, and supported, by our Government."[114] He, too, was a *ḥāfiẓ* of the Qur'an, and his scribal skills were already well known to the government. What is more, some of Yusuf Moorghay's most vociferous supporters traversed Bombay's sectarian divisions.[115] The petitioners' references to Bombay's diversity echoed Company commitments to religious neutrality and the Hastings Plan's ideas of religious legal pluralism but provided little reason to doubt Yusuf Moorghay.

Company officials reviewed arguments against Yusuf Moorghay with mild interest until they heard from his sister-in-law, Rabia Beebee. Her first petition arrived in April 1837 and delineated her experience trusting and being betrayed by him: "I placed confidence in his sweet words mixed with deceit," she recounted, "I did not think that he would follow the dictates of his nature, as the offspring of a slave girl!" As her "vakeel" (*vakīl, wakīl*), Yusuf Moorghay deceived her, stole her inheritance, and behaved dishonorably. Such a man could hardly serve as qazi for the city of Bombay: "How can a person whose principles are such . . . be fit for such an office? And how can the Mussulmans ever trust to him for the proper performance of the duties of that office? And what confidence can they place in his justice and equity?"[116] By her account, Yusuf Moorghay's deceit was so great and his character so baseless that they could not trust him to be qazi.

While Company officials all but ignored the other petitions against Yusuf Moorghay, they gave Rabia Beebee's complaints due consideration. Petitions like hers were rare, but when women voiced concerns, Company officials took them seriously. After recommending that Rabia Beebee "seek redress in the court of law," department officials then called on Yusuf Moorghay to explain himself. Toward the end of May, he submitted a detailed explanation defending himself with documents that supported his side of the story. His records gave a precise timeline for the suit; his accounts accurately reflected the related expenses; and his response clarified and contextualized his role. Rabia Beebee sent another complaint the following month, begging the government to provide her "protection and Justice," but by then it was too late. The government was satisfied with Yusuf Moorghay's explanation and "could not interfere" on Rabia Beebee's behalf. At four o'clock in the afternoon on June 7, 1837, in a special ceremony held on the steps of the Bombay Town Hall, Mahomed Yusuf Moorghay received his certificate of appointment, signed by Robert Grant, "Governor of His Majesty's Castle and Island of Bombay," along with two shawls.[117] In a sworn statement that accompanied his sanad, the qazi pledged good conduct and a faithful commitment to the office, and those who had petitioned against him received cursory replies to their unsuccessful requests.[118]

After winning the uphill battle for his appointment in 1837, Yusuf Moorghay remained qazi for the city of Bombay until his death, but he did not do so without controversy. Toward the end of his career, infighting among Bombay's Muslims brought Yusuf Moorghay's conduct into question again, yet rather than remaining within the pages of the EIC's records, these disputes instead played out in the courts of law and in the press. Reflecting the new circumstances surrounding the qazi's office, the British government's waning interest in the appointment and management of officeholders, and the growing engagement of an active Muslim public, these later controversies brought to light new conceptions of the qazi's office and his connection to Muslim legal rights and responsibilities. That story is the subject of chapter 3.

Conclusion: Three Experiences in the Context of Empire

During the first phase of Company rule, the lives and careers of individual officeholders laid the foundation for the government's continued engagement with qazis, muftis, and other legal intermediaries into the second half of the nineteenth century. While the extraordinary lives of notable, notorious, and noteworthy figures like Nur-ud-Din Husain, Shaikh Ahmad, and Yusuf Moorghay provide one perspective from which to consider this history, their exceptional stories necessarily exclude the experiences of their rivals, allies, colleagues, and coconspirators who also contributed to the Company's broader efforts to manage, administer, rationalize, and eventually do away with the qazi's office. Stepping back from the individual experiences of the exceptional figures introduced here, the next chapter examines the aggregate experience of the two hundred or so other qazis whose interactions with British officials marked the transition from precolonial, to high colonial, to postcolonial rule. Following these underdogs and unexpected allies, the discussion charts Company efforts to remove irregularities from the office; to manage the income, emoluments, and perquisites attached to old qazi appointments; and to rationalize the distribution and arrangement of appointments across the British Empire's territories—all the while balancing issues of religious difference and normative expectations bound up in the office. The relative successes and failures of these efforts laid the foundation for what would become, in many cases, a pluralistic, decentralized, and contradictory approach to the administration of religious personal law across British India.

As the discussion of Nur-ud-Din Husain, Shaikh Ahmad, and Yusuf Moorghay demonstrates, British rule ushered in an era of lasting change. Some qazis from illustrious families managed to hang on to the office, leveraging earlier entitlements under the new regime. Others fell from grace, owing either to their own failures or to their rival's successes. Many disappeared from the written record after Company officials dismissed their claims, but sometimes they reappeared, inspired by an incumbent's death, a change in policy, or the possibilities of a new legal order. For some in rural areas, land grants were the only reason to keep the title, and once the EIC successfully (for the most part) severed the qazi's office from erstwhile land grants, interest dwindled. By contrast, in urban areas, such as the city of Bombay, competition over the status, prestige, and authority kept alive fierce competition over the qazi's office. Throughout the first half of the nineteenth century, these factors combined to give the qazi's office new importance among educated Muslim elites across the subcontinent while it was receding from the records of the British government of India. The following chapters trace that transformation, not only as it unfolded in relation to the hundreds of individuals, like Nur-ud-Din Husain, Yusuf Moorghay, and Shaikh Ahmad, who struggled for Company recognition as qazis (chapter 2) but also in the context of the British Empire's changing relationship to South Asia's Muslims—as subjects of surveillance and scrutiny—across its imperial expanse (chapter 3).

2 Creating a Qazi Class

Navigating Expectations between Company and Community

In regard to the office of Cazee [*qāẓī*] [,] it is the present custom to examine the Cazees, and bestow the office upon those who best sustain the examination. But this course is attended with great injury to some poor attender Cazees. They lose their Wuttons [*waṭans*; lands] and are obliged to beg from door to door. This should not be. Rather let them be permitted to perform the duties of the office as well as they can and enjoy their Wuttons. And in order to fit them better for their office let instruction representing their duties be prepared in the Persian, Hindoostanee, Marrathee, and Goozerathee languages, and sent to them, they paying the cost of the Instructions. In this way they will be enabled to retain the Hucks [*ḥaqqs*; rights, entitlements] and Wuttons which have descended to them from their Ancestors.

—Excerpt of a petition from Gayasoodeen Mooftee of the Ahmednagar ʿAdalat, August 20, 1850

Tensions of Empire

In 1850 Gayasoodeen Mooftee [G̱ẖiyāṣ̤-ud-Dīn Muftī], then mufti for the court at Ahmednagar, sent the British East India Company's judicial department at Bombay a plan for improving the status, conditions, and qualifications of individuals holding the office of qazi under Regulation XXVI of 1827.[1] Established qazis had been cut from the Company's roster owing to their poor performance on department examinations and were now "obliged to beg from door to door."[2] To avoid this fate, Gayasoodeen recommended that the Company protect the qazis' "wuttons" (*waṭans*)—lands given to support the officeholder in his home district—and let them relearn their trade, rather than replacing them. They should "be permitted to perform the duties of the office" and encouraged to improve their skills. Instead of removing them from office, depriving them of their hereditary lands, and forcing them into penury, the Company could establish correspondence courses and outfit qazis with study materials in several of the presidency's languages, including Persian, Hindustani, Marathi, and Gujarati.[3] Officeholders would pay for these materials, so as not to drain Company accounts, and these instructional opportunities would contribute to the Company's efforts to employ only qualified qazis and strengthen the position of these otherwise displaced individuals. Gayasoodeen's plan thus involved efforts to retain local talent and to offer job training for unemployed persons.

After fixing the problems with examinations and hereditary appointments, Gayasoodeen went on to suggest that, perhaps, the Company should also reconfigure its examinations to accommodate more than book learning and rote recitation. At present, the examination evaluated qazis "only in reference to their knowledge," he explained. "It would be better if they were examined likewise in reference to their religion, so that they may be placed in authority only over those belonging to the same sect as themselves."[4] Gayasoodeen's complaints were apt. In their attempts to employ existing qazis in its new territories, Company officials paid little heed to questions of sectarian or doctrinal difference. Despite arguments from petitioners, candidates, and emerging colonial publics that different qazis represented different sects, factions, and parties, there was little, if any, effort to appoint qazis who reflected Muslim diversity in western India.[5] Subsequent campaigns to recognize legal pluralism beyond the simplistic Hindu-Muslim divide would later acknowledge these complexities, yet when it came to appointing qazis, Company officials tended to favor singularity over doctrinal diversity.[6]

Gayasoodeen's suggestions for reforming qazi appointments were well intentioned and well researched. After suggesting that the Company test its appointees on "religion" rather than "knowledge," he gave the following analogy: "Look at the Christian Religion," he began. "There are many sects belonging to that religion, but we no where see those belonging to one Sect exercising authority over those of another. So it should be among the [Muslims]."[7] Suggesting that no Christian would agree to have religious ceremonies performed by a priest from another sect, Gayasoodeen thought it absurd to assign qazis to serve communities with different doctrinal or sectarian affiliations. Although his comparison between Muslim and Christian sects might sound strange, Gayasoodeen was not alone: Company officials also referred to qazis as "priests" (perhaps recognizing that some served as *imāms*, prayer leaders, at local mosques) and described their communities as "congregations" (usually in the context of arguing that there were too many priests serving too few congregants).[8]

Yet beyond this superficial comparison, Gayasoodeen had a larger point to make: qazi appointments frequently placed Company objectives above the needs of local communities. As Mahomed Yusuf Moorghay's contested appointment from the previous chapter shows, Company favorites often received official nominations, even if community members voiced opposition. Thus, despite his efforts, Gayasoodeen's recommendations had no impact. Rather than take the mufti's proposals seriously, the secretary in Bombay rejected the portion regarding watans, asserting that "the office of Cazee is not recognized as an hereditary office either by the Regulation or by the Mahomedan Law," and suggested that he resubmit his complaints about exams to the Bombay *ṣadr ʿadālat* (chief court).[9] The proposals received no further consideration.

Whether he knew it or not, Gayasoodeen's rejected recommendations spoke to larger tensions within the Company's judicial department. These broader patterns emerged gradually, from early appointments at the end of the eighteenth century to tallies compiled in the 1860s, as Company officials acted with certain principles in mind: to keep competent individuals in office (merit); to regularize appointments, make compensation consistent, and minimize dependence on government resources (bureaucracy); and to separate the qazi's so-called private, religious functions from the public, judicial functions of the courts (administration).[10] Administrators worked toward these aims with periodic attempts to catalog, review, and organize appointments (making sure to weed out incompetent or negligent officeholders), but their efforts were far from successful. In practice, qazi appointments conflicted with Company ideals and challenged core definitions of law and religion.

While the previous chapter highlighted how elite families and prominent qazis capitalized on new opportunities arising from the British East India Company's expansion in western India, disputes in this chapter show that competing ideas about ability, status, and normativity created constant friction. Applicants exploited these tensions and drew on different strands of Company policy to make claims using hereditary titles, existing rights, and individual merits. On paper, Company officials favored merit and looked askance at hereditary titles and rights, but in practice, separating one from the others was more complicated than officials assumed. Although they fell on deaf ears, Gayasoodeen's recommendations astutely identified the larger implications of these ongoing conflicts. Qazi negotiations (1) pit Company policies against prevailing practices, (2) raised doubts about meritocratic qualifications and normative definitions, and (3) called on community support and courtroom litigation to settle disputes, producing not a handful of exceptional or extraordinary individuals (as chapter 1 might suggest) but a class of officeholders with vocal communities of supporters instead. In the longer history of Islamic legal practice, contests over qazis challenged simple definitions of Islam and law and raised vexed questions that would reappear in legislative committees and courtroom debates in the second half of the nineteenth century.

Standing for Office: Making Claims in Response to Company Policy

Before it could claim to manage its qazis, the British East India Company first had to figure out who the qazis were. Following the introduction of Regulation XXVI of 1827, officials across the presidency's several districts requested that all claimants present themselves at court to receive new, Company-issued certificates of appointment. In places like Bharuch, where the qazi family was established and well known, officeholders made uncontested claims and received their Company *sanads* (certificates of appointment; see chapter 1). Elsewhere, Company officials struggled to recognize rightful claimants and process their requests. J. A. Shaw's experiences in Ratnagiri show just how complicated this process could be. After months of inquiry and investigation, Shaw all but gave up on the task. Writing to his supervisor, he lamented,

> You are probably aware that every village which possesses three or four houses of Mussalmans [Muslims] has one or more Cazees, who according to the usual tenants of spiritual Establishments in this country or at least in this district have been accustomed to look upon themselves and to be looked upon by others as the hereditary and undispossessable [*sic*] proprietors of the office. Wuttans[11] are each divided into separate shares among many separate houses and then again subdivided among the Brethren of each House. . . . You are also well aware that, in pursuance of this view of the case, Cazeepuns [*qāẓīpans*][12] have been hitherto bought, sold, mortgaged; that persons living in the Company's territories, but out of this District, that persons living in this District (even Bra[h]mins) but holding situations and following pursuits that rendered it impossible for them personally to perform the duties of their offices have each (one and all) held the superiorities over Cazeepuns and discharged their duties by nayibs [*nāʾibs*; assistants] and that, on almost every-one of these several descriptions of claim, suits have been tried and decrees issued and enforced by the Court of Adawlut [*ʿadālat*].[13]

Detailing complaints like those Gayasoodeen would echo twenty years later, Shaw made his frustration clear: officeholders were numerous—even in villages with no discernible Muslim population—and their offices, their *qāẓīpans*, had been bought, sold, mortgaged, bequeathed, and divided among heirs so many times that it was all but impossible to tell who held what office. Non-Muslims, including the "Bra[h]mins" he mentioned, claimed the title, as did other ill-suited individuals. Such claims not only complicated Shaw's work but also made any effort to manage the office hopeless.

Across the presidency's several districts, Company administrators like Shaw struggled to fulfill directives aimed at identifying and recognizing local qazis. Depending on the nature of the original appointment, whether it had been renewed or reinstated as Mughal rule waned and successor states grew, and how many generations had managed to share, divide, sell, or mortgage the "office," district officials could face an ever-growing number of claims to jurisdictions that amounted to not much more than a couple of villages or a few households. To "prove" their claims, claimants brought piles of evidence that included certificates of appointment (authentic or fraudulent) issued by earlier regimes; documents, registers, or witness testimony showing that they did the work of the qazi and therefore deserved the title; petitions showing that local residents favored them; or results from the examinations they passed—either owing to their ability or because the evaluators were biased. Neither Shaw nor his colleagues were equipped to handle these claims.

Under normal circumstances, district judges filled qazi vacancies by making a recommendation to the registrar of the chief civil court (*ṣadr dīwānī ʿadālat*) in Bombay.[14] If there was no obvious replacement, the judge would advertise the vacancy, but in most cases, a relative, subordinate, or officeholder from a nearby district was available.[15] The judge's recommendation would describe the candidate's qualifications—noting his intellectual accomplishments, skills, character, knowledge of "the law," linguistic abilities (i.e., whether he knew Arabic and Persian), or hereditary connection to the position. He might also mention a candidate's reputation or status, as the acting judge did in 1837 when looking to fill a vacancy in the qazi's office at Surat.[16] To fill the vacancy, the district judge would request that the government at Bombay issue a sanad to the individual (figure 2.1). The court register would check his records and forward his and the district judge's recommendation to the judges of the chief court. The secretary to government for the judicial department would review and approve the

Appendix, (A.)

FORM of Sunnud to be granted to a Kazee.

To *A. B.* inhabitant of ———. (L. S.)

In conformity with the provisions of Regulation XXVI. A. D. 1827, you *A. B.* are hereby appointed to the office of Kazee in the ——— of ———; you will not be liable to be removed from your situation, while you discharge your duty with zeal and integrity under the rules contained in the Regulations which now are or hereafter may be in force.

By order of the Governor in Council,

(signed) *C. D.*,

Bombay Castle, Secretary to Government
day of 18 . in the Judicial Department.

FIGURE 2.1 Sample text for a qazi sanad (certificate of appointment), issued under Bombay Regulation XXVI of 1827, as outlined in House of Commons Paper No. 201, Regulations Passed by the Governments of Bengal, Fort St. George, and Bombay in the Year 1827. Parliamentary Papers, House of Commons, 1829, Vol. 23, 302.

recommendation; the court register would then issue a sanad. "Prepared in conformity with Regulation XXVI of 1827, on a stamped paper for the value of ten rupees," the governor in council would add his signature to the sanad, and it would be delivered to the qazi upon receipt of ten rupees (the fee for the stamp) from him.[17]

The trilingual sanad he received was modeled on earlier Mughal forms but had some distinctly British characteristics.[18] The Company's seal, embossed in red wax, appeared at the top of the page, followed by the name of the appointee. In English, the sanad announced, "In conformity with the provisions of Regulation XXVI. A.D. 1827, you [qazi name] are hereby appointed to the office of Kazee [Cazee, Qazi] in the [district/town] of [place]; you will not be liable to be removed from your situation, while you discharge your duty with zeal and integrity under the rules contained in the Regulations which now are or hereafter may be in force." It was signed and dated "Bombay Castle," "by order of the Governor in Council."[19] Following the prescribed English text, the sanad then included a similar statement in Persian and a third translation into the relevant vernacular language (Gujarati in some; Marathi/Modi in others). Where the English text began starkly, the Persian version offered more gravitas, referring to the appointee as "sharīʿāt panāh" (the shelter of shariʿa) or "sharīʿat nishān" (the emblem of shariʿa), as in figure 2.2. It defined Regulation XXVI as "qānūn-i bīst-wa-shashum" (law twenty-six), and referred to the office as "k̲h̲idmat-i qazāʾ-yi [X place]" (service of judgeship in X place). It further charged the qazi to execute his work "ba-nēk naẕrī" (with good oversight), "ba-nēk ʿamalī" (with good

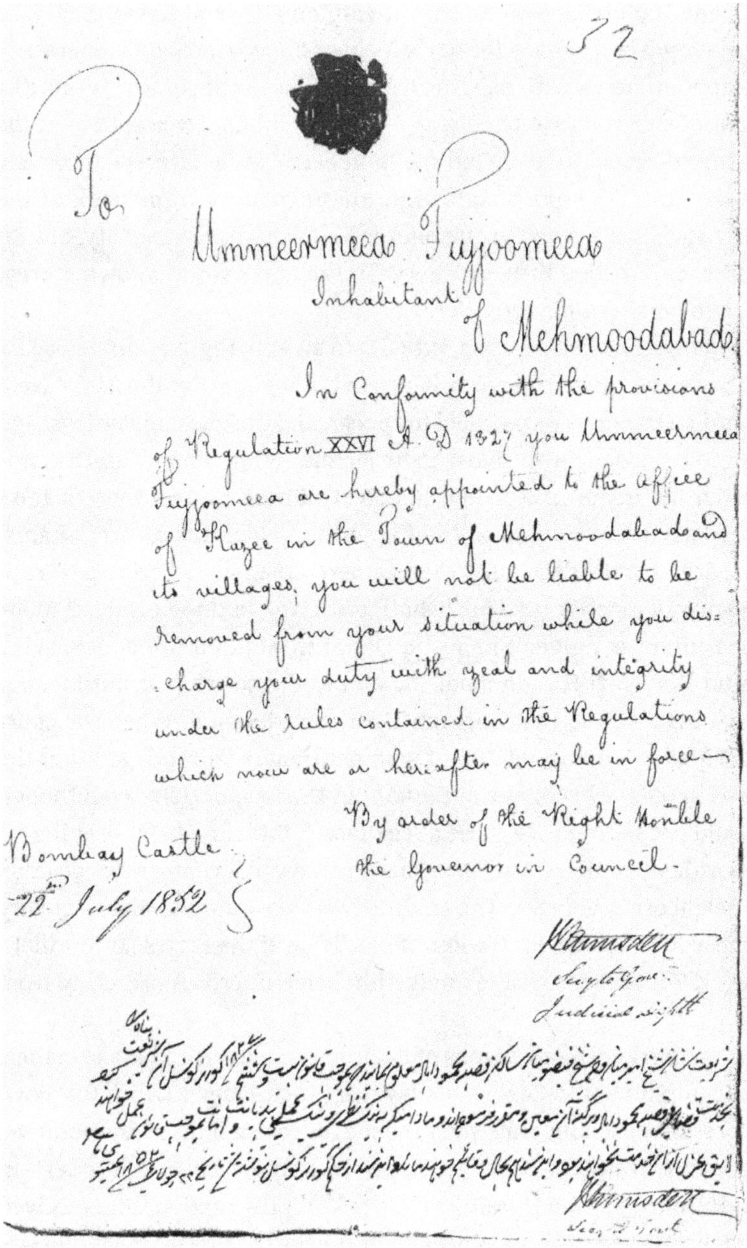

32

To

Ummeermeea Fujjoomeea

Inhabitant

of Mehmoodabad

In Conformity with the provisions of Regulation XXVI A.D. 1827 you Ummeermeea Fujjoomeea are hereby appointed to the office of Kazee in the Town of Mehmoodabad and its villages, you will not be liable to be removed from your situation while you discharge your duty with zeal and integrity under the rules contained in the Regulations which now are or hereafter may be in force—

By order of the Right Hon'ble the Governor in Council.

Bombay Castle
22nd July 1852

Secy to Govt.
Judicial Dept.

FIGURE 2.2 Facsimile of a qazi sanad (certificate of appointment), issued to Ummeermeea Fujjoomeea, under Regulation XXVI of 1827 on July 22, 1852. The third language (Gujarati) of the trilingual document has been lopped off from the bottom of the page, after being folded to fit within the volume of records. Maharashtra State Archives, Judicial Department Proceedings, 1853, Vol. 20.

actions), and "ba-diyānat wa amānat" (with integrity and sincerity).[20] Like the regulation itself, sanads for qazis melded the government's interest in orderly appointments with existing expectations for the office. Terms like *sharīʿat nishān* and *sharīʿat panāh* tapped into traditional conceptions of the qazi as the representative of God's will on earth while references to "law twenty-six" drew the qazi's status into the regulatory framework of the Company-state. Yet beyond vague references to character and duty, official appointments provided little guidance for the qazi's work, allowing great variation to persist in his activities.

While judges in some districts settled into an easy rhythm, filling vacancies as they arose, Shaw had no such luck in Ratnagiri. After the notice went out in his district, many qazis failed to appear, and usurpers, underdogs, and opportunists stepped in to make their claims. While Shams-ud-Dīn was away from his home in Kurdhe, his rival Burhān-ud-Dīn sent "a false report . . . asserting a claim to the kazeeship." Upon his return, Shams-ud-Din learned of the deceit and then gathered the town's "principal" residents to submit a petition on his behalf, testifying to these events.[21] Shaw remained unmoved, given Shams-ud-Din's initial failure to appear. Like Burhan-ud-Din, Qazi Husain made a claim to the qaziship at Kurdhe, but Shaw sent his claim to the court mufti for consideration. When the court mufti decided in Burhan-ud-Din's favor, petitioners later alleged that the mufti was in the pocket of one of Burhan-ud-Din's supporters, even though Shaw could not substantiate these allegations.[22] Burhan-ud-Din kept the office at Kurdhe, but afterward, Qazi Husain received a comparable position in two neighboring villages. The tradeoff was, according to Shaw, "a very handsome compensation for the loss of his divide of the shares [at Kurdhe]," but news of the assistant judge's makeshift solution brought scrutiny from Bombay.[23]

Shaw's inquiry inspired dozens of qazis to come forth and make claims. Shaboodeen [Shihāb-ud-Dīn] sent a "wukeel [*wakīl*; agent] with full powers" to present his claim, but when the judges rejected his representative, Shaboodeen traveled to Ratnagiri himself, only to learn that a certain Goolam Husain [G̱ẖulām Ḥusain] "made false representation" and received Shaboodeen's hereditary appointment at Rajapur.[24] Government officials told Shaboodeen to take his complaints to court to win back his office, if he desired. Similarly, Qazi Inoosbin Kazee Ahmed [Yūnas, son of Qazi Aḥmed] traveled to Ratnagiri armed with evidence of his claim to the qazi's office for several villages in the Vijayadrug region, including a grant his family received from the former Maratha government and evidence that he had continued to perform the qazi's work after the Company took over. He lost his claim after the judge, "without attending to [Yunas's] testimony," assigned half the jurisdiction to his brother and the other half to a certain Qazi Yusuf.[25] Without knowing whose claims were legitimate, whose papers were authentic, or whose excuses for failing to appear were appropriate, sorting through the claims was slow going. Shaw was rebuked for decisions he made to distribute offices or to reappoint applicants to nearby posts, and eventually he transferred to another position, leaving many of the disputes unresolved.

Ratnagiri was not the only place to suffer from competing, overlapping, and inconsistent claims, but the steady stream of disputes, contests, and rivalries that arose there turned Ratnagiri into a point of later reference for Company officials. Shaw's experiences also proved that efforts to compile a complete and accurate list of appointees were, quite often, more trouble than they were worth. His attempt to receive requests at a specified time and to reconfirm appointments in an orderly manner matched the Company's interest in regular, rational, and efficient appointments, but the procedures did not square with on-the-ground realities. Attempts to confirm existing appointments mixed hereditary entitlements, property claims, and professional qualifications without giving one claim clear precedence over the others. Interest in expediency and efficiency further meant that the first claimant often received the appointment, leaving (potentially) more legitimate claimants to work out their claims through other means.

While Shaw struggled with competing claims in the Konkan, officials in other districts wrestled with different aspects of the appointments. In the short term, it may have been easiest simply to recognize existing office-holders, but in the long term, Company officials wanted qazis to be suitably qualified for the office. Examinations became the preferred method for gauging a qazi's qualifications, but getting candidates to take—let alone to pass—the exam was a constant struggle. Muhammad Safdar's claim to the qazi's office in Pune demonstrates the difficulties Company officials faced as they tried to pivot from hereditary to merit-based appointments.

To contest the appointment in 1836 of his assistant-cum-rival, Hyatoolakhan (who appeared in chapter 1), Muhammad Safdar not only couched his hereditary claim in the language of Company policy but also rejected the examination requirement: "Your petitioner is aware that an order of the Right Hon'ble Governor in Council has been passed to the effect, that while existing rights are to be respected, and no Cauzy exercising that office at the time of passing the regulation is to be disturbed, unless convicted of some misdemeanor, every hereditary successor to the Kauzeeship, shall hence forward undergo an examination in Musulman Law before he receives a commission from the Right Hon'ble the Governor in Council."[26] Like some qazis he knew in the Konkan, Muhammad Safdar hoped to be excluded from the examination requirement. He came from a family that had held the office in Pune for nearly four hundred years, he was also "now above 70 years of age," and his work had been reduced in recent decades, such that he had "no other duties to perform, except those connected with the marriage and divorce of Musalmans." Testing him was therefore unnecessary. He "both felt it to be impossible [to pass] and could not help at the same time considering it as unnecessary that [he] should come forward and be examined."[27] Yet had Muhammad Safdar simply taken time to pass the exam, he might have avoided the lengthy dispute that awaited him.

Teasing apart the competing logics of hereditary connections and intellectual qualifications, Muhammad Safdar's claim to the position at Pune became a test case for Company officials and one that they continued to wrestle with for several years. The qazi's claim to the office was strong. As he narrated, "My ancestors have obtained Sunnuds from the ancient Pashas [*pādshāhs/bādshāhs*; kings], both of Delhi and the Deccan, as well as from their Vuzeers [*wazīrs*; governors], and also from the Rajas and [K]hwas.[28] The originals of which are still in my possession." Muhammad Safdar attached several documents, sanads granted to his predecessors by different rulers ranging from "Adil Shah" (likely referring to one of the ʿAdil Shahi sultans from the dynasty that ruled the Sultanate of Bijapur from 1490 to 1686), to "'Sewage,' Raja of Sattara" (likely referring to Shivaji Bhonsale I, founder of the Maratha Confederacy), to "'Gazeeudeen Khan,' vuzier by order of the Pasha" (possibly Ghazi-ud-Din Khan Feroz Jung, father of Nizam-ul-Mulk Asaf Jah, founder of the Hyderabad *niẓāmat* [administration]), down to the present petitioner, who renewed his father's sanad in 1790 by traveling to Aurangabad.[29] If maintaining the office lay in proving his claims to the position before British rule, then Muhammad Safdar would appear to have a legitimate claim, but Hyatoolakhan, his assistant, presented serious opposition. For four centuries, the two qazis' families had worked side-by-side in Pune, but recently, Judge Alexander Bell gave Hyatoolakhan, a better-qualified officeholder (and Shaikh Ahmad's chief rival in chapter 1), a sanad, thereby usurping Muhammad Safdar's authority.

Officials responded to Muhammad Safdar's complaint cautiously. Henry Brown, then acting register for the judicial department at Bombay, warned that "if it be true as represented by Cazee Mohomed Sufdar that he is the incumbent, he cannot in conformity with the Regulation be dismissed from his Situation except in the case of misconduct."[30] The judicial consultation echoed this advice, stating that the "petitioner [Muhammad Safdar] should be restored" and recommending that the judge at Pune conduct further inquiries into the relationship between the two qazis. It was as yet unclear whether the two were equals or whether Hyatoolakhan was Muhammad Safdar's subordinate. Furthermore, "if the matter be one of intricacy, the contending parties should be allowed to settle their claims, by law," the memorandum offered.[31] In the meantime, Robert Grant, then governor in council, cautioned the judge at Pune, not to "issue any Sannud, or in any manner give to either party any new dignity or privilege."[32] Sending the dispute back to the district, the judicial department offered three tentative recommendations: investigate the qazi's claims, issue no sanads until the issue be resolved, and advise the qazis to settle their dispute in court.

When the issue remained unresolved the following year, Muhammad Safdar again petitioned the judicial department at Bombay. In the meantime, residents at Pune began to complain about both qazis' conduct, drawing attention to the "serious inconvenience of the Mohammedan Population" that occurred because "Cazee Mohamed Sufdur . . . and Syed Hyatoolla Khan . . . are constantly quarrelling with each other."[33] A complaint submitted by a certain "Shaik Ally," for instance, made specific reference to the qazi's refusal to solemnize a marriage before receiving five rupees as his "Huk" (*ḥaqq*; right).[34] The Company had some interest in the fees qazis received but only intervened when there was evidence of impropriety.[35] A five-rupee fee was hardly grounds for investigation.[36] Secretary J. P. Willoughby confirmed that if the qazi "is guilty of gross negligence or misconduct," he could be removed from office, but suggested that "it will perhaps be considered sufficient to admonish the Cazee on this occasion."[37] The secretary gestured toward the possibility of further investigation, but the government ultimately opted for inaction.

While it may have been easy to dismiss these complaints, the dispute between Muhammad Safdar and Hyatoolakhan proved more intractable. In September 1837 Grant noted "that there is something in this case which we have not yet fully sifted." To him it was as yet unclear whether the two had equal claims; whether both were already confirmed under Section IV of Regulation XXVI of 1827; or whether the government had any right to remove one or the other claimant. Offering to inspect the qazis' family sanads, Grant asserted that "Government has full power to decide this altercation according to law and justice" and should do so, rather than allowing "a matter of public concernment to be settled by private compromise."[38] Amassing and evaluating the evidence, however, was necessary but difficult. While Muhammad Safdar made a hereditary claim, Hyatoolakhan had qualified with an exam. The two grounds for appointment conflicted, and without receiving,[39] verifying,[40] and translating[41] the relevant documents as evidence, the conflict remained impossible to resolve.

Yet even after the oriental translator determined that the two qazis were joint appointees, Muhammad Safdar did not drop his claims to superiority. In 1840 he again petitioned the government in Bombay, this time alleging that Hyatoolakhan had interfered with his business. The joint qazi had allegedly "prepared papers without the seal of the qazi being fixed thereon, nor did he pay to [Muhammad Safdar] his *Hucks* [*ḥaqqs*]." As deputy qazi, Hyatoolakhan's preparation of deeds—without the chief qazi's permission or seal—represented a clear violation: "The business of Cazee is to celebrate marriages and 'Nicas' [*nikāḥs*; marriages], to prepare bonds of separation, and settle any dispute in which the whole Mahomedan community [is] concerned while that of naib is only to celebrate marriages and nothing else," Muhammad Safdar argued.[42] Rather than intervene, the government concluded that "the proper course of action for the petitioner to adopt . . . is to bring an action against [his opponent] in the Civil Court."[43] Company officials would no longer referee.

When Muhammad Safdar eventually passed away in 1843, his son and his elder brother applied to replace him, but by that time, the government had moved on. "As a cazeeship has been decided not to be hereditary . . . and as the local circumstances . . . appear to render the office of a second cazee no longer necessary," the judge at Pune declined to appoint a successor for Muhammad Safdar's office; Hyatoolakhan was now in charge.[44] Although officials would continue to appoint family members and their descendants, Company policy no longer regarded hereditary claims as sufficient grounds for appointment. Shaw's experiences at Ratnagiri and Muhammad Safdar's insistence on his hereditary rights pushed Company officials away from treating the office as one of entitlement and continuity.

Fit for Office? Demonstrating Competence and Fulfilling Normative Expectations

Muhammad Safdar was not the only qazi to refuse examination. While Gayasoodeen's proposals for reforming qazi appointments emphasized the need to (re)educate qazis so that hereditary titleholders could learn their trade, Muhammad Safdar's opposition lay in another set of arguments: Company courts now performed much of the qazi's former work, and detailed legal knowledge was no longer necessary. Although old age was perhaps the stronger influence here, his resistance had deeper roots. In the first decades of Company rule, there was perhaps a presumption that qazis would continue to work under the British as they had under earlier regimes, but Muhammad Safdar's obstinacy forewarned impending changes. Confirming existing appointments and issuing new sanads extended Company authority into the districts easily and efficiently at first, but as time passed, officials' willingness to rubber-stamp questionable claims, overlook applicants' lack of qualifications, and ignore derelictions of duty waned. Qualifications and the ability to pass an examination assumed greater importance while at the same time the Company-state's growing legal infrastructure chipped away at the qazi's authority more aggressively.[45]

Unlike Muhammad Safdar, many candidates nonetheless agreed to be examined, though the exams they received were not standardized. District officials regularly touted candidates' successes, but there is little evidence of what the exams contained, and there was likely great variation among them.[46] Vague references, for instance, to Persian and Arabic (the languages that Company officials associated with Islam, Islamic governance, and Islamic learning) routinely appear among candidates' qualifications, but these skills were rarely sufficient. For example, when a vacancy emerged at Oomrut [Umrēṭh], Andrew Jones, who was the judge at Ahmedabad and was responsible for filling the position, recommended a candidate who "ha[d] passed an examination before the Cazee of his City and 2 others[,] who report that he is well acquainted with the Persian language and is of a respectable family."[47] Here a successful evaluation and reference to the candidate's knowledge of Persian provided Jones with sufficient evidence to recommend his appointment. Qazi ʿAbd-ur-Rahman's description of his examination in 1855 placed similar emphasis on language: "The officer in question, having handed your Petitioner some Arabic Books, desired him to read one of them, which your Petitioner did accordingly and interpreted to the said officer the substance of the same into the Hindoostanee [Hindūstānī] language."[48] Not only could ʿAbd-ur-Rahman read the text in Arabic, but he could also translate its meaning into the spoken vernacular, Hindustani, reflecting his ability to interpret, as well as to read, the text.[49] Likewise, a candidate for office in Patoda (now in eastern Maharashtra) also used language to promote his candidacy: "I can read & write Persian & have studied the Mahomedan Law. I am now studying the Arabic language. As soon as I have completed my study[,] I shall submit to an examination."[50] Here, knowledge of Persian, acquisition of Arabic, and experience studying "the Mahomedan Law" provided adequate evidence of the candidate's qualifications, and his willingness to be examined demonstrated his compliance with Company policy. Language was an easy way to signal qualification, but it was not the only factor officials considered.[51] By contrast, in 1845, a committee evaluating candidates for a vacancy at Mahableshwar (a hill station near Bombay), for example, found one nominee "not to be an accomplished man, nor yet deeply versed in Arabic lore, but still on the whole, competent in the duties of Cazee at the small station." The position was small, so advanced knowledge of Arabic was not necessary.[52] References to language thus reflected the normative expectation that Islamic legal experts would be familiar with Arabic (the language of the Qurʾan and classical Islam), Persian (the language of governance and administration throughout much of the subcontinent), and regional vernacular languages, here referred to as Hindustani.[53]

In addition to language, candidates were also expected to know "Mahomedan law" and be familiar with the relevant texts. Discussions often glossed these works as generic "law books," but specific titles occasionally appear in the reports.[54] Among these, the *Hidaya* (*Al-Hidāya; The Guidance*), a compendium of Hanafi jurisprudence compiled by the twelfth-century central Asian scholar Burhān al-Dīn al-Marghīnānī, and the *Fatāwá-yi ʿĀlamgīrī*, a compilation produced during the reign of the Mughal emperor Aurangzeb ʿAlamgir (r. 1658–1707), appear most frequently.[55] However, as the nineteenth century progressed, pointed references to specific passages within specific texts began to replace earlier, vague references to law books.[56] When questions about the qazi's office came up for debate in the 1870s, for instance, petitioners included quotations from multiple works, along with their translations into English. By then, the publication of such law books, first by European and then by native presses, in their original languages and in translation, had expanded dramatically.[57] Commercial publishing made it possible not only for jurists to refer to printed works in their opinions but also for qazis and their critics to cite their contents when making claims about the office.[58] Ready access to legal texts, as Gayasoodeen's recommendations predicted, subsequently gave the office a clearer professional standing, but the effects of print capitalism had yet to appear when Company officials put qazis to the test, and their references to law books remained vague.

If language skills and knowledge of law books demonstrated one's fitness for office, then what made a qazi ineligible for appointment? While the clamor surrounding qazi appointments—particularly in disorderly districts like Ratnagiri, introduced earlier, and Dharwar, discussed shortly—demonstrates the interests that aspirants and their supporters brought to the office, Company decisions to validate one type of claim while rejecting others reflects another set of normative expectations surrounding the office. Although Company officials ignored shortcomings during examinations, they struggled to accept nonnormative qazis, including women and Hindus. Such claimants not only reflect the messiness that administrators encountered when trying to bring order to qazi appointments but also demonstrate how difficult it was to disentangle complicated claims. There were always ways to weasel out of examinations or to defeat a rival, but there was little room to secure an appointment as a woman or a Hindu. These putatively nonnormative claims emanated from the sale, purchase, mortgage, and inheritance of property rights previously attached to the office but flew in the face of Company expectations. If examinations provided one means for weeding out inadequate officeholders, then normative expectations provided another.

Few administrators were more derisive toward unconventional claims than W. E. Frere, who oversaw the survey of qaziships in the Dharwar district in 1850. At that time, fifty-eight people claimed to be qazi, and the majority had documentary evidence—dating back anywhere from three to thirteen generations—to prove it. Yet among these claimants, some came from Hindu communities (Desais, Lingayats, and Reddiars) and some were women, including Neekajee Beebee in "Boodeelall."[59] In his report, Frere pointed out that many lacked adequate language skills, while others showed little initiative in office: "Many of the Cazees profess ignorance as to the number of their followers[,] tho' none admit to having a smaller congregation than Krishnajee Baboorow . . . to whom only fourteen Moossulmans [Muslims] spread over five villages, owe obedience."[60] For Frere, ignorant qazis could be trained (or dismissed), but those without a sufficient "congregation" reflected larger problems with recognizing existing officeholders.

J. W. Woodcock expressed similar concerns when he began "securing duly qualified persons to officiate as Cajees throughout the Khandesh Zillah" around the same time as Frere. His district had thirty-two qazis, all of whom (save one) had been "officiating without any sunnud or having passed the necessary examination."[61] He granted ten of these individuals two years to pass the exam, adding that even though "they are very ignorant," they have continued "to perform the duties of their offices either personally or through [a] Naib from the time of their ancestors."[62] Income from these offices was so small that it would be difficult to lure better-qualified candidates into these posts. Another qazi, who openly admitted "his inability to pass an examination," had so few Muslims residing near him that Woodcock recommended terminating the position. Another had jurisdiction over a set of villages, only one of which was in British territory; the others belonged to the nizam of Hyderabad's dominions. Woodcock deemed it unnecessary to grant him a Company sanad. Elsewhere, proper qazis were absent: Hoossain Beebee, "a female, the wife of the late Cazee of the Purgunnah," performed her late husband's work "through a Naib." Woodcock proposed a replacement who was "willing to contribute towards the support of the old lady." He also recommended replacing a Hindu Kunbi (farmer) with a Muslim appointee: "A Hindoo is not a fit person to hold the office of a Cazee," Woodcock asserted, but he "await[ed] orders of Government" before acting.[63] In response to Woodcock, the government at Bombay prepared twenty sanads, accepted Woodcock's recommendation to replace Hoossain Beebee, and agreed that a qualified Muslim should take the Kunbi's position. A Hindu could not be qazi, officials at Bombay confirmed.

On paper the reorganization was sound, but replacing a Hindu was one thing; requisitioning a widow's land was another. After her replacement arrived, Hoossain Beebee petitioned the government, claiming that she and her sister-in-law, Chandabee, had an equal share in her late husband's office and were reluctant to leave the land attached to it in the new qazi's hands "on any terms."[64] Having already issued the replacement's sanad, the government rebuffed Hoossain Beebee's claims, insisting that "there is no such hereditary office as a Quazee's wuttun," but agreed to investigate the question of her compensation.[65] Upon inquiry, Secretary M. Larken reported that it would be "advisable" to offer the two women Rs. 132 annually, roughly one-third of the land's yearly produce.[66] R. Y. Bazett, circuit judge in Khandesh, feared that "the old Ladies will complain of the severity of their arrangement" but could not recommend "more favorable terms for them."[67] Rejecting the idea that a woman could manage the qazi's office, the government tried to get away with offering the women a meager stipend, but the arrangement did not satisfy them.

Chandabee petitioned the government in August of that year, claiming hereditary rights to the property now attached to the new qazi's office, citing a government decree from an 1823 dispute, and pointing to a subsequent decision from 1843 that directed the women to appoint a deputy (*nā'ib*) to continue the qazi's work on their behalf.[68] With the widows claiming a sizable piece of land, with sizable annual earnings, the government could not ignore their claims—normative expectations about qazis notwithstanding.[69] Increasing his earlier amount, Judge Bazett offered the women, together, one-third of the annual income from the lands, plus any of the fees the qazi received for the remainder of their lifetimes, after which the entire amount would revert to the qazi. Officials in Bombay thought this proposal was questionable. "In fact," one commentator reported, "I cannot understand on what principle it is contemplated to deprive these ladies of their ancestral property under the pretence of its being a Quazee's Wuttun!"[70] The governor in council remained "very doubtful" that the outcome was just and demanded further explanation.[71] By the following year, it was clear that the government had made a mistake in handing over the lands to a new qazi. The widow, though "incapable on account of her sex of discharging personally the duties of the office," should nevertheless have been able to appoint a deputy, but Woodcock's intervention made reverting to this arrangement difficult.[72] In a meek gesture toward separating the land from the office, the government referred the dispute to the Inam Commissioner for further inquiry.[73] Their "sex" might have kept them from the qazi's office, but the women still challenged Woodcock's reordering. Bureaucratic objectives could not simply sweep these female claimants under the rug. Although the government would not recognize Hoossain Beebee or her sister as qazi, it would consider their property claims. The widows' persistent petitioning thus challenged the Company's ability to reorganize the qazi appointments, at least insofar as Khandesh was concerned.

Candidates who knew Persian and Arabic; who had familiarity with relevant "law books"; who came from reputable, upstanding, and regionally powerful families; and who could curry favor with Company officials made for ideal qazis, but citing linguistic acumen, familiarity with legal texts, or the ability to pass an examination did little more than paint a veneer over a messy situation. Company officials pretended that their appointments were rooted in rationality, made by meritocracy, and tied to transparency, but beneath the surface lurked exceptions, excuses, and expedient solutions.[74] Land grants, which caused many conflicts, were difficult to detach from the office. Administrators dealt uneasily with these appointments by emphasizing examinations, severing land from labor, and shuffling claimants to other districts, where they could continue the work away from longstanding grants and emoluments, but such reassignments rarely worked.[75] At the same time, administrators sidestepped requirements by granting frequent and renewable extensions and allowing candidates to remain in office while preparing for an examination that never arrived.[76] What is more, when all else failed, when merit was murky and qualifications unclear, government officials defaulted to normative expectations, meaning they rejected the claims of women and non-Muslims.

As problems with qazi appointments persisted, government officials began to consider alternative methods. The popularity of petitioning culture meant that in some cases, qazis could secure appointment by acquiring more signatures than their opponents.[77] Aggressive petitioning could also backfire, casting doubt on a claimant's sincerity and truthfulness. Rather than convincing Company officials, petitions supporting Qazi Husain's claim in Ratnagiri, for instance, resulted in the dismissal of his case. Likewise, cantonment qazi Shaikh Ahmad still lost, even after his supporters claimed greater numbers in 1859 (see chapter 1). But community support struggled against normative and bureaucratic expectations: military officers could not appoint special qazis at the request of their men who, in one case, found the local qazi "peculiarly obnoxious," but at the same time, there was no punishment for individuals who traveled to see other qazis, even if they did so "out of sheer malice" toward the local officeholder.[78] The government was equally ambivalent when it came to upholding qazis' jurisdictions. When Hyatoolakhan, qazi at Pune, and Muhammad Aslam, qazi in neighboring Junnar, reported that local Muslims refused to let them record their marriages, the government offered to make a proclamation "informing the Mahomedan Community that the appointment of a Cazee by Government is for their benefit and that if they fail to employ him in their Marriage and religious ceremonies, they or their heirs will be liable to loss in cases of disputed property," but it would not compensate the aggrieved qazis for losses. (They were, however, "at liberty to sue the parties . . . in the civil courts.")[79] In other words, community preference and personal choice provided some freedom and flexibility, but preferences for merit and bureaucratic management still dominated.

Over time, earlier approaches began to yield to popularity and public support. During the early nineteenth-century "rage for order," Company officials still favored qualifications and bureaucratic rationale, appointing qazis with skills to districts where they were needed, but popularity and community support lingered in the background.[80] Relying on petitions to determine legitimate claims muddied attempts to prioritize skill, and resolving rivalries that involved titles, lands, and emoluments was labor intensive. As the Company's dependence on local intermediaries decreased, public support and civil litigation became more prominent. This shift reflected not only new attitudes toward religious autonomy (see part II) but also the rise of legislative intervention into personal law. The seeds for these later changes were planted in the move toward adjudicating, rather than administering, disputes over the qazi's office in the second quarter of the nineteenth century.

Litigating Qazi Claims: Community Engagement and the Making of Anglo-Indian Legal Authority

Qazis routinely appeared in court throughout the first half of the nineteenth century. Those employed as court qazis (native law officers) contributed to a variety of suits, including suits related to Muslim personal law and those involving documents notarized and authenticated by qazis. As plaintiffs and defendants, however, qazi suits fell into three categories: land disputes, claims to appointment, and questions of conduct. Land disputes were the most common and had qazis in both roles: suing and being sued, making and defending their claims to property. Hyatoolakhan, qazi for the city of Pune, participated in a couple of these suits. In 1830 he successfully fended off his rival Muhammad Safdar in a fight to recover five thousand rupees—the value of one-half of the watan attached to the qazi's office at Pune.[81] Then, in 1853, Hyatoolakhan claimed the remaining half share of the watan, which he (wrongly) thought would devolve to him when the former qazi died. That case, which found its way into the *Reports of the Selected Cases Decided by the Sudder Dewanee Adawlut* for Bombay, made it clear that Hyatoolakhan's role as qazi for the city of Pune did not nullify the property rights of those who held the mortgage to Muhammad Safdar's share.[82] Suits of this kind would continue into the twentieth century, as descendants of qazis and watandars made claims to the land their ancestors held against creditors and mortgage holders.[83]

Another category of civil suit involving qazis revolved around claims to the office itself and often arose from government recommendations that claimants pursue legal action. Litigation was a contested approach to rivalries, but it nonetheless makes an early appearance in Company records. In 1832 the judges of the sadr ʿadalat contemplated whether a qazi could "sue the Officiating Priests for interference" but were divided on whether the dispute was "a fit subject for a Civil Suit."[84] The possibility of civil litigation appears again in the context of Shaw's efforts to sort claims at Ratnagiri. Acknowledging that already "suits have been tried and decrees issued and enforced by the Court of Adawlut," he suggested that "a process similar to that of a Civil Suit" might be the "only mode" by which "the rights of

Cazees can be distinctly ascertained."[85] Civil litigation was, at least for Shaw, a natural way to deal with these investigations. He reiterated these points five years later, when his successors also failed to resolve the claims at Ratnagiri: "On any mode of investigation, framed by Government, the claimants are so numerous and the evidence, offered by each, so various that a Summary inquiry, however ably executed, is quite incompetent to decide upon the merits of each claim. Nothing short of a series of investigations, each similar in elaboration and detail, to the proceedings usually held in a civil suit would ever determine the points at issue."[86] Investigations required laborious, painstaking work, and the results pleased no one. Even after months of careful consideration, decisions seemed arbitrary, and displaced claimants rarely accepted them. In the months following Shaw's remarks, officials referred several petitioners to the civil courts and declined to take any administrative action until the courts had ruled.[87] Civil litigation provided a meaningful alternative to prolonged administrative deliberation.

Complaints related to conduct arose from disputes over the qazi's income, which decreased when another interfered with his work. Misconduct could also motivate civil suits. It is hard to say whether contests over conduct made community support more important or growing community involvement contributed to the proliferation of civil suits, but both possibilities are tied to the recognition that administrative decisions were unsatisfactory and that complaints could continue indefinitely.[88] Concerns about community customs and sectarian differences were also buried within the government's preference for civil litigation over administrative determination. Not wanting to arbitrate religious definitions, Company decisions rarely acknowledged sectarian differences, even though such differences routinely bubbled in the background, as the following examples illustrate. As a result, it was not until the second half of the nineteenth century that legislative lobbying and minority community advocacy began to chip away at the illusion of the courts' neutrality toward religion.[89]

Despite its benefits, litigation was slow to gain traction. In 1837 the principal *ṣadr amīn* (chief commissioner) in the court at Thana ruled on a suit for damages brought by forty community members who were dissatisfied with their qazi. They claimed that after appointment and receipt of a sanad in 1836, the qazi stopped the hereditary "Moolna" (*maulāna*) from "carrying on the business of Naeebee [*nāʾibī*; assistantship, deputyship]." This hereditary officeholder, "who possesses old documents with seals of 70 years on them," served the local community but was technically an assistant or deputy.[90] When petitioners brought a suit for almost three thousand rupees in damages, the sadr amin dismissed it, claiming that the matter fell under Section 2, Clause 2, of Regulation XXVI of 1827 (relating to a qazi's misconduct) and was an administrative, not civil, concern.[91] When forwarding the case to Bombay, the judge flagged the doctrinal differences between the qazi (who belonged to the Shafiʿi school of Sunni jurisprudence) and the naʾib (who was Hanafi), but the government at Bombay ultimately agreed with the decision. The petitioners could not claim damages when a qazi exercised his right to appoint and dismiss his own assistants at will. They had no standing.[92]

In general, disputes over misconduct were successful not when they claimed large sums in punitive damages but when they appealed to ideas of justice. When resolving these disputes, the courts could act as neutral arbitrators to guard against qazi overreach or the spiteful claims of local litigants.[93] In one such instance, Henry Brown responded to a complaint by launching a full-scale investigation into the qazi's conduct.[94] The dispute arose when Ibrahim Khan made a complaint against Qazi ʿAbd-ul-Karim's assistant, who had allegedly granted a divorce to Ibrahim Khan's wife and performed her second marriage to another man while Ibrahim Khan was away on service. Before the divorce, Ibrahim Khan and his wife, Abeeda Nadan, had been married for about fourteen years. When he left on business for Mahim (now a neighborhood in Mumbai), Abeeda remained in the care of her father-in-law, with household utensils, grain, and property to provide for her.[95] Ibrahim Khan also claimed he sent letters and cash to keep his family informed and supported.[96] Under these conditions, he argued that Abeeda's divorce and remarriage were not permissible; the qazi disagreed.

Brown's investigation called on the full cast of characters available to him. He deposed thirty individuals (some of whom supported Ibrahim Khan; some of whom supported the qazi) and consulted native law officers at six of the district courts.[97] The legitimacy of the divorce—and the question of the qazi's conduct—hinged on whether the wife was being cared for during her husband's absence and whether the qazi had investigated her claims of neglect before granting the divorce. The issue of maintenance was questionable, but the qazi defended his actions by showing that he investigated the wife's claims "according to Law, and customs and usages of the Country," and Brown cleared him of any misconduct.[98] Afterward, the judge investigated some witnesses for suspected perjury but did not pursue formal disciplinary action against the qazi himself. Furthermore, responses from the native law officers not only revealed great consistency in their responses but also demonstrated that the qazi's conduct was not wholly improper. The law officers' answers saved ʿAbd-ul-Karim, even though the dispute cast doubt on the qazi's right to intervene on a neglected wife's behalf.

Two decades later, Mahomed Yusuf Moorghay, the illustrious and esteemed qazi for the city of Bombay, found himself caught up in a similar dispute. His trouble began in 1858, when Khuteeza Bebee [K̲h̲adīja Bībī] reportedly reached the age of puberty and came before the qazi, accompanied by her grandmother, Fatteh Bebee [Faṭiḥ Bībī], to renounce her father's *maẕhab* (he followed the Shafiʿi school of Sunni jurisprudence) and to declare herself a Hanafi.[99] Becoming Hanafi changed the guardianship requirements for her marriage. Khuteeza Bebee could now choose her own husband, without her father's consent.[100] In October, she was betrothed to Muhammad Ibrahim Purkar publicly, with the qazi and "about two hundred Muhammadans, members of the family, and others" in attendance.[101] The qazi then notified the bride's father, Ghulam Ahmad Rogay, and invited him to attend their impending *nikāḥ*. Rogay refused and instead declared the marriage illegal, presenting proof from a mufti in Ratnagiri of his daughter's betrothal to another man. The dispute thus hinged on whether Khuteeza Bebee had reached the age of maturity (she was thirteen) and whether she could represent herself in marriage after becoming Hanafi. According to the qazi, everything was legitimate; under Hanafi jurisprudence, the betrothal and marriage were entirely legal. The dispute escalated a few weeks later when Rogay, on the pretense of holding "a meeting of Moolvees [*maulvīs*; scholars]" to assess the situation, took his daughter hostage. The government then issued writs of habeas corpus against him.[102] Here, the qazi's role was minimal: he produced an affidavit but allowed the colonial legal system to handle the kidnapping. Nonetheless, his earlier involvement set in motion the chain of events that followed.

Yusuf Moorghay's involvement in Khuteeza Bebee's allegedly illegal marriage turned public opinion against him.[103] This dispute was not the first incident to spark complaints, but it "brought to a climax" the community's loss of confidence in the qazi.[104] On March 2, 1859, the qazi's opponents appealed to the government to remove him from office.[105] Ten days later, anti-qazi partisans "used abusive and indecent language with a view to provoke breach of the peace" while he was reading the *namāz* (prayers) in the city's Jāmiʿ Masjid (Congregational Mosque). The qazi brought charges against two instigators, Huckeem Macdoom Bax and Mahomed Muckba, but dropped them after the judge lectured those present not to use force but "to appeal to the legal tribunals if they had a just cause of complaint."[106] By then, formal complaints against the qazi were already in the works.

In May a petition from "a great number of the Mahomedan inhabitants of Bombay" cited "irregularities" that had "crept into the ceremonies performed at Mahomedan marriages," and resolutions to oust the qazi "passed at a meeting of the leading members of the community," which had also been printed, publicly circulated, and signed "by about one hundred and fifty leading men."[107] Complaints against the qazi referred to his refusal to perform legitimate marriages, his performance of illegitimate unions, and a reputation for participating in immoral activities, such as attending "nautch [dance]" parties. The petitioners referenced specific incidents from 1852, 1853, 1854, and 1858 to prove that the qazi "has for years been forfeiting the confidence, and meriting the contempt of nearly the whole Mahomedan community" and further accused him of being a "fasick [*fāsiq*; sinner, fornicator]."[108] The government processed the petition but was slow to respond to the complaints. As opposition to the qazi increased, public pressure began to mount. Adding "the *laissez faire* practice of the old Raj" to its list of complaints, the *Bombay Times* summarized, "This community has now been in an uproar for the last six months about this Cazee, because Mr. Secretary this, or Mr. Secretary that, does not wish to be bothered with an investigation of the matter; or worse, because one or other of them feels kindly toward the old man, against whom these complaints are lodged."[109] A government that "carried on upon such principles" could not function "without compromising the public peace," the report concluded. Finally, on August 15, 1859, the government responded by launching a formal investigation into the qazi.

The press treated the inquiry like a trial, referring to Yusuf Moorghay as the defendant and to the petitioners as the plaintiffs, but the ordeal was not a regular trial: W. Crawford, a criminal sessions judge, presided over the affair; noted attorneys represented the parties (R. A. Dallas for the qazi and J. Macfarlane for the petitioners); and each side produced witnesses and evidence to support its cause. But the commission also employed four "outstation" qazis—Nur-ud-Din Husain from Bharuch, Maulvi Muhammad Baha-ud-Din of Sangamner, Maulvi ʿAbd-ul-ʿAli Peshawari of Pune, and Muhammad Ghulam Raza of Ahmedabad—as assessors.[110] These individuals, trusted, respected, and competent qazis from elsewhere in the presidency, had to weigh the evidence and decide whether Yusuf Moorghay's conduct warranted his dismissal. Although it was not unusual to have the court qazi (or mufti) evaluate the conduct of a district qazi, it was somewhat novel to call these individuals to Bombay for the proceedings. This innovation, devised by the governor in council, helped the government address the complaints efficiently and bolstered its claims to impartiality, but the procedural innovation did not unfold without sparking new concerns.

Partway through the investigation, the petitioners complained about the choice of venue and questioned whether it was the appropriate place for investigating allegations against the qazi. They argued "that not only should this case be *decided* according to Mahomedan law, but that the enquiry ought to be *conducted* according to Mahomedan law," and should therefore take place in a mosque.[111] Judge Crawford paused to consider the meaning of conducting the trial according to Islamic legal procedure but concluded, along with the assessors, that the inquiry should continue as it began. They would assess Yusuf Moorghay as a qazi, but Anglo-Indian rules of evidence and procedure would prevail. The hybrid model seemed to work. Crawford later remarked that the assessors "were not idle spectators; but . . . took an active part in the examination of every witness."[112] They may not have been hearing evidence in the courtyard of a mosque, but the qazi assessors played a key role.[113]

After a month of proceedings, the inquiry ended, and the assessors prepared their report. When Crawford received it in October 1859, he agreed with their recommendations and "honorably" acquitted the qazi of all charges.[114] Crawford further maintained that the governor in council must "recognise Mahomed Yoosoof Moorgay alone to be lawful Cazee of Bombay"—a key point that would later bring the esteemed qazi back to court.[115] The government expressed its pleasure with the outcome, citing the "voluminous mass of evidence" collected and evaluated as part of the inquiry, and praised the entire affair for being "full and impartial."[116] With the four qazis—"who held the highest reputation for ability and good character in [their] zillah"—aiding the investigation, the government concluded that "no better tribunal could have been suggested . . . which could rightly claim the confidence of all parties . . . and the decision of which would be entitled to general respect."[117] Using the qazi assessors strengthened the government's confidence in the outcome and added to the appearance of neutrality and impartiality.

Crawford's commission may have acquitted Yusuf Moorghay, but it did not fix his public relations problem. A few days later, the *Bombay Times* reported that Yusuf Moorghay was "hardly able to keep his head above water, and has to contend against multitudinous odds." In the wake of Khuteeza Bebee's marriage, he had seen very little business: "The feelings of the greater portion of the Mahomedan community are said to have become embittered toward him . . . and most of the Mahomedan marriages are still celebrated by the newly-constituted Cazee."[118] The commission "honorably" acquitted the qazi, but it could not restore his former glory.

While unique in many ways, Yusuf Moorghay's ordeal drew from a longer history of judicial and quasi-judicial inquiries into the conduct of Company qazis. It was difficult to prove beyond a reasonable doubt that a qazi had misbehaved, but the public's contribution to judging, evaluating, and calling qazis' behavior into question demonstrated the community's continued investment in the office. At the heart of it, a long-standing schism between prominent Muslim families—and doctrinal differences between Hanafis and Shafiʿis—likely fueled Yusuf Moorghay's controversy.[119] But doctrine was not the only factor.[120] References to "leading" Muslim men concealed simmering feuds that sometimes splintered along doctrinal lines but more often reflected complicated family histories and rivalries.[121] Yusuf Moorghay was not the only qazi who fell prey to sectarian disputes, but he was one of the most prominent figures to be leveled by the pressures of public opinion that increasingly came to define the qazi's office.

By offloading administrative deliberations onto the civil courts, Company officials not only turned time-consuming evaluations into court-fee profits (relying on plaintiffs and defendants to gather and translate evidence) but also made Company courts the right site for adjudication. Qazis could no longer function without the colonial courts, nor could the community pick its qazis without government approval. During this period of transition, however, judges could not force individuals to employ specific qazis, administrators could not establish or monitor a qazi's fees, and Company favorites could not accept appointment without community support. Thus, trials involving qazis signaled evolving changes in Company policy and the qazi's status. Although Yusuf Moorghay was acquitted here, the inquest into his behavior demonstrated that the government's prized appointee was susceptible to the same squabbles, allegations, and complaints that other qazis faced. He, too, was subject to the judicial department's standards, though the civil suit he brought against his rival shows in the next chapter that he could also deploy those standards for his own purposes.

Conclusion

Being qazi in British Bombay was no easy feat. Receiving a Company sanad not only required compliance with administrative orders, the timely submission of appropriate paperwork, and a suitable demonstration of ability but also demanded the careful execution of one's duties, the protection and preservation of one's reputation, and the willingness to fight and go to court to defend one's position. Success in these areas could lead to a successful, decades-long career, exploiting the qazi's privileges and perquisites (via salaries, fees, and emoluments) before possibly passing those rights and responsibilities to a brother, son, or nephew and retiring on a Company pension. But failure lay on the other side of success, and there were opportunities to fail at every step of the way.

Failure to submit the first claim might result in losing a title, moving to another district, or waiting for the next opening. Failure to demonstrate ability might result in the rejection of one's application, appointment under the care of an older relative or guardian, or demotion to a less prestigious office. Failure to perform one's responsibilities competently might provide a rival with ammunition for a successful attack, while failure to remain respectable could attract scrutiny from British officials. Negligence in office might cause the community to lose faith in one's status, allowing Company officials to remove the underperforming qazi or giving the community reason to employ another. Without patronage from the community, the local qazi would have no access to income, no privilege or prestige, and no influence or authority. Irrelevance was, perhaps, the worst fate that could befall a qazi.

Fortunately, for the qazis of the Bombay Presidency, irrelevance was not a risk. Many continued to live and work in their home jurisdictions—as humble or inexact as they might be—until the 1860s when changes in the constitution of the Anglo-Indian courts cast doubt on the qazi's status. Practices and strategies employed in the first half of the nineteenth century would be put to the test as new forms of lobbying, and new approaches to all-India legislation, came into being. What had been a process dominated by individual applicants (and their factions of supporters) became part of a larger project of legislating and lobbying. What began as a form of personal redress with direct access to the Company and its agents became an organized effort to change the law in British India. These changes invoked the authority of Muslims with high-ranking colonial positions, lower-ranking officials scattered across the subcontinent, and increasingly vocal—and increasingly committed—Muslim publics.[122] Such efforts would produce results that had ramifications for Muslims from across the British Empire and would lay the foundations for the layered legal pluralism that would come to dominate late colonial and postcolonial legal culture in South Asia.

In the larger history of Islamic legal practice in South Asia, disputes over qazis point to several concerns that continued to define the interpretation and implementation of Muslim personal law in British India. They drew attention to local differences and to variations that ran counter to normative expectations and textbook definitions, including the presence of Hindu and female qazis. Indeed, Mufti Gayasoodeen's recommendations not only opened up debates over who and what defined the office but also pointed to questions over textual authority, classical definitions, and accurate interpretations. His analysis was prescient: it picked up on the Company's mixed allegiances toward hereditary entitlements and normative expectations; it identified problems arising from reluctance to arbitrate rivalries while striving for the orderly, bureaucratic management of appointments; and it raised questions about the Company's role in appointing religious officiants while eschewing responsibility for overseeing religious life. Gayasoodeen's recommendations attempted to split these differences between recognizing and upholding prevailing practices and implementing and enforcing normative, text-based interpretations. In the debates over continuing, changing, or abolishing the qazi's office in the next chapter, these tensions assume new forms that continue to define the landscape of religious law in British India and postcolonial South Asia.

3 From Petitions to Elections

Islamic Legal Practitioners and the Exigencies of Colonial Rule

The Cazees have no power under the Law of exacting fees; their services are to be remunerated by voluntary donations only; nor can they legally delegate their functions to Deputies as has apparently been done in Monghyr [Mungēr, now in Bihar]. These irregularities should have been brought to the notice of the Judge who has full authority to enquire into such illegal practices.

—Minute by Judge H. T. Raikes, July 5, 1859

It is the practice, we believe, of the Muhmmadan community amongst themselves to refer to and treat those entries [in the qazi's books] as proof of the several matters contained in them, and it is obviously of great public benefit to that community to possess the means of perpetuating evidence of matters so essential to the peace of families. . . . For the performance of these services for the public benefit of that community, the Kázi has never received any remuneration from the Government of Bombay . . . [but they] have been solely remunerated by a fixed fee for each.

—Chief Justice Matthew Sausse, in *Muhammad Yussub v. Sayad Ahmed*, 1861

The election of a Cazee is not, by Mahomedan law, left to the choice of the people, the Sirkar [*sarkār*; government] alone has the right to elect.

—Qazi Yusuf Moorghay, quoted in the *Bombay Times and Standard*, March 12, 1861

Defining a Profession in Law

Not long after he was "honorably acquitted" of all charges of wrongdoing, Qazi Mahomed Yusuf Moorghay went on the offensive.[1] Having been chief qazi for the city of Bombay for over twenty years, and nearing the age of ninety, Yusuf Moorghay would not accept the indignities (and accompanying loss of income) that surrounded his recent fall from favor.[2] The city's leading Muslims could attack him in the press, but they could not interfere with his right to work. Suing Ahmadshah Kashmiri for loss of income stemming from this unauthorized qazi's interference, Yusuf Moorghay took his claims to court. Meanwhile, as the judges of Bombay's Supreme Court weighed the evidence he presented, debated the nature of the qazi's office (and the authority of Yusuf Moorghay's post), and waded through law books—covering everything from the definition of an "office," to the idea of "the public good," to the possibility of electing a qazi to office—another debate, tapping into similar definitions, was unfolding around a "proposal . . . for the abolition of the office of Cazee."[3] Both deliberations would lead to similar conclusions about the qazi's office and its function, yet while the Supreme Court justices would validate Yusuf Moorgahy's claims, the home department's deliberations would lead to the passage of Act XI of 1864, "An Act to repeal the law relating to the offices of Hindu and Muhammadan Law Officers and to the offices of Kází-ul-Kuzát and of Kází, and to abolish the former offices." The office Yusuf Moorghay was fighting in court to keep was already on its last legs by the time he won his case.

In many accounts, Act XI of 1864 marks the end of Islamic law and legal practice in British India.[4] By removing "kazis" and native law officers from its courts, the government ended the employment of these native experts in *fiqh* (Islamic jurisprudence), relying instead on British-trained judges (be they Muslim or not) to interpret and apply "Anglo-Muslim law"—a constructed legal tradition that ostensibly took its substance from "original" texts in Arabic and Persian but modified its application by filtering it through Anglo-Indian rules of procedure and precedents drawn from colonial and common-law legal history.[5] Removing these native law officers not only marked a symbolic shift but also bolstered the procedural and institutional superiority of the colonial courts.[6] Certainly, Act XI of 1864 and the "abolition of the office of Cazee" affected Islamic legal practice on the subcontinent, but the transition from British East India Company–appointed qazis, to the suspension of qazi appointments in 1864, to the reintroduction of the qazi's office with new legislation in 1880 was less straightforward than most tellings relate. Qazis did not disappear altogether after 1864, and the so-called native law officers, though no longer formally employed within the courts, took new jobs—as lawyers, legislators, legal scholars, treatise writers, and political campaigners.[7] The legal system changed as new laws ushered in new institutional frameworks, but many of the participants and the players remained the same.[8]

If Company policy rested on the pretense of preserving the status quo in an empire dressed up in British clothes, then the transition to Crown rule inaugurated an era of direct legislative, procedural, and statutory intervention. British jurists began this process by emphasizing uniformity in the articulation and application of the law, implementing legal codes that ignored local and regional variation, and striving to make their decisions consistent by publishing and circulating law reports. Muslim legislators contributed to this endeavor, as debates over the Kazis' Act (Act XII of 1880) will show, by writing—and advocating for—new laws for India's Muslims,[9] and British-trained Indian Muslim judges accompanied them, calling on their British legal training and their access to Islamic legal texts in the original languages to shape law through the dissenting and concurring opinions they wrote.[10] Furthermore, an "all-India" awareness crept into legislative debates as campaigns originating in Madras and Bengal gained traction across the subcontinent and as leading Indian Muslims took responsibility for reforming, in the name of protecting, Muslim personal law. Together, these macro- and micro-processes had a profound impact not only on the nature of legal pluralism in British India but also on the making of everyday Islamic law in South Asia.

Two developments in the relationship between politics and governance foregrounded these changes. First, legislative lobbying replaced personal petitioning as the preferred mode for claims-making. Whereas qazis in the first half of the nineteenth century used personal petitions to win favor from the British East India Company, in the second half of the century, petitions representing entire communities took over. Second, religion as a category became an even more important element in colonial politics. Debates over the qazi's office took place during the moment of transition, when personal petitioning was still possible but community agitation was growing in popularity, when Yusuf Moorghay could sue his opponent and call on the government to defend him, and when the government could support his suit but decline to appoint a successor after his death, leaving the community to decide. In other words, discussions surrounding the qazi's office stood for more than the status he maintained; they also reflected the changing relationship between law, governance, and politics going forward. As such, the simple story that historians recount when talking about Act XI of 1864 requires further consideration against this broader backdrop.

In the transition from Company rule to Crown governance, public interest in the qazi's office shifted from an investment in individual officeholders to the idea of the office as a community necessity: Britain could not successfully govern its Muslim subjects if it did not provide them with adequately appointed qazis. Whether in response to the ascendance of the Anglo-Indian legal system or from fear of further demotion and diminution following the Uprising of 1857, the qazi's office became a marker of and a bulwark against further colonial encroachments. The "Muslim community" (a term predicated on inclusivity but deployed to reform nonconforming or nonelite Muslims) needed and wanted local qazis, but reintroducing the office would ultimately benefit the British government and its overburdened legal system. The Kazis' Act thus emerged through the successful articulation of overlapping interests: those of government officials (who would see a reduction in the number of nuisance marital disputes they encountered); those of the community (which required not generic civil marriage registrars but specifically Muslim qazis to record marriages); those of the registrants and vulnerable Muslim women in particular (who were left without proper facilities for documenting their marital ties);[11] those of the Crown (which the public would credit for enacting a voluntary, noncompulsory measure that responded to its subjects' needs); and those of elite Muslims (who could implement their social reform projects while appearing to represent the community's interests more broadly). In short, support for the act coalesced around political arguments that reflected the changing nature of British rule on the subcontinent, the involvement of leading Muslim men in administrative and legislative roles, and the interest of broader swaths of Muslims in staking out marriage and divorce as spheres defined by Islamic legal ideas.

When Yusuf Moorghay sued his opponent, this broader trajectory was far from clear. Instead, a plurality of ideas about what defined the qazi's office, what purpose it served, and who was responsible for it were circulating at the time. Trials like his provided a canvas on which multiple actors—colonial officials, high court judges, Muslim legislators, leading Muslim men, and non-Muslims from other communities—could paint their picture of legal pluralism and religious diversity. Legislative deliberation provided another forum for Muslims from across the subcontinent—in their capacity as legislative representatives, lower-ranking administrators, and journalists and newspaper editors—to evaluate potential risks and rewards. The burgeoning public sphere of Islamic legal publishing (see chapter 4) also played a role in defining, redefining, and reimagining the qazi's role, particularly when questions arose about the limits and extent of the qazi's jurisdiction (see chapter 7). Each of these perspectives considered the everyday practice of Islamic law and the substance of the qazi's role in relation to normative ideas about the past, in response to critical evaluations of the present, and out of a desire to enact certain changes for the future. Debates like these played out in other arenas, too, but for the history of everyday Islamic law, contests over the qazi's office and its role in British India represent a key site for mapping this transformation.

But What Do Qazis Do? Fees, Deeds, and Pleas in the Debate over Qazis

Yusuf Moorghay's suit against his competitor Ahmadshah Kashmiri was one for damages, damages amounting to several thousand rupees from the income he lost after the city's Muslims began to hire Ahmadshah as their qazi. They did so upon Ahmadshah's election to the office in December 1858, as dissatisfaction with Yusuf Moorghay mounted following the uproar over Khuteeza Bebee's marriage to Muhammad Ibrahim Purkar (see chapter 2). The marriage was only the tip of the iceberg (ill-will toward him had been mounting since 1851 when he sided with the government during the Parsi-Muslim riots), but slighting Khuteeza Bebee's father, Ghulam Ahmad Rogay, did not help. The Rogays were prominent among Bombay's Muslims; they had commercial and familial ties to the Konkan coast, Arabia, and the Shafiʿi school of jurisprudence. Yusuf Moorghay was an aging figure, a longtime supporter of the British, probably a Shafiʿi but perhaps more flexible when it came to jurisprudence.[12] Had doctrinal differences over guardianship requirements for marriage not been a core concern, the factions may have split differently, but at least on some level, doctrinal difference spurred greater animosity.

Following Rogay's dustup with Yusuf Moorghay, Bombay's leading Muslims gathered to elect a new qazi and chose Ahmadshah Kashmiri. He accepted the position and began to perform and record marriages, divorces, and other ceremonies for the city's Muslims, collecting the fees that otherwise would have gone to Yusuf Moorghay and his assistants. While Yusuf Moorghay stood trial for his alleged misdeeds, Ahmadshah worked in this capacity as qazi, but crucially for his case, the government never removed Yusuf Moorghay from office, even during the inquest. His continuity in office played a key role in persuading the court of his right to recover damages, but recovering the fees also meant proving their legitimacy in the first place.

Questions about the work qazis performed and the fees they collected were an issue even before Yusuf Moorghay's case went to trial. As changes

TABLE 3.1 Fees collected by the qazi of Bombay

	Rupees	Annas
For the first marriage	2	8
For second and subsequent marriages	5	0
For divorces	5	0
For summonses (in matrimonial causes)	1	4
For extracts from registers	2	8

Source: Muhammad Yussub v. Sayad Ahmed (1861), Bom HCR 1, at xxxviii. There are sixteen annas in each rupee.

in government policy stripped qazis of their once-diverse portfolios of fee-based practices, they complained about the changes and pleaded for exceptions or reversions to make up for the losses they suffered.[13] In addition to these complaints, Company officials also took a periodic interest in surveying the annual incomes qazis earned, but historical and regional variation routinely thwarted efforts to produce systematic accounts.[14] Indeed, it was not until the office was headed for abolition that the Bombay government finally managed to produce a "General Statement shewing [*sic*] the lands and emoluments now enjoyed by Cazees in the Several Districts of the Bombay Presidency."[15] Yet despite these complications, ample evidence supported Yusuf Moorghay's insistence on the fees he received.

For established qazis like Bharuch's Nur-ud-Din Husain and Yusuf Moorghay, fees could add up.[16] During his trial, Yusuf Moorghay presented accounts that showed him earning nearly four thousand rupees per year from fees related to performing and recording marriages and divorces.[17] As table 3.1 shows, individuals paid small amounts for each service—Rs. 2.5 for a first marriage; Rs. 5 for a second or subsequent marriage; Rs. 5 for a divorce; Rs. 1.25 for issuing a summons to appear; and Rs. 2.5 for producing an extract from one of his registers—but over the year, the fees added up.[18] Additionally, in larger jurisdictions, assistants extended the head qazi's reach, gathering fees on his behalf in exchange for a monthly stipend or a cut of the proceeds. At the time of his trial in 1861, Yusuf Moorghay employed three assistants who delivered fees to him, and he paid them Rs. 6, 12, and 25 per month respectively.[19] Ahmadshah followed the same fee schedule, signaling to the court that the fees were standardized.[20]

Yet outlining the services he performed and the fees he collected in exchange did not satisfy the judges' curiosities. If the "fees" were not required but were instead customary gratuities, then the qazi had no entitlement to them. Arguing historically, Yusuf Moorghay showed evidence of the Bombay qazi's fees "from A.D. 1776 downwards."[21] These sums were not honorary gratuities, he contended, but "certain fixed payments annexed to the discharge of official duties."[22] The honorary gifts and gratuities he received were supplemental—ranging from "clothing or shawls from the house of the husband and the wife," to cash payments anywhere from Rs. 5 from "poor persons" to "Rs. 100 and upwards . . . given by wealthy persons"—and were given in addition to (not as a substitute for) his regular fees.[23] As such, Yusuf Moorghay asserted his legitimate claim to damages.[24]

To evaluate Yusuf Moorghay's claim, the court drew from a robust body of jurisprudence regarding fees owed to individuals holding an office or a franchise. Chief Justice Matthew Sausse cited definitions from Blackstone's *Commentaries* (including the entry on "disturbance" of a franchise), *Bacon's Abridgment* (on "fees"), and *Taylor on Evidence* (for customary dues), in addition to precedents from the Privy Council in England and the Supreme Court at Bombay (including the recent decision in *Perozeboye v. Ardasser Cursetjee* on "Parsí ecclesiastical matters").[25] Yusuf Moorghay likewise provided evidence that his fees were "of an established and ancient usage . . . fixed, and certain in their amount," and he "industriously collected [various passages] from Muhammadan law-books of high authority" to show that sultans appointed qazis; ordinary Muslims did not elect them.[26] Working across these bodies of law, Yusuf Moorghay proved his right to collect fees, denied Ahmadshah Kashmiri's claims to the office, and won his case.

Although the Bombay Supreme Court sided with Yusuf Moorghay and his right to collect fees, this entitlement did not remain unchallenged. Regarding him less as a toll-road operator than as a baptismal registrar, judicial officials around this time began to question more broadly whether qazi appointments were still necessary. Under the "regulations passed many years ago," qazis may have been "partly of a judicial and partly of a social and religious character," but there was little need to continue their appointment, one official argued.[27] Others echoed these concerns, suggesting that the qazi's fees were "purely optional," "perfectly voluntary," and possibly "quite illegal." As a result, suits "being instituted by Pergunnah Cazees against interlopers . . . to recover the amount of the fees to which they (the Cazees) considered themselves entitled . . . were invariably dismissed."[28] Yusuf Moorghay may have been successful in court, but other qazis were not, and interested parties struggled to arrive at a consensus over whether qazis were public officials (with a right to claim fees) or religious officiants (and therefore exempt from government interference). Eventually, legislation intervened, but the two perspectives remained contested.

Toward the Abolition of the Qazi's Office

In 1859, as Yusuf Moorghay's legal troubles began, concerns over the qazi's office shifted away from minor administrative conflicts to sweeping proposals for abolition. Conflicts, like those over fees, remained unresolved (only to surface in later proposals for the qazi's reintroduction), but arguments for abolition coalesced around three key issues. The first of these issues was necessity—that is, whether qazis still performed functions that were vital to the administration of justice in British India. Secretary of State for India Charles Wood summed it up nicely when he remarked that "all of the judicial and executive functions formerly discharged by the Cazees are now vested in other Officers specially appointed for the purpose."[29] Judge E. Jackson, stationed at Midnapore, expressed a similar sentiment, explaining that qazis in his district "are employed in reality as Registrars of Deeds."[30] Judge H. T. Raikes shared this sentiment, pointing out that "the only Official acts" qazis performed "consist of the attestation and registry of deeds of transfer of property" but that "deeds so attested derive little or no weight in our Courts."[31] The judicial system depended on the proper registration of documents, but facilities created by specific registration acts (including XIX of 1843 and IV of 1845) made the qazi's involvement unnecessary.[32] Qazis were "cheaper" and "more easily accessable [*sic*]," but their involvement increased the risk of fraud—and efforts to check that risk had so far failed.[33] If qazis no longer performed the "public acts" of registering and recording deeds, there was little reason to continue employing them to do so.[34]

If the work of qazis as document registrars was negligible, then judicial officials turned to their status as religious officiants, the second issue around which abolition advocates circled. For Raikes, abolishing the office was necessary, given the "impolicy of keeping up such Officers in connection with the Government of the Country, while the Government professes to recognize no distinction of creed, and to place its subjects on an equality in all matters of religion."[35] Denuded of its judicial functions, the office of the qazi had become "a priestly one," since "all its functions [were] of a religious nature."[36] It would therefore go against government policy to "interfer[e] in such matters," let alone "to oblige the Christian Judge to invest the Mahomedan priest."[37] Beyond objecting on principle to the government's involvement in religion, there was also the question of equity: if the government appointed qazis ("a preferment . . . exclusively bestowed upon the Mahomedans"), it risked offending other communities. Furthermore, it was unfathomable for a British (Christian) judge to appoint a Muslim religious official; it would be better, they argued, to change the qazi into a "Mahomedan legal officer" who would hold a civil, rather than a religious, position.[38] This two-pronged argument, which first made qazis religious officers and then made marriage a civil ceremony (despite marriage being a category of personal law), not only minimized the qazi's role but also sidestepped any appearance of religious interference. "To suppose that there is anything approaching to State interference with Religion, in the appointment by Government of Officers before whom, accordingly to immemorial custom marriage contracts shall be signed, and by whom they shall be sealed and registered, is not reasonable," E. H. Lushington asserted.[39] If marriage was a civil contract, as in "a Scotch marriage," then there could be no objection to the government's appointment of civil (Muslim) marriage registrars.[40]

While issues one and two of the abolition argument related to the qazi's purpose and function, the third issue dealt with legal substance. In the first half of the nineteenth century, the British government of India had transformed vague references to existing judicial practices into robust bodies of substantive and procedural law. With "valuable text books already in existence" and plans to compile digests of Hindu and Muslim law that would "leave but few questions of common interest untouched," there was little reason to continue employing native experts. Written sources were safer anyway, as "there [were] as many opinions as commentators."[41] Consensus suggested that decades of experience had equipped colonial officials to interpret and apply personal law, but the issue of expertise was complicated. Many agreed that the government could remove low-level qazis from small towns and villages, but some recommended retaining them in the appellate courts.[42] Others suggested that even if the government removed law officers from its courts, it should sponsor academic professorships in Hindu and Muslim law instead.[43] Proposals like these popped up in the abolition debate, but ultimately they received little traction. As case law and textbooks expanded access to Anglo-Muslim legal substance, there was little interest in "do[ing] anything to prolong the vitality of these [legal] systems" through education or appointment.[44]

Not all voices supported abolishing the qazi's office. Some of those who were hesitant wondered whether they fully understood the office and its functions—or the broader consequences of abolition. They supported additional inquiries before making any decisions.[45] Others challenged the qazi's involvement in the attestation of deeds generally but recognized his importance when it came to recording marriages and documents tied to marriage, such as contracts of dower (*kābīn-nāmas*).[46] Related arguments advocated expanding this aspect of the qazi's work: if the government recognized Muslim marriage as a civil contract, it could continue to appoint qazis as civil marriage registrars, Lushington suggested.[47]

A small minority pushed to abolish the qazi's office while retaining native law officers as "expounders of law." If they worked as legal expounders, they would lose their "priestly" character but still contribute to the administration of justice. Furthermore, the government could do away with village and town qazis, who had little knowledge to offer, but should retain the services of these legal experts in the district and chief courts as needed. Their services remained necessary, as recent efforts to produce comprehensive digests of Hindu and Muslim law had yielded lackluster results: "Although the gist of the original question and answer is generally correctly given . . . the language in which it is clothed requires in almost every instance more or less correction, and is in most of the longer and more intricate questions so confused as to render it almost unintelligible."[48] Progress on the Hindu law digest was disappointing, but work on the Muslim volume was, by contrast, "entirely at a stand still" following the death of the Mahomedan law officer assigned to the task.[49] Qazis and law officers made similar arguments, pointing to the lack of available materials and questioning the British judges' ability to access the full range of texts the law officers used. These experts opposed abolition, arguing that "justice will never be fully meted out" with the existing law books. From the perspective of justice alone, qazis and law officers should remain employed. Furthermore, the offices cost little to maintain, and government support was important if Hindu and Muslim law were not to become "but a dead letter."[50]

In the end, arguments for abolition won out, and with a series of enactments, the government divested itself of any further involvement with qazis. The Code of Criminal Procedure, which came into effect "on January 1, 1862, . . . rendered the services of the Mahomedan Law Officers unnecessary."[51] Then, with the passage of Act XI of 1864, the government "repealed the Regulations and Acts relating to the offices of Hindoo and Mahomedan Law Officers, with a view to the abolition of those offices," and terminated its appointment of qazis.[52] Citing how "unnecessary" and "inexpedient" it was to keep those offices or to have appointments "made by Government," legislators presented the measure not as something new but as an act of repeal.[53] Specifically, the act "repealed" a series of regulations, including sixteen from the Bengal Code introduced between 1793 and 1829; four from the Madras Code dated from 1802 to 1828; and two from the 1827 Bombay Code, including the whole of Regulation XXVI "for the appointment and removal of Cazees."[54] The act further repealed Act XXVII of 1836, Act VII of 1843, and Act V of 1845—all of which related to the role of law officers in court.[55] Oddly enough, the act explicitly stated that nothing in it "shall be construed so as to prevent a Cazee-ool-Cozaat or other Cazee from performing, when required to do so, any duties or ceremonies prescribed by the Mahomedan Law."[56] Act XI of 1864 terminated the government's involvement in the appointment of qazis but did not directly interfere with "any duties or ceremonies" they might perform.

The 1864 act thus followed earlier precedents, preserving the status quo (up to a point) while changing the government's role. The British East India Company may have been willing to wear the shoes of the erstwhile Mughal emperor, adopting the title of "Company *Sarkār*" and allowing petitioners to address its agents as "ṣāḥib bahādur" (brave lord), but the Crown government was less wedded to the symbolism of earlier regimes and less dependent on the authority of local intermediaries.[57] After successfully quashing a native uprising and reasserting its authority with the full backing of the British Crown, the new government of India had little to gain from continuing to appoint qazis.

The repealing power of Act XI of 1864 effected a minor regime change, but the act's full influence would not be felt until later. Qazis and law officers who were eligible could retire and receive government pensions. Those who were not yet eligible for retirement could apply for a job as district magistrate, supernumerary magistrate, district collector, or other low-level government servant. Government officials calculated these possibilities when considering abolition and seamlessly folded many of the displaced officers into new positions.[58] Thus, by the time Yusuf Moorghay passed away in May 1866, the relationship between the government and its qazis had changed almost entirely. The government no longer appointed individuals to the office or granted their records special status in court. (After all, without native law officers, there was no one to read or inspect their records.)[59] The government also, at least officially, stopped mediating disputes involving qazis and local communities, unless they brought their disputes to court. Accordingly, when the leading Muslims of Bombay nominated Muhammad Husain Moorghay, the late qazi's nephew, to take over, the government declined to recognize the chosen successor. One official even noted on the backside of the petition, “What has gov’t to do with the appt. of the Cazee of Bombay?”[60] A new Qazi Moorghay now held the title, but after 1864, it was not clear what that title meant. In the decades that followed, confusion over the implications of Act XI of 1864 and the “consternation” that accompanied its introduction inspired legislative lobbying that unwittingly united the interests of elite Muslim men and the colonial state in a new measure aimed at the private, domestic life of Muslims—with ramifications that reached from British India across the empire.[61]

Toward the Qazi’s Reintroduction

There was just one hitch to the government’s graceful exit plan: qazis required government appointment. As Yusuf Moorghay testified and excerpts from the *Hidāya* confirmed, communities could not just choose their own qazis.[62] The government’s hands-off approach not only disrupted centuries-old practices but also left Muslims in the lurch. Thus, shortly after Act XI of 1864 went into effect, reports began to surface about the inconvenience Muslims faced when legitimating their marriages, and legislative proposals quickly sprang up to address the issue.[63] What began in Bengal as a simple proposal for Muslim marriage registrars expanded into an all-India campaign to resume the government appointment of qazis. The corresponding bill, which eventually became Act XII of 1880, the Kazis’ Act, drew from the legislative influences of elite Muslim men and capitalized on the contributions of a robust public sphere that supported, debated, and critiqued the proposal. Not only did the Kazis’ Act signal a new phase in Anglo-Indian lawmaking, with the production of new laws aimed to meet the needs of specific communities, but it also reconfigured the evolving interdependence between Islamic legal practice and the colonial state.[64] By the end of the nineteenth century, it was clear that the Anglo-Indian legal system was paramount and that the laws of British India were remaking Indian society in profound ways. Making marriage registration central to the politics of representation, the Kazis’ Act put Islamic law at the center of colonial governance.

Evidence of the “inconvenience” Muslims experienced without qazis to register their marriages glued together several interests in the legislative campaigns that followed.[65] Elite Muslims balked at the instability of family structures among the “lower classes” of Muslims and advocated greater oversight. District and subordinate court judges complained about the volume of cases crowding their dockets, owing to the perceived “loose notions regarding the marriage tie" and the range of dubious criminal "offenses against marriage" they produced: "The remarkably small number of convictions obtained in such cases, taken together with their increasing numbers, seemed to indicate the existence of a grievance which the criminal Courts are at present unable to redress," one commentator observed.[66] Legislators in Bengal rose to meet these challenges with "A Bill to Provide for the Voluntary Registration of Mahomedan Marriages and Divorces" and a proposal to create "an authorized system" using a registrar who would "take the place . . . [of] the old kazis." Extracts from the registers would provide "prima facie proof of the facts" of the marriage, so the courts would be able to settle marital disputes. Registration would be optional and "all questions of remuneration" would be "settled between the Registrar and the parties," to avoid any appearance of favoritism or religious interference.[67] Furthermore, failing to register would not invalidate an otherwise valid marriage, nor would registration validate an otherwise invalid marriage. Registration would simply confer the benefits of a written record.

Proposals like these harked back to the abolition debate and to questions of whether qazis were religious or civil officials and whether marriage was a religious rite or civil contract. Introducing a new mechanism—or "machinery," as officials described it—for marriage registration sidestepped these questions by implementing a neutral title: registrar.[68] Registrars would be licensed, and any Muslim could apply for a license. Much like the erstwhile Company qazis, the government would grant licenses to applicants who were respected and well versed in the law, yet from the get-go, there were doubts about whether the neutral registrar title would be sufficient. Although the first draft bill from 1873 referred exclusively to "registrars," by the time an amended version appeared in 1875, the term "Kazi" had replaced "registrar" and had come to signify "any person who is duly authorized under this Act to register Mahomedan marriages and divorces."[69] The 1875 proposal also included details about how these qazis-cum–marriage registrars would produce, maintain, store, and deposit their registers; how many registers they would maintain; what each register would include; and how they would verify and certify (with witness attestations and signatures) the validity of the marriages they recorded. This proposal, which became Bengal Act I of 1876, signaled the extent of the problems created by the loss of government-appointed qazis and prompted wider interest in marriage registration, not just in British India but throughout the empire.

Following the Bengal proposal, the central government requested input from local governments in Madras and Bombay.[70] The Bombay government initially declined to follow in Bengal's footsteps, claiming there had been no dissatisfaction among its Muslims. This report was not entirely accurate.[71] In 1879 Muhammad Ali Rogay sent a letter to the General Department, in his capacity as vice president of the Anjuman-i Islam (Islamic Society) of Bombay, to ask about (1) earlier discussions to "abrogate the right of Government" to appoint qazis, (2) the compensation qazis previously received, (3) whether the government confiscated the grants formerly attached to the qazi's office upon its abolition, and (4) whether the government issued any proclamations stating its reasons for abolition.[72] After transferring his inquiry to the judicial department, the government endeavored to answer the second, third, and fourth points but declined to state its reasons for discontinuing qazi appointments.[73] Delivered on the anjuman's stationery, Rogay's submission had little influence but demonstrated continued interest in the qazi's office, despite the local government's statement to the contrary.

The Madras government read the Bengal bill with different interests in mind. C. G. Master, acting chief secretary, argued that the "bill fail[ed] to remove the evils which the virtual abolition of the office of Kazi has created, and that it [was] calculated to give rise to other evils." Summarizing the Madras government's opinions, he objected to any government involvement in "prescrib[ing] the forms and ceremonial necessary to make [a marriage or divorce] valid," criticized the appeal structure provided in the bill (whereby disputes went before a "European or Hindu" officer), and stressed that registration would be "of no real value" if not "compulsory . . . [and] penal." Master rejected the Bengal proposal for registrars and advocated for the qazi's return: "The office, as is well known, was not abolished because its holders were unfit, or because the discharge of the duties were in any way prejudicial to the State, but ceased to exist merely from the circumstance that by Muhammadan Law it needed the confirmation of the sovereign power."[74] He drafted a proposal for the qazis' reintroduction and sent it along with his reply.

Given the Madras government's response—and a growing recognition that the qazi question could only be addressed through imperial legislation—attention shifted from the provincial governments to the imperial legislative council.[75] The reply from Madras also prompted a reconfiguration of the scope and scale of the legislation: The Bengal act was too specific about how to validate and record marriages and veered into the territory of religious interference. By contrast, the revised proposal from Madras was brief (and vague). It included reasons for reintroducing the qazi, procedures for granting licenses using community input, procedures for appointments without community support, and an acknowledgment that licenses would continue until revocation.[76] The bland Madras proposal was thus "superior to the [more specific] Bengal Act" because "it [left] all technicalities of dower, divorce, and marriage untouched."[77]

In the imperial legislative council, Sayyid Ahmad Khan (1817–1898)—venerable Indian Muslim statesman and scholar known for his work founding the Muhammadan Anglo-Oriental College (now Aligarh Muslim University) in 1875 and promoting Muslim social and educational reform—became the bill's sponsor, advocate, and public face. Like his fellow Muslim legislator Nawab ʿAbd-ul-Luteef, Sayyid Ahmad also "fel[t] strongly about the inconvenience caused by the operation of the Act of 1864" and thought "there would be advantage" in introducing a measure to restore the qazi.[78] He thus introduced his "bill for the appointment of persons to the office of Kazi" to the imperial legislative council on January 23, 1880. When it passed, the Kazis' Act was only six hundred words long, but Sayyid Ahmad prefaced it with a lengthy "Statement of Objects and Reasons" in which he not only outlined the qazi's trajectory under the British but also summarized his precolonial history: "Under the Mohammedan Law the Kází was chiefly a judicial officer. His principal powers and duties are stated at some length in the Hedaya, Book XX. He was appointed by the State, and may be said to have corresponded to our Judge or Magistrate. In addition, however, to his functions under the Mohammedan law, the Kází in this country, before the advent of British rule, appears to have performed certain other duties, partly of a secular and partly of a religious nature."[79] None of these duties, he conceded, was "incumbent on the Kází as such" but instead extended from his "official position" and knowledge of the law. In other words, duties that were "originally in some sense an accidental adjunct of his office" became "his principal and only duty," such that for many, "the presence of a Kazi at certain rites and ceremonies appear[ed] now to be . . . essential." Keeping with the British government of India's interest in separating "secular" and "religious" functions, Sayyid Ahmad advocated the qazi's return, though his bill would not "confe[r] any judicial or other powers on a Kazi, or mak[e] his presence necessary at any marriage or other ceremony at which his presence is not now necessary."[80] His was a permissive measure aimed at restoring rather than creating.[81]

After introducing the proposal, Sayyid Ahmad formed a select committee to review the bill and urged the government to solicit public feedback by delivering copies to local governments for circulation among colonial officials, translation into the vernacular languages, and advertisement in government gazettes. Dozens weighed in, and their opinions varied in predictable ways.[82] Some welcomed the measure with open arms, while others voiced legitimate concerns. Over six months of discussion, however, these opinions coalesced around three points. First, colonial officials worried about the government's right to make these appointments and whether government involvement was necessary. Stripped of his "executive" or "judicial" functions, all that remained were the qazi's "social" and "religious" functions.[83] If a marriage registrar could provide the "social" function of recording marriages, was government involvement in qazi appointments still necessary? To allay these concerns, Muslim organizations, such as the Anjuman-i Panjab (Punjab Society), produced detailed documents, drawing from expert opinions and Arabic sources, to provide the necessary assurances that government involvement was necessary and would not constitute religious interference.[84] Such replies validated the government's investment in textual authorities and called on the representative status of burgeoning civic associations.

The second point arose from Muslims who worried about qazis' qualifications and their responsibilities. Those worrying about the former advocated greater government involvement in the certification of qazis to prevent ignorant or untrained individuals from misbehaving in office. Those concerned with the latter worried about asking qazis to record marriages if they could not also settle marital disputes. Allowing qazis to perform some—but not all—of the tasks related to Muslim marriage and divorce left the door open to future conflicts and confusion.[85] Although each position reflected concerns over the government's appointment of qazis and the mechanics of those appointments, their contradictory aims—one fearing too much lenience and the other worrying about too many restrictions—canceled each other. Neither affected the legislative council's deliberations.

The final point of contention was over whether marriage registration should remain optional or be made compulsory. For the most part, British commentators were wedded to the idea that registration remain optional and permissive, owing to the government's stated commitment to noninterference (see interlude II). An act that merely permitted Muslims to have their marriages and divorces recorded by a local qazi would sidestep any potential interference, yet for many Muslim commentators (and for a few judges who heard marital disputes in court), voluntary registration would scarcely fulfill the reform objectives embedded within the act. After all, "looseness in the marriage tie" and marital "disputes and feuds" were the primary motivations for improving registration.[86] Voluntary registration would not suffice.[87] A penalty for failing to register was one solution, but here again, the recommendation fell on deaf ears. After several months of debate, the bill passed and became Act XII of 1880.

Commentary on the Kazis' Act came from Muslims across the subcontinent. Some of the commentators were former qazis, muftis, or legal experts; others worked in nonjudicial offices as honorary surgeons or district commissioners, while some contributors headed civic organizations, voluntary societies, and anjumans. The issue was confined neither to Muslims within a particular region nor to those representing particular interests. Their responses instead demonstrated that debates over Muslim marriage in one part of British India affected Muslims living and working in other areas and that Muslims were neither unified nor unanimous in their opinions, despite their recognition of the issue's importance. In turn, lobbying over the act reflected and inspired greater mobilization of an all-Indian Muslim community, which resurfaced in later campaigns, too. Paradoxically, however, the Kazis' Act invited greater government involvement in the conduct and registration of Muslim marriages precisely at a time when "secular" governance was reaching its apogee and when imperial attitudes toward Muslims were laden with fear and suspicion.[88] While most colonial accounts treated the Kazis' Act as a marginal success, the measure had lasting effects on the practice of everyday Islamic law and the status of religious legal pluralism on the subcontinent.

First India, Then the Empire: Evaluating the Kazis' Act

After adoption, the Kazis' Act of 1880 followed a meandering path as administrators across the subcontinent extended it to their districts in fits and starts. In 1881, the year after the act's introduction, the Bombay government reported the partial adoption of the act in parts of Sholapur, Satara, and Pune.[89] Inhabitants at Ratnagiri had also expressed an interest in having their former qazi reappointed to the office, but as yet, the government had taken no action, other than to inform them about the new procedures. To add more confusion to the act's extension, at Surat there was some doubt about "whether Government can extend the Kazis Act to a place where a Kazi is already in existence." The answer was yes, but the government first had to determine (a) "whether a Kazi appointed [by government] is really requisite according to the usage of the Muhammadan community" and, if not, (b) "whether there [were] otherwise sufficiently strong reasons to justify Government's interfering."[90] In other words, the Bombay government asked the magistrate at Surat to reconsider the very questions that motivated the Kazis' Act in the first place. By contrast, in Thana, Kolaba, and Nasik, the report concluded that there was little reason to extend the act, as "present arrangements . . . work well."[91] Act XII's extension thus depended on administrators' perception of its relative usefulness and on local inhabitants' commitment to it.

The following year, 1882, after extensive debate about extending or withholding the act in various districts, towns, and villages—and receiving petitions so numerous that officials began referring to them by number (rather than by name or location)—the government appointed over fifty qazis for the Ahmednagar District in one fell swoop, notifying the public of their appointment by printing the qazis' names and "jurisdictions" in the *Bombay Government Gazette*.[92] Great pains went into compiling the printed notification,[93] but little interest remained in organizing or rationalizing the qazis' territories: some of the appointments encompassed entire districts (*taʿalluqas*),[94] others listed only a single village,[95] and some included lengthy lists naming eighty or even ninety villages individually.[96] After a glut of appointments in 1882, the Bombay government continued for the next several years to make periodic appointments, after which point evidence in the archive tapers off, meaning interest may have waned (on the part of administrators or among qazis) or, more likely, responsibility for dealing with appointments fell to district-level administrators, as records from other regions suggest.[97]

Elsewhere, reports on the working of the Kazis' Act were similar. In Madras, where inspiration for the act originated, collectors in fifteen districts appointed people to the office of qazi "in consultation with the principal Muhammadan residents" in September 1880. The following year, the government reported that "Act XII of 1880 appear[ed] to be working in a satisfactory manner," though Secretary Master was still awaiting additional input from district collectors, which would offer a more "decided opinion."[98] Then, in 1882, the Madras government produced a thorough analysis of the act's operation there: approximately twenty administrators, working as collectors and district magistrates, submitted their (generally favorable) preliminary observations on the local workings of the act.[99] Most reports indicated the number of qazis appointed and offered brief comments on the nature of those appointments—whether they included long-standing officeholders; whether they emerged in response to petitions or public agitation; and whether there were any difficulties or controversies when making the appointments.[100] Magistrates like N. A. Roupell in Anantapur responded that "no persons have been appointed" but that "no dissatisfaction [was] reported" from among local Muslims.[101] Others praised the act for working "satisfactorily," acknowledging that "the Mahomedan community have generally appreciated the advantages resulting from its operation," as W. S. Whiteside, collector for North Arcot, did.[102] Some remarked that hardly enough time had passed to provide an accurate assessment, while those more deeply involved in fielding and processing requests mentioned ongoing deliberations and solicited government approval for disputed appointments.[103] Here again, "previously existing private arrangements" or disputes between factions could necessitate the act's extension or could render the government's intervention unnecessary, depending on local circumstances, and as in Bombay, references to orders and notifications in the official government gazette accompanied these reports.[104]

In the short term, then, the post-1880 appointment of qazis was reminiscent of earlier periods. A small collection of files from the commissioner's office at Allahabad shows applicants to the office claiming rights (*ḥaqq, ḥuqūq, istiḥqāq*) to perform similar work (*nikāḥ-k͟hwānī* [reading marriages]; *pesh namāz-i ʿīdain* [reading the ʿEid prayers]) and making similar appeals to status, ability, family connections, and moral character in their claims.[105] Instead of issuing exams, the district commissioner now appealed to the opinions of respectable Muslims, who self-identified in their appeals as the "ṣāḥib-zāda-hā-yi nāmdār" (descendants of the nobility), the "nabīra-hā-yi ʿalá waqār" (grandchildren of those of highest character), principal inhabitants, gentry (*raʾīs, ruʾasāʾ*), and members of the great families (*k͟hānadān*).[106] Appeals to popularity and public support were the new modus operandi for qazi appointments, with concerns about "whether the petition is a genuine expression of the wishes of a majority of the respectable Muhammadan inhabitants of the locality" accompanying every inquiry.[107] When public support was lacking, the commissioner might decline to make an appointment. If a town was too small to support a qazi, he might recommend that petitioners visit a more populous town nearby, and when there were multiple candidates, officials would evaluate their merits and gauge their support from among prominent families. Petitioning culture thus gave way to a new type of electoral politics, rooted in community support and popular opinion.

Generally speaking, patterns of appeal and appointment were the same now as before but with a few modifications. For example, when the death of Dilawer ʿAli in 1885 created an opening for the position of qazi in the

Fatehpur District of the North-Western Provinces, six individuals presented themselves to the commissioner at Allahabad. Immediately, he rejected two candidates for living outside the district; another two were quickly dismissed for their failure to attend a public meeting. As a fierce rivalry emerged between the final two candidates, Zahur-ul-Hasan and Muhammad Moosa, the local magistrate received numerous petitions from the candidates, each discrediting the other and asserting his own claims based on lineage, training, and public support. After several rounds of inquiry, and a public contest in which district residents voted for their preferred candidate, the magistrate tallied the votes. The two were virtually tied, so he split the position between them.[108] For this and other contested posts, officials might decline to make any appointment, divide the position across multiple candidates, or offer to appoint separate Sunni and Shiʿa qazis.[109] They thus opted to defuse possible conflicts, rather than searching for the sole rightful claimant.

If public support went against the government's choice, other criteria would come into play. When looking to fill a vacancy at Chibramau (south of Farrukhabad between Agra and Lucknow), the collector faced two candidates, each of whom claimed descent from "the old Kazi family." ʿAbd-ul-Kayum [Qaiyūm] had a head start "in applying for the appointment by accident," but Kamr-ud-Din [Qamr-ud-Dīn] made a better case. When the votes were tallied, ʿAbd-ul-Kayum had 156 and Kamr-ud-Din had only 127 supporters. Despite the difference, Kamr-ud-Din was older and wiser, and he had access to rent-free lands that would support him while in office, so Officiating Collector G. I. Nicholls nominated him for the position.[110] As these examples illustrate, new criteria like vote tallies came into play after 1880, but the government continued to privilege many of the same criteria as before: family background, ability, and reputation.

Exchanges about these appointments reveal that qazis were coming from the same families as before, and many also had ties to legal work, recordkeeping, and education—jobs that overlapped with the qazis' (former) responsibilities.[111] Likewise, the mechanisms for appointment were surprisingly consistent across time and space, with only a few changes to reflect new politics and new circumstances. The opinion of "respectable Muslims," for instance, now affected administrative decisions, reflecting the rhetoric of social reform and respectability that accompanied earlier legislative debates. The public's active involvement was also important: the act's wording made its extension contingent on the government's acceptance of an application from local Muslims, leading to a piecemeal introduction based on interest and involvement. This petition-response-appointment process further made the qazi's presence dependent on government recognition, reducing the once-esteemed office to one of negotiation and favor.

Beyond a few files from districts like Allahabad, government correspondence says little about the work these qazis performed after the 1880 act. To flesh out that part of the analysis, in chapter 6 I turn to the records qazis produced and instead focus in the rest of this section on critical evaluations of the operation of this legislation in British India and its influence on subsequent imperial policies. Across several metrics, marriage registration laws in British India failed to deliver the desired results, yet their failure did not prevent similar legislative acts relating to Muslim marriage (and to marriage registration) from appearing across the British Empire, from the Straits Settlements in 1880 to Trinidad and Tobago in 1961.

The most extensive inquiry into the workings (or failings) of marriage registration laws came from Bengal, where H. J. S. Cotton spearheaded a committee to evaluate the local 1876 Muhammadan Marriages and Divorces Registration Act.[112] The committee met five times during the months of January and February 1881, eventually producing a twenty-two-page report. The typed, single-spaced report began with a sweeping introduction to the qazi's office, described earlier regulations for the office, and compiled opinions on and collated information regarding recent regulations, before concluding with a draft for new, improved legislation that included twenty-eight separate sections (each with its own subsections) and an additional "Schedule" prescribing the form each register should take. "Unfortunately," the report concluded, the act had "not succeeded according to the sanguine expectation of its authors and promoters." With the Muslim population for the districts covered by the act totaling 11.2 million, the number of marriages recorded for the previous year (1879–80) barely reached seven thousand.[113] Beyond that, some marriage registrars recorded fewer than fifty ceremonies over the course of the entire year, and "in nineteen offices less than 10 were registered." Numerically, the act was a failure.[114] Committee members disagreed on the reasons for the act's failures, with ʿAbd-ul-Luteef arguing most animatedly that there was no flaw inherent to the act's wording or structure but that its execution was to blame.[115] Other committee members, however, felt that the "principle of the Act [was] radically defective" and that "mere modification of procedure under the present Act" would not solve any of the problems they observed.[116]

Notwithstanding these criticisms, the Bengal act became a template for legislation that traveled to the Straits Settlements and Ceylon (Sri Lanka)

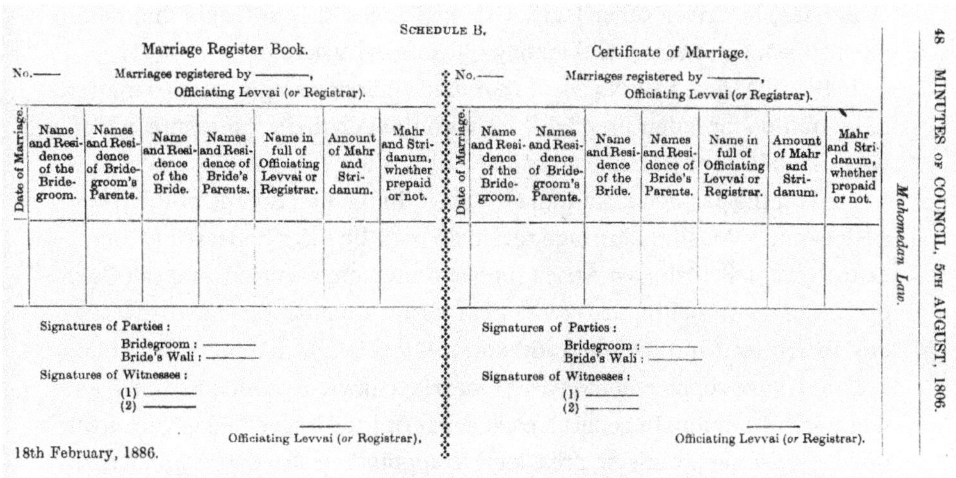

SCHEDULE B.

Marriage Register Book.

No.—— Marriages registered by ———, Officiating Levvai (*or* Registrar).

Date of Marriage.	Name and Residence of the Bridegroom.	Names and Residence of Bridegroom's Parents.	Name and Residence of the Bride.	Names and Residence of Bride's Parents.	Name in full of Officiating Levvai or Registrar.	Amount of Mahr and Stridanum.	Mahr and Stridanum, whether prepaid or not.

Signatures of Parties :
Bridegroom : ———
Bride's Wali : ———
Signatures of Witnesses :
(1) ———
(2) ———

——— Officiating Levvai (*or* Registrar).

18th February, 1886.

Certificate of Marriage.

No.—— Marriages registered by ———, Officiating Levvai (*or* Registrar).

Date of Marriage.	Name and Residence of the Bridegroom.	Names and Residence of Bridegroom's Parents.	Name and Residence of the Bride.	Names and Residence of Bride's Parents.	Name in full of Officiating Levvai or Registrar.	Amount of Mahr and Stridanum.	Mahr and Stridanum, whether prepaid or not.

Signatures of Parties :
Bridegroom : ———
Bride's Wali : ———
Signatures of Witnesses :
(1) ———
(2) ———

——— Officiating Levvai (*or* Registrar).

48 MINUTES OF COUNCIL, 5TH AUGUST, 1886.

Mahomedan Law.

FIGURE 3.1 Recommended register layout for recording Muslim marriages under Ceylon Ordinance No. 5 of 1886, as revised by Ordinance No. 2 of 1888. *A Revised Edition of the Legislative Enactments of Ceylon 1707 to 1879*, volume I (Colombo: H. C. Cottle, 1907), 48.

and then to Africa and the West Indies. The Straits Settlements Ordinance (Ordinance No. 5 of 1880), which was contemporaneous to the Kazis' Act, mirrored both the Bengal act (especially in Part I, Registration) and the Kazis' Act (in Part II, Ka[d]is),[117] while incorporating additional measures relating to the "effect of marriage on property" (Part III).[118] The organization, wording, and intent of the Straits Ordinance are too similar to suppose separate origins for these laws, especially since the two acts appear together in a single file.[119] British Ceylon, where general laws for marriage registration (Ordinance No. 15 of 1876) and marital property already existed but explicitly excluded groups like Muslims,[120] introduced Ordinance No. 8, "An ordinance to provide for the Registration of Mohammedan Marriages contracted in this colony," in 1886. Inflected by the history of Dutch colonialism, the 1886 ordinance differed from the Bengal act but included key sections (for example, those on appointments and dismissals, supply of books, fees, and rules for correcting errors) that paralleled the Bengal act. Dower, which is absent from the Bengal regulation (despite its centrality to the marriage registration project), appears in section 19 of the ordinance, as do examples of the registrar's tabulated forms—forms that map directly onto those qazis in British India used.[121] (See figure 3.1.) The direct connection between these two measures is not as obvious as the Straits Settlements ordinance, but given other legislative exchanges, it is probable that notes on India's act also circulated among officials in Ceylon.[122]

In South Africa, Law No. 25 of 1891 made marriage registration a matter of regulation for indentured laborers with this "civilizing" measure, which was, much like the Kazis' Act, designed to eradicate "loose" marriages contracted on the passage from India.[123] Then, in the first decade of the twentieth century, Muslim marriage registration ordinances appeared in Sierra Leone (1905), British East Africa (present-day Kenya) (1906), and the Gold Coast Colony (1907) in nearly identical forms. Comparable measures traveled to Trinidad and Tobago (1961) and to Gambia (1941), though these later acts may have supplemented earlier marriage laws, as subsequent revision was not uncommon. In general, each act permitted a specified government official (governor, minister, president) to appoint registrars who would then validate the marriage, verify the parties' identities, and create a record in his register, following the prescribed format. The registrars' titles, their registration procedures, the languages they employed, the procedures for submitting and reviewing their records, and the legal status of their records varied, but much of the substance was identical across these acts.

In Sierra Leone, registration constituted "proof of the existence, past or present, of a Mohammedan marriage, or of the dissolution of a Mohammedan marriage, [that] shall be received in evidence by all the Courts in the Colony."[124] (Qazis in India struggled to have their registers treated this way.) In the Gold Coast, marriages could not be valid unless they were registered under the act, and any person required to register a marriage or divorce who failed to do so without "good cause . . . shall be guilty of an offence and shall be liable to a fine not exceeding five pounds."[125] The penal element that was lacking in British India's legislation thus found its way into the Gold Coast law. These two ordinances also included sections on the succession of property for people dying intestate, which was in Part III (effect of marriage on property) of the Straits ordinance.[126] The ordinance from East Africa, which followed the Bengal act closely, also included a "saving" clause, like the one added to the second version of the Bengal act. Beyond this, each measure referred to the abstract idea of "Muslim" or "Muhammadan" law as well as to specific laws and institutions present in the individual colonies and territories, showing how law applied to people (i.e., personal law) intermingled with law applied to territories.

Scholars who work on comparative imperial law already know that laws—and lawmakers—traveled around the empire and carried ideas from one context to another.[127] Macroscopically, the Muslim marriage registration acts reflected imperial anxieties over the nature and status of Muslim marriage and kept it separate under Muslim personal law while at the same time subjecting it to greater legislative oversight and scrutiny. Microscopically, each act reflected unique elements of the legal structures, hierarchies, and systems in different locations. What is unique about the marriage registration laws' travels, then, is that they made Muslim marriage a unique problem that necessitated a specific legislative intervention. Against this larger backdrop, the Kazis' Act of 1880 stands out in that it appointed qazis, not "registrars," and did less in terms of marriage reform than advocates might have desired. The act delegitimized qazis as judicial officers while it upheld and reinforced paradigmatic views about their work in relation to personal law. Precisely by declining to intervene in that work, the act left open the possibility for these individuals to define their own role alongside—but outside—the formal, colonial legal system and to imagine Islamic legal practice not as Anglo-Muslim law but as something that existed outside, beyond, and in addition to the Anglo-Indian courts. How those notions and discourses of law came into being and circulated in British India is the subject of part II.

Conclusion

Often cited but rarely interrogated, the legacies of these legislative interventions into the qazi's office remain surprisingly overlooked. Not surprisingly, such oversight tracks with the many observations noted in but ultimately sidestepped by the debates surrounding the 1880 act: Should appointees receive more or less authority? Should their responsibilities be expanded or contracted? Should they be popularly elected or administratively appointed? Should they be government employees or independent contractors? Should the public have a say or only those representing the "respectable" classes? Could the government trust its appointees or would suspicion always follow the office? Even after independence, these questions continue to surround the qazi's office.

Such complaints are not new; they draw on a long history of criticism and ridicule assigned to qazis—a history much longer than the century-long narrative outlined in these chapters. Yet rather than reflecting some unchanging truth about the qazi, such criticisms tend to reflect other anxieties—about the liabilities of outsourcing legal authority, normative family structures threatened by the "looseness" of the marriage tie, and misguided prejudices about the inequality (and extralegality) of unilateral male divorce.

When mixed with anti-Muslim bias, scanty evidence provided ample pretext for legislative intervention, increased surveillance through registration, and the general diminution of nonstate legal experts. Whether the Kazis' Act could have succeeded if set on steadier footing remains to be seen, but its influence remains not only in postcolonial India but also in marriage registration ordinances across the former empire and in immigration policies tied to proof of marriage. Setting aside shortcomings in these legislative fixes, the next three chapters look at how Islamic law operated outside and alongside legislation to remedy gaps and inadequacies in the Anglo-Indian legal system. Doing so, the narrative moves away from the offices of judicial, legislative, and home department officials toward those of the madrasa, *dār-ul-iftāʾ* (fatwa institute), and printing press and away from the Bombay Presidency and into North India and the Deccan.

Part II Paperwork

Interlude II

Crown Rule in the Context of Noninterference

Whereas, for divers weighty reasons, We have resolved by and with the advice and consent of the Lords Spiritual and Temporal, and Commons, in Parliament assembled, to take upon Ourselves the Government of the Territories in India heretofore administered in trust for Us by the Honorable East India Company: . . .

We hold Ourselves bound to the Natives of Our Indian Territories by the same obligations of Duty which bind Us to all Our other Subjects; and those Obligations, by the Blessing of Almighty God, We shall faithfully and conscientiously fulfil [*sic*].

Firmly relying Ourselves on the truth of Christianity, and acknowledging with gratitude the solace of Religion, We disclaim alike the Right and the Desire to impose our Convictions on any of Our Subjects. We declare it to be Our Royal Will and Pleasure that *none be in any wise favored, none molested or disquieted by reason of their Religious Faith or Observances; but that all shall alike enjoy the equal and impartial protection of the Law*: and We do strictly charge and enjoin all those who might be in authority under Us, that they *abstain from all interference with the Religious Belief or Worship of any of Our Subjects*, on pain of Our highest Displeasure.

And it is Our further Will that, so far as may be, Our Subjects, of whatever Race or Creed, be freely and impartially admitted to Office in Our Service, the Duties of which they may be qualified, by their education, ability, and integrity, duly to discharge.

—"Proclamation of Queen Victoria on the 1st Day of November 1858, to the Princes, Chiefs, and People of India" (emphasis added)

Text and Context: The Queen's Proclamation of 1858

The Queen's Proclamation of 1858 marked the end of Mughal rule on the subcontinent and announced the arrival of a new sovereign: Queen Victoria.[1] Issued after the disturbances of the 1857–58 Uprising had mostly been subdued and the British East India Company relieved of its responsibilities for governing Britain's South Asian territories, the proclamation made "Victoria, by the Grace of God of the United Kingdom of Great Britain and Ireland, and of the Colonies and Dependencies thereof in Europe, Asia, Africa, America, and Australia, Queen, Defender of the Faith," sovereign for millions of Indians. Now, instead of governing through the offices and officers of a trading company, the United Kingdom would rule India through the queen's cabinet and her secretary of state for India, who would, in turn, oversee local affairs through the viceroy.[2] Not only did the proclamation put the queen at the top, but the transition from trading company to crown also paved the way for sweeping legal reforms. Alongside experiments in legal codification like the Indian Penal Code (1860), the government also introduced codes of civil and criminal procedure (1858, 1861) and acts relating to contracts (1872) and evidence (1872), overhauling the existing legal system almost in its entirety.[3] In addition to the proclamation's symbolic implications, these acts had indelible effects on the organization of the courts and the adjudication of cases—substantively and procedurally.

The Uprising had multiple causes. Complaints against recruitment and compensation for Indian soldiers in the Company's army provided the kindling, but the spark that set off over twelve months of fighting between soldiers, rebels, and civilians on both sides of the conflict was a rumor surrounding the introduction of Enfield rifle cartridges that were offensive and injurious to the religious sentiments of Hindus and Muslims.[4] Although the uprising had multiple systemic causes, religious offense became the cause célèbre in subsequent accounts, marking British insensitivity—and insensibility—toward Indians' religious sentiment.[5] Accordingly, the Queen's Proclamation was an attempt to acknowledge, apologize for, and prevent any future such incidents. Despite the sweeping legal reforms that followed (many of which had been imagined before 1857), the proclamation—a pronouncement asserting royal, sovereign authority in the name of Christianity and for a queen who ruled "by the Grace of God"—made it clear that religious life was to remain free from government interference. The status of religious sentiment as one of the Uprising's chief causes demonstrated the problems that could arise from interference in the liberties of the empire's Indian subjects, and the proclamation sought to attenuate those risks.

The principle of "noninterference," as it later became known, guarded against government interference in religion and kept religion from interfering with good governance, but the proclamation did other things as well. It affirmed the queen's lack of desire to extend her "present territorial Possessions"; vowed to "respect the Rights, Dignity, and Honour of Native Princes"; and confirmed the validity of existing treaties with native princes, effectively transferring the Company's treaty obligations to the Crown. It condemned the "evils and misery" that Indians had suffered at the hands of "ambitious men" who "led them into open Rebellion" and expressed a desire to show those men "Our Mercy" by granting them pardon. In an effort to quell ongoing disturbances, it further offered "unconditional Pardon, Amnesty, and Oblivion of all Offence against Ourselves, Our Crown and Dignity" to those who gave up their arms.[6] In short, the proclamation offered royal benevolence in exchange for willing surrender to and recognition of the queen's sovereign authority. It followed in the footsteps of earlier declarations by introducing broad changes in the structure of government while at the same time upholding and affirming much of the status quo.

Toward a New Politics of Secularism

Read alongside the Hastings Plan of 1772, the Queen's Proclamation fits with but offers a subtle reconfiguration of earlier approaches to religious difference and diversity in South Asia. References to being free from favor, molestation, or disquiet here parallel the Company's approach to religious legal pluralism in the past, cordoning off areas of private life from government intervention. Yet the proclamation changed the definition of religion, reflecting new developments in secular thought and imperial policy. While the earlier judicial plan named, identified, and pledged to govern individuals belonging to two distinct categories (Hindus and Muslims), the proclamation, by contrast, sought to divide the political life of British rule from the private life of religious belief. Subjects were free to maintain any "faith" they desired and were to be unencumbered in their "Religious Belief," but governance would now occur alongside, rather than through, those ideas of "Belief or Worship." In other words, the proclamation embraced the secular division between religion and politics.

To be sure, the proclamation did not make British India a secular state, nor did it establish Britain's government of India as a secular entity, but the wording of the proclamation—in its recognition of religious difference, in its acknowledgment of religious diversity, and in its overt contrast between the ruling sovereign's Christian "Conviction" and the native inhabitants' non-Christian "Belief"—made it clear that religious practices and principles were no longer the basis for government policy or rule. At the same time, by pledging noninterference and recognizing religion as an area into which government would (and should) not interfere, the proclamation also made religion a space for cultural, legal, and social autonomy. In the years following the Queen's Proclamation, these dynamics—between religion as a separate, private sphere for "Belief and Worship" and religion as a space free from colonial interference—played out across South Asia's variegated social landscape. Self-identified "religious" institutions created spaces of autonomy by undertaking projects (educational, ideological, political) in the name of religion.[7] Leading elites, including Sayyid Ahmad Khan and Nawab ʿAbd-ul-Luteef, pushed reformist efforts through local and imperial legislative councils by leveraging their ability to speak for religious communities.[8] And religious legal practitioners, as the following chapters show, engaged with questions about the category of "religion" and where the lines of Muslim "Belief and Worship" lay.[9] In this way, the Queen's Proclamation, symbolically if not practically, set in motion the project of separating religion from law, politics, and economics that would play out across the second half of the nineteenth century and into the postcolonial period.[10]

While much of the fanfare surrounding 1858's symbolic and practical reconfiguration of power and authority on the subcontinent focuses on the last Mughal emperor Bahadur Shah Zafar's deposition and exile to Burma, other reconfigurations of power were taking place on the ground.[11] Social scientific approaches to policy, replete with statistics, demographics, surveys, and summaries, replaced earlier interests in precedent, custom, or tradition. The colonial knowledge-production project shifted from an earlier interest in how things were to an emphasis on how things *ought to be*. In some respects, these changes encouraged the homogenization of practices, principles, and approaches. Efforts to minimize regional variation and to rationalize aspects of governance (like law) across British India's expansive territory resulted in new, pan-Indian projects (like the Kazis' Act), with varying degrees of success. In others, these efforts contributed to fractious politics and increased factionalism.

In law, religion became a space protected from interference and defined by exception. It was an arena to which one could appeal for accommodation, as Muslim legislators did in the context of the Kazis' Act. It was also a mechanism through which one could make claims for exception or exemption. In this way, the proclamation's attempts to minimize the role of "Religious Belief or Worship" in the definition, constitution, or construction of British rule had the inverse effect: it made religion central to any legal debate or policy prescription. Read in conjunction with the late nineteenth century's turn toward legal codes and codification, the proclamation thus pushed debates over the correct interpretation of religion to the forefront, inviting Indian Muslim judges and legislators to strive for the accurate and authoritative instantiation (or establishment) of Islam through law. Legislators were empowered to enshrine specific interpretations of scripture into law, judges were authorized to adjudicate the proper way to pray,[12] and dissenters learned that the best way to disagree was to litigate or to lobby for new legislation.[13] Winning the battle in court thus meant gaining control over what Islam was.

Debates along these lines continue today in India, Pakistan, and Bangladesh with Islamic legal scholars and experts routinely pointing to the shortcomings, failures, and misinterpretations of the colonial state's efforts to get Islamic law "right." What these debates fail to acknowledge, however, are the ways in which the quest for "right" interpretation still relies on the authority of the state to dictate the terms of that debate. And with a few exceptions, the participants in these debates largely accept ideas about the status of religion found in statements like Queen Victoria's Proclamation.[14] While much of the scholarship on South Asia's legal history focuses on the construction of religious personal law in response to changing colonial policies, the social history of law outlined in the following chapters explores the contributions of ordinary individuals to the definition and constitution of "personal law" beyond the bounds of legislators, lawmakers, and litigation, beginning with a question about the very idea of who counts as "Muslim." Although the 1858 proclamation pledged noninterference in religious affairs, fulfilling that promise required accepting a stable definition of religion, qua religion, as something apart from the state, separate from politics, and outside the framework of law. The British colonial state may have had one definition in mind, but nonstate legal actors respected, adopted, and developed a range of definitions that shaped their day-to-day work and produced alternative visions of Islamic legal practice. Everyday Islamic law emerged at the intersection of these competing definitions.

4 Personal Law in the Public Sphere

Fatwas, Print Publics, and the Making of Everyday Islamic Legal Discourse

What say you, scholars of the faith and muftis of the *sharīʿa*, located in Lucknow, may God have mercy on you, in these issues . . . ?
—Amir Khan, writing to ʿAbd-ul-Hayy, 1881

Defining Legal Categories

In 1881 tensions were mounting between two factions of Muslims in Amīr K̲h̲ān's hometown of Haliyāl in the Kanaṛa region of South India. One faction, the "royal butchers" (*sulṭānī qaṣṣāb*), called themselves Muslims (*musulmān kehlātē hain̠*) and behaved (mostly) like other Muslims, but they kept themselves separate. They said the *kalima-yi shahādat* (the profession of faith), read the Friday prayers, celebrated ʿEid, prayed five times daily, kept the fast during Ramadan, had their *k̲h̲atna* (circumcision) performed and their *nikāḥ* (marriage) read. Yet despite performing the five pillars, these butchers did not intermingle with others. They would not share food or drink with other Muslims (*Musulmānōn̠ kē āb-ō-ṭaʿām sē parhēz kartē hain̠*), nor would they use the same water at the mosque to perform their ablutions before prayer (*masjid kē pānī sē wuẓū tak nahīn̠ kartē*). Were these butchers Muslims or were they blasphemers? Amir Khan wondered.[1] To quell tensions between the groups (and to set his mind at ease), Amir Khan did what any madrasa employee might: he wrote to a fellow scholar for advice.[2] Traveling 1,600 kilometers from Haliyal in the south to Lucknow in the north, Amir Khan's letter described a local situation that tapped into timeless anxieties about who belongs to and what defines the category "Muslim." To answer that question, he drew on the expertise of a scholar whose prestige crossed regional and sectarian divides, whose reputation was well established, and whose status was unmatched, even under British rule. He turned to Muḥammad ʿAbd-ul-Ḥayy Farangī Maḥallī of Lucknow.[3]

In the first half of the nineteenth century, disputes involving qazis took for granted the existence of a "Muslim" community, allowing those who cared about qazis to represent Muslim interests and concerns by default. As British rule became more entrenched and pan-Indian legislation homogenized regional variation,[4] questions about who spoke for Muslims, who represented the community, and who belonged to the category assumed greater importance, as the "rule of colonial difference" gave seemingly simple definitions new meaning.[5] Answering the question, "Are they Muslim or are they blasphemers?" not only determined who belonged to the community but also determined the group's legal status.[6] Over one thousand years after Muhammad's followers founded a new community of believers in Medina, the question of whether to call someone a Muslim was not new, nor was Amir Khan the only one to ask it, but in the context of British rule and the colonial state's expanding intervention into everyday life, the question assumed new meaning.[7] While some of these questions—about who or what defined Islam—made their way into courtroom proceedings, others spilled over into the public sphere, where experts and nonexperts engaged in their debate.[8] Dispatched to a prominent *muftī* (legal scholar), Amir Khan's question belonged to the latter category.

In the second half of the nineteenth century, the courts of British India became increasingly strident in their abilities to settle religious law disputes, yet questions like the one Amir Khan posed complicated the courts' ability to adjudicate.[9] Common-law precedents and Anglo-Indian procedures, mixed with ad hoc references to partially translated Islamic legal texts, made the legal field uneven, as the courts remained deferential to religious difference, even though recognizing the authority of religious experts undermined the courts' own interpretive superiority.[10] Amid the colonial courts' efforts to articulate and apply "the law" accurately, Islamic legal practitioners entered the fray to evaluate the laws of British India, consider the courts' application of them, and assess colonial legal processes in relation to Islamic jurisprudence (*fiqh*). While the courts took the categories of "Hindu" and "Muslim" for granted, muftis like ʿAbd-ul-Hayy evaluated the nuances of these very categories. As jurists (not judges), muftis were obligated to reply "in light of the *sharīʿa*," but they did so with the entire toolbox of Islamic jurisprudence at their fingertips. Writing legal opinions (fatwas), not binding judicial decrees, muftis had the freedom to chart alternative paths that considered context and complications, and in his answer, ʿAbd-ul-Hayy adopted this approach. Rather than relying on the colonial state's black-and-white definitions, he embraced indeterminacy, chastising but not casting Haliyal's butchers out of the community. Imperfect Muslims were still Muslims.

Amir Khan was not the only one to raise questions about categories and definitions; they flowed through the discourse of Islam's nineteenth-century revival as experts, nonexperts, scholars, students, legislators, lawmakers, and administrators debated who counted as a Muslim, what being Muslim meant, how Muslims should behave, and who should decide. The answers that arose reflected a growing awareness that British rule required new understandings of law, religion, state, and society and that answering these questions meant looking beyond the particularities of a given place and the customs of a certain community. Finding answers necessitated looking elsewhere, to other parts of the subcontinent, and across the empire. The collapsing of time and space in the era of steam and print not only brought everyday life to the forefront of legal debate but also brought ordinary individuals into the conversation.[11] Everyday Islamic law thus unfolded spatially and conceptually, following the threads of communication and networks of exchange that fatwa seekers like Amir Khan and muftis like ʿAbd-ul-Hayy employed. These networks expanded as communication capabilities grew and contracted as factionalism created new politics of inclusion and exclusion, but throughout this history, seeking and receiving fatwas persisted.[12]

Exploiting emergent print technologies and expanding information networks, inquiries, answers, conversations, and exchanges like those captured in ʿAbd-ul-Hayy's *Majmūʿa-ul-Fatāwá* (*Collection of Fatwas*) traversed the subcontinent, moving from intellectual hubs to rural outposts, across and between British Indian territories and those of the native princely states, and into and out of the subcontinent through postal, rail, sea, newspaper, and telegraph networks. The route Amir Khan's question traveled from Haliyal to Lucknow is only one example of the many paths legal questions took in late colonial South Asia. As new communications circuits replaced older intellectual networks and reached across and beyond the subcontinent, they incorporated larger lay audiences—merchants, educators, government employees, pensioners, professionals—who used the fatwa genre to make Islam compatible with the changing world in which they lived and to make the changing world compatible with Islam. Everyday Islamic law thus emerged from these exchanges. It was at once permanent and malleable, timeless and modern, and could reach an expansive community, respond to shifting frames of reference, and address growing uncertainties.

Exchanges between scholars and students, experts and laymen, accelerated from the late nineteenth into the early twentieth century (and have continued to accelerate into the present with the addition of radio, television, internet, and mobile phone technologies).[13] They created networks of authority that were intensely local and self-consciously global, grounded in particular locations yet increasingly mobile, rooted in intellectual traditions and classical texts, but steadily shaped by new scholarly perspectives and a new corpus of reference works.[14] Experts and professionals lost their monopoly over Islamic legal discourse as ordinary individuals flocked to these debates. Emphasizing the contributions of scholars and political leaders, history has largely ignored the involvement of these ordinary individuals in the making of everyday Islamic law, but the pages of published and unpublished fatwas they requested record their contributions. Their reflections on the colonial legal system carried Islamic law beyond the courtrooms of British India and made it relevant outside madrasa networks.[15] Their reluctance to cede interpretive authority to the colonial state made Islamic law respond to the everyday demands of modern life. Their everyday engagements with Islamic law brought public law questions into the arena of private religious practice and pushed debates over personal law into the public sphere. In short, the broader transformation they inspired was less about separating law from religion (as secularism might suppose) and more about bringing law together with the new category of "religion."

As the courts of British India narrowed the scope of Muslim personal law, Islamic legal practitioners and their interlocutors became more outspoken about the application of *sharīʿa* (divine guidance) to everyday life, blurring the courts' neat understanding of legal concepts and categories.[16] Exchanges between expert jurists and ordinary individuals raised questions about the "legality" of British law for everyday life, the ethics of accepting judicial decisions as Muslim litigants, and the sufficiency of state enforcement for living according to Islam. As fatwas became part of public discourse, communications networks catapulted legal discourses across the subcontinent and the professional roles and responsibilities of a growing cadre of muftis changed accordingly.[17] Qazis were not the only legal practitioners to professionalize in response to British rule. Muftis, the experts in jurisprudence who formerly worked alongside qazis in the adjudication of cases but were cast aside by the colonial courts' common-law understandings of textual authority, also responded to professional expectations, popular demands, and institutional opportunities.[18] ʿAbd-ul-Hayy's trajectory was emblematic of and at the same time prefigured the mufti's transformation from marginal figure to mainstream public intellectual.

From Private Inquiry to Public Debate: The Changing Landscape of Fatwa Writing in British India

Debates about the connection between Islamic legal discourse and Muslim social life have been long standing and are ongoing.[19] Those skeptical of the relationship between legal theory and everyday life, for instance, contend that Islamic law is but "a speculative system of religious thought, thoroughly imbued with idealistic norms."[20] Such views emerge from the supposition that after the classical period (and following the metaphorical closing of the gates of *ijtihād* [independent reasoning]), nothing meaningful developed in Islamic jurisprudence, and that, in the words of the influential yet controversial Islamic studies scholar Joseph Schacht, Islamic legal (and administrative) practice became "rigid and set in its final mould" in the century following the Prophet's death.[21] It is easy to see why scholars like Schacht came to this conclusion given the forms of discourse that survive, but plumbing the depths of a more expansive Islamic legal archive provides opportunity to recover its social history.[22]

All of law's textbook writings (i.e., those that exist as "models *of*" legal practice, to use Brinkley Messick's categorization) demand abstraction, generalization, and categorization, but the generic conventions of the fatwa make it especially vulnerable to vagueness.[23] The genre demands certain acts of erasure and generalization that allow the expert to glean the legal question from its real-world origins and to transform the specific question into an abstract rule.[24] Removing details, reframing events, and substituting proper names with relational terms make law possible; they also detach legal records from everyday affairs. Fatwas that survive in manuscripts copied by student jurists decades, if not centuries, after they were originally issued include few particulars. Abbreviated into legal maxims, these records make it difficult to connect legal principles to actual events.[25] Yet law often works through the process of abstraction, as it transforms the messiness of everyday life, with extraneous details, ill-defined relationships, and unclear legal categories, into precise, narrowly defined questions and clear legal answers.[26] Recording, compiling, editing, and preserving fatwas erases the connection between legal interpretation and lived experience at the same time that it drives Islamic legal change.

Scrutinizing extant fatwa collections, Wael Hallaq has demonstrated that messy, "primary" fatwas contributed to the making of substantive jurisprudence after being "stripped" of their particulars, but his argument about how each round of compilation and revision moves answers further from the particular (opinion) and closer to the universal (law) has yet to inspire social histories that acknowledge the content of fatwa questions alongside their answers.[27] Moving beyond Hallaq's medieval jurists, my history of colonial legal change takes seriously the proliferation of fatwa writing as a vehicle for substantive legal change, even when the engines of colonial law were traversing another track.[28] What is more, this approach reveals that legal change emerged not from the top down but from the bottom up; it was driven as much by those who answered legal questions as by those who asked them.[29]

Two moves accompany this making of everyday Islamic law. The first is a shift in moral focus away from the state and onto the individual. The shift took place gradually, but the deposition of the last Mughal emperor, Bahadur Shah Zafar, following the 1857 Uprising marks a decisive moment symbolically, if not practically,[30] and questions over the status of British India as *dār-ul-ḥarb* (abode of war) or *dār-ul-Islām* (abode of peace) exemplify the effects of this shift, as Indian Muslims publicly debated the moral authority of the British government in India.[31] The second is the penetration of state law, governance, and governmental institutions into everyday life.[32] Colonial governmentality and the rise of the modern state brought government authority "into the lives of the colonized," leaving some to wonder whether it is still "useful to make a distinction between the colonial state and the forms of the modern state."[33] Everyday Islamic law rose in response both to colonial (i.e., foreign, British, Christian) rule and to the rise of the modern state as Indian Muslims grappled with the effects of these changes.[34]

Although religious personal law still applied to some areas of life and the British government still allowed Muslims to practice their religion, colonial governance reconfigured the relationship between state law as "law" and personal law as "religion."[35] Colonial secularism replaced shariʿa as the substance of law and public policy,[36] but it did not, as others have argued, destroy or "decimat[e]" shariʿa by reducing it to a category of personal law.[37] Instead, it shifted the site of shariʿa from the seat of sovereign power onto the body of the community, reinvigorating Islam as a discursive tradition in the public sphere.[38] The social, political, and legal histories of fatwa writing in colonial South Asia thus show that Muslim personal law did not replace other engagements with "law." Instead, it challenged the supremacy of state law as an adequate or sufficient source of authority and brought the question of law to a broader community of interlocutors. Taking seriously the process of seeking, receiving, and circulating fatwas, this chapter demonstrates how legal discourse brought state law into conversation with religious life, raised questions of religious authority in response to colonial hegemony, and contributed to substantive legal change through state and nonstate venues. These exchanges not only challenge conventional narratives about the retreat of Muslim life into areas of personal law, piety, and religious practice but also explain how and why attempts to separate the secular from the religious, state from nonstate, and public from private remain contested today.

Print technologies and engaged audiences pushed fatwas into the public sphere and gave new shape to the traditional legal form. When a person (the *mustaftī*) seeks a fatwa, he (or she) approaches a mufti, an expert who has studied *iftāʾ* (legal consultation) and is trained to provide an answer.[39] The mustafti may present the question (*istiftāʾ*) orally or in writing. (Oral [*zabānī*] requests tend to be shorter and simpler but nonetheless require the mufti's careful attention.)[40] A mufti might receive questions at the mosque where he works, the madrasa where he teaches, or at home.[41] He may even receive questions while walking or traveling.[42] With few exceptions, muftis answer the questions they receive in the order they are received and strive to treat those who approach them equitably and fairly, without favoring the rich and powerful.[43]

Generic conventions guide the exchange, from the first line of the mustafti's request ("What do the ʿulama say in this matter?") to the end of the mufti's response ("And God knows best"). Conventions also dictate the language, tone, structure, and evidence that muftis use, though he will change his language, vocabulary, tone, and modes of expression to accommodate the mustafti's abilities.[44] Muftis answer oral questions orally and written (*taḥrīrī*) requests in writing, using the bottom portion of the original page to provide the answer.[45] No record survives for thousands of oral and written fatwas produced through these exchanges, but records do survive from muftis who kept notebooks, employed disciples to transcribe their conversations, or worked in institutions that later kept detailed records.[46] In the past, a mufti might have provided an official version of the *suʾāl* and *jawāb* (question and answer) for matters tied to court cases or royal inquiries.[47] Nowadays, institutes employ digital technologies to scan, copy, and preserve these exchanges, typically setting them aside for subsequent compilation and publication,[48] though even with these efforts to duplicate and preserve the muftis' words, countless fatwas have been lost.[49] Nonetheless, the archive of fatwas from British India and postcolonial South Asia remains a relatively unexplored source for socio-legal history.

Although variation exists across institutions and circumstances, certain rules govern all muftis' conduct. Literature on the conduct and responsibilities of muftis (*ādāb al-muftī* literature), for instance, stresses the importance of understanding each question before providing an answer.[50] Mustaftis must write neatly, and "a mufti should not accept questions that are written on cut, torn, or dirty paper."[51] Upon receipt, the mufti must read the question carefully. If anything is unclear, he must ask the mustafti to clarify. If the mufti is confident, he may answer immediately, but if the question is complicated, the mufti should ask the mustafti to return later for an answer. Muftis who take their work seriously will refer to relevant verses from the Qurʾan and Sunna (traditions of the Prophet). Muftis might also draw on outside knowledge when questions refer to current events or touch on legislative or political concerns. Muftis must, however, remain cautious, avoid entering into disputes, exercise additional caution when inheritance is involved, prevent mustaftis from leaving out important details, and answer only the questions they are competent to answer. Issuing fatwas is serious business, and many muftis experience tremors of fear before commencing a response.[52]

At their most basic level, fatwas reflected an exchange between mufti and mustafti. When a mustafti presented his question in person, the mufti could ask for additional information to clarify any uncertainties on the spot. When questions arrived by post or telegraph, muftis in British India would employ those same networks to answer follow-up questions, as the files from the *dar-ul-ifta* (fatwa institute) in Hyderabad show (see chapter 5).[53] Even with telegraph lines and steam-powered postal services, exchanges between mustaftis and muftis were private: questions arose from personal experiences and answers applied to those specific cases. Print made these exchanges public.

Histories of Islamic revival and reform in British India demonstrate how print and publishing affected Islamic scholarship. Not only did print make religious texts accessible to wider audiences, but lithography also made them affordable.[54] Rather than gaining mastery through methodical memorization and time-intensive tutoring, readers were able, with the rise of commercial printing, to buy texts, read them without a teacher's supervision, and pick and choose references at random. Responding to the threat of "protestant" Islam, scholars (*ʿulama*) embraced print for their own purposes as well.[55] In addition to publishing pamphlets, tracts, and treatises, many institutions also published their own journals that included columns dedicated to answering legal questions. *Al-Imdād*, the monthly periodical for Ashraf ʿAli Thanwi's *khānqāh* (lodge) at Thana Bhawan, printed commentaries, religious treatises, fatwas, and letters. The Dar-ul-ʿUlum Nadwat-ul-ʿUlama in Lucknow published its own journal (*An-Nadwa*), and the Jamʿiyat-ul-ʿUlama-yi Hind's *Al-Jamʿīyat* included an "iftāʾ" column with fatwas written by Mufti Kifāyatullāh.[56] The casual inclusion of legal opinions within these publications publicized the jurists' opinions and made seeking, receiving, reading, and writing fatwas part of everyday Muslim life.

Publication also spurred the broader circulation and consideration of fatwa literature. Once they were public, fatwas became the subject of disputation, disagreement, and discord that characterized the "pamphlet wars" of Islamic legal revival and reform.[57] They traveled across contexts not just from South India to the north, as Amir Khan's question moved, but from British India to Burma, South Africa, and Scotland. As they traveled across the British Empire, they produced new ideas about law, new understandings of what it meant to be Muslim, and new conceptions of Indian Muslim identity. They acknowledged the authority of the colonial state but wondered what else Muslim life might entail. In the following sections, I trace these practices using printed fatwa collections to highlight the fatwa's dialogic form and its contributions to the making of colonial (and postcolonial) society.

Publication, Republication, and Reception: Toward a New Corpus of Islamic Law

Amir Khan's brief exchange with ʿAbd-ul-Hayy appears in the second volume of the *Majmūʿa-ul-Fatāwá*, which was published under the direction of the mufti's nephew, Maulvī Muḥammad Yūsuf, in 1887 CE (1305 AH), shortly after the mufti's death. This multivolume edition printed the mufti's legal opinions in chronological order. The first dated fatwa comes from 1868 CE (1285 AH); the final date is Rabiʿ-ul-Awwal of 1886 CE (1304 AH), the month of the mufti's death.[58] Organized this way, the *Majmūʿa* places the mufti's experience at the center of the text. The questions and answers proceed in the order the mufti received and responded to them. Mufti-centric ordering means that the text focuses on single inquiries on prayer (*ṣalāt*) and *jihād* (struggle) before switching to marriage for several questions, then jumping to *uẓḥīyat* (sacrifice, the slaughtering of sheep for ʿEid al-Aẓḥa) and purity for one exchange each, before returning to prayer.[59] Arranged in this order, the volumes offer not a comprehensive treatise on law but a collection of answers to questions as they arose.

Rather than ordering the questions by topic, as works of jurisprudence do, the editor identified legal concepts and categories in the margins, forcing the reader to flip the volume from top to bottom, side to side, to find a relevant reference. For some questions, the names of mustaftis and the dates their questions arrived or answers departed also show up in the margins. The questions move between Persian, Urdu, and Arabic, reflecting the mufti's multilingualism, and are punctuated by quotations from Arabic sources, ranging from a few words to several pages in length. Later editions would change this presentation, as ʿAbd-ul-Hayy's *Majmūʿa* moved from an author-centric text to a reader-centric reference, but the initial edition did little more than put the mufti's handwritten notes onto the printed page.[60]

The lack of editorial intervention is not surprising. Located somewhere between prized manuscript and printed notebook, this first edition reflects ʿAbd-ul-Hayy's place within the changing landscape of Islamic leadership and authority. Born into the Farangī Maḥall family of Lucknow during the reign of the last nawab of Awadh, Wajid ʿAli Shah (r. 1847–56), ʿAbd-ul-Hayy was, in the words of Francis Robinson, "the last outstanding scholar" to complete training in the rational Islamic sciences before the traditional *dars-i niẓāmī* (Nizami curriculum) gave way to colonial education.[61] During his lifetime, he witnessed the annexation of Awadh, the Uprising of 1857, the transition to Crown rule, and the segregation of educated Muslim elites into social reformist and Islamic revivalist camps, but his scholarly status was assured. His opinions on current issues were nuanced and well reasoned to the extent that he could be misquoted to support one side in a debate, despite his ultimate support for the other.[62] As a mufti, he not only offered fatwas that responded to questions about everyday life in British India but also participated in meta-juridical debates on juristic independence and imitation (*ijtihād wa taqlīd*) and on the role of history in determining Muslim responses to the present moment.[63]

The compiler's introduction to the *Majmūʿa* refers briefly to the mufti's handwritten fatwas but says little about the labor that went into the publication of the first edition. Compared with extant notebooks in other collections, and the compiling and arranging work that other editors performed, the compiler's contributions were minimal here.[64] At the end of the volumes, he provided an index (*fihrist-i maẓāmīn*) in which he summarized each question. Subsequent editions replaced the chronological ordering and sorted the questions according to topic, but in the interim, indexes helped readers navigate ʿAbd-ul-Hayy's opinions. Useful as it was, the index was also crude: it reduced Amir Khan's multipart question to a single subject (i.e., "buying meat from a non-believer when you believe the butcher is a Muslim and the debate between the non-believer and the Muslim customer") and ignored the question's more pressing discussion of whether the butcher was a Muslim or a nonbeliever (*kāfir*).[65]

Later editions continued the process of abstraction. After being republished in the same form in 1891 CE (1309 AH) and with slightly different pagination again in 1911 CE (1330 AH), a new edition of ʿAbd-ul-Hayy's text came out in 1926 CE (1345 AH) that not only advertised itself as a translation into Urdu (eschewing the multilingualism of earlier editions) but also arranged the questions into thematic chapters and subchapters, grouping questions on similar issues together. Those on beliefs (*ʿaqāʾid*) made a hefty chapter, and questions on *ʿilm* (knowledge) and the *ʿulama* (scholars) had their own section.[66] Ḥafīẓ-ur-Raḥmān Wāṣif describes a similar process for his preparation of Mufti Muhammad Kifayatullah's fatwas for publication fifty years later: after writing subject headings at the top of foolscap-size paper, he systematically went through the mufti's four-thousand-plus individual fatwas to sort them by category.[67] These reflections not only describe the herculean feat Wasif accomplished, gathering and sorting the mufti's fatwas for publication, but his method also reflects the citational practices and archival approaches that developed among the Indian ʿulama in the decades following ʿAbd-ul-Hayy's death. This outlook is evident not only in the records muftis kept—for example in Kifayatullah's records (which assigned serial numbers to individual mustaftis and included meticulous notes about dates and addresses) and in the fatwa files of the state dar-ul-ifta in princely Hyderabad (see chapter 5)—but also in the way readers responded to fatwas by similarly referring to dates, editions, and page numbers.

When Amir Khan's question appeared in the redesigned 1926 edition of ʿAbd-ul-Hayy's *Majmūʿa*, it was thrown into a lengthy chapter, over two hundred pages long, on "permission and prohibition" (*kitāb al-haẓr wa al-ibāḥa*) and appeared alongside a range of supposedly similar questions on everything from riding elephants, to smoking opium, to shaving one's beard.[68] The question that preceded it asked whether it was permissible to dig up and level an old graveyard in order to build new houses, and the one that followed it voiced concerns about the publication of insults relating to Imam Abu Hanifa, the eponymous founder of the Hanafi school of jurisprudence.[69] The later edition preserved the content of Amir Khan's question and the mufti's answer, but the new layout erased any reference to the question's context or origins. When published with the marginal note naming Amir Khan and identifying his location as Haliyal, the question was rooted in a particular time and place, the dispute was tied to regional histories of migration and assimilation, and ʿAbd-ul-Hayy's response accounted for these contingencies. The question's *yahāṉ* (here) referred to a specific location (Haliyal), and its "us" and "them" referred to specific groups. For the historian, these contextual clues undo the abstraction of legal rule-making and make legal debates about real-world concerns. They enable close engagement with the imagined communities of legal practice and treat everyday lawmaking not as an inevitability but as a process that unfolded through the circulation of newspapers, journals, and other printed texts; that flowed through fatwa questions and the answers they inspired; and that emerged from exchanges between Amir Khan in Haliyal and ʿAbd-ul-Hayy in Lucknow.

As later editions removed particularities from the questions ʿAbd-ul-Hayy received, they contributed to the making of a new legal literature. Producing a vernacular-language legal corpus may not have been on editor Muhammad Yusuf's mind when he commissioned the first printing, but by the turn of the twentieth century, the *Majmūʿa* was a commercial and intellectual success. While multiple printings in the first decades of its existence signal the work's commercial success, its intellectual success stems from the broader circuits its traveled. Not only did ʿAbd-ul-Hayy's audience span the subcontinent, but his writings also resurfaced amid later inquiries into the meaning and interpretation of everyday Islamic law. Such engagement is a testament to ʿAbd-ul-Hayy's influence and to the contested, constructed, and critical evolution of Islamic legal discourse that took place in concert with and in opposition to the Anglo-Indian legal system. Fatwas played a central, though often mischaracterized, role in this process.

Affirmation, Repetition, and Accretion: Fatwas and Substantive Legal Change

Modern legal systems thrive on rules, clearly articulated, universally applicable, and expertly codified.[70] In British India, such rules abound in the Indian Penal Code, the Indian Evidence Act, the Indian Contract Act, and codes of civil and criminal procedure.[71] Legal codes like these work through idealized forms.[72] They construct legal worlds from the top down, mapping lawmakers' projected ideals onto an imagined society. Such codes rarely reflect socio-legal realities and rely instead on robust institutions, penalties, and enforcement mechanisms to uphold their ideal visions. Fatwas reflect a different kind of legal project, one that also has ties to an ideal world but finds expression in individual cases.[73] Rooted in individual questions and tied to specific circumstances, muftis craft law not in the black-and-white terms of law codes but in the gray stippling and cross-hatching of law that emerges through the wording of a question, the characterization of events, or the alignment of an analogy.[74]

Muftis are not judges. They do not decide cases or issue decrees, but they do offer opinions and give answers in response to specific questions. Their process of making law uses the lawmaker's tools to craft bespoke answers to the questions before them. They decide whether a crime belongs to the category of manslaughter or murder, whether an act described is categorically "forbidden" (*ḥarām*) or simply "discouraged" (*makrūh*), whether a proposed remedy is permissible or possible.[75] Muslims engage in ifta because they want the mufti's advice; they accept fatwas as law because they want to follow "the law." But there is more to it than that. Fatwas are a discursive practice.[76] They require the interplay of abstract rules and specific circumstances; they demand that the mustafti produce a question and the mufti write an answer; and they require both parties to recognize that the world in which fatwas circulate is clouded by the imperfections of circumstances and situations. Fatwas are a framework for making the ideal forms of law's abstractions fit everyday Muslim life.

The specific mechanisms for seeking and receiving fatwas illuminate these connections between law and everyday life. Fatwas are nonbinding opinions that interpret how Islamic jurisprudence should or ought to be applied to a particular case.[77] They are rooted in particularities but operate through generic terms. "Someone," "a person," "your devoted servant" (*fidwī*), "a man" (*mard*), "a woman" (*ʿaurat*), or a "friend" might be the subject of the question. When a question requires a name, men become Zayd, Bakr, or ʿAmr[ū]; women become Hind[a] or Zainab.[78] Blank spaces, ellipses, or filler words like *fulān* and *kaẕā* (so-and-so; such-and-such) also take the place of proper names.[79] Identifying individuals by function, whether one of kinship (husband, wife, mother, father, son, daughter, uncle, aunt, in-law, etc.), profession (prayer leader, trader, student, scholar, pensioner, etc.), or legal position (buyer, seller, landlord, tenant, mortgager, mortgagee, etc.), also facilitates the mufti's work as he transforms complicated interpersonal affairs into abstract legal principles. Personal names do appear, when questions are complicated or inheritance is involved, but convention dictates the use of generic names when possible.[80]

Muftis employ several techniques to produce their answers, but even after production, answers remain nonbinding. Fatwas are lawlike but do not carry the same threat of punishment or enforcement as state law. Instead, they shape behavior through the individual and collective recognition of their law-bearing content.[81] Put another way, fatwas make law by virtue of being interpreted as law. Individually, fatwa seekers support this process by pledging to accept, follow, and implement the mufti's recommendation.[82] Collectively, Muslims use fatwas to create and maintain community norms. The compilation and publication of fatwa collections in the nineteenth century not only accelerated these lawmaking practices but also brought Islamic legal norms into conversation with expanding state law and accompanied the demarcation of Muslim personal law.[83]

Not all fatwas had the same effect on lawmaking. Change at the level of making and redefining community norms—that is, changing the substance of law—required additional mechanisms. Earlier, scholars who followed the principles of *tajrīd* (stripping, the process of making questions abstract), *tal̲kh̲īṣ* (abbreviating), and *tak̲h̲rīj* (educing, bring out a new ruling) transformed individual opinions into universal maxims.[84] In British India, as the pace of legal change accelerated, and as vernacular publishing created new audiences, the processes I define as affirmation, repetition, and accretion transformed individual juridical opinions into the substance of law.[85] None of these practices was new, but each assumed new meaning in response to colonial legal change.

With affirmation, other muftis simply added their signatures to a given opinion. When the Anjuman-i Mustashar-ul-ʿUlama (Society of Consulted Scholars) in Lahore published its short collection of fatwas in 1907, it included affirmations from a dozen or so individuals for each answer.[86] The affirmations included the statement "the answer is correct" (*al-jawāb ṣaḥīḥ*) followed by the signatory's name and title (figure 4.1).[87] For the anjuman, affirmation and collective authorship provided an opportunity to emphasize scholarly consensus and to combat theological factionalism. Posthumous affirmation was another approach. When editing and compiling a mufti's *majmūʿa* (collection), disciples, scholars, and students would (re)affirm the correctness of an answer by adding their seals and signatures. ʿAbd-ul-Hayy's *Majmūʿa*, for instance, included printed, seal-like affirmations from individuals including Muḥammad Masīḥ-ud-Dīn K̲h̲ān (seal dated

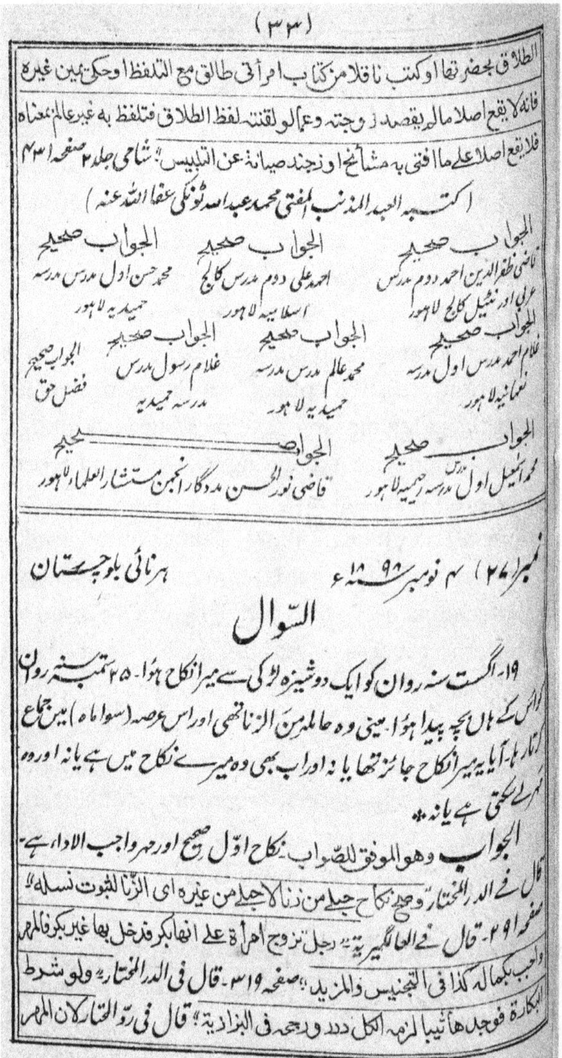

(۳۳)

الطلاق بحضرتها او کتب ناقلا من کتاب امرأتی طالق مع التلفظ او حکی یمین غیره فانه لا یقع اصلا ما لم یقصد زوجته وعما لو لقنته لفظ الطلاق فتلفظ به غیر عالم بمعناه فلا یقع اصلا علی ما افتی به مشائخ اوزجند صیانة عن التلبیس" شامی جلد ۲ صفحه ۴۳۱

(کتبه العبد المذنب المفتی محمد عبد الله ٹونکی عفا الله عنه)

الجواب صحیح — قاضی ظفر الدین احمد دوم مدرس عربی اورنٹیل کالج لاہور

الجواب صحیح — احمد علی دوم مدرس کالج اسلامیہ لاہور

الجواب صحیح — محمد حسن اول مدرس مدرسہ حمیدیہ لاہور

الجواب صحیح — غلام احمد مدرس اول مدرسہ نعمانیہ لاہور

الجواب صحیح — محمد عالم مدرس مدرسہ حمیدیہ لاہور

الجواب صحیح — غلام رسول مدرس مدرسہ حمیدیہ

الجواب صحیح — فضل حق

الجواب صحیح — محمد اسمٰعیل اول مدرس مدرسہ رحیمیہ لاہور

الجواب صحیح — قاضی نور الحسن مددگار انجمن مستشار العلماء لاہور

نمبر (۲۷) ۴ نومبر ۹۸ء — ہرنائی بلوچستان

السوال

۱۹ اگست سنہ رواں کو ایک دوشیزہ لڑکی سے میرا نکاح ہوا۔ ۲۵ ستمبر سنہ رواں کو اس کے ہاں بچہ پیدا ہوا۔ یعنی وہ حاملہ من الزنا تھی اور اس عرصہ (سوا ماہ) میں جماع کرتا رہا۔ آیا یہ میرا نکاح جائز تھا یا نہ اور اب بھی وہ میرے نکاح میں ہے یا نہ اور وہ مہر لے سکتی ہے یا نہ؟

الجواب وهو الموفق للصواب۔ نکاح اوّل صحیح اور مہر واجب الادا ہے۔ قال فی الدر المختار "وصح نکاح حبلی من زنا لا حبلی من غیره ای الزنا لثبوت نسله" صفحه ۱۹۰۔ قال فی العالمگیریة "رجل تزوج امرأة علی انها بکر فدخل بها فاذا هی غیر بکر فالمهر واجب بکماله کذا فی التجنیس والمزید" صفحه ۳۱۹۔ قال فی الدر المختار "ولو شرط البکارة فوجدها ثیبا لزمه الکل درر وصححه فی البزازیة" قال فی رد المختار لان المهر

FIGURE 4.1 Printed fatwa from the *Majmūʿa-yi Fatāwá-yi Ṣābriya*, published by the Anjuman-i Mustashar-ul-ʿUlama in Lahore. Note the printed format of the collective fatwa, including multiple signatories after the expression "al-jawāb saḥīḥ" (the answer is correct) in the top portion of the page and the (incomplete) elements of record keeping for the next fatwa in the bottom portion of the page. The heading for that fatwa includes the number (27) and date (November 4, 1898), along with the location of the fatwa seeker, Harnai, Balochistan. Other fatwas in this collection included the name, profession, and address of the fatwa seeker as well. Ṭōnkī, *Majmūʿa-yi Fatāwá-yi Ṣābriya*, 33, © The British Library Board, Asia, Pacific and Africa Collections, VT 3784.

1265 AH/1848 CE), Muḥammad ʿAlīm-ud-Dīn (seal dated 1276 AH/1859 CE), and the author (seal dated 1281 AH/1864 CE).[88] The introduction of institutional seals, like the one the Dar-ul-ʿUlum at Deoband began to use after opening its dar-ul-ifta in 1893, also affirmed decisions, letting the seal represent the community's collective authority.[89] Lithographic printing thus allowed authors and editors to embrace traditional forms of affirmation and attestation while preparing texts for new audiences.[90]

Affirmation was also common in the context of political fatwas—that is, those aimed at changing, amending, or supporting British policies.[91] In 1909, for example, over ninety signatories confirmed the pro-British message of support contained within a set of fatwas presented to the chief secretary to the government of the Punjab by Ḥakīm Raẓī-ud-Dīn and Maulavī ʿAbd-ul-Ḥaqq of Delhi.[92] Ten years later, during the noncooperation movement, the Jamʿiyat-ul-ʿUlama-yi Hind produced a fatwa urging Muslims to boycott and to refuse employment in or cooperation with British government agencies.[93] Blending elements of legal opinion and political petition, fatwas aimed at government policy used the accumulation of signatures to demonstrate collective support. Such practices blurred the lines between fatwas as public politics and fatwas as private law, negating any neat divisions between "law" and "religion."

While affirmation was a popular tactic for acknowledging accepted opinions, repetition guided scholars toward the creation of new legal principles, often in response to new circumstances or situations.[94] Writing fatwas for novel circumstances—new laws, new political configurations, new technologies—required practice.[95] Repetition clarified the question's core legal principles as jurists' answers became more uniform.[96] Published fatwa collections tend to hide these processes of sorting, discerning, and distilling, but looking across contemporary collections provides some clues about the process, and the arrival of telegraphic technology provides an illustrative example.[97]

Year after year, fatwa seekers requested answers about the telegraph's role in communicating information about the appearance of the crescent moon at the start or end of the month of Ramadan. The new moon's appearance would signal the arrival of ʿEid, but cloud cover routinely thwarted attempts to see the moon with the naked eye, and Muslims looked for other options. Growing awareness that the telegraph linked Muslims across vast spaces raised questions about whether a telegram sent from one location could convey the necessary information to Muslims living elsewhere.

Accordingly, the dozens of questions on this issue that appear in printed fatwa collections from this period thus signal that the ʿulama were still in the process of developing a principled answer.

Naẕīr Ḥusain Muḥaddis Dehlavī (1805–1902) received multiple versions of the question. The first asked simply whether it was permissible to believe testimony (*shahādat*) about the sighting of the crescent moon by way of "wire" (*ba ẕarīʿa-yi tār*).[98] The second referred to "the matter in which news of the sighting of the crescent moon . . . comes from another place by way of telegram [electric wire; *tār-i barqī*]." And a third wondered, "When news of the *hilāl* [crescent] moon comes from Bombay, etc., is it permissible to act on this information, believing it to be trustworthy, or not?"[99] The questions expressed concern about whether relying on the telegraph was "acceptable or not," requested answers "according to the Qurʾan and Hadith," and wanted the opinion of "the scholars of the faith," but variation in the details they contain demonstrates how repetition enabled muftis to distill precise legal principles. Each referred to the "news" (*k̲h̲abar*) of the crescent moon's sighting and questioned this news in relation to the necessary "testimony" (*shahādat*); and each asked whether it was possible to "believe" (*mānnā*), "accept" (*maqbūl*), or "trust" (*muʿtabar jān-kar*) the information for the purposes of starting or ending the fast (*rōza*).

To arrive at the correct legal principle, Nazir Husain first clarified that sighting the crescent moon was not "news" but belonged to the category of "testimony," which carries strict legal requirements. The witness must use the expression "I testify" (*ashhadu*) in the presence of a qazi to confirm the proper origin (*niṣāb*) of the information.[100] Transmission by telegraph, however, makes the information not legal testimony but "nonbeliever news" (*k̲h̲abar-i kāfir*). In the context of worldly affairs (*muʿāmalāt*), nonbeliever news is acceptable, but in the context of religious affairs (*diyānat*), it is not: "Shahādat, kāfir kī, diyānat main̲ muʿtabar nahīn̲." Drawing on passages from the "*Durr Muk̲h̲tār*, etc.,"[101] Nazir Husain then explained that even if the employees in the telegraph department were Muslim and equitable (*ʿudūl*), the transmission would still not be reliable for ritual purposes. In other words, using the telegraph was permissible but not in the context of transmitting testimony about the sighting of the new moon.[102]

Three other muftis affirmed Nazir Husain's answer to the first question, but their affirmations did not settle the matter.[103] Writing in the decades following Nazir Husain's death, ʿAzīz-ur-Raḥmān ʿUṣmānī (fl. 1911–15) responded to several nearly identical questions on this issue, fatwas numbered 637, 638, and 639 in his collection.[104] Mufti Kifayatullah also received several versions of this question, adding nuance and detail to the issue. One question referred to a *maulvī* (learned man, scholar) who announced the end of Ramadan, and another referred to the spread of news about the sighting of the crescent moon in Rangoon, Burma.[105] In each instance, some people celebrated ʿEid and others continued the fast. Kifayatullah evaluated these additional details but confirmed the general principle outlined earlier: telegrams, prone to errors and shortcomings (*kamī bēshī aur g̱halaṭ̤ī*), do not provide adequate testimony for the purposes of ending the fast, and acting on such information is incorrect.[106]

Repetition of this question, with details drawn from multiple instances, allowed scholars like Kifayatullah, ʿAziz-ur-Rahman, and Nazir Husain to clarify the legal principle at play. Their repeated analysis of and response to this common issue confirmed that the telegraph worked for some contexts but was impermissible and unacceptable in others, and their discernment of the legal rule paved the way for later scholars to address questions of transmission via radio and telephone.[107] Clarification, elaboration, and repetition of the muftis' answers thus transformed a hodgepodge of concerns tied to specific contexts into abstract, legal rules that became a part of everyday Islamic law. Attending to the nuances of this process shows not only how uncertainty contributed to the adaptation and evolution of law but also how extant compilations and printed records reflect moments of indecision, rather than proof of established doctrine.

Like repetition, accretion also produced substantive change over time. This approach made previously uncommon, circumstantial, or unconventional interpretations standard or commonplace. During the transition from individual question, to abstract legal principle, to written response, muftis have the opportunity to analyze topics from different perspectives, to foreground particular pieces of the puzzle, to emphasize certain legal principles over others, and to incorporate personal or judicial preference into their fatwas.[108] Individual muftis may be drawn to certain legal maneuvers or mechanisms, but over time, their recourse to such mechanisms or maneuvers (referred to as *ḥīla*, or tricks, by cynics) validates an interpretation or approach that might have otherwise been novel or exceptional, thereby creating a new benchmark or point of departure for future decisions.[109] Judicial literature identifies and recognizes these maneuvers under the umbrella of *ijtihād*, which includes specific practices like *istiḥsān* (juristic preference), *istiṣḥāb* (presumption of continuity), and *istiṣlāḥ* (consideration of public interest).[110] In addition to these approaches, changing political, social, and economic circumstances popularized other methods as well.[111]

Talfīq, the process by which jurists "piece together" new interpretations by borrowing from other schools of jurisprudence for instance, became popular among South Asian jurists in the context of reforming Muslim marriage laws.[112] For cases involving absentee husbands with unknown whereabouts, the Hanafi school of jurisprudence (the main Sunni school in South Asia) takes the view that a woman must wait until all of her husband's contemporaries have passed away before she is eligible for judicial separation (*tafrīq*) and remarriage.[113] The Maliki school, by contrast, says that when her husband's whereabouts are unknown, a woman may seek a judicial separation after waiting only four years for his return.[114] When contemplating legislative reform for Muslim marriage laws in British India, the Indian ʿulama advocated this second interpretation, it being much more accommodating to the needs of a woman who is legally tied to but has been physically, emotionally, and financially abandoned by an absentee husband (cases referred to as *mafqūd-ul-k̲h̲abar*).[115] Legislative reform may have required extensive deliberation and juristic investigation, but even before the Dissolution of Muslim Marriages Act (Act VIII of 1939) came into force, Hanafi jurists had already embraced the shortened waiting period.[116] In fatwas from 1937, for instance, Kifayatullah refers to a four-year waiting period without comment, signaling that this position, rooted in talfiq but accepted through accretion, was already commonplace.[117] Textbooks on Muslim personal law support this observation. In his treatise *The Personal Law of the Mahommedans: According to All the Schools* (1880), Syed Ameer Ali (1849–1928) explained that women who declare "before the magistrate . . . that the husband had disappeared for four years without leaving any trace behind" would receive permission to remarry.[118] He concluded that because Abu Hanifa (d. 767), eponymous founder of the Hanafi school of jurisprudence, held the "startling" view that women "ought to wait one hundred and twenty years," Hanafi jurists in India routinely followed the Shafiʿi school's seven-year waiting period.[119] Accretion conferred legitimacy on this alternative interpretation, despite its departure from traditional, canonical, or doctrinal perspectives.

Muftis employ strategies like affirmation, repetition, and accretion to transform individual questions—rooted in the messy circumstances of everyday life—into the abstract rules and guidelines of legal substance. For each fatwa, the process commences with the conversion of specific experiences into legal questions through abstraction and anonymization. From there, collective affirmation invests individual answers with personal and institutional validation, repetition allows scholars (individually and collectively) to distill disparate questions into clear legal principles, and accretion provides an opportunity to move the benchmarks of legal substance forward. These processes were not invented in the nineteenth century, but they did find new life as individuals turned to the fatwa genre and as cheap lithography make it possible to publish, disseminate, and debate legal points in the emerging vernacular public sphere. Thus, reading published collections against the grain—not for the answers they provide but for traces of the deliberations they involved—provides some evidence of how private law intersected with public debate in nineteenth- and twentieth-century South Asia. Other sources—unpublished, uncataloged, and unexamined—provide another means for charting these practices in greater detail. Those sources move to center stage in the next chapter.

Conclusion: Rereading ʿAbd-ul-Hayy and Debating a New Corpus of Islamic Legal Literature

The social life of the fatwa did not end with publication. Instead, publication was the first step in the process of everyday Islamic lawmaking. Individually, mustaftis responded to the fatwas they received by either accepting or rejecting the mufti's advice (or, at times, submitting a follow-up question). Collectively, Muslims across British India responded to fatwas by making them the subject of broader public debate: Did the mufti answer the question correctly? Did his answer account for this or that special circumstance? Did his answer account for this factor, or does this detail necessitate another inquiry? Secondary engagements like these—questioning, scrutinizing, and reflecting on fatwas as they circulated—gave life to everyday Islamic law. Well-known muftis responded to a range of questions and concerns from headmasters at local madrasas looking for outside opinions, government employees settling disputes, pious believers confronting complex problems, and others. Time has erased many of these subsequent inquiries, but sifting through published and republished editions provides some evidence that further exemplifies the social history of the fatwa, as subsequent generations called earlier opinions into question or made them address new circumstances.

The posthumous career of ʿAbd-ul-Hayy's fatwas provides a case in point. In February 1936, fifty years after his death, ʿAbd-ul-Hayy became ensnared in another debate about Muslim identity and belonging. Although it would have been difficult for him to write a new fatwa at the time, he became part of the conversation through the mustafti's willingness to read and cite his work. That mustafti, Maulana Aḥmad Buzurg of the Jamiʿa Islamiya in Dabhil (Ratnagiri, Maharashtra), was dealing with a controversy over whether a child born out of wedlock could be buried in a Muslim cemetery.[120] Specifically, the maulana wondered whether "Zayd" was correct that having one Muslim parent meant that the child was Muslim and should be buried in the Muslim cemetery or whether "ʿAmrū's" hesitancy—about the sources Zayd cited and the simple answer he provided—required further consideration. To round out his question, Maulana Buzurg made two additional points: first to state that jurists generally recognize the mother's lineage; and second to quote ʿAbd-ul-Hayy's fatwa on the issue.[121] So important was ʿAbd-ul-Hayy's opinion that after noting the volume, chapter, and page number, Maulana Buzurg reproduced the entire question and its answer verbatim in the fatwa request he sent to Mufti Kifayatullah in Delhi.[122]

Drawn from the 1926 edition of ʿAbd-ul-Hayy's *Majmūʿa*, the question Maulana Buzurg cited appears in the section on shrouding and burying (*tajhīz wa takfīn*) in the chapter on funerals (*janāʾiz*), alongside other questions about how to bury a woman and child who die during the child's birth, financial responsibility for burying women, and how to recuperate burial costs from family members. On the surface, the fatwa in question—about how to bury the product of illicit sex between a Muslim and an unbeliever (*kāfir*; *kāfira*)—certainly belonged to the same chapter, and Mufti Kifayatullah's compiler agreed, similarly categorizing this question in a section on funeral prayers (*namāz-i janāza*) in the chapter on funerals (*janāʾiz*).[123] In other words, the sorting and organizing of these questions tied their substance to broader rules about funerals and burials, yet there were other ways to read this fatwa.

Fatwas grow from experience. They emerge from the questions mustaftis submit and the answers muftis offer. Even with their subsequent organization, categorization, and compilation, fatwas are rarely systematic or comprehensive the way law codes or statutes might be. Instead, they take entire bodies of knowledge for granted, relying on the assumption that their audience already knows how to behave in routine cases. Amir Khan, for instance, knew that Muslims belong to a single community—the *ummah*—and that internal divisions and divisiveness were problematic. Likewise, Maulana Buzurg knew that only Muslims should be buried in a Muslim cemetery (and knew how to perform such burials). Their questions do not address these underlying assumptions. Instead, they attend to the aberrant, the irregular, and the extraordinary and call on noteworthy experts to provide answers. In this way, Amir Khan's and Maulana Buzurg's questions have more in common than their placement in unrelated chapters might suggest.

Like Amir Khan's, Maulana Buzurg's question also revolves around concepts and categories. It opens not with "a woman," "a man," or "a person" but with Zayd's original argument ("Zayd says"), followed by ʿAmrū's rejoinder ("ʿAmrū says"), and a section on what "the jurists say," with a reference to ʿAbd-ul-Hayy's fatwa at the end. Taking the question's content for granted, the compiler placed the fatwa in the chapter on funerals. A more meaningful sorting, however, might have placed it in the chapter on belief and nonbelief (*kitāb al-īmān wa al-kufr*) or in the one on knowledge (*kitāb al-ʿilm*), since the nuances of the substance have more to do with validating scholarly sources. Sorted this way, Maulana Buzurg could easily locate ʿAbd-ul-Hayy's original opinion on parentage, but the categorization simultaneously erased the question's parallels with Amir Khan's one about community, making the issue of "Muslim" identity less relevant than that of burials.

Such categorizations seem straightforward, but they are also subjective. When Ḵẖurshīd ʿĀlam published a revised edition of ʿAbd-ul-Hayy's *Majmūʿa* in 1964, he removed Amir Khan's question from the chapter on "permitting and prohibiting" and placed it in a catchall chapter on "miscellaneous issues." Thus, categorizing fatwas was about more than making them accessible to later readers; it was also about drawing lines between religious practice and legal life. As personal law became restricted to areas of religious practice, redefining questions or re-creating categories in religious terms both accorded with the rules of colonial secularism and challenged those rules at the same time. Later chapters will reveal more clearly how classifying questions using categories of Muslim personal law (e.g., marriage, divorce, inheritance) allowed Islamic legal experts to reclaim authority over them and then to use that authority to expand Islamic legal practice to other areas of life (e.g., contracts, property, commercial law), but already those processes are evident in the making and citing of ʿAbd-ul-Hayy's *Majmūʿa*. The categorization of Amir Khan's fatwa may seem immaterial, but in the context of colonial legal change, such classifications were also strategic. Seeking and receiving fatwas not only brought Islamic jurisprudence to bear on new issues as they arose but also made consideration of those issues through Islamic jurisprudence relevant to Muslim public life. The public efflorescence of Islamic legal debate in British India was not the natural by-product of innate Muslim religiosity but the result of a concerted effort to bring Islamic law into conversation with everyday Muslim life.

5 From Files to Fatwas

Procedural Uniformity and Substantive Flexibility in Alternative Legal Spaces

Times are strange today. Wonder is here to stay. Without prophetic updates, without interest in consensus or comparison, without taste for the roots or branches [of knowledge], without any skill for solving problems, half-*maulvīs* [scholars], on the whole, think writing fatwas is easy work and right or wrong copy from whatever book they please. They have no knowledge of the ways of the mufti, nor the etiquette of answering questions [*iftā*ʾ], nor have they mastered the books of the trade. They lack the skill to distinguish between worthy and unworthy texts. They know not the status of the jurists, the teachers of perfection, the types of *ijtihād* [reasoning]; the lords of elucidation and preference; nor the bases for rebuffing and rebutting. Nevertheless, they've rolled up their sleeves to write fatwas [legal opinions] and are eager to answer *istiftā*ʾs [legal inquiries]. Their pens are ready with every breath and they await an *istiftā*ʾ at every instant. These are the very things with which maulvis are not generally familiar, and few are such who know the answers to these questions, though they all know quite well the penny, the dime, and the dollar that the fatwa-foundry mints.

—ʿAbd-ul-Awwal Jaunpūrī, *Mufīd-ul-Muftī* (1908), 2

Taming the Wild World of Fatwa Writing

ʿAbd-ul-Awwal Jaunpuri (1867–1921) may have been exaggerating when he opened his multipart compendium *Mufīd-ul-Muftī* (*For the Benefit of the Mufti*) in 1908 CE (1326 AH) with a scathing critique of the dim-witted "half-maulvis" he observed writing fatwas (Islamic legal opinions). Not only were these profit-seeking individuals untrained and unskilled, but they were also in it only for the money. Sensing a need for his intervention, ʿAbd-ul-Awwal set out to school these upstarts and to give them the knowledge they needed to do *iftā*ʾ (legal inquiry) accurately and lawfully. After slyly outlining the four principal sources of law—Qurʾan (revealed text) and Sunna (prophetic example), consensus (*ijmā*ʿ), and analogy (*qiyās*)—and demonstrating his own adroitness in a series of lyrical statements, ʿAbd-ul-Awwal addressed the amateurs who had willy-nilly entered the juridical profession: there was neither honor nor etiquette in their work; neither care nor consideration in the way they answered questions; and to top it all off, they could not tell a legitimate source from an imposter reference. They knew nothing of the history or heritage of their Hanafi predecessors such that for them, "writing fatwas was illegal and impermissible" (*nā-jāʾiz aur ḥarām*).[1] Yet for all his ranting and raving, ʿAbd-ul-Awwal had little tangible guidance to offer. For him, the solution to the era's problems lay neither in recovering prophetic experiences nor in constituting a council for consensus. Rather, the solution he proposed in the two-hundred-plus pages of text that followed was to catalog and commemorate the intellectual ancestors and textual antecedents that formed the canon of Hanafi jurisprudence. To approach the art of ifta in the modern age was to show deference to the school's founder, disciples, and intellectual descendants, and to learn about the reliable works they authored. ʿAbd-ul-Awwal's approach was meritorious, but it was decidedly outdated.

By the first decade of the twentieth century, countless madrasas—new and old—with facilities to train young scholars in the Qurʾan, Hadith, and *fiqh* (jurisprudence) littered the subcontinent.[2] They housed dozens of experts who were trained in the art of ifta and employed to answer legal questions.[3] As a disciple of the famous ʿAbd-ul-Ḥayy Farangī Maḥallī (see chapter 4), ʿAbd-ul-Awwal knew all of this.[4] He was part of their networks, trained in their institutions, and associated with their founders and benefactors. He patronized the same small-town presses and participated in public exchanges with them, yet the strength of Islamic learning in South Asia had little impact on the frustration he felt.[5] Instead, to remedy the wrongs he observed, ʿAbd-ul-Awwal dragged his readers through an encyclopedic history of the Hanafi tradition, beginning with the biographies of the school's founders and contributors from the first to the fourteenth century Hijri and ending with a list of the reliable titles they produced. Fixing scholarly sloppiness lay in recovering respect for and indoctrinating young scholars in the ways of the past.

To say that ʿAbd-ul-Awwal overlooked a key aspect of Islamic scholarly success in the early twentieth century would be an understatement. By the time he published *Mufīd-ul-Muftī* in 1908 CE (1326 AH), the legal landscape of British India was quite different from that encountered by the past generations ʿAbd-ul-Awwal venerated. While the roots of scholarly authority still lay in traditional rubrics of achievement, success as a mufti ultimately depended on much more. Fetishizing the intellectual lineages and biographies of Hanafi jurists, ʿAbd-ul-Awwal missed entirely the urgent need for a jurist's flexibility, adaptability, and most importantly, accountability.

With hordes of "half-maulvis" standing with pens poised and sleeves rolled up, ready to write fatwas at the blink of an eye, institutional accountability brought more than collective accreditation to the fatwas they wrote. If anyone with a pen and a proverb could write a fatwa, then leading institutions (*dār-ul-iftā*ʾs) needed to offer more than a hasty response scribbled on a scrap of paper. Institutional prestige gave some offices more clout than others. A public presence, political engagement, and proximity to power could also help. Yet the main factors that separated upstart muftis from the bigwigs were paperwork and procedure. Nowhere is the role of paperwork more notably demonstrated than in the dar-ul-ifta of the princely state of Hyderabad. While the previous chapter showed how published fatwas made their mark on Islamic legal substance more broadly, moving the benchmarks of practice and interpretation in response to new contexts and new challenges, this chapter focuses on the practices and procedures that granted formality, credibility, and legitimacy to the individual answers these institutes provided.

Anxieties, like those ʿAbd-ul-Awwal expressed, over who had the authority to write and whose fatwas were legitimate accompanied the proliferation of Islamic legal publishing and opinion writing in the late nineteenth century. Affirmation, accretion, and repetition provided one set of strategies to support muftis as they worked through common questions to arrive at answers that were authoritative but still accommodated changing circumstances.[6] Yet amid the changing landscape of colonial law, and in response to the rapid expansion of the state's regulatory and administrative structures, muftis did more than respond to "religious" concerns. They also navigated concerns about jurisprudence, jurisdiction, legal institutions, and the legitimacy of the legal system.[7] In other words, fatwas also became a means for questioning whether "the law" was legal. While debates over worship, ritual, and belief brought the nuances of religious practice and theology into the public sphere,[8] questions over legal practice and legal process challenged the separation of "law" from "religion."[9] In this context, the dar-ul-ifta blossomed into a clearinghouse for all manner of questions about where to go, whom to consult, and which forum to approach to resolve legal, familial, interpersonal, and administrative conflicts.

Concerns about legal process were not confined to British India. Muftis in the princely states also responded to inquiries about Islamic authority in relation to broader legal change.[10] In Hyderabad State, where judicial reforms followed models from British India, the state maintained a formal dar-ul-ifta within the Ecclesiastical Department and employed a mufti at the high court.[11] Other states like Bhopal and Tonk employed Islamic legal experts, called on them to evaluate proposed law reforms, and appointed them to serve in institutions like Tonk's *sharīʿa ʿadālats* (shariʿa courts).[12] Hyderabad's dar-ul-ifta likewise fused the bureaucratic procedures of a state institution with the moral authority of the mufti's office, making it possible to trace the dar-ul-ifta's work through its paperwork. Moving away from published collections, established answers, and agreed-on consensuses (like those examined in chapter 4), files from Hyderabad's dar-ul-ifta demonstrate the processes of conversation, investigation, and negotiation that went into the making of a fatwa. Rather than emphasizing the mufti's answer, these files highlight the back-and-forth relationship between the dar-ul-ifta and its clientele, as *mustaftīs* (fatwa seekers) posed questions and the dar-ul-ifta worked to provide answers.

While Hyderabad's demi-official dar-ul-ifta is unique for several reasons—including for its ability to conduct interdepartmental inquiries, to evaluate evidence independently, and in some cases to intercede directly on a petitioner's behalf—the procedures it followed were comparable to those found in British India's nonofficial dar-ul-iftas. Within these institutions, muftis worked to respond to fatwa requests quickly and efficiently, to provide answers that were accurate and consistent but accommodated individual circumstances, and to operate seriously and professionally despite their unofficial status. These aspects of the mufti's work are often omitted from discussions that focus on decisions alone, but they are vital to understanding how muftis served their communities. Maintaining files, moving cases through the process, keeping tabs on named and numbered mustaftis, executing correspondence with order and consistency, and providing the best answer were not duties unique to the dar-ul-ifta in princely Hyderabad, but the archive it produced provides unique access into the deliberative, investigative, and consultative functions it performed.

Situating the Dar-ul-Ifta

The institute for issuing fatwas in princely Hyderabad (the dar-ul-ifta of the Ṣadārat-ul-ʿĀliya [Noble Secretariat]) traced its origins to the post of the *ṣadr-uṣ-ṣudūr*, who was, under the Mughals, an appointed official responsible for maintaining religious institutions. After Nizam-ul-Mulk Asaf Jah I claimed de facto sovereignty over the province in 1724, the state initially retained many former Mughal institutions, but as the threat of British interference into Hyderabad's affairs grew, the nizams subsequently called on their prime ministers to implement wide-ranging reforms.[13] These judicial and administrative transformations, first initiated under Salar Jung I (d. 1883), resulted in the reorganization of the Sadarat-ul-ʿAliya according to the state's new administrative schema. From the late nineteenth century onward, the office belonged to various departments: Miscellaneous, Religious Affairs, Ecclesiastical Affairs, Judicial and Public Affairs.[14] It retained the Sadarat-ul-ʿAliya name, but with each reorganization, the dar-ul-ifta became more governmental. By the start of the twentieth century, the day-to-day work it performed bore little resemblance to that of the erstwhile *sadr-us-sudur.*

Whereas the department's eighteenth-century predecessors left behind little paperwork, the twentieth-century dar-ul-ifta created thousands of files that trace the route legal questions followed as they went from shapeless descriptions of troubling situations and a fatwa seeker's request for advice, to an official department file and matter of inquiry.[15] Most of these inquiries were internal and drew on the expertise of office employees, but occasionally, files necessitated external or interdepartmental inquiries. From there, each inquiry became the basis for a draft answer and a formal response. Files sprouted from the supplicant's initial inquiry as assistants (*madadgārs*) and employees added underlining, marginal notes, follow-up inquiries, citations, correspondence, outside information, witness statements, and other communications. Once these investigations concluded and the answer was ready (after it had been drafted by an assistant and reviewed and corrected by the chief mufti), the office produced a formal response (figure 5.1), composed alongside the original question on stationery bearing the department's seal. As questions became files, and files moved through the dar-ul-ifta, they were lumped into categories, dated, enumerated, and deposited. The office repeated this process over and over: receive a request—in person, on a postcard, in a letter; from Hyderabad city, Hyderabad State, British India, or abroad—distill the narrative into a legal question, research, respond, and repeat at the rate of one or two new inquiries per day.[16]

Extant files lend the department's ordinary routines to historical investigation and carry the history of everyday Islamic law in new directions, but Hyderabad's dar-ul-ifta was not alone in adopting these procedures. Other fatwa-granting institutions and independent muftis received questions at comparable rates and followed similar procedures.[17] In Delhi, Mufti

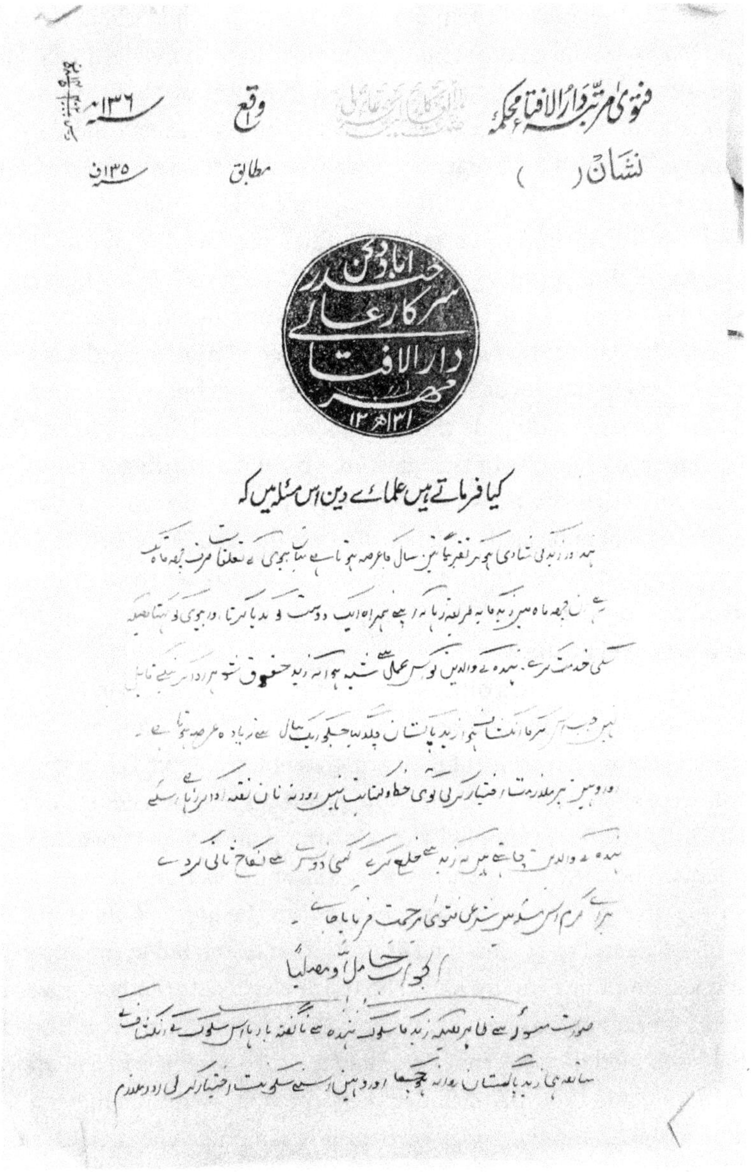
فتویٰ مرتبہ دار الافتاء محکمہ
نشان ( )
وقع
مطابق
سرکار عالی حیدر آباد دکن دار الافتاء مہر
کیا فرماتے ہیں علمائے دین اس مسئلہ میں کہ

FIGURE 5.1 Formal fatwa issued by the dar-ul-ifta of the princely state of Hyderabad on special stationery featuring the institute's seal in the center of the page. Record-keeping elements at the top include spaces for the file number (*nishān*) and date of the fatwa, according to the Hijri and Fasli calendars, which remain blank in this example. Andhra Pradesh / Telangana State Archives, Fatwa No. 22/5, 15 Dai 1359 F; photograph by the author.

Kifāyatullāh kept records of the requests he received at his primary workplace, the Madrasa Aminiya, assigning a number to each mustafti who approached him.[18] He received and responded to fatwas at about the same rate as the dar-ul-ifta in Hyderabad. Elsewhere in Hyderabad, the dar-ul-ifta of Jamiʿa Nizamiya kept registers of the fatwa requests it received, interleaving the register's pages with correspondence and other documents as needed.[19] In Tonk, the shariʿa ʿadalats, which produced legal rulings in the fatwa form, numbered its opinions and its clients.[20] The Anjuman-i Mustashar-ul-ʿUlama, a much smaller organization based in Lahore, received fewer fatwa requests overall but followed similar record-keeping procedures.[21] When it published a small volume of its opinions in 1907, it printed each question alongside the name, location, and occupation of the mustafti and noted the date of the question's receipt according to the Hijri and Gregorian calendars. Fatwa files or daily registers no longer exist for many institutes, but published evidence suggests that similar record-keeping practices prevailed across these institutions as muftis received requests, deciphered and distilled legal questions, researched and investigated the issue, and provided an answer.[22]

The Hyderabad dar-ul-ifta differs from these other institutes in its demi-official status—a status that marked its origins in Mughal India and made its twentieth-century governmental incarnation notable. From the first mark on the file's cover sheet to its closure, the processes and procedures of the Hyderabad dar-ul-ifta resembled those of the state's other government departments. The files' cover sheets were the same as those on any government file, except that these files belonged to the *daftar* (office) of the Sadarat-ul-ʿAliya and were classified as *iftāʾ*—that is, related to the answering of a question of law (figure 5.2). The office also used standard government forms for its internal memos. Figure 5.3 shows the printed, bilingual page that contained its print run, date, and number of copies in the upper left-hand corner and typically included the form name—"form number 2"—in the upper right-hand corner. A vertical line separated the memo's substance from its subsequent commentary, with the right column labeled "Office Note" (*kaifiyat*) and the left side labeled "ORDERS" (*ḥukm*), allowing lower-level employees to write their comments before their superiors responded (often with a simple "munāsib," or "agreed").[23] The dar-ul-ifta also had its own, specialized forms, including one for writing draft fatwas—which had the words "al-jawāb ḥāmidān wa muṣalliyān" printed at the top along with fill-in-the-blank spaces for the date, the file number (*nishān-i miṣl*), and the department (*ṣīgha*) (figure 5.4)—and another for

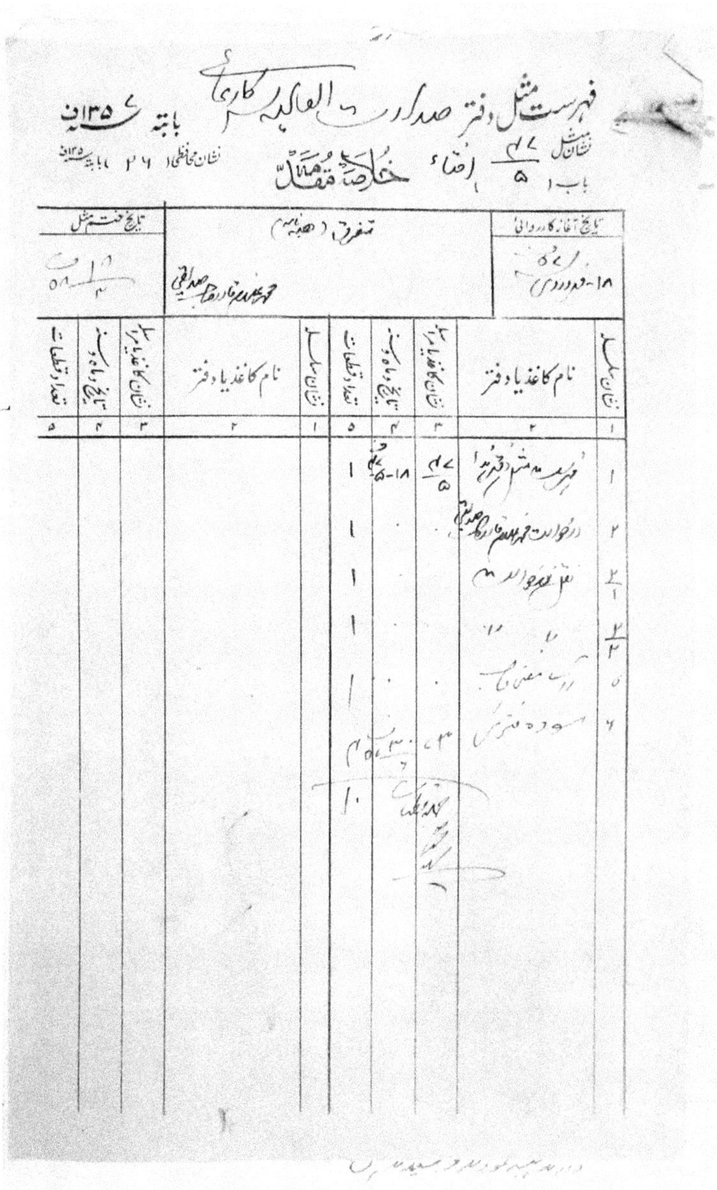

FIGURE 5.2 Cover sheet for a fatwa file from the dar-ul-ifta of the Sadarat-ul-ʿAliya in Hyderabad. Note the preprinted record-keeping elements in the header and the growing list of contents in the right-hand column. This file belongs to the *mutafarriq* (miscellaneous) category regarding a *hiba-nāma* (gift deed). Andhra Pradesh / Telangana State Archives, Fatwa No. 47/5, 18 Farwardin 1357 F; photograph by the author.

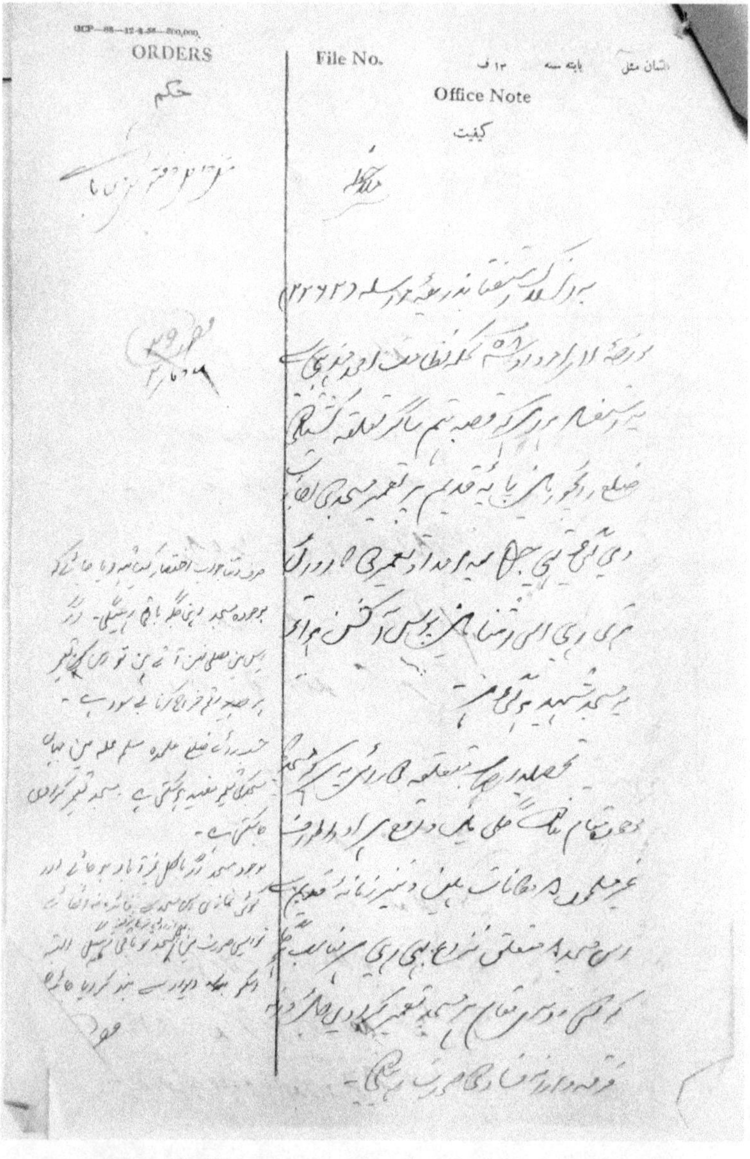

FIGURE 5.3 Internal office memo, produced as part of a fatwa file in Hyderabad. Note the division of the page between the preliminary comments and recommendations on the right (under "Office Note" [*kaifiyat*]) and the follow-up comments and recommendations in the column on the left, with accompanying dates and signatures, under the "ORDERS" (*ḥukm*) column. Andhra Pradesh / Telangana State Archives, Fatwa No. 127/5, 19 Murdad 1358 F; photograph by the author.

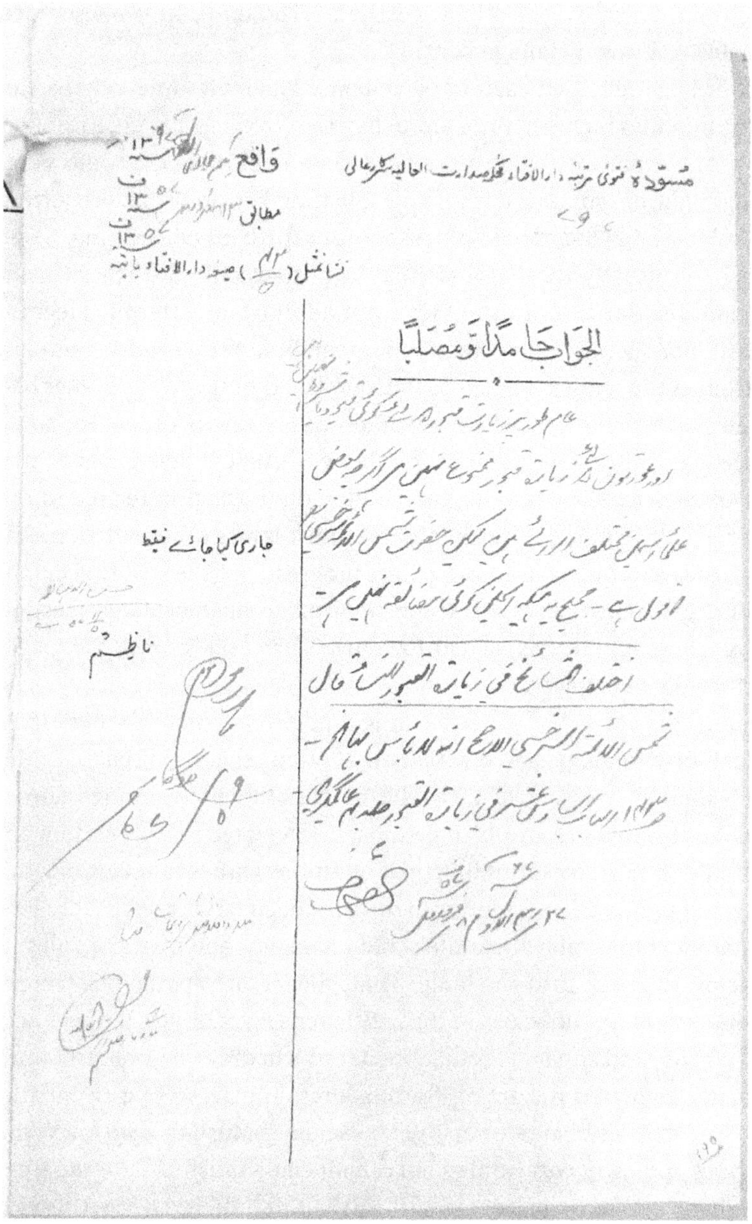

FIGURE 5.4 Draft fatwa (*musauwada fatwa*) written before preparing the final, formal fatwa to send or deliver to the fatwa seeker. Note the printed heading at the top of the page and the record-keeping elements in the upper left-hand corner. Andhra Pradesh / Telangana State Archives, Fatwa No. 43/5, 7 Farwardin 1357 F; photograph by the author.

writing the final fatwa, mentioned earlier.[24] The office also maintained files related to its own management.

A cover page recorded each file's contents. Thick files had long lists of contents; thin files included little more than the coversheet itself. Most files began with the mustafti's question. Employees read these questions carefully, highlighting, summarizing, and evaluating key points before jotting down their recommendations for a response or further investigation. Some questions—especially those transmitted by post—required further clarification, and the dar-ul-ifta would transmit a follow-up letter or telegram to request more detail. Others required research. Assistants added notes to the bottom of the question paper to indicate whether the fatwa seeker had provided postage or whether they would need a money order. For some cases, the dar-ul-ifta sent inquiries to other government departments, like the *dār-ul-qaẓā* (qazi's office), to get additional information related to the case—especially when questions ran up against issues of jurisdiction. Additional research could slow down a file's progress, but the steady accumulation of papers nonetheless marked its progress from amorphous question to concrete answer. The second date (on the left-hand side of the cover page) marked the file's completion.

Beneath this veneer of paper-pushing and bureaucracy lay a world of legal flexibility, analogy, and creativity that often remains obscured in the quest for final answers. In fact, the dar-ul-ifta's tidy file-keeping belies a world of legal ambiguity, in which petitioners attempted to coax certain answers from the mufti by sprinkling their questions with legalese or fudging key pieces of information.[25] Muftis, in turn, prodded fatwa seekers for more details, worked to establish parallels and analogies, and bent the rules to find a helpful answer, to aid an indigent supplicant, or to pinpoint a technicality that would tip the scales in the petitioner's favor. It was in these acts of legal sorting and sussing out that the dar-ul-ifta drew on its status as an office and invigorated the art of ifta to address the needs of a twentieth-century clientele—a clientele comprising ordinary Muslims who knew the dar-ul-ifta's authority was waning but remained dissatisfied with the legal system that stood in its place. Here, the dar-ul-ifta offered a legal service that not only answered questions in line with Islamic jurisprudence (the focus of this chapter) but also offered advice on how to pursue further legal action in other fora (see chapters 7 and 8). Together these activities represented a skillful solution to the problems created by legal change in British India and the princely states.

Representing Self and Society to the Dar-ul-Ifta

Individuals introduced themselves to the dar-ul-ifta in the questions they asked. They expressed their knowledge of the law in the stories they narrated, the details they provided, and those they neglected to provide. They demonstrated their legal knowledge by strategically deploying legal terms in their writings and hinted at the way they thought the law should work by guiding the mufti toward one interpretation or another. They responded to interpretations as they challenged the legitimacy of decisions produced by the courts, their adversaries, and their loved ones. They wrote about themselves, their families, and their friends, calling on the mufti's sympathy in some cases and artfully dodging personal responsibility in others. Whether visiting the dar-ul-ifta in person or corresponding from afar, they yearned for the right interpretation, begged for assistance, and hoped for simple solutions. They looked to venerable institutions like the Sadarat-ul-ʿAliya for guidance as they navigated the uncertainty of changing legal landscapes, and called on the mufti and his assistants to decode problems and determine the next steps. They asked friends, neighbors, amateurs, and experts to craft their complaints and let the dar-ul-ifta fill in the remaining gaps. The fatwa requests they submitted thus did more than spell out simple legal questions; they also situated law in society. How they wrote about, referred to, challenged, and questioned "the law" shaped the dar-ul-ifta's activities and rendered its opinions legally relevant.[26]

Manuals for epistolary etiquette formally differentiated between fatwa questions (*istiftāʾs*), petitions (*ʿarẓīs*), and letters (*k̲h̲aṭṭs*), but submissions to the dar-ul-ifta blended these genres. At the top of the page, mustaftis commonly addressed the office by name (adding the appropriate honorifics) and opened their requests with supplicating expressions: "ba-ʿārẓ mī rasānad" (the petitioner submits).[27] Many employed the third-person voice of a truly humble petitioner: "The cherisher of the poor, with hands clasped in expectation, requests that you clarify for your humble servant the *sharʿī* orders [*aḥkām-i sharʿī*] related to the incidents [*waqiʿāt*] and statements [*fiqrāt*] below [in the form of] a fatwa."[28] Another began, "Forgive this worthless [*nā-qābil*] individual's impoliteness [*bī-adabī*] for bringing this strange and astonishing [*ʿajīb-nāk wa ḥairat angēz*] occurrence before you, in search of a solution [*ḥal*]."[29] A few used cover letters to introduce the question and asked for answers "by way of kindness" (*ba-rāh-i karam*).[30] Others simply opened with a straightforward, "The request is that . . ."

(*guzārish hai ke*).[31] Letter-writing mechanics also appeared at the end of their missives. They concluded with requests to have the response sent "to the address below" and used house numbers, neighborhoods, and other landmarks to direct the dar-ul-ifta's return correspondence. They signed their names with English, Perso-Arabic, Devanagari, and Telugu scripts or plopped smudgy finger- or thumb-tip impressions on the bottom of the page. Fatwa seekers drew on a range of epistolary conventions that placed their requests within the broader context of petitioning and supplication, and in exchange for laying bare their embarrassing, shameful, personal, or private experiences, they expected to receive an accurate, acceptable, and shariʿa-compliant answer that would also "solve" the problem for them.[32]

Ordinary Muslims brought a range of questions to the dar-ul-ifta. Many of these questions concerned family disputes, sometimes surrounding marriage and divorce, other times relating to separation and child custody, and almost always involving property—its possession, division, or distribution.[33] When describing their problems, petitioners spoke from personal experience (even if they used the third person) and almost always deployed some form of legal language.[34] They referred to their documents as legal statements (*iqrār, iqrār-nāma*) and contracts (*ʿaqd*). They asked whether practices were permissible (*jāʾiz*) or necessary (*wājib*). They sought permission (*ijāzat*) to interpret the law in particular ways and wondered whether behavior—theirs or others'—was correct (*ṣaḥīḥ*), appropriate (*munāsib*), legal (*ḥalāl*), or lawful (*mubāḥ*). As they described their experiences, they shared intimate details about their personal and marital lives, naming individuals when necessary, or veiling personal involvement with generic names—Zayd, Bakr, ʿAmru, and Hinda.[35] For some questions, kinship terms replaced personal names, making individuals legible to the dar-ul-ifta as husbands and wives, parents, or in-laws (e.g., *bīwī, shauhar, k̲h̲āwand, wālidain, susrāl*). In others, fatwa seekers opted for occupational terms or professional titles that classified individuals—and their legal obligations—by title (e.g., *malāzamat, imāmat*). References to social rank (e.g., *aik buzurg, aik imām*) also worked in this way, particularly when disputes arose over competing interpretations or intergenerational differences. When all else failed, petitioners resorted to vague descriptions like "a person" (*aik shak̲h̲ṣ*), but the ordinary language they employed to describe a circumstance (*ṣūrat*), occurrence (*wāqiʿa, wāqiʿāt*), situation (*bāt*), or problem (*masʾala*) masked the legal knowledge they brought to the table.

Fatwa seekers employed multiple strategies to translate life's messy complications into legal concepts and categories relevant to the dar-ul-ifta. They called on the roles and responsibilities of husbands, wives, parents, and other family members to assert their rights and to frame another's wrongdoings. They summarized established patterns and noted sudden changes to prove or challenge an act's finality. They included copies of legal documents for the dar-ul-ifta's inspection. Petitioners described their interactions with other offices and organizations, including the courts, the police, the jails, local qazis, the *waqf* (endowment) board, banks, credit cooperative societies, and insurance companies. In these cases, they invoked the religious authority and bureaucratic acumen of the dar-ul-ifta to help them navigate the procedures, regulations, and limitations of government offices. Outside Hyderabad, fatwa seekers also called on muftis in this way, but within Hyderabad, employees at the dar-ul-ifta had access to internal channels of communication to investigate petitioners' claims, and in some cases they could also intercede directly on the petitioner's behalf.[36] When deciphering this mishmash of fatwa requests, the dar-ul-ifta identified relevant details, highlighted applicable principles of jurisprudence, and either offered an answer or advised supplicants on the relevant next steps. Occupying the interstitial spaces between law, society, and the state, the dar-ul-ifta translated everyday encounters into legal questions, calling on its bureaucratic practices and government status to serve as a legal clearinghouse, receiving, sorting, solving, and making recommendations for each question.

Most of the time, the answer was the easiest part. All muftis are trained to provide answers using their knowledge of the Qur'an and Sunna and applying this knowledge to novel situations by constructing legal analogies and identifying generalizable principles. But running an effective dar-ul-ifta also required another set of skills. Turning messy personal narratives into abstract legal questions and applying relevant legal principles was one part of the process; managing the paperwork of the bureaucratic office was the other. Employees at the dar-ul-ifta not only had to provide appropriate answers for each question, but they also had to investigate details connected with each case, follow office procedures and protocols, and stay on top of their paperwork.[37] Such paperwork included drafting orders; making recommendations; sending postcards, letters, and telegraphs; and keeping accurate and up-to-date records on the status of each file as it passed through the dar-ul-ifta. These were the procedures that set the bureaucratic dar-ul-ifta apart from its premodern predecessors and also the ones that have kept it alive into the present.

Describing Circumstances

Despite the variety of requests it received, the dar-ul-ifta's procedures were uniform. After "Hinda" passed away, her relatives wondered about the 1,100 rupees her husband owed her as *mahr* (dower).[38] Hinda had (allegedly) forgiven her husband's debt before she passed away, but there were no witnesses. Before her passing, Hinda's husband, "Zayd," informed "some relatives" (*baʿẓ qarābat-dār*) that the debt was forgiven and even swore to that fact while holding the Qurʾan on his head. Looking for the dar-ul-ifta's guidance, Sayyid Ḥaidar Riẓwī, whose connection to "Zayd" and "Hinda" remains unclear, wondered whether Zayd's oath was reliable according to shariʿa (*sharīʿa main̠ muʿtabar*).[39] The dar-ul-ifta opened its file on the fifth of Bahman (the third month of the Nizam's Persian Faṣlī calendar).[40] Adding Rizwi's letter to the file, an office assistant underlined passages relating to Hinda's forgiveness and to concerns about the legitimacy of Zayd's oath. The following day, he drafted an answer explaining which types of oaths were acceptable and which were not.[41] His supervisor made a slight change to the text—amending the phrase "Qurʾanic oath" to read, "an oath, [that] also included swearing on the Qurʾan"—and then passed it up the bureaucratic ladder. The following week, on the twelfth of Bahman, the registrar (*nāẓim*) produced an official fatwa and added his signature under the printed phrase "so issued." Rizwi's request was almost complete when the office ran into a snag. Mail receipt coupons indicate that the dar-ul-ifta contacted Rizwi to request a money order to cover postage expenses. He replied the following week (on the nineteenth of Bahman) with another letter and the requested money order. A note in the file confirms the money order's receipt and calculates the amount due back to him, after deducting the expenses for registering and transmitting the fatwa via certified mail. Three employees confirmed the recommendation to return the amount with a new money order and affixed their signatures to the recommendation. An insured mail receipt, the final item in the file, confirms the fatwa's transmission.[42]

What began as a simple question about the legality of an oath tied to marital debts and inheritance prompted a series of internal and external communications that accompanied Rizwi's request from beginning to end. Receipts and "coupons" added to the file make it clear that bureaucratic practice, as much as Islamic legal interpretation, shaped the dar-ul-ifta's response. Yet in Rizwi's case it is not clear whether the detailed correspondence was worth the effort. His revised question restated the situation in plain language and focused not on the placement of the Qurʾan during Zayd's oath but on the in-laws' presence during his oath-taking. In other words, Rizwi seemed to be asking whether Hinda's parents could legitimately confirm the debt's forgiveness. Unfortunately, the dar-ul-ifta did little to change its answer after receiving the updated request. The draft fatwa focuses on the Qurʾan's placement and does not go into the in-laws' presence. Bureaucratic procedures could thus serve fatwa seekers who were excluded from other legal venues, but they could also interfere with petitioners' access to a more meaningful, straightforward response.

Beyond requests for payment, exchanges between the dar-ul-ifta and its patrons fulfilled substantive functions as well. G̱ẖulām Aḥmad Ḵẖān's inquiry about the division of heritable property was one of these cases. His request began with a cover letter addressing the "honorable employees" of the dar-ul-ifta and introducing its employees to Muḥammad Ḵẖwāja ʿAlī's descendants. In the family tree he provided, he listed sons (Muḥammad Bahādur ʿAlī and Muḥammad Jaʿfar ʿAlī) and daughters (Afẕal Bī, Amīna Bī, Raḥamū Bī, Maḥmūda Bī, Rābiʿa Bī, and Zainab Bī), and then added that Amina Bi was also deceased.[43] Upon receipt, the office assistant began to parse the question, using the family tree and narrative description for guidance. Noting an anomaly, he underlined Amina Bi's name and highlighted the sentence referring to her death.[44] On the backside of the letter, the clerk made a note to request more information about the date of Amina Bi's passing. Had the petitioner come to the dar-ul-ifta in person, the assistant would simply ask for clarification, but since he could not ask in person, he sent a follow-up inquiry using the same postal and telegraph networks the petitioner originally used to submit his query.

Ghulam Ahmad Khan lived outside Hyderabad in the town of Karimnagar, and the dar-ul-ifta's mail reached him a few days later. He promptly replied by postcard, including the file number for his case and the date of the dar-ul-ifta's message to him, alongside the additional information it had requested: Amina Bi passed away maybe seven or eight years *after* her parents, he noted on the blank backside of the preprinted card. A few weeks later, having considered the matter further, he sent a second postcard now saying that Amina Bi died ten years after her father.[45] The fact that she had died after her father meant that Amina Bi's children would be eligible to inherit from his estate. Satisfied with this clarification, the dar-ul-ifta now had the information it needed to divide the estate and respond to Ghulam Ahmad Khan's fatwa request. Here again, Ghulam Ahmad Khan knew that an answer to his question required information about Khwaja ʿAli's family members and whether they were living or dead, yet in his first communication, he forgot to include the key detail of when Amina Bi had passed away, which prompted the dar-ul-ifta to contact him for additional information. Relying on postal and telegraph networks, the dar-ul-ifta communicated with its fatwa seeker to answer the remaining question. Such exchanges allowed the dar-ul-ifta to account for petitioners' limited legal knowledge and to fill in details that were missing from their original submissions. Thus, expanding telegraph and postal networks not only allowed fatwa seekers to submit their inquiries quickly and efficiently but also facilitated the dar-ul-ifta's work, as employees navigated the particularities of individual cases in relation to relevant juristic principles.

When Ṣālim bin Nāṣir wrote to the dar-ul-ifta, he began by asking forgiveness for sharing a salacious story about "some of his relatives" that brought him shame (*k̲h̲ẉud is bāt par sharm hōtī*).[46] His subsequent narration then introduced a couple who had been married for fifteen years. They had lived happily together with their son, and at some point they had invited a relative to live with them and added a partition in their home to accommodate him. Salim bin Nasir was not sure of this relative's exact relationship to the couple, but he noted that the wife called him *dēwar* (husband's younger brother).[47] The houseguest had a good relationship with the couple, but in the husband's absence, he grew especially close to the wife. Their closeness continued until news of the relationship surfaced and "disturbed" the neighborhood. The husband "[went] into a rage." He threatened to beat his wife to death (*qātilāna ḥamla*), but when the neighbors held him back, he threw her out of the house instead. The dewar and exiled wife lived together in an "unknown location" (*nā maʿlūm maqām*), and she gave birth to a son who lived for a few days and then died. The wife never married her dewar, nor did her husband grant her a divorce, but after her dewar passed away, she had nowhere to go and returned to her husband, apologetic and repentant. Out of weakness, he forgave her. Salim bin Nasir's question for the dar-ul-ifta was whether the two could lawfully live together again as husband and wife.[48]

In recounting this lengthy and shame-filled narrative, Salim bin Nasir shields his own role. He may have been the husband, afraid to declare himself a cuckold. He may have been the couple's son, willing his parents to reconcile, or he may have been an onlooker, entrusted to remedy the couple's marital woes. Regardless, his reason for approaching the dar-ul-ifta was clear: after describing these surprising and astonishing (*ʿajīb-nāk wa ḥairat angēz*) circumstances, he wondered whether reconciliation was possible.

Unfortunately, however, Salim bin Nasir never received his answer; the dar-ul-ifta requested additional postage from him and the request went unfulfilled. The completed, typed fatwa remains attached to the file in the archive.[49]

Like other fatwa seekers, Salim bin Nasir uses a confessional tone that implies remorse, confusion, and moral uncertainty about the implications of the events he describes. Beyond the narrative's reversal of typical gender roles (i.e., describing the wife's, rather than the husband's, infidelity), it is interesting to note the apologetic tone he evokes and the detached, almost disinterested, frankness the dar-ul-ifta employs in the response. There is no scolding, shaming, or criticizing. Instead, the employees prepared a frank, straightforward answer to what they identified as the core question: whether the couple needed to contract another marriage to make their reconstituted relationship legal. In response to this and other confessional tales, the dar-ul-ifta's employees sifted through accounts of infidelity, anger, disappointment, and moral confusion to provide answers that addressed the petitioner's concerns in light of the shariʿa and in response to the social context.

Not all questions were as effusive as Salim bin Nasir's, but all fatwa seekers strove to provide sufficient information to establish and explain their legal issues. Before responding, employees parsed lengthy narrations to identify the central question and any relevant details. Muftis could only produce accurate answers if the inputs they received were accurate and sufficient. For marital disputes, these details might include descriptions of abuse, abandonment, or infidelity. When questions arose over inheritance, petitioners called on fragmentary memories of marital histories, death dates, and the ties of distant, adopted, or otherwise unconventional family members. If a question involved property, fatwa seekers listed the property's boundaries, its ownership history, and its status as privately owned or as part of an endowment. They affixed diagrams, maps, and, in a few rare instances, black-and-white photographs to support their statements. Copies of legal documents (sometimes redacted to remove confidential details) also accompanied these verbal descriptions, as did hand-drawn diagrams, which added another layer of legal knowledge to their requests. These statements not only reflected fatwa seekers' (educated yet nonetheless nonexpert) understandings of the law but also reflected their hopes that the dar-ul-ifta would resolve the problems they presented.

At times, the dar-ul-ifta's answers confirmed supplicants' understandings of the law, but many responses refracted their amateur knowledge and captured law's complicated intersections with society instead. When Muḥammad Sardār Ḵẖān sought the dar-ul-ifta's advice about how to divide his paternal uncle's property, he narrated the family's history around the edges and in between the two family trees he drew. His uncle, Maḥmūd Ḵẖān, was childless when he passed away in 1946. He left behind his wife, Āmina Bī, an adopted son named ʿAbd-ul-Jabbār, and two full brothers (*ḥaqīqī bhāʾī*), both of whom had multiple offspring. The first brother, Ibrahīm Ṣāḥib, passed away during the uncle's lifetime, leaving behind two sons, the fatwa seeker, Sardar Khan, and his brother, Ismaʿīl Ḵẖān. The second brother, Ādam Ḵẖān, was alive at the time of his brother's passing but had since passed away, leaving behind four sons and one daughter. The estate included movable property (jewels, cash, etc.) and immovable property (a house), and Sardar Khan wondered how it should be divided. Following Adam Khan's recent passing, it was time for the family to sort through the remaining inheritance.[50]

Despite his diligent efforts to sketch the extended family structure across two family trees, Sardar Khan neglected to mention a widowed aunt, who was also entitled to a share of the estate. After his first set of statements, he added a second page, mentioning this aunt, and then retroactively wrote her name at the edge of his original diagram. Unlike the petitioner, the dar-ul-ifta did not forget Fāṭima ʿAlī, the neglected aunt. Rather, it started the fatwa response by mentioning her first. After that, the dar-ul-ifta had no problem dividing the heritable property; it was fully competent to divide complicated estates. Yet here again, the dar-ul-ifta depended on accurate inputs. Had Sardar Khan excluded other relatives—distant or otherwise—employees at the dar-ul-ifta would not know to include them in its calculations. The proper functioning of the dar-ul-ifta—and the production of legal answers—depended not only on the institute's authority but also on the probity and honesty of the fatwa seeker's requests. Getting a clear picture sometimes required amending earlier statements.

Fatwa seekers included personal details and intimate knowledge in their requests for advice, yet they did not always know how to present that information. Some questions, like Salim bin Nasir's, adopted a confessional tone, laying bare the juicy details of a wife's infidelity and her husband's willingness to forgive her. Other fatwa seekers, like Sardar Khan, included diagrams and detailed descriptions yet missed important pieces of information—like a widowed aunt. Occasionally, fatwa seekers sent second requests with supplementary details, hoping to provide clarity or to place an event in its context. The dar-ul-ifta read these questions, underlined important points, asked for clarification, and drafted responses. It offered moral guidance but sidestepped moralizing critiques, opting for straightforward explanations instead. Following these exchanges helps to highlight law not as fact but as process, not as rote rules but as guidelines drawn from unique situations or mitigating circumstances. Legal innovation was not unheard of in the dar-ul-ifta, but it was also not necessary in most cases. Instead, the dar-ul-ifta focused on its core tasks of deciphering, distilling, and clarifying the questions it received. Turning messy personal narratives into digestible legal questions was the heart of the dar-ul-ifta's work, and it pursued this work in response not only to intimate narrations but also to written legal documents—another genre of lay legal writing that found its way into the dar-ul-ifta's records.

Displaying Legal Documents

Copies of legal documents provide another framework for exploring everyday Islamic law in the dar-ul-ifta. On the one hand, documents that accompanied fatwa requests demonstrate how ordinary Muslims thought about and articulated aspects of law using attestations, declarations, deeds, and other documents as they secured themselves and their legal interests in writing. On the other hand, the dar-ul-ifta's engagement with documents shows how different fora engaged separately with substance and procedure. British India's modern courts—and their princely state cognates—were obsessed with questions of authenticity (i.e., whether a document was "true," "original," and "properly" executed).[51] Muftis, by contrast, tended to evaluate the document's substance and to answer questions about whether the document's contents performed the legal actions executors or signatories envisioned.[52] In most cases, they accepted the document as a legitimate, "authentic" expression of the executor's legal wishes and desires and looked to confirm that the text was accurate, its terms legally permissible, and its intention in accordance with jurisprudential norms. Doing so, Islamic legal institutes stood apart from the law courts; they evaluated, interpreted, and advised, rather than merely accepting "authentic" documents and rejecting "forgeries."

Fatwa seekers shared their legal knowledge in the documents they presented. They included specific details, legal terms, conditional statements, promises, and pledges. They also omitted important points, overlooked key issues, and wondered how the manner and mode of execution affected a document's legal status. Did sending a divorce decree by registered mail make it legally binding? mustaftis like Muḥyī-ud-Dīn Ṣāḥib wondered.[53] In British India, with the regulations for registering, validating, and stamping legal documents changing constantly, questions about the validity of written divorce decrees became so numerous that fatwa collections started to group them under separate headings.[54] Similarly, when fatwa seekers brought these questions to the dar-ul-ifta in princely Hyderabad, they affixed the original document (or a replica of it) to the istifta and offered details about its execution or transmission. Such details allowed petitioners to draw on the dar-ul-ifta's consultative function, to look beyond the contents of their question into the finer points of the documents themselves, and to take seriously the possibilities of juristic deliberation.

For Muhyi-ud-Din, the dar-ul-ifta's consultative function was key, and enclosing a copy of the divorce decree expanded the institute's ability to issue its answer. The redacted document opened with the husband's declaration, "I . . . by way of this notice . . . grant irrevocable divorce and separation." Drawing on the language of contracts (*aḥkām*, *sharʿ*, *k̲h̲ilāf*, etc.), he then explained that the wife's disobedience was the root cause of the separation and stipulated his terms for the divorce: she must return the jewels and clothing he gave her, and their small child must be returned to his care.[55] The decree concluded by advising the wife to retain this "nōṭis" (transliterated from the English) as proof of their separation and mentioning that he also gave a copy to the "protector of the *shariʾa*" (most likely the local qazi) for safekeeping.[56] In its phrasing, structure, and substance, the document displays the husband's familiarity with legal conventions and hints at the broader legal world in which such writings operated.

In his declaration, the husband recognized the legal content of certain terms (*sharīʿa*, *ʿaqd* [contract], *ṭalāq* [divorce], etc.) and used them throughout, so that there could be no doubt about the seriousness or intent of his deed. Muhyi-ud-Din, the fatwa seeker, also recognized the document's legal implications and its potential to grant the husband's divorce without any input from the wife. Yet for him, the question lay not with the document's contents but with its mode of transmission. His primary reason for seeking a fatwa seems to revolve around the husband's reliance on registered mail for its transmission. With a copy of the text in hand, the dar-ul-ifta offered another interpretation: paying little attention to the question of registered mail, the dar-ul-ifta accepted the legal validity of the document, while rejecting the husband's terms. Responding to Muhyi-ud-Din's istifta, the dar-ul-ifta explained that the wife need not fulfill the husband's demands to return clothing, jewelry, or young children to his custody. In fact, the child should remain in her care, while the husband continued to provide support.[57] With access to the text of the document, the dar-ul-ifta was thus able to validate the husband's general intent to divorce his wife but to reject his terms. Even without any enforcement power, the dar-ul-ifta could be a powerful intermediary, validating the legal desires expressed in informal legal documents while clarifying the limits of those rights as well.

In another example, an unnamed couple sent matching divorce decrees to the dar-ul-ifta for evaluation. As Jaʿfar ʿAlī explained in his cover letter, the husband and wife executed their decrees after a recent dispute, and he included redacted copies of the documents, using generic names (Zayd and Hinda) and obscuring other details with ellipses and the Perso-Arabic expression "fulān" (so-and-so). "Zayd's" *ṭalāq-nāma* (divorce decree) clearly stated his desire to divorce "Hinda," and Hinda's parallel *k͟hulʿ-nāma* (divorce decree for female-initiated divorce) confirmed the couple's intent, acknowledging Zayd's statement and further releasing him from any marital obligations. For all intents and purposes, it looked like the couple's marriage had ended by mutual consent, except for the fact that "all of a sudden," Jaʿfar ʿAli explained in his istifta, the couple had decided to reconcile. "What are the shariʿa commands [*aḥkām*] for this situation?" Jaʿfar ʿAli wondered.[58]

Whereas the courts of law typically assessed a document for authenticity (Was it knowingly and properly executed? Was it an original, a true copy, or a forgery?) and procedural accuracy (Was it issued on stamp paper of the correct value? Was it properly registered with the government registrar?), the dar-ul-ifta tended to evaluate it according to the authors' intent and the legitimacy of its terms.[59] Employees scrutinized the document's contents, attending to whether its demands were just and legally valid. They also considered its context, knowing that references to anger were enough to have the mufti reconsider the finality of a divorce.[60] In this case, however, anger was not an issue, as the couple was clearly level-headed enough to execute sober legal documents. Instead, the office assistant looked for other clues that would provide the couple with a legitimate means to reconcile. First, he noted that Zayd's talaq-nama only stated his intent to divorce once, not the three times that would make a divorce decree final and irrevocable. Second, he observed that the documents were executed recently, on the eighth day of Bahman, a mere twenty-one days before Jaʿfar ʿAli brought his question to the dar-ul-ifta. Accordingly, the waiting period (*ʿiddat*) had not yet ended, and the couple was free to reconcile.[61] Calling on his extensive legal knowledge and ability to interpret the couple's statements directly, the office assistant validated their wish to resume marital relations in spite of the legal documents they had signed. Before approaching the dar-ul-ifta, the participants knew that these documents carried legal content and that signing them could result in legal consequences, yet they did not know precisely how or when those legal consequences went into effect and needed the dar-ul-ifta to clarify. Writing to the dar-ul-ifta provided them with an opportunity to receive the expert input they needed to fix the potential problem their amateur documents created.

Along these same lines, Shujāʿ-ud-Dīn sent a pair of questions concerning the validity of a divorce. In the first, he described a husband issuing in writing "three talaqs at once" (*ba-waqt-i wāḥid tīn ṯalāq*), in essence executing an irrevocable divorce (*ṯalāq-i bāʾin*). During the waiting period, the husband wanted to reconcile and wondered whether it was possible or whether the couple would need to renew (*tajdīd*) their marital union. Under normal circumstances, divorce takes place across several months, during which the husband must utter the words "I divorce you" three times before the divorce is finalized.[62] Reconciliation is both possible and encouraged during this period, and muftis in Hyderabad routinely found ways to facilitate reconciliation, as the previous case demonstrates. In this case, however, the employee interrogated the divorce decree, underlining three lines of the six-line text referring to the *ṯalāq-i bāʾin* and to the question of reconciliation. He then scribbled a note to ask for a copy of the decree itself. The fatwa seeker, Shujaʿ-ud-Din, promptly supplied a copy of the divorce decree, allowing the office assistant to see—and to underline yet again—the words "ṯalāq-i bāʾin (yaʿnī tīn ṯalāq)" (irrevocable divorce—that is, three divorces). With documentary evidence in hand, the assistant could now prepare a response, confirming the couple's divorce.[63]

In most cases, supplicants knew something about the law, but they were not experts. Sometimes they missed key details or overlooked possibilities, but they revealed their lack of expertise in other ways too. In 1946 Sayyid Aʿẕam ʿAlī, who resided in house number 1429 in ʿAmbarpēṭ, Gōlnāka (then a suburb of Hyderabad), wrote with a question about "a person's" wife who had disappeared with some cash and jewelry. When she did not return after roughly six months, he wondered whether their marriage was over. Writing in a passable Urdu script, Aʿzam ʿAli used terms like *mankūḥa bīwī* (lawfully wedded wife) and *faskẖ* (marital dissolution) yet betrayed his unfamiliarity with legal terminology by writing the word "fatwa" (not once but twice) using *baṛē ḥē* instead of *alif maqṣūra* and writing *faskẖ* with *qāf* instead of *kẖē*.[64] Likely more familiar with English orthography than with Urdu, Aʿzam ʿAli (who signed his name in English at the end) followed the words' pronunciation, rather than their Arabic etymology. Nonetheless, the dar-ul-ifta could parse his meaning and provide details about the additional steps required to dissolve this marriage.[65] Spelling errors may seem small in relation to a wife's disappearance, but they reflect a particular approach to legal problem-solving. Ordinary individuals like Aʿzam ʿAli had some basic knowledge of the law and knew they could ask the dar-ul-ifta for advice, but the dar-ul-ifta often had to fill in gaps in the fatwa seeker's knowledge.

By the middle of the twentieth century, fatwas were fodder for the masses. Not only did they travel across the subcontinent, between British India and the princely states, but they were also published in newspapers and other venues.[66] As a result, requests came from a range of individuals, from those knowledgeable enough to dispute prominent muftis' opinions, to those barely able to spell the word "fatwa" itself. Inexpert legal writings and poorly executed legal documents reflected the reach of everyday Islamic law's net, which included Muslims deeply invested in religious knowledge and those only marginally concerned with the legal implications of an informal decree. In this way, fatwas became not a separate sphere of legal discourse but an integral part of everyday legal life. The dar-ul-ifta in princely Hyderabad was but one institute engaged in these practices, but its archival remains demonstrate how these negotiations played out.

Facilitating Inquiries and Investigations: A Hyderabadi Exception?

In addition to evaluating legal documents, employees at the dar-ul-ifta also took steps to intervene when possible. Such interventions, however, often arrived at the end of a long legal battle, after petitioners had pursued every other option. Even in princely Hyderabad, fatwas were unenforceable, meaning the law courts remained the first port of call for many complainants. Yet the courts also tended to privilege money, status, and power, so those who were disadvantaged by or excluded from the masculine habits of adversarial law tended to seek refuge in the dar-ul-ifta, where they could air their complaints directly, in plain language, without relying on a hired representative.[67] Women took advantage of those aspects, but they were not the only supplicants to benefit from the dar-ul-ifta's accessibility. Others gained from the ability to ask questions differently, explore disputes from other perspectives, and employ the full arsenal of juristic maneuvers to locate equitable solutions.

G̱hulām Muḥammad Ḵẖān was one of these individuals. In 1946 CE (1356 Fasli) he executed a *waqf-nāma* (endowment deed) to ensure the safety and sanctity of his property after death and promptly registered the deed with the Waqf Board of the Religious Affairs Department in accordance with the board's rules.[68] While these rules may have served the government well, the Religious Affairs Department's zealous quest for oversight created problems for unsuspecting registrants like Ghulam Muhammad Khan.[69] A year after he executed his deed, the Waqf Board swooped in to seize his property. Unfortunately for Ghulam Muhammad Khan, this intervention not only went against his intentions but also put his life and livelihood at risk. As he explained to the dar-ul-ifta, if the Waqf Board took over his property, he would be left with nothing.[70] The board remained intractable, so Ghulam Muhammad Khan turned to the dar-ul-ifta for help.

The Waqf Board's legal claim to Ghulam Muhammad Khan's property rested in the idea that Islamic endowments are permanent and irrevocable, meaning jurists considered later emendations and alterations to be illegal.[71] To ensure that endowments fulfilled their primary (charitable) objectives and did not simply turn into tax havens, governments in British India and the Ottoman Empire implemented programs to manage waqf properties.[72] Hyderabad followed suit. Yet unlike the general opposition other measures sparked, Ghulam Muhammad Khan's disagreement did not lie with the Waqf Board in general; his disagreement lay specifically with its interpretation of his deed. Fortunately for him, the dar-ul-ifta had a few tricks up its sleeve. Examining the text of the deed, employees at the dar-ul-ifta noted that not just once but twice Ghulam Muhammad Khan referred to this endowment as a future desire, rather than a present act. Generically speaking, Islamic legal documents perform the actions they describe. They buy, sell, gift, grant, endow, marry, divorce, and bequeath.[73] A waqf written in the future tense cannot perform the act of endowing; it can only signal the executor's intent to entrust. By virtue of this simple distinction, Ghulam Muhammad Khan's original deed was invalid. Both the Waqf Board and the dar-ul-ifta belonged to the Religious Affairs Department and followed similar bureaucratic routines, using registers to record and organize their work and following rules rooted in Islamic jurisprudence but modified to meet the state's administrative needs. Yet when it came to interpreting shariʿa, the two offices had different degrees of authority. The Waqf Board was hidebound to follow the rules laid out in the Hyderabad Endowments Regulation; the dar-ul-ifta had more freedom. Not only could its employees visit the Waqf Board's records to verify Ghulam Muhammad Khan's information, but it could also push back against the rigidity of the board itself. Once the dar-ul-ifta questioned the validity of the original deed, it could unstick Ghulam Muhammad Khan from the sticky situation into which the Waqf Board's rules had put him.

Marital disputes were another area in which the dar-ul-ifta could intercede because, in addition to evaluating legal documents, it could also access and interrogate documentation from other government offices. In December 1948 the widow Ruqaiya Bī wrote to the dar-ul-ifta to find a solution for her daughter's unhappy marriage to a distant relative, which she characterized in terms of arguments, abuse, and material neglect.[74] Physical abuse and failure to provide support were grounds for divorce according to Islamic jurisprudence and under statutes adopted in British India (following the Dissolution of Muslim Marriages Act of 1939) and in princely Hyderabad, yet the mother and her daughter were still struggling to escape the union.[75] When they went to court, they faced obstacles and opposition from (male) relatives who had better resources and therefore needed the dar-ul-ifta's help. In response to Ruqaiya Bi's complaint, the dar-ul-ifta had a few options. It could advise the two on how to pursue further legal action or conduct its own investigation into the complaint. If witnesses corroborated their complaints about abuse and neglect, the dar-ul-ifta could then issue a judicial separation (*tafrīq*), but opposition in court suggested that this route might be difficult.

Noting that Ruqaiya Bi had not originally consented to her daughter's union ("duk͟htar kē ʿaqd unkī marẓī kē k͟hilāf hūʾa hai"), one employee recommended another possibility: "If given permission, I can then provide . . . a detailed opinion [about the status of the marriage] after examining the marriage register" (*agar ḥukm hō, tō main̲ siyāha kō dēkhnē kē baʿd mufaṣṣal rāʾi kar sakūnga*). Upon receiving permission, the employee called up the original marriage contract, Number 25734 in the register, and noted that the bride's grandfather had served as her guardian (*walī*) during the *nikāḥ* (marriage).[76] This detail was a bit unconventional, so the employee followed up with Ruqaiya Bi to find out whether the qazi had contacted her, whether she had been at the ceremony, and whether she had accepted the union. Ruqaiya Bi replied in the negative.[77] Owing to a technicality in Hanafi jurisprudence according to which an error in the marriage contract would render it invalid (*g͟hair ṣaḥīḥ*), the employee concluded that the couple's marriage was illegitimate. Relying on the grandfather's guardianship, instead of the mother's, meant that the qazi had not followed proper procedure.[78] Ruqaiya Bi's daughter could now escape her unhappy marriage, owing to the dar-ul-ifta's inquiry and its ability to consult—and interrogate—the original marriage register.

In both examples, the dar-ul-ifta's solution arose from its ability to access original documentation and to draw on the full range of interpretive possibilities. For Ghulam Muhammad Khan, the question was not whether the Waqf Board could take control of his property but instead whether the original deed was legally binding as executed. His use of future-tense verbs confirmed that it was not, in fact, legitimate and should therefore be deregistered and returned to him. For Ruqaiya Bi, a solution to her daughter's problem lay not in proving spousal neglect and abuse but in questioning the original marriage contract. Once the dar-ul-ifta was satisfied that the original contract was invalid, it could offer a solution to this otherwise intractable conflict. The dar-ul-ifta was thus able to redefine the questions it received along other axes to provide meaningful solutions. Not all the dar-ul-ifta's investigations were successful, but it benefited from being able to consult records from other departments, interpret evidence independently, and leverage its institutional status to push back against other departments' intransigence. Although these investigative abilities set Hyderabad's official dar-ul-ifta apart from the unofficial, nongovernmental institutes in British India, unofficial status did not mean these other institutes were impotent. They, too, worked to help petitioners find solutions within and despite the courts' judicial dominance. Although competition between state and nonstate legal institutions closed some paths for formal investigation, nonstate dar-ul-iftas nonetheless found ways to fill some of these gaps informally. That is, when formal paths of investigation were closed, informal routes opened for guidance, counseling, and advice.

Conclusion

While some visitors to the dar-ul-ifta expressed familiarity with the legal concepts in their cases, many struggled to pinpoint exactly which details mattered and how they should be organized into a legal question. To supplement their narratives, they quoted direct speech, oaths, and sworn statements; they provided diagrams, outlines, and detailed descriptions of family trees, properties, and legal experiences; they couched their legal questions in the language of humility and deference, supplicating themselves to the expertise and authority of the dar-ul-ifta and the answers it provided; and they referred to other legal encounters that preceded or might follow their consultation with the dar-ul-ifta. These statements, descriptions, and documents—expert and inexpert, formal and informal—entered the dar-ul-ifta and became a part of its paperwork. As files moved through the office, they followed the princely state's administrative protocols and drew from the employees' Islamic legal training. Assistants highlighted key passages, wrote questions at the bottom of the page, and corresponded with fatwa seekers to obtain answers. Once the assistant drafted a response, the chief mufti reviewed it, making necessary corrections, emendations, and additions in bright red ink before adding his signature to the page, putting a reference to it in the office register, and passing the file along so that the completed answer could be returned to the fatwa seeker.

Muftis working elsewhere in British India engaged in these processes as well, but their records are more fragmentary, captured in printed volumes and the occasional handwritten register. Printed compilations sometimes capture back-and-forth exchanges between fatwa writers and fatwa seekers and sometimes refer to histories of readership and reception as well. In rare instances, publications identify fatwa seekers by name or location, offering a few more clues to help historians put the process of seeking and receiving legal advice back into its social context, but the process of piecing together the embedded history of late colonial fatwa culture remains difficult and the results have been fragmentary at best. For these reasons, the paperwork from princely Hyderabad's dar-ul-ifta and the analysis of its processes and procedures for receiving and responding to fatwa seekers' questions show that there was more to the social history of late colonial fatwa literature than the answers muftis produced and the publications they authored. Fatwa seekers not only carried extensive knowledge of the law with them, but they also saw the dar-ul-ifta as a particular type of institution, capable of addressing, if not solving, the problems they presented.

Yet despite its utility, the authority of the dar-ul-ifta remained uncertain. Many fatwa seekers pledged to follow or to implement whatever answer the dar-ul-ifta produced, but that did not mean their kin or others implicated in the answer would also respect the dar-ul-ifta's decision. Fatwas responding to concerns over the distribution of heritable property bound multiple generations of family members into a single unit linked by biology and sociology, but fatwas could not always withstand challenges from uncooperative heirs or competing claimants. Husbands, wives, parents, children, and others brought marital disputes to the dar-ul-ifta, but a fatwa seeker could only narrate the situation from his or her perspective, leaving open the possibility that the truth behind the confessional narrative might not be exactly as the fatwa seeker made it seem. The dar-ul-ifta could investigate when the information did not add up, and it could ask for clarification when the pieces did not quite fall into place, but it was limited—as are all legal fora—in its ability to ascertain the truth from uncooperative or unwilling participants.[79] Fatwa seekers acknowledged these limitations by drawing their interlocutors' attention to intentional omissions, missing details, and one-sided accounts, and fatwa writers admitted the limitations of their answers by referring to the "situation in question" and framing their responses in terms of the information provided. Each side recognized the constraints under which the other operated.

These limitations notwithstanding, the practice of seeking and receiving fatwas was alive and well in late colonial South Asia. The 1,200 extant files consulted for this chapter all come from the final years of the dar-ul-ifta's operations between 1940 and 1950, with most of the individual files belonging to the second half of the decade (1946–50). Records for other offices and authors are similar. Mufti Kifayatullah began writing fatwas at the end of the nineteenth century, but fatwas in his nine-volume collection tend to come from the late 1920s into the 1940s. While the historical record may never provide definitive evidence about the rates for and numbers of fatwas produced in British India, the extant evidence overwhelmingly suggests that the practice gained and maintained popularity throughout this period, precisely as the rates of litigation and interest in the courts grew. In other words, legal reforms in princely Hyderabad likely contributed to, rather than detracted from, the popularity of the dar-ul-ifta, just as they did in British India. Legal codification and procedural formalism did not erase other modes of legal action but instead contributed to the making of a cacophonous playground of overlapping options and competing conventions.

The dar-ul-ifta of the Sadarat-ul-ʿAliya of the princely state of Hyderabad may have been an exception in terms of its institutional status, access to other government departments, and pride of place among the state's redesigned judicial structure, but in the context of making everyday Islamic law, its practices were comparable to those found elsewhere. Furthermore, the bureaucratic patterns and processes it embraced mirror those found within postcolonial dar-ul-iftas, which continue to receive, to respond to, and to offer advice in relation to questions that individuals regularly submit about their interpersonal, familial, religious, and ethical concerns. How these questions interacted with other ideas of law and governance in late colonial South Asia is the focus in part III.

6 Accounting for Qazis

Negotiating Life and Law in Small-Town North India

Because the first marriage is established, the second marriage is illegal.

—Inʿam Allah Khan, renouncing his marriage to Shah Jahan Begum, 1910

From Law to Action: Qazis in Meerut

Ten years after he took over from his predecessor, Qazi Muḥammad Bashīr-ud-Dīn had a pesky problem to address. His rival, Munshī ʿAbd-ul-Ḥalīm, had published an advertisement (*ishtihār*) to deceive the public (*pablik kō dhōkē maiṉ ḍālna*) and make it difficult for Bashir-ud-Din to perform and record marriages for the approximately fifty thousand Muslims who lived in the North Indian town of Meerut where he resided.[1] Like other qazis appointed under Act XII of 1880, Bashir-ud-Din worked at the intersection of government authority and the messiness of everyday life in rural India. As with his ancestors, who worked as qazi before him, Bashir-ud-Din's success depended on his recognition from the state and the satisfaction of the local Muslims he served. Unlike his predecessors', however, Bashir-ud-Din's work now revolved almost exclusively around performing and recording marriages, and even with his government appointment, his position was ambiguous. His was a constant struggle to meet the legal needs of his clients and to remain within the circumscribed bounds of the legal authority that the state granted him. Facing his conflict with ʿAbd-ul-Halim head-on was but one of his struggles.

While muftis built robust institutions and developed complex bureaucratic procedures for receiving and responding to fatwa requests (using newspapers, pamphlets, and other platforms to address the panoply of problems Muslims presented to them), qazis—now appointed under the Kazis' Act (Act XII of 1880) and its patchwork application across British India—also developed strategies to meet the current moment's needs.[2] And despite disruptions from interlopers like ʿAbd-ul-Halim, most qazis adapted with ease to their roles as marriage registrars, embracing the state's classification of marriage as "religious" while also noting its central role in everyday life and its ties to other areas of law like property.[3] Over several decades, marriage registration underwent a transformation from an ad hoc practice to one involving elaborate forms and detailed records. Following extant records from the family collections of qazis, it is possible to see not only how the practice of recording marriages changed over the course of British rule but also how qazi records remained similar across space and time. What is more, these records mirror the recommended and prescribed forms appended to marriage registration laws from across the British Empire.[4] In other words, qazis adapted to legislative interventions not by reducing the meaning of their records but by making their records more elaborate and more representative of modern bureaucratic record-keeping. The examples presented here come from two collections of records, but snippets of evidence from other collections suggest that they were not unique.[5] Looking at how they evolved parallel to but separate from the state's legal system not only shows everyday Islamic law in action but also reveals how state and nonstate legal fora intersected at different stages of the legal process.

Surveying the archive of marriage registers from one family of qazis in Meerut, this chapter delves into the experience of everyday Islamic law not at the level of administrative discourse or legislative intervention but at the level of a regular, routine marriage register entry. It looks at the registers local qazis produced, the form they took, the types of data they included, and the signs and symbols they incorporated to appear legitimate and authentic. It uses that evidence to consider why and how individuals called on the local qazi to perform a marriage or to make an entry in his register. Evidence from these registers not only complicates prevailing narratives about the failure of the Kazis' Act (a narrative that commenced immediately after the act's introduction) but also draws attention to the multiple, manifold, and intermingled legal worlds in which marriage registration operated. The British government of India limited qazis' authority when it reintroduced them to record marriages, but marriage provided them with plenty of room to shape local legal life.[6] There are, after all, few areas of law not affected by marriage and the relationships it fosters. In short, marriage registration was always about more than marriage.

If muftis tackled areas of Islamic legal life by transforming messy interpersonal affairs into abstract legal questions, then qazis performed similar work when they took complex socio-familial relations and captured them in an abbreviated form. Doing so, qazis navigated narrow terrain between the authority of the colonial state (with detailed procedures for registering and stamping documents), the limited sphere in which they were authorized to work, and the needs of the communities they served. Their path was treacherous and littered with landmines that challenged the accuracy of their records, left litigants hanging with incomplete records, or made the record keepers themselves subject to litigation or police investigation. Any one of these incidents could damage the qazi's character—and the status of his office—irreparably. At the same time, and as the following account relates in more detail, providing one legal service without being able to offer others put qazis like Bashir-ud-Din in the middle of an unresolved debate over the meaning of Muslim personal law and who had authority over it. With statutes like the Kazis' Act defining their work, qazis became pawns in the larger debate over law, society, and the colonial state.

Locating Qazis between the State and Society

For Bashir-ud-Din, there was little time to debate the nuances of the qazi's role. Work kept him busy from the start of his career as an assistant to his time as chief qazi.[7] Like many of the government's appointees, Bashir-ud-Din descended from a long line of qazis. His ancestors traced their lineage back to the family of the Prophet Muhammad through his father-in-law, Abu Bakr, and their employment on the subcontinent commenced during the reign of Muhammad Shah (r. 1719–48), when Sharīʿat Panāh (Shelter of Shariʿa) Qazi Ilāhī Bak̲h̲sh held the post of *qāẓī-ul-quẓāt* (chief qazi).[8] After working as assistant qazi for some time, Bashir-ud-Din became chief qazi for the town, district, and military camp at Meerut (*shahr wa kaimp wa pargana-yi mēruṭh*) in 1915. Putting him in the place of his predecessor, "Muḥammad ʿAbd-ul-Hādī, son of Muḥammad ʿAbd-ul-Bārī, both deceased," the tahsildar (district collector) confirmed Bashir-ud-Din's promotion by issuing a proclamation addressed to the elites (*ruʾasāʾ*), landlords (*zamīndārs*), traders (*tājirān*), cultivators (*kāshtkārān*), and "other inhabitants and Muslims of . . . Meerut" (*dīgar bāshandagān-i ahl-i Islām*) under the authority of the lieutenant governor of the United Provinces of Agra and Awadh.[9]

Although it was not called a sanad, the document performed the same function as one. Issued according to government letter No. 900/341-7, dated August 14, 1915, the "announcement" (*iʿlān*) gave the qazi control (*un kē sipurd [main̲]*) of the following activities: leading congregational and ʿEid prayers (*imāmat-i jumʿa wa ʿīdain̲*), reading marriages and granting divorces (*nikāḥ-k̲h̲wānī wa ṭalāq*), and performing other religious rites (*wa-g̲h̲aira marāsim-i maẕāhib*). It further advised all classes of Muslims (*har ṭabqē kē muslimān*) to "take benefit" (*fāʾida uṭhāvain̲*) and to make use of the qazi and his services "because these days, matters relating to marriage and divorce more often than not lead to fights, [so] it is advisable for Muslims to have the qazi, or one of his assistants [*nā'ibs*] read their marriages and to obtain a marriage 'certificate' [*sārṭīfikaṭ*] from him."[10] The announcement further confirmed that the qazi's certificate (*qāẓī ṣāḥib mauṣūf kā sārṭīfikaṭ*) was authoritative (*mustanad*) and that his "legal marriage certificate" (*bā-ẓābiṭa nikāḥ kī sanad*) would be accepted as proof at the collector's office.[11] The announcement thus confirmed many of the duties that petitioners cited in connection with the office, such as reading marriages, reciting the ʿEid payers, and performing other rites, which he did for the "benefit" of local Muslims.[12] Bashir-ud-Din acknowledged the government of India's authority by subsequently reproducing the announcement in his marriage registers.

Owing to his status as a government appointee, Bashir-ud-Din was not hesitant to call on local officials when ʿAbd-ul-Halim circulated an ad against him in August 1925. In response, the magistrate at Meerut, P. W. Marsh, issued an order (*ḥukm*) the following month in which he again certified Bashir-ud-Din's status as the legally appointed qazi (*qānūnān̲ muqarrar shuda qāẓī*), acknowledged his appointment under Act XII of 1880, and cautioned that no individual could legally interfere in the performance of his duties (*kō'ī shak̲h̲ṣ un kē farā'iẓ kī anjām dahī main̲ qānūnān̲ mudāk̲h̲alat nahīn̲ kar saktā*). The magistrate's order, issued under Section 144 of the Criminal Procedure Code, prohibited ʿAbd-ul-Halim from printing "any kind of advertisements or announcements" (*kisī qism kē ishtihārāt aur iʿlānāt shā'iʿ na karain̲*) that would cause the qazi harm and ordered him not to do so again. The tahsildar at Meerut amplified the magistrate's order by issuing a proclamation to notify the public (*ʿawāmm un-nās kī iṭṭlāʿ kī g̲h̲araẓ sē*), condemn ʿAbd-ul-Halim's actions, summarize the magistrate's restraining order, and reconfirm Bashir-ud-Din's status as qazi.[13] If running a successful legal practice depended on gaining the right to publicity, then the qazi won this round.

In this instance, government officials stepped in to defend Bashir-ud-Din, but it did not take much to cross the line between eliciting support and drawing ire from the state. In 1910 one of Bashir-ud-Din's then-fellow assistant qazis recorded the marriage between two individuals, Inʿām Allāh K̲h̲ān (the groom) and Shāh Jahān Begum (the bride). At first glance, the marriage was unremarkable. The couple came before the qazi, and he recorded their *nikāḥ* (marriage). Were it not for a subsequent note in the last column of the marriage register, there would be little reason to question this union: it looks like a routine entry on a regular page in the register. Yet behind this innocent-seeming marriage lay a seedier story, one whose full telling escapes the archival traces it created, but whose intrigue appears elsewhere in the qazi's archive.

On opposing pages in the separate notebook he kept for copying legal documents, Bashir-ud-Din's predecessor, Qazi ʿAbd-ul-Hadi, reproduced two sworn statements from Shah Jahan Begum's dueling husbands.[14] In the first, Inʿam Allah Khan explains that on February 1, 1910, he married Shah Jahan Begum before one of the qazi's assistants. Unfortunately, even though the assistant backdated the register entry to read January 31, the marriage between them was illegal: as later reports made clear, by the time Shah Jahan Begum contracted her marriage with Inʿam Allah Khan, she was already married to another man. Because the first marriage already existed, the second was illegal (*nikāḥ-i ṣānī sharʿā͟n jāʾiz nahī͟n*), and Inʿam Allah Khan had to relinquish his marital claims. In word and in deed, Inʿam Allah Khan washed his hands of Shah Jahan Begum (*us sē mai͟n dast bardārī hōtā hū͟n*), terminated their spousal relationship now and for the future (*āyanda mujhkō kōʾī taʿalluq yā kōʾī ḥaqq nisbat-i nikāḥ-i maẕkūr . . . na hōgā*), and declared Shah Jahan Begum and the other man, Nathē, to be husband and wife (*zan wa shauhar*). Inʿam Allah Khan willingly made his statement to satisfy Nathe and so that it might serve the couple in the future (*āyanda kām āvē*).[15] On the opposing page, Nathe provided similar testimony.

No more than three days after the couple first approached the qazi, the two grooms—and several witnesses—signed these affidavits. Combining elements of everyday Islamic law with trappings of the colonial legal system, these statements stand out as a clear example of the fringe legal work that qazis performed in conjunction with their routine practice of recording marriages. The qazi not only updated the marriage record with a marginal note about its nullification but also included elements of colonial legal document-making in his notebook copies, with references to the stamped paper the grooms used for their statements.[16] (Such details would aid any subsequent testimony in court.) Adding another layer of intertextuality to the mix, Inʿam Allah Khan also claimed to be making his statement "because the matter reached the police" (*chū͟nke yeh muʿāmala pōlīs tak pahūnchē gayā hai*).[17] While the statement does not provide any additional details about the charge against him or the subsequent police involvement, Inʿam Allah Khan suggests that, at the very least, the threat of criminal charges kept him from pursuing his marriage to Shah Jahan Begum.

Given the qazi's care in producing these supplementary documents, it is hard to believe that the assistant who recorded the marriage simply wrote the wrong date (January 31, 1910) rather than the correct one (February 1, 1910). In all likelihood, the registrants had something calculating in mind when they first approached the qazi. They may have duped him into writing the wrong date after declaring that their marriage had been performed on the previous day, or they may have simply convinced him to backdate the entry.[18] Either way, the chances are slim that the wrong date entered the record "by mistake" (*g̱halaṭī sē*).[19] One clue to the possible "truth" of the situation lies in Nathe's statement, which declares that he married Shah Jahan Begum with her acquiescence (*ba-istirẕāʾ*) and with her father's permission (*ba-walāyat-i Muḥammad K̲ẖalīl, pidar-i musammāt*).[20] By referring to her guardian's involvement, Nathe contrasts his legitimate nikah to the illegitimate one with Inʿam Allah Khan. Indeed, a closer analysis of the qazi's register reveals that Shah Jahan Begum had no guardian when she married Inʿam Allah Khan. Instead, the assistant relied on a "special statement" from the bride (*iqrār-i k̲ẖāṣṣ-i musammāt-i maẕkūr*).[21] It was not uncommon for widowed or divorced women to represent themselves when contracting second marriages, but that was not the case here. Rather, Shah Jahan Begum's "special statement" suggests elopement or, at the very least, marriage against her guardian's wishes. While the assistant qazi may have indulged the young couple by making an official record of their "secret" marriage, the faulty register entry could not override threats of police involvement. The qazi thus corrected the problem and nullified the marriage using the same tools that created it: documents and writing.

These two encounters with the colonial state and its enforcement powers—one backing the qazi and his work and the other casting doubt on the legitimacy and accuracy of his records—illustrate the Scylla and Charybdis between which the qazi steered his ship in British India. On the one hand, colonial legislation reduced the qazi's role to recording marriages (and divorces) among Muslims living in or near his loosely defined jurisdiction. On the other hand, marriage sat at the heart of law-and-society relations, and he could not rightfully record marriages without venturing into other legal territory. Making sense of these tensions pushes the history of everyday Islamic law beyond legislative debates and disputes over appointments and into the records qazis kept. A close reading of these records shows that in taking control over marriage, the qazi's work intersected, overlapped with, and at times replaced other forms of legal activity that belonged to the colonial state. These tensions continue into the present and remain central to debates about Islamic legal reform and secularism today.[22]

Writing Records, Making Marriages

While the state kept the chief qazi in check from above, subordinates supported his work from below. These marriage readers (*nikāḥ-k͟hwāns*) and record keepers (*indirāj-kunandas*; entry-doers) discharged the qazi's day-to-day responsibilities performing and recording marriages, and in exchange for their work, they either received monthly stipends or collected fees directly from their clients, as earlier petitions suggest.[23] Depending on the size of his jurisdiction, the chief qazi might have joined his subordinates as they performed and recorded marriages, as Bashir-ud-Din's predecessor did, or he might have given them responsibility for recording marriages while he pursued other business, as Qazi Zain-ul-ʿĀbidīn, the last qazi who appears in this collection of records, did.[24] In Meerut, qazis and nikah-khwans overlapped, sharing the same registers and making their entries one right after the other in the same books until the 1920s or so. Later, more elaborate register layouts, which placed each entry on a separate page, kept the volumes shorter, with fewer entries in each. During this phase, registrars kept their own notebooks, suggesting a more decentralized approach to record-keeping.[25] Even though they are fragmentary, these registers nonetheless provide a rich picture of the socio-legal world in which qazis lived and worked.

Records from the earlier period (roughly 1880–1915) show, for instance, that before becoming chief qazi, Bashir-ud-Din worked as an ordinary record keeper, signing the records he made "*al-ʿabd* Muḥammad Bashīr-ud-Dīn ʿAlī."[26] A volume of marriages recorded between January 1909 and November 1910 includes ceremonies that Bashir-ud-Din oversaw alongside those signed by his predecessor (Muhammad ʿAbd-ul-Bari, qazi for the city of Meerut) and several other marriage registrars. Signatures are notoriously difficult to decipher, but the volume suggests that six or seven marriage readers worked alongside the qazi at the time. Of the 400-plus records included in the volume, Bashir-ud-Din recorded about 80 (20 percent) and the qazi recorded roughly 30 (less than 10 percent). The most prominent registrars recorded 105, 75, and 24 ceremonies, respectively, while two additional registrars recorded around 15 ceremonies each.[27] Other individuals—with indecipherable signatures—recorded only a handful of ceremonies each. The data are incomplete, given that some of the entries are missing the nikah-khwan's signature and that the volume is so badly torn and damaged by mold, mildew, and rot that many of the entries—and the corresponding entry numbers—are missing, but these figures provide a rough estimate for how the qazi and his assistants recorded marriages.

Marriage registers like these were a (seemingly simple) transcription of the (necessarily more elaborate) marriage contract.[28] The couple would keep the original marriage contract, and the qazi would preserve an abbreviated record in his register.[29] For elites, marriage contracts could be elaborate documents with gold leaf, ornate orthography, and extensive decoration. For ordinary individuals, the simpler marriage contract might include the qazi's seal or another invocation at the top, followed by a statement about the marriage process. Contemporary handbooks for writing legal documents describe the groom taking responsibility for the bride at a ceremony (*majlis*) in which witnesses heard the "offer and acceptance" (*ījāb wa qabūl*) and gave the couple congratulations.[30] The deed would also include details about the *mahr* (dower) amount—to be paid immediately (*muʿajjal*) or at some point in the future (*muʾajjal*)—and the names of the witnesses. After participating in the ceremony and witnessing the signing of the marriage contract, the marriage registrar would create a brief transcription of the event.

Records from 1881 (when Bashir-ud-Din's predecessor's predecessor, ʿAbdul-Bari, was in charge), arrange the information horizontally, as shown in figure 6.1.[31] A heading at the top of the page describes the contents as "Copy-register for Marriages, connected to the Qazi for the City, Camp, and District of Meerut" (*naql-rajasṭar-i nikāḥ, mutaʿallaq-i qāẓī-yi shahr wa kaimp wa pargana-yi mēruṭh*), beneath which lie a series of supra- and subheadings. From right to left, the columns give a serial number and date for each entry, situating them in the qazi's archive, and then identify the participants. Under the crude labels for "man" (*mard*) and "woman" (*ʿaurat*), the registrar recorded the name, father's name, community, and place of residence for each party. Details related to the amount of mahr, pledged or paid, followed in the next columns. One page of entries from 1881 shows mahr in the amount of two thousand rupees for the marriage between Yūsuf Ḥusain and Luṭf-un-Nisāʾ; thirty-two rupees in the marriage between ʿAlī Bak̲h̲sh and Naṣībān̲; five thousand rupees in the marriage between Shaik̲h̲ Amīr ʿAlī and Kulṡūm; one hundred rupees in the next marriage recorded on December 10, 1881; and five hundred rupees in the entry at the bottom of the page, recording the marriage between Raḥīm Bak̲h̲sh and ʿIṣmat-un-Nisāʾ. All of these payments were marked "deferred."[32]

In the next two columns, the registrar recorded details of guardianship—that is, by whose permission the couple married. On this page, the *walī-yi mard* (man's guardian) and *walī-yi ʿaurat* (woman's guardian) columns are

نقل رجسٹر نکاح متعلق قاضی شہر و کیمپ و پرگنہ میرٹھ

کیفیت

FIGURE 6.1 Page from the registers of Muslim marriages produced by the qazis of Meerut. This page records four marriages, numbers 175–78, recorded in June 1881. Family History Library, Muslim Marriage Records, Microfilm 1307221, Vol. 1.

mostly empty. (Nasiban represented herself, and ʿIsmat-un-Nisa's father acted as her guardian.)[33] Grooms frequently wed without noting their guardians, but as the dispute surrounding Mahomed Yusuf Moorghay's "illegal" marriages demonstrates (see chapter 3), a bride's guardianship could be contested. On the following page, at least three of the brides served as their own guardians and one was married under the guardianship of her father. The form indicates that the registrar should identify the guardians with the same details as the bride and groom (i.e., name, father's name, community [*qaum*], and place of residence), but registrars tended to ignore this requirement, writing "by permission of the aforementioned lady" (*ba-ijāzat-i musammāt-i mazkūra*) or "by permission of the father of the aforementioned" (*ba-ijāzāt-i pidar-i musammāt-i mazkūra*), or simply "So-and-so, father of the lady" (as in "Muhammad ʿAbd-ul-ʿAzīz, pidar-i musammāt") instead.[34] Here the register's status as a "copy" of the marriage contract is clear; improper guardianship was grounds for nullification in Hanafi jurisprudence, so registrars were unlikely to overlook such details as a matter of course.

After recording the guardians, the registrar recorded the name of the marriage broker, the *wakīl,* who orchestrated the union. Here again, the form instructs the registrar to include the father's name, community, and place of residence for each broker, and although the form provided space for the groom's broker (*wakīl-i mard*) and for the bride's (*wakīl-i ʿaurat*), the groom rarely had a wakil. Accordingly, for the entries introduced earlier, Buniyād ʿAli, a *sayyid* from the town of Meerut, represented Lutf-un-Nisa; Amīr K͟hān, who lived near Bāg͟hpat Gate, represented Kulsum; Ḥusain Bak͟hsh, originally of Aurangabad but residing in Kishanpura, represented the bride ʿAẓīmān̤ on December 10; and Turāb ʿAlī [?], also a resident of Meerut, represented ʿIsmat-un-Nisa. Additional details about the broker might tie the marriage to an extended family or social network, but the register entry leaves these relationships up to the reader's imagination.

The final columns gave details about the ceremony itself. Before recording the name of the marriage reader in the penultimate column, the form required the names of two witnesses, lumping them together in a single box. The final column, labeled "kaifiyat" (particulars, detailed circumstances), allowed for additional details. When the marriage between Inʿam Allah Khan and Shah Jahan Begum became illegitimate, for instance, the qazi made a note in this final column explaining the "circumstances" surrounding their separation and noting the legitimacy of Shah Jahan Begum's union to Nathe. This column, as the later discussion will show, allowed qazis and marriage registrars to move from the abbreviated "facts" of the marriage to the broader context of the couple's union. The space, which appears to be no more than a small square on the edge of the page here, became bigger and more prominent in subsequent versions of the register, letting the qazi extend the marriage record from the "facts" of the marital union to its context, its history, and its relationship to other legal activities.

Legislative debates surrounding the 1880 Kazis' Act suggest that appointing qazis would provide the "lower classes" of Muslims with facilities for recording their marriages. When disputes arose, judges would theoretically be able to refer to the qazi's register to find out whether a marriage had taken place, whether it was legal, and whether it had been subsequently annulled or terminated. Act XII of 1880 provided little explicit guidance about the form the qazi's register should follow, but pieces of legislation enacted elsewhere in the empire were much more explicit.[35] Yet despite these details, it is unclear whether late nineteenth-century legislation followed existing practices or whether subsequent practices followed the legislation, since there is ample evidence that even before the Kazis' Act, marriage registration was a key part of the qazi's work. During his civil trial, Yusuf Moorghay not only referred to marriage registers as proof of the income he formerly collected but also showed his predecessor's registers dating back to the eighteenth century to demonstrate the importance of marriage registration. The court's published decision does not provide additional information about those registers, what they looked like, or how the entries were arranged in them, but their use as evidence in this high-profile case confirms their existence and testifies to the court's recognition of them as meaningful documentary records.[36] The qazis at Meerut (and elsewhere) merely continued this practice after 1880.[37]

Making Marriage Registers: Outlines and Signs in Bharuch

Additional evidence of the records qazis kept comes from the family collection of Qazi Nur-ud-Din Husain, the exemplary government qazi who lived and worked in Bharuch and was Yusuf Moorghay's contemporary (see chapter 1). After his predecessors made complaints about the government's decision to take away their right to collect fees for authenticating a range of legal agreements, including *wakālat-* and *muk͟ht̤ār-nāmas* (deeds of representation; powers of attorney), the qazis of Bharuch doubled down on their involvement in marital record-keeping.[38] Throughout the 1840s and 1850s, they filled dozens of registers with marriages and several others for divorce (referred to as *fārig͟h-k͟haṭṭī ṭalāq-nāmas*, or deeds of dissolution-divorce) and property exchanges (*ẓamānat-nāmas* and *bark͟hāst-nāmas*).[39] Unlike the qazis at Meerut, who used lithography to print their forms, the qazis in Bharuch made their registers by hand, using blank notebooks and drawing the lines they needed to organize the records. Yet even if their forms differed in appearance, in principle they overlapped with later examples from Meerut. Looking back to these earlier registers not only follows a longer historical arc from early colonial registration practices to late and postcolonial ones but also suggests that the qazis in Meerut were not alone in their record-keeping practices.[40] Robust archives like theirs might not be readily available today, but they were not alone in their approach to marriage registration.

Like the qazis in Meerut, Nur-ud-Din Husain's family in Bharuch also employed na'ibs. When recording marriages, one of these assistants, Shaik͟h G͟hulām Muṣṭafá, signed his records with the statement, "Nā'ib Shaik͟h G͟hulām Muṣṭafá bā-ijāzat-i sharī'at panāh nikāḥ k͟hwānda" (The *nā'ib* . . . with permission of the shelter of *sharī'a* [i.e., the qazi] read the *nikāḥ*).[41]

These entries began with the date in the top right corner of the page, following the convention for the Perso-Arabic script, which reads from right to left. Writing in the middle decades of the nineteenth century, Ghulam Mustafa included the English-Gregorian date alongside the Islamic-Hijri one. In the next column, he then recorded the name and other identifying details about the "nākiḥ," the one who marries, the groom. Ghulam Mustafa recorded the groom's name, his father's name, his place of residence, and his approximate age. The groom would then add his "sign" (*ʿalāmat*) below. In many of the entries, the groom's sign was a line or squiggle, suggesting his limited literacy (figure 6.2). Some of the grooms signed in Gujarati script (even though the record was in Persian); others wrote in Persian, and the expression "ba-dast-k̲h̲aṭṭ-i k̲h̲wud" (by his own signature) would appear before his name. In this volume, which contains ninety-four entries, seventy-five grooms gave their "sign," fifteen wrote in Gujarati, and only four gave signatures in the Perso-Arabic script.[42] The use of multiple languages and scripts shifted across time and space, but linguistic mixing was common throughout South Asia's corpus of legal documents, with local scripts and languages frequently appearing alongside Persian and Arabic.[43]

After recording the details of the groom, Ghulam Mustafa would move to the next column and record details about the "mankūḥa," the one being married, the bride. Again, he would write the bride's name, her father's name, her place of residence, and her approximate age. The bride here resided in Bharuch (*sākina-yi bandar-i Bharūch*) and was seventeen years old (*tak̲h̲mīnan ba-ʿamr-i 17 sāla*).[44] With guardians and brokers facilitating their nuptials, brides did not "sign" the records, and the scribe frequently wrote the location of the ceremony beneath her information: "the *bāzār* [market] of Ḥajjī K̲h̲ān Ṣāḥib," "in the neighborhood of Kahushwāṛa [?]," "in the neighborhood [*maḥalla*] of Tahūlia [?]." These locations, all but indecipherable to outsiders today, hint at the social and geographical worlds in which qazis and their assistants operated.

After listing the bride's and groom's information, the record then detailed the amount of dower pledged or paid. To protect against later manipulation, the scribe wrote these numbers in long form: "one hundred and twenty and seven rupees" (*yak ṣad wa bīst wa haft rūpiya*), "forty rupees" (*chihil rūpiya*), "seven hundred and fifty rupees" (*haft ṣad wa panjāh rūpiya*).[45] Reference to the symbolic "mahr-i Fāṭimiya," the amount of mahr the Prophet's daughter Fatima accepted when she married ʿAli, is also common in these volumes—appearing with those words or as an equivalent monetary

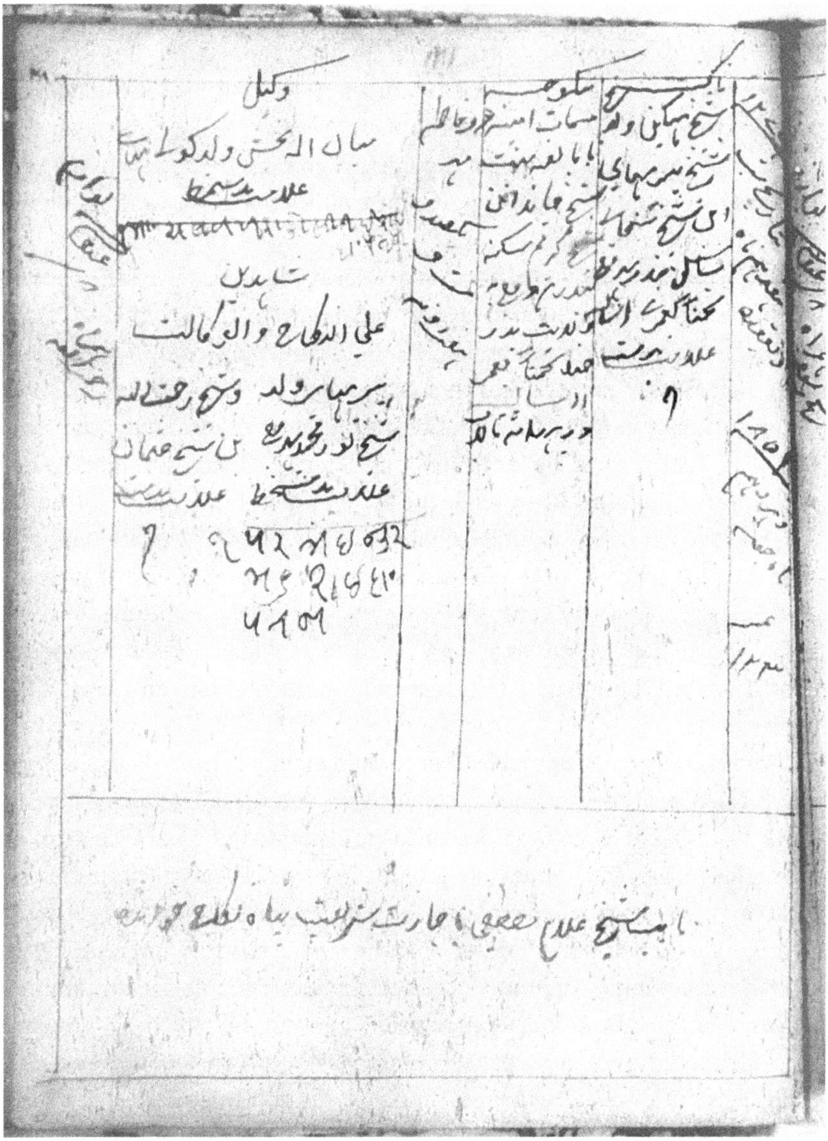

FIGURE 6.2 Marriage register entry from Bharuch, recorded by the naʾib qazi (assistant qazi) Ghulam Mustafa. Note the use of Persian and Gujarati script, as well as the reference to mahr in the amount of "yak-ṣad wa bīst-o-haft" rupees (Rs. 127). Entry number 123, recorded on June 18, 1859 (17 Ẕūʾl-qaʿda 1275 AH). Courtesy of the National Archives of India, Microfilm Acc. No. 850, Sr. 40, Nikah-namas from Broach (Bharuch).

amount in many of these records (Rs. 127 in this volume; Rs. 108 in earlier volumes).[46] Mahr amounts varied according to family status and were not always provided in terms of cash or currency. Grooms also included movable or immovable property either in their original pledges or in their subsequent payments.[47] The relatively narrow column dedicated to mahr in these registers thus belied its significance within the wider world of family, property, and economics.[48]

As in the subsequent registers from Meerut, the scribe used the penultimate column to record the marriage broker and two witnesses (the *shāhidain*) "of the marriage and of the brokerage" (*ʿalá al-nikāḥ wa al-wakālat*), along with their fathers' names. They then added their signatures or "signs." With a single column for recording multiple participants' information, the registers were not the most elegant. Signatures from one witness might overlap with details about the other, while the broker's details sat awkwardly at the top. In one entry, the Gujarati signature of Mālik G̱ẖulām Muḥammad spills over into the space reserved for his co-witness.[49] The naʾib qazi's memory could clear up any later confusion over who performed what role, but here again, the register's status as a "copy" of the actual marriage contract is evident. The final column noted the receipt of the qazi's or nikah-khwan's fee, his *lawāzim*.

The registers from Bharuch incorporated elements from narrative legal deeds (such as witness signatures and signs) and those from later bureaucratic forms (such as columns and grids to separate individual pieces of information). They did not narrate the nikah, record the marriage offer and its acceptance, stipulate the marital duties or responsibilities of each party, or annotate the witnesses' presence at the *majlis*, but they did retain some narrative elements—such as the tissue connecting names with families, places, and ages. Later marriage registers omitted these phrases, breaking individual identities into separate points of data, but the hand-drawn Bharuch registers were more flexible than those later printed forms: qazis and their nikah-khwans could adjust the spacing of the columns to include additional details or to explain mitigating circumstances. At the bottom of one entry, a certain Aḥmad Muḥammad testified to the death of the bride's previous husband and swore that she had not taken another husband since then.[50] When the registrar ran out of room at the bottom of the first page, he carried the statement over to the top of the next page. Narrative statements like these allowed marriage registrars to determine a bride's eligibility for marriage while also creating a legal record of past legal events (e.g., divorce, death, conversion). Qazis and nikah-khwans were responsible for adequately documenting these details, so that if later questions arose over the legality of a particular union (for instance, in the case of Shah Jahan Begum and Inʿam Allah Khan), the qazi could call on these witness statements to supplement the marriage record. Keeping accurate records served the qazi's—and his clients'—best interests.

Looking at registers from Meerut and Bharuch, it is easy to identify similarities and differences in their format and arrangement. While the assistant qazi in Bharuch tended to record each marriage on a single page, using handwritten headings (*nākiḥ, mankūḥa, wakīl*) to identify the contents of each column, the qazis and nikah-khwans in Meerut used forms with printed headings that clearly marked the contents of each column, recorded multiple marriages on a single page, and introduced the *kaifiyat* (circumstances) column to record additional notes about the union. This type of transcription allowed them to preserve hundreds of entries in a single volume but also made it difficult to search the records quickly or efficiently. Despite their similarities, the connections between the qazis of Bharuch and Meerut and the longer history of legal document writing and local legal practice in nineteenth- and twentieth-century South Asia remain obscured. Without clearer narrative sources, it is impossible to learn more about the motivation and mechanisms involved in the design and production of the registers, but from the evidence that survives, it is clear that qazis across several locations had a shared understanding of what each register should include and how the entries should work independently and in relation to the broader corpus of legal deeds and documents. These concerns continued into later phases of record-keeping.

From Columns to Grids: Documentary Specificity in Meerut

After Bashir-ud-Din took over as qazi in Meerut, the layout for the marriage registers changed dramatically, ushering in a new phase of marriage registration. If drawing columns on a blank page helped the naʾib qazi in Bharuch produce orderly marriage registers, then Bashir-ud-Din multiplied this intent by turning columns into grids, as figure 6.3 illustrates. Rather than having a single heading at the top of the page, the new format now presented the information as a grid, with labels across the top and along the side of the page. This arrangement further separated marriage registration from the narrative *nikāḥ-nāma* (marriage contract) and brought the qazi's record-keeping in line with government bio-data forms and identity cards introduced around this time.[51]

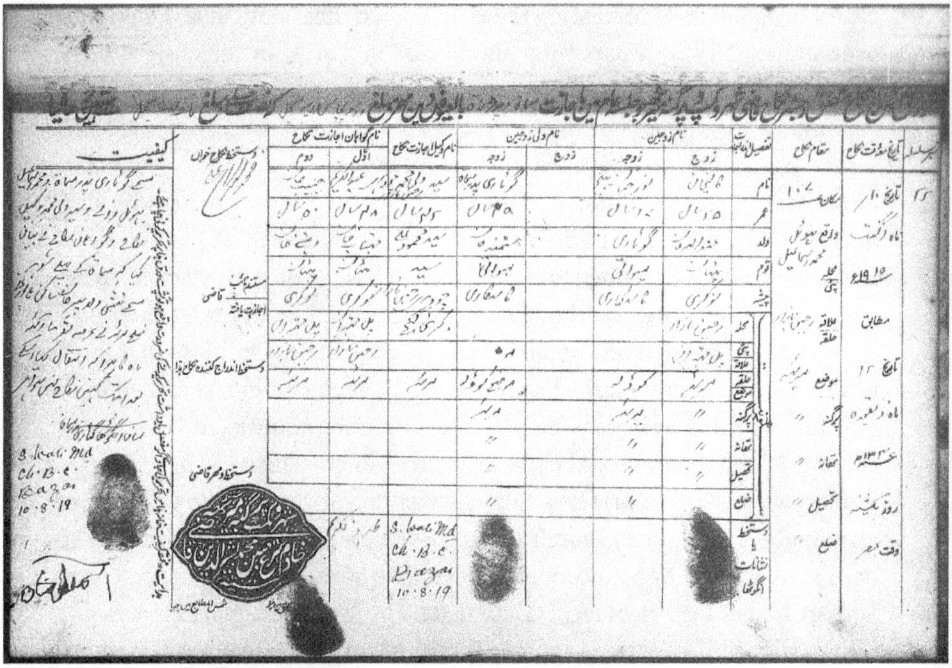

FIGURE 6.3 Marriage register entry produced by Qazi Bashir-ud-Din in August 1919. Note the inclusion of fingertip impressions at the bottom of the page, along with signatures in Urdu and in English. The left-hand column includes a statement regarding the bride's former husband's death. Family History Library, Muslim Marriage Records, Reel 1307224, Vol. 28, Entry 22.

Lithographic printing made this complex layout possible, and evidence suggests that the qazis of Meerut privately commissioned the printing of their registers, the way businesses hire presses to print business cards, stationery, and specialized forms. Toward the beginning of his tenure, Bashir-ud-Din employed Shaik͟h ʿAbd-ul-Ḥaqq, printer at the Shams-ul-Maṭābaʿ, to produce the registers. Another set of registers refers to printing by the "Nāmī Prēs" of Meerut under the direction of Munshī Maḥbūb ʿAli, "prinṭar" (printer).[52] Even though the records mirrored those outlined in contemporary acts of Muslim marriage registration legislation, there is no evidence that the government supervised or participated in the production of these registers.[53] Instead, their printing and design appear to have been orchestrated entirely by the chief qazi.

As with previous versions, the new layout labeled each page's contents with the heading "waraq-i indirāj-i nikāḥ mutaʿallaq-i rajasṭar-i nikāḥ-i qāẓī-yi shahr wa kaimp wa pargana-i mēruṭh" (page recording the marriage connected to the qazi for the city, camp, and district of Meerut). Turning the narrative nikah-nama into a fill-in-the-blank form, the heading continued with details about the ceremony and the agreement: "Jalsa-yi ʿām main̲, ba-ijāzat-i . . . biʾl ʿiwaẓ-i dain-i mahr-i mablag̲h̲ . . . ke niṣf jiskē mablag̲h̲ . . . hōtē hain̲ [nikāḥ] paṛhā gayā" (in a public ceremony, with the permission of . . . in exchange for mahr debt in the amount of . . . half of which is . . . [the nikah] was read).[54] The qazi's register was no longer a "copy-register" (*naql-rajasṭar*) but was instead a "page" (*waraq*) recording the marriage, and the narrative heading brought many of the performative elements of the marriage contract back into the register entry, referring to the "public ceremony" (*jalsa-yi ʿām*) in which the nikah "was read" (*paṛhā gayā*), for instance.[55] Different printings modified this heading slightly, but the text remained fairly stable across several decades of records. Registers from 1941, for instance, renamed the records "nikah register of the dar-ul-qaza for the city, camp, and district of Meerut" (*rajasṭar-i nikāḥ, dār-ul-qaẓā-yi shahr wa kaimp wa parganah-i Mēruṭh*) and added Bashir-ud-Din's name but otherwise kept the same details about the ceremony, granting of permission, and exchange of mahr in the heading.[56]

Bashir-ud-Din's successor, Zain-ul-ʿAbidin, who took over around 1945, continued to use registers with similar layouts. In some of his later registers, he replaced the Urdu heading with one that stylistically imitated Arabic calligraphy and later added a supplementary statement regarding his title and authority as qazi that said, "Under the authority [*zīr-i nigrānī*] of Maulvī Muḥammad Zain-ul-ʿĀbidīn Ṣiddīqī (*maulvī fāẓil*), Qazi of the City, and Camp, and District of Meerut, appointed [*muqarrar shud*] on behalf of the Government of U.P., by way of Order 1614 (1) / 251-7, under section 2 of Act 12 of 1880."[57] Beneath this heading, the document then recorded details about the public ceremony, guardianship, and mahr amount (and half amount) with which the marriage was contracted (*munʿaqid*), according to the rules of *sharīʿa* (*ḥasb-i qawāʿid-i sharʿīya*).[58] Zain-ul-ʿAbidin's many assistants continued to use these registers to record marriages in Meerut until the 1980s.[59]

Writing out the mahr amount, often in words and numerals, along with its half amount, not only tied the exchange of mahr to the marriage ceremony but also cautioned against possible fraud. When Nanī married her second husband in March 1920, she represented herself; agreed to mahr in the amount of two hundred rupees "upon request" (*ʿind-uṭ-ṭalab*), half of which was "one hundred rupees upon request"; and gave a sworn statement before Muḥammad Ḥasan, the nikah-khwan, stating that her first husband (*pahalē k͟hāwand*) had passed away two years ago and she had not entered into a second contract (*ʿaqd-i ṡānī*) since then.[60] With the mahr amount stated at the top and Nani's testimony summarized in the kaifiyat column along the left-hand side, the entire page contributed to the making of the marriage.

Nani's entry was typical. While the header outlined key features, the devil of the record was in the details below. Moving from right to left, the first columns gave the "order number" (*nambar-i silsila*), the "date and time of the nikāḥ" (*tārīk͟h maʿa waqt-i nikāḥ*), and its location (*maqām-i nikāḥ*). Within these categories, the form provided room for the date, month, and year according to the Hijri and Gregorian calendars, followed by the day of the week (*rōz*) and time of day (*waqt*) at the bottom. Nani's marriage took place at eight o'clock in the evening. For place, the form specified the house (*makān*), its location (*wāqiʿ*), its neighborhood or address (*maḥalla/paṭṭī*), and its area or circle (*ʿalāqa/ḥalqa*)—designations made more meaningful with the development of the postal system—along with the corresponding township (*mauẓaʿ*), district (*pargana*), division (*taḥṣīl*), and province (*ẓillaʿ*). The next column repeated the same list for the participants' residential addresses. The qazi's ambit was mostly local, so like Nani's, many of the records (and registrants) had "Meerut" for the township, district, division, and province, and the registrar would either write the word hastily or employ the ditto marker (") across several rows. Occasionally, however, one or more parties came from outside Meerut. In another instance, from September 1941, a bride who resided in the princely state of Tonk (*riyāsat-i Ṭōnk*) married a groom from Agra.[61] In November of that year, a groom from Meerut wed a bride from Khurja, a town roughly one hundred kilometers to the south.[62] Longer distances became possible as changes in transportation facilitated greater mobility, but for most records, one or both parties resided in Meerut.

The next column, the fourth from the right, simply said "details of the recorded" (*tafṣīl-i indirājāt*) and signaled the move from details about the ceremony to details about the participants. Beginning with the groom, the following columns referred to the "names of the husband and wife" (*nām-i zaujain*), the "names of the guardians of the husband and wife" (*nām-i walī-yi zaujain*), the "name of the wakil permitting the marriage" (*nām-i wakīl-i ijāzat-i nikāḥ*), and the "names of the witnesses for the marriage" (*nām-i gawāhān-i nikāḥ*). Except for that listing the wakil, each of these columns had subheadings for the groom (*zauj*) and the bride (*zauja*). The witnesses (here identified with the Persian plural *gawāhān*) were simply "one" (*awwal*) and "two" (*duwum*). After naming each of the parties—*zauj*, *zauja*, *walī-yi zauj, walī-yi zauja, wakīl, gawāh-i awwal, gawāh-i duwum*—the form then used the penultimate column for the signature of the nikah-khwan (who read the marriage), the acquiescence of the qazi or his naʾib (*mustanad nāʾib / qāẓī ijāzat yafta*), the signature of the recorder (*indirāj-kunanda*; entry-doer), and the signature and seal of the qazi (*dast-k̲h̲aṭṭ wa muhr-i qāẓī*). Bashir-ud-Din had his seal printed (rather than stamped) on the page.

In total, then, each register entry required dozens of pieces of information. To create a complete entry, the recorder would write three details at the top; twelve pieces relating to the order, timing, and location of the ceremony; and eleven pieces of information for each of the seven participants. If he entered information into each of the boxes on the grid, then, he would produce roughly one hundred data points for each entry. Numbers could vary if there were no guardians or if everyone lived in Meerut, but making a complete record required dedication and diligence. When registrars made mistakes or could not complete a record, they would draw an "X" through the entire page, and sometimes even make a note about the quarrel that broke out between the bride and groom and prevented their union, for instance.[63] Record keepers employed other strategies to ensure accuracy as well. Sometimes, they would report accidentally recording the information for one participant in the column reserved for another,[64] or they might try to catch a mistake and fix it by crossing out some details and writing others in their place, as one registrar did when entering details about the bride's guardian.[65] In addition to using forms that required detailed information for each entry, efforts like these, to catch mistakes and to fix them in the written record, suggest that qazis and nikah-khwans were invested in the project of producing accurate and verifiable records—despite criticisms to the contrary.

Once the scribe completed the entry, the participants would add their signatures or finger- or thumb-tip impressions in the final row at the bottom of the page. Participant and witness signatures were traditional, but with the introduction of forensic fingerprinting, the biometric imprint quickly became standard across various forms of documentation.[66] Marriage registers from Meerut began to add them around 1915, after Bashir-ud-Din's takeover and the introduction of the new register layout. Around this same time, the princely state of Hyderabad also added finger- and thumb-tip impressions to its marriage records and trained assistant qazis (and police officers) in the practice.[67] Again, the mixture of signatures, signs, and finger- or thumb-tip impressions varied across the entries, depending on the registrants' literacy levels. For some entries, all participants signed their names; for others, everyone used fingertip impressions; for some there was a mixture.[68]

The bride's column was the one most likely to remain empty, possibly indicating her absence at the time of registration, but brides were not always passive registrants.[69] In many cases, they presented registrars with evidence of their past legal lives and current legal status as eligible brides. Capturing these statements—along the edges of the marriage record—extended the qazi's practice into other areas of law, beyond the mere production of documents and data points and into the social world of marital relations and the expansive experiences of everyday Islamic law. Moving away from the data-driven form, the final part of this discussion considers the narrative, documentary, and marginal strategies that qazis and marriage registrars employed to reconnect the administrative functions of the marriage register to the broader context of family affairs and the wider world of colonial legal life. These details demonstrate how marriage registration constantly overlapped and intersected with other forms of legal activity and shaped everyday encounters with Islamic law and with the colonial state.

Reading beyond the Register Entry: Legal Life at the Intersections of State and Society

Marriage registers dictated the information registrars recorded and the arrangement of that information on the page, but even with its dozens of boxes laid out in precise columns and rows, marked by headings and subheadings, and certified with signs, signatures, and fingertip impressions, the register could not guarantee the legitimacy or legality of a union. There was more to legitimating a marriage than simply recording names, dates, and ages. A woman who was already married, for instance, could not legally marry again unless her husband had passed away or had granted her a divorce. Contractual mechanisms like delegated divorce (*ṭalāq-i tafwīẓ*) allowed some women to escape unhappy marriages when their husbands broke certain conditions, but the legal status of these agreements (which could be spoken, not written) was often unclear.[70] Working at the margins of the formal legal system, qazis and marriage registrars navigated these fuzzy legal areas, even though their authority remained ambiguous. (Would the court accept the qazi's evidence or reject it? Would his testimony lend support or invite scrutiny?) In this context, marriage registers became an archive of legal entanglements, as evidence of other legal events, experiences, and encounters punctuated the seemingly straightforward practice of recording marriages. Looking at the broader context in which these registers operated, as muftis, qazis, and colonial judges attempted to adjudicate marital issues, further serves to illuminate the qazi's socio-legal role.

With their columns, grids, and abbreviated statements, marriage registers provide a sanitized version of marital life. Contemporary fatwa literature, however, is filled with juicy details about how marriages failed and the legal conundrums they created—especially in the context of proving or disproving divorce and dissolution. In one instance, the mufti at Deoband weighed in on a situation in which the husband promised not to engage in adultery (*zinā*) or to consume alcoholic "toddy" (*tāṛī*; country liquor), and vowed that if and when he did so, his wife would become *ḥarām* (forbidden) to him, meaning their marriage would no longer be legitimate. He then cheated on his wife, and the mufti had to decide whether this meant the couple was divorced.[71] In another instance, a fatwa seeker wondered whether a *kābīn-nāma* (dower deed) was legitimate if it contained the following conditional statement: "If I become impotent [*nā-mard*], or go missing [*mafqūd-ul-k̲h̲abar*], end up in jail [*qaid*], or move to a foreign country [*pardēs*] and stop visiting you, and do not provide for your food and clothing [*nān-pārcha*], then, having waited two years for me, you may take the right that I have to divorce you and give [yourself] three *ṭalāqs*, before marrying another person."[72] Fortunately for the wife, there was a written document in this case, but finalizing the divorce would still require investigating (and proving) that the conditions had been met, holding a public meeting to confirm the divorce, and waiting two years. If anyone refuted her claims, she would still be stuck in her marriage.[73]

Local qazis, and the marriage readers and registrars they employed, operated in this world in which informal legal documents, divorce decrees, pledges, and promises were constantly subject to debate and open to interrogation. Like the muftis described in chapters 4 and 5, these legal practitioners also looked for equitable solutions to the conflicts they faced and the problems they encountered, slotting individual experiences into the blank space at the margins and on the backsides of their register entries. Without a robust legal infrastructure dedicated to grassroots, everyday Islamic legal practice, it was difficult for ordinary individuals to make sense of the rules and regulations that affected the legal status of their relationships. Qazis and marriage registrars stepped in here, breaking free from the constraints of the enumerated, tabular register layout to address these issues, and gave documentary life to these often indeterminate and sometimes fuzzy legal categories.

Witness statements were the most common—and most readily available—form of evidence that registrars could capture, summarizing the substance of the witnesses' statements and asking for their names and signatures to make them legally binding. In 1919, for instance, a bride's father and two witnesses certified that her husband died eight months ago and that she had not been married since then. Her father placed a fingerprint underneath his name, while the other witnesses, Sayyid Walī Muḥammad and Muḥammad Ismāʿīl, added their signatures, the first in schoolboy English cursive and the second in a messy Urdu *nastaʿlīq* (suspended script).[74] When Rustam and Imtiyāz Begum married later that year, a statement from the bride's father and two other witnesses (Shēr Muḥammad Ḵẖān and ʿAbd-us-Samīʿ) made the union legitimate. The bride also testified ("wa nīz musammāt nē bayān kiyā") to say that her former husband (*sābiq shauhar*) died roughly nine months ago and that she had not contracted another marriage since then.[75] In another instance, the qazi recorded the bride's statement from behind a curtain; she stated that her husband had passed away and she was getting "happily" (*ḵẖwushī sē*) remarried.[76] Statements like these allowed the qazi to document the bride's participation or lack thereof. When Ḥusunī married Nāṣir Ḵẖān, she was not present to give testimony, and the qazi noted her absence.[77] Witness statements like these rooted marriage within the broader context of social knowledge and community participation and fulfilled the qazi's need to certify the bride's eligibility for marriage. Of course, witnesses could lie, but their statements nonetheless served a vital function, linking the legal union to the world of social relations.[78]

In addition to making statements, witnesses also testified to the validity of written documents presented to the qazi in connection with previous marriages or legal agreements. Qazis mentioned documents coming before them (*sāmnē, ḥāẓir*), gave them names that categorized and legitimated their contents (*iqrār-nāma, ṭalāq-nāma*), and noted other elements that made them authentic (e.g., seals and stamps). In some cases, they copied these documents in full, as in the case involving Inʿam Allah Khan and Shah Jahan Begum described earlier.[79] In other cases, they simply summarized the contents, form, and context of the documents they saw. One woman, Raḥīma, brought a copy of her *ṭalāq-nāma* (divorce decree) on stamped paper to prove her eligibility for remarriage. Witnesses also came forth to testify to the legitimacy of the document and to observe her new marriage.[80] Not all women had such robust documentary records. ʿAzīz Fāṭima did not have a *ṭalāq-nāma* and instead relied on a basic *iqrār-nāma* (affidavit) that confirmed her eligibility for remarriage.[81] In another instance, the qazi conducted an independent inquiry into the woman's marital status and called on a fatwa from the "ʿulama of the Ṣadr Bāzār" that confirmed her divorce on August 26, 1937.[82] Outside evidence reached qazis and nikah-khwans in a variety of forms, and they made diligent notes in the kaifiyat (circumstances) column to protect against later recrimination and to make a legal record for their clients.

The kaifiyat column also allowed the qazi to describe transactions and exchanges after the marriage ceremony, particularly in relation to payment of mahr or maintenance (*nān-ō-nafaqa*). When ʿAbd-ul-Qādir and Sulṭān Begum married in 1936, the registrar recorded the execution of an *iqrār-nāma* on that same day, designating the wife's maintenance as ten rupees.[83] When Shāh Jahān and "Ḵẖātūn" married later that year, he pledged one thousand rupees in *mahr-i muʿajjal* (immediate dower), and then, in exchange for her *jahīz* (dowry), he gave her half of a house (*niṣf-i makān*).[84] When ʿĀlamgīr Ḵẖān got married, he promised his wife five thousand rupees in mahr, half of which he gave to her immediately and half of which was "deferred." Qazi Bashir-ud-Din made a note of this accounting in the kaifiyat column, under which the groom signed his name.[85] Noting the execution of sworn statements, documenting the exchange of property, and clarifying the relationship between immediate and deferred payments, the marriage register did more than record the construction of new marital unions; it also recorded the exchange of property—exchanges that butted heads with the legal and documentary authority of the colonial state.

When evidence from the qazi's register was presented in court, judges greeted it skeptically,[86] but on at least a few occasions, women successfully used such evidence to stand up for their rights and to make legitimate claims to the property their husbands owed them.[87] The colonial legal system may have attempted to sideline marriage—and marriage registration—under the separate heading of "personal" or "religious" law, but it was difficult to keep these spheres separate. Small-town qazis used their marriage registers to blur these lines, referring to external legal documents and devices that belonged to the legal apparatus of the colonial state and appropriating their legal content as part of their records. To look at legal life from the level of a register entry, then, is to consider the ways in which individuals used the resources they could access and found ways to create legal records, even when the colonial legal system erected obstacles that thwarted their efforts to render everyday life legible in legal concepts and categories.

To record a legitimate marital union was to create a snapshot of the participants' legal pasts, presents, and futures, while addressing questions of permissibility, acceptability, and legality that brought qazis and marriage registrars into contact with other aspects of local legal life. Death (*intiqāl*, *faut*), divorce (*ṭalāq*), and disappearance (*mafqūd*, *mafqūd-ul-k̲h̲abar*) all appear in the registers, as do references to being a widow (*bewa*), a divorcee (*muṭallaqa*), an out-of-towner, a convert (*nau muslima*), or a rightful property owner. Together with the witnesses they brought and the documents they displayed, registrants shared their legal histories with the qazi to secure their present marital union and their future legal status. By recording and archiving these encounters, qazis and registrars not only connected marriage registration to other forms of legal activity but also extended the marriage register into other areas of legal life.

Conclusion

Working alongside local qazis, na'ibs, nikah-khwans, and indiraj-kunandas performed work that was in some respects similar to, but in many ways quite distinct from, that of the jurists and scholars described in the previous chapters.[88] Both qazis and muftis took the messy details of everyday life and corralled them into legal categories to make family relationships, personal histories, and other legal arrangements legible. Both took ideas from jurisprudence (*fiqh*) and connected them to everyday life and experience, and both provided services from the bottom up, rather than dictating behavior from the top down. But there were differences as well. If muftis took unnamed individuals—"someone" (*kō'ī*), "a person" (*aik shak̲h̲ṣ*), or a "friend" (*dōst*)—and turned them into buyers and sellers, prayer leaders and followers, traders and travelers, then marriage registrars had the more complicated task of turning a "public gathering" (*jalsa-yi 'ām*), a statement (*bayān*, *iqrār*), or a document (*dastavēz*, *nāma*) into the information needed to make a marriage ceremony complete. Their writings turned participants into brides and grooms (*zaujs* and *zaujas*), parents (*wālidain*), guardians (*walīs*), brokers (*wakīls*), and witnesses (*shāhid*, *gawāh*). Like the jurist's conversion of a messy fatwa narrative into a clear legal question, marriage registration also turned individuals with different backgrounds, stories, and life experiences into formal registrants with prescribed roles and responsibilities, and the documentary forms they employed when executing this work mandated the precise, explicit, and complete application of those terms.

While the introduction of new documentary forms constrained the qazi's work in some ways, it could not account for the many marital situations that arose. In these situations, nikah-khwans drew on the availability of the kaifiyat column to add context and to situate the details they recorded in separate rows and columns that marked the participants' legal pasts and marital futures. Contextual clues broke away from the enumerative, tabular arrangement that the printed form prescribed and challenged the idea of record-keeping as an administrative, fact-producing process. Stories about religious conversion, relocation, property exchanges, divorce, death, and disputes filled these pages. References to legal deeds produced elsewhere, authenticated with colonial stamps and fees, presented in person, and validated by witness testimony filled the blank spaces on the margins and backsides of the register's pages. Qazis and marriage registrars did not receive instructions about how to record these details in the legislation under which they served or from the government officials who appointed them. How to keep track of these external elements; how to bring the legal authority of the marriage register together with the additional legal documents, agreements, and experiences that contributed to its validity; and how to keep their work relevant for the generations of clients they served were challenges they faced directly. When it came to designing the registers, Bashir-ud-Din and his assistants were likely improvising, drawing on past models and incorporating new features (like printed seals and fingertip impressions), but their improvisations made it so that marriage registration could exist neither independently of, nor apart from, the larger legal apparatus of the colonial state. With these references, records, annotations, and announcements, qazis pushed back against the colonial state's neat division of legal life into religious-personal law and secular-public law, and they inserted themselves into local legal life at the critical juncture where everyday life and everyday law intersected. Bringing together the processes of registration, documentation, and legal inquiry outlined in part II, the final chapters consider how ordinary individuals moved between and across different legal venues to solve everyday legal problems and illustrate how colonial legal processes and Anglo-Indian judicial practice shaped these maneuvers.

Part III Possibilities

Interlude III

Analyzing Shari'a, State, and Society

WHEREAS it is expedient to make provision for the application of the Muslim Personal Law (Shariat) to Muslims; it is hereby enacted as follows: . . .

(2) Application of Personal law to Muslims.—Notwithstanding any custom or usage to the contrary, in all questions (save questions relating to agricultural land) regarding intestate succession, special property of females, including personal property inherited or obtained under contract or gift or any other provision of Personal Law, marriage, dissolution of marriage, including *talaq*, *ila*, *zihar*, *lian*, *khula* and *mubaraat*, maintenance, dower, guardianship, gifts, trusts and trust properties, and wakfs (other than charities and charitable institutions and charitable religious endowments) the rule of decision in cases where the parties are Muslim shall be the Muslim Personal Law (Shariat).

—"An Act to Make Provision for the Application of Muslim Personal Law (Shariat) to Muslims," 1937

Text and Context: The Muslim Personal Law (Shariat) Application Act of 1937

Like much of the legislation passed in the final decades of British rule, the Muslim Personal Law (Shariat) Application Act (Act 26 of 1937) was the product of special interests, nationalist politics, and ideological alliances. Following on the heels of a similar measure recently adopted by the Frontier Legislative Council, the Shariat Application Act that came into force across British India in October 1937 appealed to multiple interests for its promises to restore "shariʿa" as the rightful source of personal law and to advance the interests of Indian Muslims, freeing them from the "paralysing hold of custom."[1] While political transformations and military upheavals precipitated the first two interludes (the Hastings Plan of 1772 and Queen Victoria's Proclamation of 1858), this one, the third, was born of another political context and represented another political project. Yet while its origins may have differed—emerging not as a unilateral proclamation or one-sided plan but through political negotiations and parliamentary debates—its content and scope hardly strayed from the generic promises and pledges of those earlier measures. Some even asserted that the law's promises were already "clearly stated" in Victoria's proclamation, though the British government of India had, "for some reason, receded from that position."[2] Reading the act today, it is difficult to discern the change it represented or effected. Commentators at the time made similar remarks. Claiming to make "Muslim Personal Law (Shariat)" the "rule of decision in cases where the parties are Muslim," the Shariat Application Act echoes much of the sentiment expressed in those earlier statements of legal pluralism and religious difference. This act differed, however, in its specificity—applying only to one religious community—and in the collaborative politics of its origins.

Laying out the bill's objectives, H. M. Abdullah emphasized how the measure reflected "the cherished desire of Muslims in British India" to make clear "that the customary law should in no case take the place of the Muslim Personal Law." Not just Muslims but the Jamʿiyat-ul-ʿUlama-yi Hind, "the greatest Muslim religious body," also "supported the demand." "Custom," assemblyman Ghulambhik Nairang explained, had a "ruinous" effect on litigation, and the courts' willingness to accept it as a source of law "offered temptation to invent customs and thus mislead the courts into doing injustice instead of justice."[3] As a result, the "law" being applied to Muslim personal law cases not only deviated from but also made an abomination of Muslim personal law. The Shariat Application Act sought to remedy those problems.[4]

Yet when it came to making specific interventions into the interpretation and application of Muslim personal law, the measure said very little. Aside from Clause 2, excerpted at the beginning of this interlude, the only other substantive part of the act was Clause 3, relating to the "power to make a declaration," which stipulated that any Muslim "competent to contract" under the Indian Contract Act (Act 9 of 1872) and resident of the territories included in the act "may . . . declare that he desires to obtain benefit" from the act. Clause 5, which related to the "dissolution of marriage by Court in certain circumstances," contained relevant substance, but it was merely standing in for the more substantive measure that resulted in its repeal a mere two years later: the Dissolution of Muslim Marriages Act of 1939. Clause 4 referred to the rule-making power of the state governments, and Clause 6 listed the "Acts and Regulations" that were inconsistent with (and accordingly repealed by) the new measure. In other words, it was short on substance.

Furthermore, the Shariat Application Act was one of several measures considered, debated, and approved by the Central Legislative Council at this time.[5] In addition to regional measures, such as the Frontier Provinces Muslim Personal Law Act, assembly members considered the Shariat Application Act alongside measures relating to the property of intestate and heirless Muslims, the dissolution of Muslim marriages, Parsi divorce, amendments to the Child Marriage Restraint (Sharda) Act of 1929, the property rights of Hindu widows, and the validation of Hindu and Arya marriages.[6] It also appeared alongside proposals and enactments related to the Bombay Kutchi Memon community and the Mappila Muslim community of Malabar.[7] In contrast to other contemporary proposals relating to religious and personal law, however, the Shariat Application Act was relatively superficial. Its sole power lay in its declaration that custom would not stand in the way of "Muslim personal law (*Shariat*)" for cases concerning the issues it listed.

Despite its lack of substance, though, the bill had several strong supporters who considered the proposal necessary not only for Muslims but also for the nation. Maulana Zafar Ali Khan claimed the measure would contribute to "Muslim solidarity and national unity" and urged the Congress Party to support the measure to "show that they were prepared to allow Muslims to follow the *Shariat*." Without supporting shariʿa, the Congress Party had no right to rule. Others argued on behalf of India's women, whose economic status would increase once they were released from the hold of custom. Men should "stand up for establishing the law of the *Shariat*," Shaukat Ali declared; it was "unnatural" for women to "be deprived of a share in their parental property."[8] Despite these strong stances of support, when it came down to the nuts and bolts of the bill, plenty of questions about what it meant and what it would accomplish remained unanswered.

Situating Shariʿa in Muslim Personal Law

While most of the assembly members were willing to take the bill's equivalence between "Muslim personal law" and "shariat" at face value, others, like Yamin Khan, questioned the inclusion of that term: "Shariat," he suggested "was interpreted in different ways by different sects and might therefore lead to wasteful litigation in the future."[9] Mahomed Yakub expressed similar concerns, arguing that "the object of the original Bill was to remove restrictions imposed by Anglo-Muslim law on Muslim law but the Bill as amended was certainly going to interfere with Muslim law."[10] They were not wrong in their objections. Even though it claimed to restore shariʿa and to liberate Muslim women from the "dead hand" of custom, the act provided none of the expected safeguards that would ensure or protect the interpretation of shariʿa. Just as recourse to custom, "an indefinite thing differing often from one part of a village to another," according to one assemblyman, allowed litigants to make false claims to practices that favored their interests, so too did emphasis on shariʿa have the potential to favor specific interests and particular interpretations.[11]

Like the Kazis' Act of 1880, the Muslim Personal Law (Shariat) Application Act left unanswered many of the practical questions about who and how the legal establishment might interpret shariʿa. During one of the bill's debates, a suggestion arose to allow the states to appoint specific boards or agencies to interpret shariʿa, but specific rules regarding the establishment of these boards did not make it into the final act.[12] Furthermore, in the push to get the act passed, Muhammad ʿAli Jinnah proposed they remove the word "law" from Clause 2, thereby allowing for—if not inviting—further "statutory modification" of Muslim personal law.[13] Likewise, the bill specifically exempted "agricultural land," meaning it left the large estates of "powerful landholding families" untouched.[14]

While symbolically the measure may have carried a great deal of weight—promising to unify Indian Muslims under the banner of shariʿa, rather than allowing them to live under the divided laws of local custom—practically, the measure packed little punch. As Julia Stephens points out, the exemption of agricultural lands alone meant "99.5 percent of all property in India" was excluded, as it was classified as "agricultural lands."[15] Furthermore, when placed alongside earlier statements of religious noninterference and legal pluralism, the act's contributions become even fuzzier, given that the Hastings Plan already made the Qur'an (and by extension shariʿa) the source of law for Muslims and Queen Victoria's proclamation pledged noninterference for all communities. Despite its subsequent interpretation by historians, the act did not, as Stephens rightly contends, "codif[y] Muslim personal law."[16] It did not specify whose interpretation of shariʿa would count for the purposes of adjudication, nor did it specify *how* shariʿa would be interpreted. It did not provide a list of books or texts from which judges could draw, nor did it identify titleholders or officeholders who would provide interpretations. Lack of capacity was not the cause of these shortcomings. Founded in 1919, the Jamʿiyat-ul-ʿUlama had the resources, status, and clout to undertake the necessary interpretive work. Likewise, the Imarat-i Shariah, founded in Bihar in 1921, could have provided the institutional model for shariʿa adjudication, and those who passed the relevant "qualifying tests" could have provided the personnel.[17] But these possibilities were not part of the act.

Embracing the ambiguity and circularity of earlier policies, the Shariat Application Act thus contributed to the larger secular project found in British India's personal law system and its religious legal pluralism. The act not only accepted the state's definition of "shariʿa" as "personal law," but it also used the mechanisms of state law to make shariʿa the source of that law. Rather than disentangling the two sources—state law and shariʿa—the act brought the two even closer together in ways that have since complicated and confounded efforts to reform, revise, or reinterpret Islamic law.[18] Nor did it answer any of the questions relating to Muslim personal law's intersections with Anglo-Indian legal procedure or the legal substance for documents, registrations, contracts, or deeds. These aspects of legal practice remained beyond the bounds of legislators' considerations here but were nonetheless central to the administration and adjudication of cases. Likewise, as questions over jurisdiction reveal in the next chapter, defining and categorizing legal complaints was just as important to the outcome of a case as the content of the law applied to it. Even if Muslim personal law *should have* been the basis for deciding a case, judges—including well-trained Muslim judges—could easily move cases into and out of personal law categories at will. These moves not only reflect the many legal paths litigants and those affected by litigation could pursue but also confounded efforts among Muslim politicians, litigants, and the ʿulama to make a case for *sharʿī* adjudication.

Today, critics of the Shariat Application Act, and of the personal law system more generally, raise concerns over personal law's interference with individual legal rights, such as those guaranteed under broader legal frameworks like the Indian Constitution. Such criticisms, however, tend to occlude aspects of law in action, either by misrepresenting other forums' ability to achieve gender equality or by overlooking the benefits of Islamic legal bodies' lower barriers to entry (i.e., through lower fees, limited dependence on paid professionals, and ability to keep disputes within the community). These arguments now feature in debates over whether to grant more authority to state courts or to nonstate legal bodies to settle personal law disputes, not only in South Asia but in other plurilegal societies as well.[19] By conflating shariʿa with Muslim personal law, recognizing the state's authority to apply that law, and accepting the secular definition of religious law in relation to personal status, the Muslim Personal Law (Shariat) Application Act of 1937 further entangled state institutions and religious legal practice. Keeping this framework in the background, the following chapters show that there was more to religious adjudication than looking to sources of law—be they "custom" or shariʿa. Making, defining, and articulating legal questions and categories also shaped litigants' access to legal remedies and influenced their satisfaction with legal outcomes. Part III thus follows the possibilities and problems that emerge from a more expansive definition of Islamic legal practice, beyond the bounds of state institutions, to reveal the contests that remain when multiple actors attempt to define everyday legal life.

7 Of Judges and Jurists

Questioning the Courts in Islamic Legal Discourse

> Those qazis, who normally read marriages and ʿEid prayers in Hindustan, according to *shariʿa* [*sharʿān*], they are not qazis who possess judicial powers to grant orders and issue decrees. As a result, none of their decisions will be judicial decisions and in matters [*masāʾil*] that necessitate judgment [*qaẓāʾ*], their order [*ḥukm*] will never be sufficient. For Jumaʿ [Friday prayers] and ʿEid, and in these types of religious issues, the one who Muslims make qazi can be qazi and his decisions will be sound because the present government has granted freedom [*āzādī*] in religious affairs.
>
> —Mufti Muhammad Kifayatullah, 1917

> Moreover—and this is the most important point—most of the passages relied upon by [Justice] Markby relate[d], not to substantive law, but to procedure, and in particular to the duties of the Cazi [*qāẓī*] in matters connected with partition, compromise, composition, and other similar subjects.
>
> —Justice Syed Mahmood, 1885

Defining Jurisdictions

After witnessing the workings of local dispute resolution in the small town of Sagar in what is today Madhya Pradesh, Muḥammad ʿAbd-us-Salām had a few questions about jurisdiction. Opening his inquiry with a quick reference to the "jurisdiction" (*ʿamal-dārī*) of the British government of India (Sarkār-i Qaiṣar-i Hind, Angrēzī), ʿAbd-us-Salam quickly turned to the real jurisdictions he wanted to probe: those of the local council (*panchāyat*) and the qazi.[1] In a letter addressed to Mufti Muḥammad Kifāyatullāh in October 1917, ʿAbd-us-Salam narrated what he had observed when the local qazi granted an unnamed couple a judicial separation (*tafrīq*) to resolve a contentious dispute. Apparently, "Zayd" (the unidentified husband) had accused his wife, "Hinda," of infidelity and took his complaint to the local council, the panchayat. The husband asserted his claim and the wife denied the allegations; both parties swore before the council that they were speaking truthfully and accused the other of lying. The council then conducted an inquiry and concluded there had been false accusations against Hinda. Four or five days after the council's ruling, Zayd expelled Hinda from their house, which prompted the qazi to issue the separation on the council's recommendation. ʿAbd-us-Salam wanted to know whether this decision was valid in British India, "when there were no '*shariʿa* judges' [*sharʿī ḥākim*]."[2]

ʿAbd-us-Salam's question emerged from specific events he witnessed, but its implications extended beyond this single incident. Quoting articles written by Indian National Congress leader Maulānā Abūl Kalām Āzād (1888–1958) and activist Maulānā ʿAbd-ur-Raʾūf,[3] ʿAbd-us-Salam pointed to the incongruities that existed between the judicial administration of the "English" (*Angrēzī*) government in India and panchayats that existed to resolve intracommunal disputes.[4] In an article printed in the newspaper *Ṣadāqat* in 1916, Abul Kalam Azad, for instance, explained that "the courts that exist in British India today cannot stand in for those of the qazi or [Muslim] judge [*ḥākim*] and wherever the guidelines of sharīʿa [*aḥkām-i sharʿīya* (*sic*)] use the words 'qāẓī' or 'ḥākim,' they are not referring to the courts that exist today."[5] He further observed that Muslims in British India were not the only ones who needed a solution to this problem, which he explained "causes Muslims either to turn to the *ʿulama* [religious scholars] or to make use of the *panchāyats* to solve their *sharʿī* cases [*muqaddamāt*]." The second commentator, ʿAbd-ur-Raʾuf, chimed in to say that the jurists (*fuqahā*) considered it legitimate for Muslims to appoint their own qazis and that Muslims living "under Christian dominion" (*ʿīsāʾī salṭanat kē mā taḥt*) in other parts of the world had already done so. In his inquiry to Kifayatullah, ʿAbd-us-Salam wondered whether these opinions had any bearing on the way the qazi in Sagar worked, and if so, did they validate or undermine the marital separation he had witnessed?

On paper, regulations implemented in the first half of the nineteenth century (chapter 1), followed by new pieces of legislation toward the end of the century (chapter 3), had turned the Swiss Army knife–style qazi of the precolonial period who worked across religious communities to resolve different kinds of legal contests and disputes into a registrar with authority to perform only the putatively nonjudicial tasks delegated to him under the Kazis' Act of 1880, but as the analysis of the qazis' marriage registers in chapter 6 demonstrated and ʿAbd-us-Salam's question confirms, separating the "judicial" from the "nonjudicial" was easier said than done. Nearly forty years after the government of India reclaimed its role in the appointment of qazis, ʿAbd-us-Salam, a guest in the local qazi's house, remained confused about the extent of the qazi's jurisdiction. He was not the only one. Between 1917 and 1934, Kifayatullah responded to multiple questions about the qazi's jurisdiction, and he fielded inquiries about the status and authority of different legal bodies throughout his career.[6] In addition to those that explicitly referred to the office of the qazi, Kifayatullah received countless others on topics related to the jurisdiction of the courts, their role in the interpretation of Islamic law, and the legitimacy of their decisions in relation to shariʿa. His answers addressed the substance of the legal conflict, as well as the procedures involved in different venues, reflecting his training in Islamic law and his knowledge of the Anglo-Indian legal system. Kifayatullah was not alone in these debates. The jurisdiction of qazis, courts, and panchayats was a vexing problem for the public (which advocated localized and state-centric solutions to dispute resolution) and for the Indian ʿulama (which promoted legislative intervention and autonomous authority). These positions remain unsettled and open to debate, even today.[7]

Questions about jurisdiction also traveled in the other direction, as British judges (and British-trained Indian Muslim judges) quarreled over the meaning of religio-legal doctrine and the courts' right to implement and interpret that doctrine. Debates at both ends of the spectrum point to a key contest that shaped Muslim personal law in British India: the relationship between substance and procedure. As the discussions presented here will demonstrate, while this issue remained of principal importance for personal or family law disputes, other areas of law came into question as well. Property, taxation, administration, and adjudication all traveled along this uneven terrain as high court judges grappled with their responsibilities in relation to those of the qazis. Qazis, too, tested the limits of their authority, even though they lacked comparable jurisdictions. Rather than outlining the path colonial administrators followed in the construction of Muslim personal law, these debates reveal the questions—and contestations—that remained unsettled, even after decades of engagement with Islamic jurisprudence, and the conflicts they sparked continue to influence debates on religious law, secularism, and the limits of state and nonstate legal authority today.[8] Untangling the interplay between substance and procedure taps into these ongoing debates while at the same time unearthing new ideas about the connection between legal action, legal actors, and legal outcomes.

Part II took a tour through the office of the qazi and the institute for issuing fatwas (*dār-ul-iftāʾ*) to demonstrate how these institutions developed in the late nineteenth and early twentieth centuries in response to changing judicial institutions and growing public need. Whether in the context of recording and legitimating a marriage or resolving a dispute among heirs, these offices reconfigured precolonial legal practice within robust (predominantly private) institutions that adapted and embraced bureaucratic procedures.[9] These new institutes acknowledged the influence of and followed models provided by the colonial state and made their day-to-day operations resemble those of government offices, but rather than drawing clear boundaries that divided one institution's jurisdiction from that of another, the superficial similarities of the paperwork they produced and the procedures they followed only increased the competition—not to mention the confusion—between the two. Bureaucratic innovation was more than mere imitation; it was a strategic form of camouflage that cloaked the unofficial records of the qazi's registers and the mufti's file-making in the clothing of government officialdom. The two looked so similar in practice that ʿAbd-us-Salam and others wondered whether they could, in fact, perform the same functions.

Navigating New Juridical Terrain

If conversations toward the end of the nineteenth century revolved around whether government-appointed qazis were necessary (see chapter 3), then debates at the beginning of the twentieth century turned toward questions about what those qazis could do. Marriage and divorce belonged to the qazi, but marital infidelity (adultery) was a criminal offense under Section 497 of the Indian Penal Code.[10] Technically speaking, qazis had no jurisdiction in that area, yet by appointing qazis, the government hoped to reduce the number of marital infidelity and adultery cases that entered its courts. Who was responsible for maintaining which aspects of marital harmony remained unclear. Given these competing ideas over jurisdiction, it is no surprise that observers like ʿAbd-us-Salam struggled to decipher whether local qazis had the right to issue judicial separations for cases involving charges of adultery (*zinā*). The decision followed the qazi's perspective on what was "right," and followed the principles of justice, equity, and good conscience that previously guided British judges, but was the outcome legal? Moreover, did the qazi's action carry any legal implications for the couple? Would the courts now recognize the woman's right to remarry and to deny her (former) husband conjugal access?

Kifayatullah began his answer rather cautiously, determined to set the record straight: "According to shariʿa [*sharʿā̱n*], they are not qazis who possess judicial powers . . . [and] none of their decisions will be judicial decisions," adding that qazis could perform many religious functions but could not settle disputes, as the first epigraph outlines.[11] In response to ʿAbd-us-Salam, he then elaborated, "However, in the present case, in which 'Zayd' and 'Hinda' appointed an outside individual to settle their dispute, and the parties were satisfied with the separation order, in this case, [the qazi] was an arbitrator [*ḥakam*] and the separation was correct and reliable."[12] Offering a rather circuitous explanation, Kifayatullah thus confirmed that qazis had no judicial powers to settle disputes but that parties could appoint one to serve as arbitrator, in which case his decision would be final.[13] The answer may have settled ʿAbd-us-Salam's mind about the validity of the local qazi's actions, but it left open many questions about the limits of the qazi's jurisdiction. Could the qazi step in as arbitrator in any type of case or only for those involving marital disputes? Must the parties be content (*rāẓī*) with the qazi's decision for it to be valid, as Kifayatullah implies here? And were the other experts (i.e., Abul Kalam Azad and ʿAbd-ur-Raʾuf) correct or incorrect in their assessments of the situation? Kifayatullah left these questions unanswered.

When it came to defining the qazi's jurisdiction, Kifayatullah had no skin in the game, but he was expertly poised to weigh in on the issue. By the time he received ʿAbd-us-Salam's letter in 1917, he was already well established as a mufti in Delhi and would remain so until his death in 1952. Born around 1875 in the town of Shahjahanpur in what is now Uttar Pradesh, Kifayatullah graduated from the Dar-ul-ʿUlum at Deoband in December 1897.[14] After graduation, he returned to his hometown, where he worked for a few years under the direction of his first teacher at the Madrasa ʿAin-ul-ʿIlm. There, Kifayatullah taught classes and practiced the art of *iftāʾ*, or the art of legal inquiry and fatwa writing. When his mentor passed away and the madrasa's finances began to falter, Kifayatullah headed to Delhi to continue his career teaching and writing fatwas. In Delhi, he found work at the Madrasa Aminiya, where he remained for the next fifty years. While there, he also contributed to the organization of the Madrasa ʿAliya Fatehpuri and later became a founding member of the Jamʿiyat-ul-ʿUlama-yi Hind (est. 1919), through which he contributed to nationalist and Muslim politics and extended the reach of his fatwa writing by authoring the fatwa column for the jamʿiyat's thrice-weekly newspaper, *Al-Jamʿīyat*.

According to one account, Kifayatullah wrote 4,500 fatwas during his lifetime, which were collated, compiled, and published after his death. Ḥafīẓ-ur-Raḥmān Wāṣif edited and published the resulting nine-volume,

3,700-page collection under the title *Kifāyat-ul-Muftī* (*Sufficiency of the Mufti*), drawing from Kifayatullah's fatwa registers at the Madrasa Aminiya, his columns from *Al-Jamʿīyat*, and miscellaneous documents and writings found at the mufti's home in Delhi.[15] Surveying fatwa literature from the subcontinent, Mujib Ahmad describes Kifayatullah's fatwas as erudite and easy to understand, soundly reasoned, and accessible to lay readers.[16] Eulogists offered similar praise, crediting Kifayatullah with producing fatwas that were practical and well grounded in the science of Islamic legal reasoning, relevant to the challenges of twentieth-century modernity, and well regarded not only in Hindustan, where Kifayatullah was best known, but in other parts of the world as well.[17] Like other Deoband-trained muftis, Kifayatullah adjusted his fatwas to match the fatwa seeker's knowledge and expertise.[18] He was skilled and respected among the ʿulama and was among those experts Ashraf ʿAli Thanwi consulted when revising his now-famous fatwa on the relationship between apostasy, conversion, and marriage in 1931.[19] Indian Muslims also consulted Kifayatullah when they encountered conflicts or questions while living abroad, sending their questions to him by post or by telegram, much the same way fatwa seekers communicated with the dar-ul-ifta in Hyderabad.

A reasonable and well-reasoned scholar, Kifayatullah commented on a range of topics, including some that received only cursory treatment in other fatwa collections. The *Kifayat-ul-Mufti*, for instance, includes an entire chapter on legal judgments and inquiries (*kitāb al-qaẓāʾ wa al-iftāʾ*)—a rare feature among contemporary collections. References to the role of the qazi and the "Muslim judge" (*Musalmān ḥākim*) found their way into other chapters, too.[20] What is more, his opinions demonstrate how Islamic legal experts (including muftis and qazis) shaped the legal landscape in late colonial South Asia, even when they were formally detached from and worked outside the courts. In contrast to muftis formally employed in Ottoman shariʿa courts, say, muftis in British India worked independently, offering advice at the behest of individual litigants in relation to their cases. Kifayatullah was thus one of several privately employed muftis who fulfilled this consultative function in conjunction with, but apart from, the formal legal system.

Legal consultation was not limited to British India. Litigants from princely states (including those with Muslim and non-Muslim rulers) also sought advice from Islamic legal experts, often crossing (and challenging) jurisdictional boundaries in the process.[21] For instance, Raḥam Bībī and Muḥammad Shāh lived in the princely state of Bahawalpur, where they had been married with the permission Raham Bibi's parents (ʿInāyat Shāh and Tāj Bībī).

Shortly after giving birth to their first child, Raham Bibi was summoned from the marital home back to her natal home. Muhammad Shah followed and moved in with his wife's family, even though his in-laws disliked him. To mollify their animosity toward him, Muhammad Shah composed a legal statement (*iqrār-nāma*) on eight-anna stamp paper on June 24, 1898—an informal legal document much like the ones surveyed in chapter 5.[22] In it, he promised to stay by his wife's side and to do as his father-in-law asked. He vowed never to leave home without his in-laws' blessing, adding that if he ever did go somewhere (*kisī ṭaraf chalā jāʾūn̲*), he would, in effect, grant his wife a divorce and cease to make any marital claims to her. Everyone involved recognized the statement as legally binding, yet none foresaw what would follow when ʿInayat Shah's niece, who harbored "ill-will" toward Muhammad Shah, showed up and forced him to move out. His departure set the terms of his iqrar-nama into motion.[23]

Given his earlier pledge, the family considered the couple divorced, but Muhammad Shah did not agree and took the matter to court. Not knowing quite how to resolve the case, which involved questions of marriage, family, religion, and contracts, the court *sarrishtadār* (clerk) sent for expert advice in the form of a fatwa, and when the Bahawalpur state muftis could not arrive at a consensus, he looked beyond the princely state's borders for an answer. Writing to the dar-ul-ifta of the Anjuman-i Mustashar-ul-ʿUlama in Lahore, the sarishtadar called on the expertise he could access beyond the Bahawalpur court as he looked outward (and upward) for input.[24] Along with his request, he summarized the events leading up to the case and included a copy of Muhammad Shah's statement. Although the anjuman did not reprint the full text when it published a reply to the sarrishtadar's inquiry, references to the text and its context provide some insight into the dar-ul-ifta's consultative function here. Like Hyderabad's dar-ul-ifta, the anjuman gave an answer focused on the phrasing of Muhammad Shah's document (he used the future tense) and the motivation behind his legal suit (he wanted marital relations to resume). With statements like "I will leave my wife and will not make a claim," Muhammad Shah's intent to divorce his wife remained hypothetical (*iḥtimālī*), rather than certain (*yaqīnī*). As such, Mufti ʿAbdullah Tonki reasoned, "when there is proof of a couple's marriage but their divorce remains hypothetical, then there can be no doubt that their divorce did not take place." On top of this, Muhammad Shah's suit clearly demonstrated a desire to stay married. Taken with the fact that it was his right to resume marital relations during the waiting period, the mufti urged the court to allow the couple to reconcile—meddling in-laws or no.[25]

It was not uncommon for questions—and cases—to cross jurisdictional boundaries between British India and the princely states or to move from a village council, to a local qazi, to a dar-ul-ifta, to a colonial court, but just as the use of the future tense blurred the lines between the legal intent and legal effect of Muhammad Shah's statement, so too did the travels of questions from one jurisdiction to another blur the lines of legal authority. Where fatwas might have been only consultative and advisory in British India, they could be adjudicative and determinate in a princely state, and where the qazi might have no jurisdiction to decide suits, he could still issue decisions as an arbitrator. Thus, even in British India, where the authority of the state courts may have been hegemonic on paper, in practice, the interplay between formal adjudication, informal advice, and exchanges across fora complicated the compartmentalization of cases. Efforts to define the scope and extent of religious personal law produced an awkward, and at times untenable, separation of religion from the secular state, and the overlap between "secular" legal forms and "religious" legal categories (like Muhammad Shah's iqrar-nama, for instance) made it difficult to separate the substance of religious law from the procedures of the secular courts.

Separating the Qazi's Substance from the Court's Procedure

Separating the wheat of the substance from the chaff of procedure often proved more difficult than it might have originally seemed, as Justice Syed Mahmood (1850–1903) realized when writing opinions from his position on the Allahabad High Court. Syed Mahmood was the youngest son of the illustrious social reformer and "well-wisher of the Raj," Sayyid Ahmad Khan (1817–98), who was also the legislator behind the Kazis' Act (Act XII) of 1880 (see chapter 3). Syed Mahmood grew up in Delhi and Moradabad (where his father was posted with the Indian Civil Service at the time). He studied in Government College (Delhi), Queen's College (Benares), and the University of Calcutta before traveling to England to continue his education at Cambridge University, joining Lincoln's Inn in 1869, and being called to the bar in 1872. He returned to India shortly thereafter and began his legal career as a barrister enrolled at the Allahabad High Court. From there, he went on to receive Lord Lytton's appointment for the position of district and sessions court judge before rising to the ranks of puisne judge at the high court in Allahabad.[26]

Well versed in English law, owing to his training in the United Kingdom, and competent in Persian and Arabic, Syed Mahmood was a well-respected member of the Allahabad bench yet remained an outlier nonetheless. He took an active interest in shaping the interpretation of Muslim personal law not only by authoring his own lengthy, independent opinions in response to cases that came before the court but also by conducting his own research, using original, untranslated sources and including in his written opinions extensive citations and lengthy footnotes in Arabic when necessary.[27] As Alan Guenther writes, "In his use of authoritative works of *fiqh*, he refused to be limited to the two or three sources that had been translated into English and were accepted as the standard sources utilized by the English judges."[28] In fact, as his decision in one particular case from 1885 shows, Syed Mahmood not only took it upon himself to conduct the research he felt was necessary to answer the questions facing the court, but he also corrected and contextualized the references on which his "learned brethren" on the bench relied.[29] By this token, Syed Mahmood used his position on the bench—and later while serving on the Legislative Council for the North-Western Provinces and Awadh—to shape Islamic legal practice "in translation, in legislation, and in adjudication."[30]

The 1885 case in which Syed Mahmood revealed his independent streak began in 1878, when ʿAli Muhammad Khan died intestate. He left behind him as heirs his parents, his wife, two sons, three daughters, and a brother. He also left behind him a debt owed to his son-in-law, ʿAbd-ur-Rahman, husband to his daughter Jafri Begam.[31] No doubt the division of ʿAli Muhammad Khan's property fell under the jurisdiction of Muslim personal law and should have followed Islamic rules of inheritance, yet certain claims regarding unpaid debts complicated what might otherwise have been a simple division of the estate. Rationalizing these competing influences, the courts struggled to disentangle the Islamic devolution of the estate from its other legal encumbrances. Determining which rules applied to which part of the case complicated its status as a personal law dispute.

The basic principles of Islamic inheritance law come from the fourth chapter of the Qurʾan, Surat An-Nisa, which not only lists the family members who are eligible to inherit property but also describes the process for dividing the property among them:

> As for the children, God decrees that the share of the male is equivalent to that of two females. If they consist of women only, and of them more than two, they will get two-thirds of the inheritance; but in case there is one, she will inherit one half. The parents will each inherit a sixth of the estate if it happens that the deceased has

> left a child; but if he has left no children, and his parents are his heirs, then the mother will inherit one-third; but if he has left brothers, the mother will inherit one-sixth after payment of legacies and debts. Of parents and children you do not know who are more useful to you. These are the decrees of God who knows all and is wise. (4:11)[32]

The next verse (4:12) then outlines the division of a wife's property, depending on whether she leaves behind children, parents, or siblings. Evidence from the Hadith (sayings of the Prophet) further supplement these verses, as do centuries of scholarship and commentary on the subject of inheritance. To complicate matters further, Muslims could bequeath up to one-third of their heritable property through wills and other legal instruments, provided these documents were (1) properly executed according to the Indian Contract Act and other rules relating to registration and stamps and (2) issued in accordance with the Hadith and treatises like *Al-Sirajiyyah* (one of the preferred texts on Sunni inheritance law in British India).[33] Needless to say, Islamic inheritance law was a robust field of legal scholarship, bolstered and enhanced by the British East India Company's early interest in property rights and ownership.

As the Qur'an outlined and expert commentaries elaborated, the number of survivors and their relative degrees of kinship determined the distribution of the deceased's estate, which led to complicated forms of division—particularly when the estate included movable and immovable, divisible and indivisible property. Fortunately, Islamic jurists were well versed in calculating these divisions and guiding descendants. They were also, as the exchange between Hyderabad's dar-ul-ifta and Ghulam Ahmad Khan over the timing of Amina Bi's death demonstrated (see chapter 5), able to address other complicating factors, since Islamic inheritance law stipulates that if a descendant passes away before his or her ancestor, the descendant's descendants will not inherit from that ancestor. These principles, grounded in the Qur'an and Hadith, were thus the substance that applied to the division of ʿAli Muhammad Khan's estate. What complicated this case when it came before the Allahabad High Court on appeal, however, was not the division of the estate per se but the handling of a debt held against the estate—and a certain Muslim judge's feeling that the Anglo-Indian courts had yet to address the matter fully.

When the case came before the court on appeal, Syed Mahmood referred it to the full bench for deliberation not necessarily because the case was complicated but because the existing case law was contradictory and incomplete.[34] He wanted to correct the record, particularly when it came to settling the deceased's debts through the estate. The case originated from the claims of one heir, Amir Muhammad Khan, brother to the deceased, who felt his share should be larger than what he had received. In addition to the portion he claimed as a direct inheritance from his brother, he also claimed another portion of the estate indirectly through his parents, Panna Bibi and Ghulam Muhammad, after they passed away.[35] Panna Bibi was the first to pass. Of the 28 portions she received from her son ʿAli Muhammad's estate (which had been divided into 168 shares originally), she passed 21 (three-fourths) of her shares to her other son, Amir Muhammad, and seven to her husband. When her husband then passed away, Amir Muhammad claimed those additional seven shares. There was little to dispute here. Instead, Amir Muhammad's challenge arose from his claims to an additional portion of the estate, which he thought had been unduly wrested from him when the family decided to settle ʿAli Muhammad's debts before assigning portions to his parents (a valid practice recognized under Anglo-Indian and Islamic jurisprudence).

Most of the estate consisted of land in the village of Bakhtiyarpur, and the debts ʿAli Muhammad owed were held by ʿAbd-ur-Rahman, his son-in-law. When the family paid off those debts, it sold a portion of ʿAli Muhammad's lands, shrinking the overall size of the estate and therefore diminishing the amount Amir Muhammad eventually received. Amir Muhammad thought his portion should be bigger, since he was not party to the sale, which went toward the debt repayment that reduced the share he received through his parents. Initially, the lower court sided with him and decreed that the sale-cum-debt-payoff had no right to interfere with his inheritance. Yet his niece Jafri Begam, wife to her father's creditor, disagreed and appealed the ruling. After hearing the appeal, Justices Syed Mahmood and Douglas Straight referred three questions to the full bench for deliberation, which I paraphrase here:

1. Does the estate of a Muslim who dies intestate devolve immediately to his heirs, or is devolution contingent on (and therefore suspended until) the payment of his debts?
2. Does a decree relative to his debts bind the other heirs, who were excluded from the debt settlement?
3. If not, is the (original) plaintiff in this case (i.e., Amir Muhammad) entitled to recover a portion of the property sold to pay the debt

> without recovery of possession being rendered contingent on payment by him of his proportionate share of the ancestor's debts for which the decree was passed, and in satisfaction whereof the sale took place?[36]

In other words, the final question probed, should Amir Muhammad receive a larger portion of the estate, even though he played no role in settling the estate's debts? When it came time to answer the questions before them in February 1885, the judges agreed that shares devolved immediately but did not agree with Amir Muhammad's claim to additional shares. All the heirs should have been liable for the repayment of the deceased's debts, even if the settlement of that debt took place through a court decree to which Amir Muhammad was not party. Although Justice Mahmood "agree[d] generally" with his colleagues' opinion, he had more to say on the matter and "reserved the reason of [his] judgement" for a separate opinion.[37]

A month later, Syed Mahmood found the time to write his twenty-page opinion on the case, and commenced not by criticizing his fellow judges for their misinterpretation of the law but by taking issue with the "paucity" of sources available to them.[38] He decried the lack of authoritative information on the matter, as existing sources were "either incomprehensive [*sic*] compilations or abbreviated translations, and, in some cases, translations of translations," and lamented the fact that "the language of the highest Courts in India is not the language of the people, and consequently the veast [*sic*] majority of advocates . . . are not likely to refer to the original Arabic authorities."[39] His complaints were not too dissimilar from ones British East India Company employees had voiced a century earlier. After weighing the available evidence and consulting "original authorities" on the first matter, he thus supported his decision regarding an estate's immediate devolution by including footnotes in Arabic.[40] Yet when it came time to address the second and third questions in the case, Syed Mahmood chose another approach: "I do not consider it necessary to cite the original texts which go to maintain these propositions [regarding the debt repayment suit], because I am satisfied that these rules of law are provisions which go only to the remedy . . . being matters purely of procedure as to array of parties, production of evidence, *res judicata*, and review of judgment, &c."[41] In other words, despite his ability to assess and evaluate relevant works of jurisprudence "by citing original authorities," he concluded that the question had more to do with legal procedure than with substance. Rejecting "certain passages of the Hedaya [*Hidāya*]" that clarified the distinction between contested and consensual suits for the recovery of debts, Syed Mahmood argued "those passages [from the *Hidaya* and other texts] lay down rules of *procedure* which are not binding upon us, [and] which are in many important respects inconsistent with the rules of the Civil Procedure Code."[42] For him, the *Hidaya* had little to offer about the outcome of the dispute, so the court should defer to Anglo-Indian rules of procedure here: "I would reject the rules of the [Islamic] Law of Procedure in connection with the binding effect of decrees upon absent heirs," Syed Mahmood concluded, siding with the rest of the bench in his answer to the second question. Using his authority as the relative expert on the bench, he advocated a strict separation of substance and procedure, giving precedence to the procedures of British Indian law and undermining the substantive contributions of Islamic jurisprudence accordingly.[43] The fact that procedure could affect substance was apparently lost on him.[44]

If the difference between substance and procedure determined Syed Mahmood's answer to the second question, his answer to the third question took an even bigger departure from the original status of the case. Here, he rejected engagement with Islamic legal sources wholesale, opting instead to frame the question in relation to "the general principles of equity." Citing Anglo-Indian case law alongside several extracts from American jurist Joseph Story's by then classic *Commentaries on Equity Jurisprudence* (1835–36), Syed Mahmood argued that it would only be equitable for the original plaintiff (Amir Muhammad) to "obtain a decree for possession of his share" if that decree were "rendered contingent upon payment by him of such proportion . . . as would represent his proportionate share of the liability to the ancestor's debts liquidated by the proceeds of the auction-sale."[45] That is, Amir Muhammad should only receive a larger share of the estate if he also made a proportional contribution to repayment of the estate's debts; the heirs were jointly liable for repayment of the deceased's debts.

As someone competent in Islamic and English legal principles, Syed Mahmood's decision to make this case one of equity rather than of Muslim personal law was incongruous with the attention he directed toward "original" Arabic sources at the beginning of his judgment. Needless to say, as the son of a prominent social reformer, he was also invested in the project of Anglo-Indian legal pluralism, and he apparently saw no conflict in the court's ability to answer questions of Islamic legal substance following Anglo-Indian legal procedure. In fact, he even criticized his fellow justices for failing to differentiate between the two aspects. Justice W. Markby, whose minority opinion in *Assamathem Nessa Bibi v. Roy Lutchmeeput Singh* influenced the court's decision in this case, for instance, made the mistake of relying on passages from the *Hidaya* that "relate[d], not to substantive law, but to procedure, and in particular to the duties of the Cazi [*qāẓī*]," as quoted in the second epigraph.[46] It was not the court's responsibility to follow the procedures of the qazi, Syed Mahmood suggested, but to answer questions of law.

Syed Mahmood's decision to write a separate opinion may have been the product of his unique perspective, but he was not the only justice to do so. Syed Ameer Ali and Badruddin Tyabji, two equally prominent Indian Muslim barristers and judges, also functioned as intermediaries, translating their cultural knowledge about Islam and the Muslim communities they represented into judicial decisions and legal textbooks.[47] Nor was the practice of engaging with Islamic legal authorities restricted to Muslim judges. Justice F. C. O. Beaman, for instance, wrote a lengthy opinion in one case not only to clarify the distinction between the concept of gifts in Islamic and English law but also to explain the subtle distinction between a simple gift (*hiba*) and a gift for consideration (*hiba bi'l ʿiwaẓ*).[48] Yet judicial musings over the meaning of technical terms and their application for particular disputes were perhaps less transformative than the casual manner in which British India's judges made themselves synonymous with Islamic legal practitioners.[49] Syed Mahmood's decision in *Jafri Begam* was unique not only for deciding the final question according to the principles of equity jurisprudence but also for severing Islamic legal practice from Anglo-Indian legal procedure so concretely. More typically, justices overlooked the distinction between substance and procedure, letting themselves—or their colleagues on the bench—stand in for the qazi when deciding cases that fell under Muslim personal law. These substitutions not only affected decisions in British Indian courtrooms but also raised questions about the authority of Islamic legal actors outside the courts.

In some cases, like *Moosa Adam Patel v. Ismail Moosa* (1909), the term "judge" would simply replace the term "qazi," which allowed the former to take the place of the latter without further comment.[50] In others, the court explicitly framed its action in relation to the qazi's role: to appoint a trustee in *Ramzan Mistri and Ors. v. Haji Zahur Hossein*, Justices H. Holmwood and E. P. Chapman reasoned that Anglo-Muslim law was "perfectly clear that the power of appointment of mutwalli [*mutawallī*; trustee] lies in the first place with the wakif [*wāqif*; testator], on the death of the wakif it lies with his executors and on the failure of executors the appointment rests solely with the Kazi or District Judge under our present system."[51] Dozens of cases followed this pattern, referring to the "kazi or judge," "the District Judge as Kazi," "the ordinary Courts having taken the place of Kazis," "the place of the Kazi . . . now taken by the Court," "the Court which represents the power of the Kazi," "the civil court . . . vested . . . with the powers exercised by the Kazi under the Mahomedan regime," "the powers of the Kazi . . . ordinarily exercised by the District Judge," "the Kazi's power" now "vested in the Court," or "the district Judge who takes the place of the Kazi in Muhammadan Law."[52] Using these terms interchangeably—that is, defining "qazi" in different contexts as "judge," "district magistrate," or "district judge"—the courts operated as if procedure had no effect on the substance or outcome of a case. It was a routine substitution that provoked little comment.

Yet even with district judges taking the qazi's place, it was not always clear that Muslim personal law would apply when cases came before the court. In *Srimutty Jamila Khatun v. Abdul Jalil Meah and Another*, Judges T. W. Richardson and H. Walmsley argued that the court could not address the petitioner's request to be appointed mutawalli because even though "it may well be conceded that the District Judge has the powers of Kazi . . . the endowment in the present case is admittedly a public endowment" and was subject not to the law of Muslim endowments but to Section 92 of the Civil Procedure Code (relating to public trusts).[53] A few years later, however, the Calcutta High Court came to the opposite conclusion in *Mohiuddin Chowdhury v. Aminuddin Chowdhury and Ors.*, arguing that Section 92 had no bearing on that case (again involving the appointment of a trustee) because "the District Judge was carrying out a duty imposed upon him by the founder" of the trust.[54] Here instead, Richardson reasoned that the appointment was a matter of administration and that "the present case . . . raises . . . no such question as is contemplated by Section 92 of the [Civil Procedure] Code."[55]

Despite recognizing endowments as a matter of religious personal law, judicial decision-making was, as Justice L. P. E. Pugh laid out a decade earlier in *In Re: Halima Khatun v. Unknown*, ambiguous at best, given the "conflicting decisions as to the power of the Court."[56] Overlaps between the English law of trusts, Anglo-Indian statutes like the Indian Trustees' and the Trustees' and Mortgagees' Powers Acts of 1866, and the "native substantive laws" relating to trusts and endowments clouded the courts' ability to act consistently.[57] Rejecting the application before him, Pugh concluded that the question was "really one of procedure." For him, framing the question as "purely a matter of procedure" made Anglo-Indian law paramount: "The procedure of this Court is regulated by its own Orders and Rules and the

Code of Civil Procedure, and even, when administering Mahomedan law, this Court does not vary its practice with regard to Mahomedan cases."[58] Others, like Justice Richardson, took the matter one step further, arguing that appointing a mutawalli was not a judicial matter but one "of an administrative character."[59] By this token, as cases moved between the lower and appellate courts, district judges and high court justices alike not only claimed the qazi's authority for themselves but also diminished the extent to which personal law applied in each case.

Justices like Richardson, Beaman, Markby, and Mahmood wrote opinions that reconfigured judicial expectations not necessarily because they had an activist interest in rewriting Anglo-Muslim law but because plaintiffs brought their complaints to court and appealed their cases to the regional high courts and Privy Council in London when they disagreed with the lower courts' decisions.[60] Such appeals enabled the justices to author independent decisions, reevaluate earlier precedents, compile evidence from original sources, and ultimately influence subsequent outcomes. Yet appealing unfavorable decisions was not the only way to challenge the courts' interpretation of Muslim personal law. For many ordinary Muslims, local councils, informal inquiries, and advisory opinions not only provided an accessible means to address legal complaints but also offered responsive and accessible outlets for their uncertainty about how to bridge the divide between Islamic law and legal adjudication in British India.

As the courts incrementally redefined Muslim personal law through the separation of substance, procedure, and administration, they sparked a number of contests and debates beyond the courtroom. In these debates Muslim litigants, those contemplating litigation, and those affected by litigation questioned the courts' ability to decide cases in accordance with Islamic jurisprudence. They also questioned their ability as Muslims to accept the courts' decisions as legally valid. Muftis across British India (and the princely states) responded to fatwa requests on these and other matters, drawing their expertise in Islamic jurisprudence into conversation with their understanding of the Anglo-Indian legal system. In these exchanges, *mustaftīs* (fatwa seekers) expressed concerns about the moral—if not legal—implications of following the courts' decrees and brought their interests in the private life of religious law into the public framework of courtroom adjudication. They made everyday Islamic law not by accepting the separation of substance from procedure nor by acknowledging the authority of Anglo-Indian law over some aspects of life and Muslim personal law over others but by bringing the two together in their approach and response to formal and informal legal actions.

Judges, Legislators, and Jurists

Across successive phases of policy and practice, the courts may have decided that Anglo-Indian procedure and British-trained judges could replace Islamic legal experts, but Muslim jurists—and the ordinary individuals who sought their counsel—were less convinced by this straightforward substitution. In their exchanges, "qazi" and "judge" were decidedly not synonymous. Instead, the terms referred to two distinct entities: the *qāẓī*, who was defined by Islamic jurisprudence, and the *jaj*, who worked in the British Indian courts. For jurists like Kifayatullah, a *jaj* would only count as a qazi if he were Muslim, had knowledge of Islamic jurisprudence, and was competent to resolve a suit. Such qualifications did not deny the courts' authority to hear cases or to settle disputes, but they did raise questions about the religio-ethical implications of adhering to court decrees. If litigants simply followed the ruling, were they doing all that was required of them as Muslims? A fine line separated legitimate decisions from illegitimate actions, and muftis took great pains to delineate the distinction clearly. Fleshing out the limits and powers of the law court's authority as qazi and the qazi's authority as court called on the mufti's ability to navigate the subtext of the questions he received.

Thus, for jurists like Kifayatullah, clarifying these distinctions was an ongoing struggle. In response to a question about who could grant a couple's judicial separation (*tafrīq*), he began by affirming the court's competence: "Yes, absolutely, Muslim judges and *munṣif*s [subordinate judges] in the English [*angrēzī*] courts could act as appointed, shariʿa qazis [*qāʾim maqām qāẓī, sharʿī kē*]." They could settle disputes related to Muslims' personal legal matters (*muʿāmalāt-i makẖṣūṣa-yi ahl-i Islām*) in accordance with shariʿa because the government (*ḥukūmat*) gave them the authority (*ikẖtiyār*) to do so.[61] Pegging the judge's status as qazi to his ruling in accordance with shariʿa (*sharʿiya kē muwāfiq faiṣala*), Kifayatullah defined the judge as qazi tautologically. A ruling by a Muslim judge was not a shariʿa ruling by default, he seemed to suggest.[62] What is more, "if a Muslim judge, arbitrator [*ḥakama*], or local council [*panchāyat, ṣāliṣ*] is not familiar with the matter, then they must seek guidance from a mufti or an *ʿālim* [scholar] before deciding," he cautioned in another fatwa.[63]

Questions like these arose as individuals probed the authority and ability of the British Indian courts, but the issue went both ways. With British and Hindu judges appointed to hear Muslim personal law cases and colonial policy expressing renewed interest in community adjudication, curious litigants wondered whether one possible solution was to establish separate councils. Similar to the community qazis discussed in chapter 1, these officiants would be chosen by the people to hear their cases and settle their disputes. The mufti was hesitant to accept this approach because, in his mind, the power to appoint a qazi lay not with the people but with the ruler (*bādshāh*) and the *imām* (prayer leader).[64] If "people themselves appoint a qazi, he will not be a qazi because . . . he will not have the authority or power to enforce his orders" (*lōg agar k̲h̲ẉud qāẓī muqarrar kar lain̲, tō voh qāẓī na hōgā kyōn̲ke [us] kō tanfīẕ-i aḥkām kā ik̲h̲tiyār aur qudrat na hōgī*), he reasoned.[65] Without the ability to enforce his decisions—and without the backing of the state—a community-appointed "qazi" was not a qazi. Furthermore, even though some jurists argued that any *ʿālim* could act as qazi, Kifayatullah, for one, did not buy this argument.[66] In British India, "the government gave the ʿulama no such authority" (*gōvarnmanṭ kī ṭ̤araf sē, ʿulamāʾ kō kōʾī ik̲h̲tiyār nahīn̲ diyā gayā*), and none of their decisions would be valid (*un kā kōʾī faiṣla muʿtabar nahīn̲*).[67] In other words, just like a British-trained judge could not simply assume the qazi's position unless he was Muslim and knew the relevant doctrine, a self-appointed community qazi could not be a judicial qazi because the government had not granted him the right to make decisions, nor would it uphold them.

Knowing that the qazis' judicial powers had been supplanted by the Anglo-Indian courts was one thing, but expressing satisfaction with the courts' decisions was something else altogether. In fact, litigants frequently called on local muftis' expertise to approve, ameliorate, or sidestep courtroom decisions. Yet rather than undermine the courts' rulings outright, these inquiries instead served to bring courtroom litigation in line with stricter, and more "authentic," interpretations of Islamic law.[68] They also added to the plurality of legal orders active in British India.[69] For some cases, individuals simply wondered how to square court decrees with Islamic law. When the trustees of a mosque in Chhota Shimla took a dispute to court, the court ordered that a formal committee take charge and entrust the mosque's funds to a bank. Incidentally, the dispute also made the mosque subject to government oversight, meaning the committee was now also responsible for paying taxes (land and water). The committee complied with the decree and placed the mosque's funds in an interest-earning account at

Lloyd's Bank but wondered how to square judicial compliance with prohibitions against taking interest (*sūd*).[70] Kifayatullah's brief response offered a compromise: use the interest from the bank account to pay the taxes. The solution was not perfect, but it would meet the demands of the court decree without threatening the moral authority of the mosque (or its committee members). The mufti's recommendation provided an adequate solution.

Court decrees presented similar quandaries for individuals, too. In 1925 Shaukat ʿAli loaned thirty thousand rupees to an unnamed Hindu borrower. When the debtor did not return the money, the dispute went to court and, in 1928, the lender won his case. Shortly thereafter, the debtor appealed the decision, and the dispute eventually reached the high court.[71] Shaukat ʿAli's case was strong, but after overcoming multiple hurdles (*mutaʿaddid marāḥil ṭai karnē kē baʿd*), he won the appeal. By that time, the original debt had skyrocketed to the astounding sum of eighty-two thousand rupees, according to the court's calculation. Shaukat ʿAli wondered whether accepting the court-decreed interest (*sūd lēnā*) was permissible or not (*jāʾiz hai yā nahīn̲*), whether there was any sin (*ḥaraj*) in spending that money, and how the amount should be calculated for his annual zakat (alms).[72] Kifayatullah's fatwa confirmed Shaukat ʿAli's concerns about accepting the interest (even from a Hindu) but added that he could rightfully take the original amount along with the amount he spent on court fees (*muqaddama bāzī kē maṣārif-i wāqiʿa*)—both of which should then be included in his calculation of zakat.

Shaukat ʿAli found this answer unsatisfying and sent a follow-up to the mufti: "I recall [*mujhē yād paṛtā hai*] seeing in a past issue of the *Ak̲h̲bār-i Zamzam* one of Sir's [*janāb kē*; meaning your] fatwas on this subject, which [said that] in *dār-ul-ḥarb*, it is permissible to take *sūd* from non-Muslims [*g̲h̲air Muslim*]. Obviously, I must have misunderstood. Nevertheless, please explain [*farmāʾiyē*] whether interest from non-Muslims should be relinquished and whether at a minimum it is still not permissible to take the money and to spend it on good works."[73] Kifayatullah could not recall this particular fatwa, published in the newspaper Shaukat ʿAli cited, but he did admit that in some cases, he acknowledged the permissibility of accepting interest owing to British India's status as dar-ul-harb (abode of war; i.e., non-Muslim territory).[74] Yet two factors complicated Shaukat ʿAli's situation. First, the payment of interest was not voluntary. The Hindu debtor was being forced by the court to pay the amount. Therefore, Shaukat ʿAli should exhibit caution. Second, the ʿulama were not unanimous when it came to designating India dar-ul-harb; therefore, the mustafti should remain cautious when it came to demanding interest. As a consolation, however, the mufti conceded that if the lender and his debtor could come to a private settlement, say seventy thousand rupees instead of the eighty-two thousand decreed by the court, he could accept the payment. For Kifayatullah, a private agreement was more equitable than a court-decreed award.

In criminal cases, too, individuals wondered how the courts' punishments squared with Islamic remedies.[75] In 1933 a certain Sayyid Shāh Maḥmūd asked Kifayatullah whether an innocent (*bē gunāh*) man who had been convicted of murder under the Indian Penal Code and sentenced to serve seven to ten years in prison would be absolved of his crime according to shariʿa without paying blood money to the family of the victim.[76] Kifayatullah's assistant offered the first response: If the person actually committed the crime, the family of the victim had the right to claim "retribution" (*qiṣāṣ*) or "compensation" (*diyat*) in exchange for their loss (*k̲h̲ūn kā muʿāwaẓa*). Jail time would not absolve him.[77] Kifayatullah answered next: Guilty verdicts in the courts of British India, provided under the Indian Penal Code, were not equivalent to those produced by shariʿa courts (*bā-qāʿaida sharʿī ʿadālat*). The family could only demand blood money if the defendant confessed (*k̲h̲wud qarār karē*) or if his guilt was proved with proper shariʿa evidence (*shahādat-i sharʿīya* [*sic*] *sē*). Before that, people (*ʿāmm Musulmān*) should not refer to him as a murderer, nor should individuals pursue additional compensatory actions against him.[78] The man may have been found guilty in the British Indian courtroom, but until he had been found guilty in a shariʿa court, the community had no right to claim additional payment. Thus, in contrast to the previous example, Kifayatullah cautioned against taking any out-of-court action. While both legal systems regarded *qatl* (murder, homicide) as a serious transgression, they employed different types of evidence and argumentation; a guilty verdict in one system did not make a man a guilty in the other.[79] Whether to shield the defendant from community retribution or to distinguish between Anglo-Indian justice and Islamic law and procedure, Kifayatullah allowed the court's decision to suffice here. After all, the mustafti said the man was innocent.

Mosques and murder were not the only contexts in which Muslim litigants brought complaints about the courts to nonstate experts. Ordinary Muslims also questioned the courts' rulings in personal matters and did so frequently. While living in Port Blair, ʿAbd-ul-Aḥad married a young woman, pledging to pay her five thousand rupees as *mahr* (dower). At the time, he was unemployed and did not have the means to pay, but his in-laws assured him that he need only pledge that amount for display (*dikhāvē kē liyē*), and afterward, his wife would forgive the dower debt. Sure enough, three or four months into the marriage, the wife went before the local council (*panch*) and forgave the mahr debt. She also produced a signed statement, onto which the document writer (*ʿarẓī-nawīs*) affixed a "one-anna ticket." ʿAbd-ul-Ahad thought he was in the clear.[80]

The in-laws chafed at his wife's decision to forgive the debt and snatched her one day while he was at work. She returned three years later, and upon her return, ʿAbd-ul-Ahad gave her a divorce owing to her "conniving behavior" (*bad-chāl chalan*). Shortly thereafter, the mahr debt came back to haunt him. His wife demanded payment, and to make matters worse, she also claimed that she had been a minor when she was forced to forgive the marriage debt. ʿAbd-ul-Ahad, who by now had misplaced the deed of forgiveness, brought forth the five members of the council as witnesses. The court rejected his ex-wife's claim about being a minor, accepted the witnesses' testimony, and decided in ʿAbd-ul-Ahad's favor. The family appealed, and the appellate court rejected the original decree. ʿAbd-ul-Ahad appealed the appeal, taking the case to the high court, where again the court concluded that the wife was not a minor and had forgiven the debt voluntarily. It looked like ʿAbd-ul-Ahad was about to win until the court came to the particularities of the debt forgiveness: Under the Indian Contract Act, the court asserted, forgiveness of the mahr debt required a signed contract, executed on five-rupee stamp paper.[81] Without such written documentation, the court could not dismiss the wife's complaint and thus ordered ʿAbd-ul-Ahad to pay the original five-thousand-rupee sum. With nowhere else to turn, ʿAbd-ul-Ahad reached out to Kifayatullah.[82]

This was not ʿAbd-ul-Ahad's first fatwa request. He had requested a fatwa from Kifayatullah earlier in the process and had been pleased with the mufti's confirmation that a written document was not necessary to forgive a mahr debt. Again, the mufti attempted to ameliorate the mustafti's woes: Indeed, written documentation was not required to forgive a dower debt, he began. The husband simply had to provide adequate proof of the wife's forgiveness—such as testimony from the original council. However, "the English courts [*angrēzī ʿadālat*] make demands according to their rules."[83] These rules, the mufti emphasized, did not square with Islamic jurisprudence, so "it is up to all of the people of this nation [*tamām ahl-i mulk*] to change the law . . . [so] that when reputable witnesses provide evidence of [the debt's] forgiveness, the courts will issue a decree to that effect." Acknowledging that a single act of defiance would do little good, Kifayatullah pledged to have the Jamʿiyat-ul-ʿUlama-yi Hind take up the matter "where ever they can, and as far as they can."[84]

Across these examples, Kifayatullah provided the fatwa seekers with advice in relation to the court's procedures and determinations. He provided the mosque committee with a reasonable compromise, cautioned Shaukat ʿAli not to claim the court's interest-heavy settlement for himself, warned community members not to seek retribution unless they could prove guilt according to (stricter) Islamic rules of evidence, and urged ʿAbd-ul-Ahad to follow the law now but to work for its revision in the future. Thus, accepting or rejecting the courts' authority was not an all-or-nothing proposition. Each case required cautious deliberation and careful consideration. Nor was Islamic jurisprudence confined to matters of "personal law." Debts, contracts, criminal proceedings, and other legal issues also required Islamic legal expertise, and in the absence of a better legal system, the mufti's informal guidance became a well-trod path for pursuing these aims. Recognizing the authority—and the limitations—of the colonial courtroom, muftis and mustaftis made everyday Islamic law part of British India's plural legal landscape, complicating the neat separation of substance and procedure, and rejecting the limited application of Islamic jurisprudence to matters of family and religion.

Conclusion

The question of jurisdiction in British India was one that felt straightforward but never was. Rather than producing a clear response to questions of jurisdiction, judges and jurists wavered about the types of cases that belonged in each forum and the extent to which different bodies of law obtained in each. To answer questions about the fit for each case, judges and jurists established equivalencies and analogies between qazis in the past and magistrates and judges in the present and drew on legal sources from both traditions. Yet as disputes over inheritance, endowments, and gifts persisted, the courts' methods tended to produce more, rather than less, confusion. For all the scholarly hullabaloo over the effects of codification and precedent (*stare decisis*), the courts left ample room for litigants (and jurists) to maneuver—and maneuver they did.

As high court judges hemmed and hawed over technical terms to address the finer points of jurisprudence, they laid bare the weaknesses of the state's legal apparatus and its inability to handle not only the run-of-the-mill problems of everyday life but also the nuances of the personal laws it vowed to preserve and protect. Fatwa seekers like ʿAbd-us-Salam, whose question about the effective jurisdiction of the local council opened this chapter, exploited gaps in authority created by the courts' inadequacies and made strong arguments for other types of legal action. Although the expert he called on was not willing to overrule the courts' authority to decide cases, muftis like Kifayatullah nonetheless admitted that a degree of ambiguity existed in the wording of the government's pledge to respect religious personal law and its simultaneous refusal to authorize the proper functionaries (namely qazis) to perform that work.

Muftis were not the only ones interested in these debates. Justices in the high court engaged in them as well, moving issues into and out of Muslim personal law not always on a case-by-case basis but sometimes on a point-by-point basis, as Syed Mahmood's opinion in *Jafri Begam* shows. These back-and-forth debates not only weakened the authority of the courts but also demonstrated that even within the Anglo-Indian legal system, there was room to maneuver, and while muftis tended to uphold the courts' authority to resolve legal disputes, they nonetheless conceded that in many cases, the courts were less than perfect. Continuing with the theme of back-and-forth, the next chapter examines the role muftis played in guiding litigants and those affected by litigation through various forms of legal action within, across, and between legal fora to explain what legal uncertainty meant for ordinary individuals trying to get their lives back on track.

8 Whose Law Is It, Anyway?

Navigating Legal Paths in Late Colonial Society

Ab mēra k̲h̲ayāl hai ke kisī sē ʿaqd kar lūn̲.

—Maryam Bi, expressing her desire to remarry, 1950

Looking at Life through Law

By the time Maryam Bī traveled to Hyderabad in 1950, she had run out of options.[1] Her husband was "missing" (*lā pata*), and she had not heard anything from him for the last "two, or two and a half years."[2] He had sent no letters, telegrams, or messages to explain his whereabouts. To put it another way, he was, in legal terms, *mafqūd-ul-k̲h̲abar*, or "vanished without a trace." For a woman with little access to employment outside the home and dependent on the income and financial support of her husband, there was not much Maryam Bi could do. For the past couple of years, she had been living in her father's home, where she received support from him, but his eyesight was now failing, and as a result, his employment opportunities were also diminishing. It was time for Maryam Bi to make a change, so she traveled to Hyderabad to do just that by bringing her situation before the *dār-ul-iftāʾ* (fatwa institute) of the erstwhile princely state.[3]

Maryam Bi's situation was hardly unique. By the middle of the twentieth century, ordinary Muslims across the subcontinent had grown accustomed to presenting their moral, ethical, and legal dilemmas before well-known scholars and jurists. Nor was it strange for her to approach the office that had once been the official dar-ul-ifta for a state that no longer existed. Many such institutions continued to operate after independence with little or no change, and the dar-ul-ifta of princely Hyderabad received a steady stream of fatwa requests up to 1950, when the dar-ul-ifta of the Madrasa Jamiʿa Nizamiya took over as Hyderabad's premier institute for issuing fatwas.[4] Yet in this particular moment, there was something unique about Maryam Bi's case that spoke not to the finality of British rule on the subcontinent but instead to the ongoing entanglements of religious law, everyday life, and the regulatory structures of the postcolonial state. Arising as it did out of a peculiar combination of institutional, political, and personal circumstances, Maryam Bi's case was legally straightforward but circumstantially complex.

Unlike the fatwa questions other muftis received in the first half of the twentieth century, Maryam Bi's request was not so much aimed at picking the muftis' brains over legal puzzles as it was geared toward the institute's ability to provide legal advice and potential intercession on her behalf. The language of her plea mirrors this intent, commencing not as a question but as a supplication: "The petitioner submits" (*ba-ʿarẓ mī rasānad*), her scribe wrote across the top of the page, before introducing her request, her "guẕārish."[5] The petition gives no pretext about seeking the expert's command (*kyā farmāte hain̲*), nor does it wonder how the scholars of the faith (*ʿulamāʾ-yi dīn*) might offer guidance for the present scenario (*is masʾalē main̲*).[6] Instead, the transcript recounts the simple story of a woman whose husband got caught up in the police action at the end of the nizam's reign and never returned home.

Maryam Bi recounts her tale in plain prose. Her husband (*mērē shauhar*) had been missing "since the time of the Raẓākārs' [action]" (*raẓākārōn̲ kē zamānē sē*), and she had heard nothing of or from him since then.[7] That was two years ago, and as she was a self-described "parda nashīn" (sitting in seclusion) woman who did not work outside the house, her husband's two-year absence made her worry-stricken (*muṣībat zada*) and worthless, like all the other helpless fugitives (*muhājirīn*) flocking to the city from their districts (*aẓlāʿ sē*).[8] With her parents' aging fragility and her father's failing eyesight, she had neither food to fill her stomach (*pēṭ bhar*) nor clothing to cover her body (*tan*). She and her parents "endured every kind of difficulty from every direction" (*har aik bātōn̲ sē aur har ṭaraḥ sē muṣībat*). She wanted to remedy the situation the only way she knew how: through remarriage to a second husband. Doing so, however, required permission—permission that only a valid legal authority could grant. To that end, she approached the dar-ul-ifta.

What Maryam Bi colloquially cites as the "Razakars' time" refers to several months of violence and instability across Hyderabad State that most textbooks describe as the "police action" Operation Polo. Independence and Partition in August 1947 created the new states of India and Pakistan (with the latter further divided into West Pakistan and East Pakistan, now Bangladesh) but left the fate of several princely states uncertain.[9] Many of the smaller princely states had no option but to join the new, independent nations, but Hyderabad and Kashmir covered enough territory to resist forcible integration—at least for a while. Led by Syed Qasim Razvi, the Razakar militia (initially formed as the nizam's private police force) rejected Hyderabad's accession to India. To them, Hyderabad was a characteristically Muslim territory, and they wanted, at the very least, to see the princely dominion join the Muslim-majority Pakistani state, rather than the Hindu-majority Indian state.[10] In the months leading up to Operation Polo, the Razakars took up arms, attacking villages in the western part of Hyderabad State in an effort to prevent the Indian military from claiming de facto control of the territory.[11] The disturbances cut off mail services, constrained supply transports, and made travel through the state so difficult that the Indian army stepped in to escort convoys of goods.[12] The forces threatened trains and travelers into and out of Bombay, and as the violence continued, villages around the edges of the nizam's dominions began to declare independence and to self-accede to India.[13] The government of India cited over three hundred incidents of violence in the lead-up to its invasion of the prince's territory. In the end, the ragtag militiamen were no match for the Indian army, but the political maneuvering and disordered violence that surrounded the Razakars' action tied the circumstances of Maryam Bi's missing husband to the contested origins of Hyderabad's place in the Indian nation. Many of the Razakars who participated in the raids and skirmishes were arrested and put in jail. Others perished. But two years after Operation Polo ended, the whereabouts of Maryam Bi's husband remained unknown.

The end of British rule marked a moment of profound change in the political history of the subcontinent. No doubt, colonial rule was a period of tremendous rupture, characterized by a break with the past and the advent of global modernity, tinged by the racial and economic inequalities of foreign rule. To deny these ruptures would do a disservice to those who lived through—or continue to live with the legacies of—this subjugation. At the same time, it would be equally irresponsible to overlook the continuities. Laws that passed in British India remained on the books in independent India. The ad hoc administration and appointment of qazis continued into the post-1947 period; the dictates and expectations of the Muslim Personal Law (Shariat) Application Act of 1937 remained in place—and even inspired offspring in West Pakistan.[14] The confusing array of textbooks, statutory interventions, and case-law precedents remained in effect, allowing judges to draw from earlier citations or to reason independently from original sources. The codes of civil and criminal procedure, the Indian Penal Code, and the unsystematic additions and accretions to these acts continued to provide the backbone for the legal system. Stamp paper and its accompanying fees continued to operate (and have only grown since independence).[15] In short, for all that changed with independence, much remained the same.

What is more, for women like Maryam Bi, it was not altogether apparent what was different. Certainly, the political changes that accompanied the drafting and adoption of the Indian Constitution and its guarantees of "equality of status and of opportunity" could not undo centuries of gendered inequality, nor did the introduction of postcolonial industrial and economic development create a wellspring of employment opportunities for women like Maryam Bi who were accustomed to working at home.[16] Yet the new nation, filled with promise and potential, should have been able to provide Maryam Bi with some remedy. After all, the nation was, at least in part, responsible for her husband's disappearance.

Rather than think about legal history on the subcontinent as one bounded by the momentous landmarks of political history and the subsequent triumphs of postindependence, constitutional lawmaking, the experiences of ordinary individuals like Maryam Bi push historians to consider not only what remained the same but also what historical moments felt like for those who were less fortunate, for whom independence did not bring triumph but instead brought personal tragedy, and whose personal tragedies did not fit within the recognized traumas of partition and transborder migratory violence.[17] Understanding these experiences as part of the subcontinent's larger legal history requires reading "law" with a different lens and thinking about legal conflict (and resolution) as affected but not necessarily bounded by legislation and litigation. Maryam Bi's tale is but one of many that could occupy this space.

Everyday Advice and the Making (and Unmaking) of Islamic Legal Categories

Personal crises like missing husbands and lack of resources were not the only ones that brought ordinary Muslims to the dar-ul-ifta. The making of everyday Islamic law necessitated that these institutions and their experts have the capacity, ability, and willingness to respond to requests about everything from religious rituals to employment, contracts, compensation, sales, banking, finance, construction, agriculture, trade, migration, civic associations, voting, politics, and so on. In most cases, these requests were minimal, laying out the situation in stark terms and asking the jurist for a response "according to Islamic law."[18] In other cases, disputes were ongoing, problems unresolved, and the conflict between the rules and regulations of the state and the capacities and capabilities of the individual particularly entangled.[19] In these cases, muftis responded not only in accordance with shariʿa but also in relation to the law of the land (*qānūn*), the specific political context, and the legal landscape that Muslim litigants would navigate to resolve their disputes.[20] Through the regular and repeated exchange of questions and answers, ordinary Muslims placed everyday life in relation to Islamic law and made Islamic law apply to their ordinary, everyday affairs. The interplay between the two, between private morality and public life, between Islamic guidance and state law, not only disrupted the compartmentalization of personal law but also created a pluralistic and multivocal legal landscape that continues to operate today.

Questions about employment and profession demonstrate the evolving scope of these concerns, as private religious questions spilled out into the public labor market.[21] Muslim marriage registers (discussed in chapter 6) provide some evidence of these changes, as labels like "student" and "pensioner" filled the box for *pesha* (vocation, profession). Rather than referring to *who* one was, this term (*pesha*) now referred to *what* one did. Recognizing employment as occupation, rather than identity, muftis fielded various questions: Was it permissible for a Muslim to work as a "subinspector," given that subinspectors collected debts and recorded accumulated interest (*sūd*)?[22] Was it acceptable to work as a *taḥṣīldār* (revenue collector) when the job required following rules other than those of Allah?[23] Others wondered more earnestly about the possibility of transforming religious service (e.g., reading marriages, reciting the call to prayer, giving Qurʾan lessons, or slaughtering animals) into paid labor.[24] Was it permissible to take wages for this work? What about compensation for other forms of immaterial labor, such as working as a storyteller or performer?[25] Questions about employment, profession, and compensation demonstrate some of the ways fatwa seekers blurred the lines between religion, identity, and public life.

For those who sought fatwas on these topics, the idea that "religion" only applied to one's confessional belief or ritual practice did not make sense. Being Muslim was not something one turned on or off, on a particular day, at a particular time, or in a particular place; it applied to all aspects of life and extended beyond those areas encapsulated in secular concepts like "Muslim personal law." Engagement with legal questions that blurred these distinctions also reflected growing awareness of the state's involvement in and regulation of everyday life. Petitioners were not simply taking the threads of nineteenth-century Islamic revival and dressing up their everyday lives in Islamic clothing (though clothing itself came up in their questions). Instead, they were trying to understand how to live in accordance with state law without forsaking God's. Contrary to secularists, who believe the separation of church and state or religion and politics is possible, these fatwa seekers saw law and religion not as incompatible but as intertwined, and they called on Islamic legal experts to explain those intersections.[26] Using the avenues of informal inquiry available to them through postcards, letters, and telegrams, these individuals stretched the canvas of Islamic legal practice from the personal, to the professional, to the political, making and remaking the substance of everyday Islamic law in conjunction with their daily routines and ordinary activities. Despite the colonial state's repeated attempts to limit Islamic law to a subset of "personal" legal matters, such limitations were meaningless for the ordinary individuals who sought fatwas and the muftis who provided them.

Reconfiguring the Mufti in Relation to "Law"

Yet Muslims' desires to connect everyday life to religion in ways that exceeded the state's interpretation of religious personal law are not a sign of separatism or extralegality.[27] Instead, the questions they posed and the answers muftis provided reveal an overwhelming desire to make commensurate two systems of law and two approaches to life—one public and one private; one formal and one informal. References to the courts, judges, laws, bills, and the material trappings of everyday legal activity (contracts, legal statements, stamp paper, registration) proliferate within Islamic legal writings from this period. Questions about a mosque's right of preemption and the sale of adjacent land refer to the stamp paper on which the sale deeds are written.[28] Disputes over pending, completed, or abrogated sales refer to the dates of agreement and those of the sale's official registration, the legal "notice" (*nōṭis*) sellers issued or received, and the "advertisements" (*ishtihārs*) they made for sale and rental properties.[29] Their concerns over buying and selling property are mixed together with questions about government regulations for taxing, distributing, and regulating land.[30] In short, *mustaftīs*' (fatwa seekers') ready reference to a range of competing and overlapping legal regimes demonstrates their desire to bring together these multiple legal orders.

Incorporating elements across legal orders looked back to an earlier era in which muftis played a more direct role in the adjudication of cases, but departed from that model in several meaningful ways. When muftis worked as native law officers in the first half of the nineteenth century, the courts called on them to answer questions of legal substance. In 1811 the *ṣadr dīwānī ʿadālat* (chief civil court) at Calcutta heard a case about the right of preemption (under Islamic law) and referred two sets of questions to the court mufti: the first to determine whether the sale of the property without notifying the preemptor was legitimate, and the second to assess whether the preemptor's actions were sufficient to establish his claim of preemption. After consultation, the justices ruled in favor of the preemptor "in consideration of the *futwas* of their law officers" and on the basis of evidence presented in the case.[31] In another instance, the court "rel[ied] on the law, as exposed in [the law officer's] *futwa*," to determine that a deed need not make "express use" of the term *waqf* in order to assign land as part of a religious endowment.[32] Likewise, when the court called on its mufti to determine the division of property in an inheritance dispute, the mufti complied and provided an explanation of the property's divisions that occupied nearly 40 percent of the entire published case report. The mufti's calculations went right into the court's ruling.[33] In each of these examples, the court mufti responded to questions of substance, leaving matters of procedure open the courts.

By the end of the nineteenth century, questions that reached muftis in relation to court proceedings were decidedly different. While muftis' interpretations of points of law could enter the judicial record as evidence (perhaps akin to expert testimony for personal law cases), they had no formal role or responsibilities within the court. They neither advised judges nor supervised litigants, yet as colonial legal procedure evolved, their expertise influenced legal practice in other ways. Muḥammad ʿAbd-ul-Ḥayy Farangī Maḥallī, for instance, responded to several questions about the legal status of court fees.[34] When "Zayd" took "Bakr" to court to recover a one-hundred-rupee debt, he appended the stamp fees for filing and his attorney's fees to the original amount and won a judgment from the court in the amount of Rs. 125. Was it permissible to accept the full award? ʿAbd-ul-Hayy's answer was no.[35] Nor was it permissible to borrow money from (and pay interest to) a Hindu moneylender (*mahājan*) to cover expenses when one was unwillingly drawn into a legal dispute.[36] In other words, going to court did not relieve one of other religious obligations.

While working as chief mufti at the Dar-ul-ʿUlum Deoband in the 1930s, Muḥammad Shafīʿ also answered questions similar to those ʿAbd-ul-Hayy had answered the previous century. Departing from the Lakhnavi jurist's parsimonious rulings, Shafīʿ, however, turned to the prominent Damascene Ottoman Hanafi jurist Ibn ʿĀbidīn (d. 1836) to grant litigants permission to recover court fees and fines as part of their debt reclamation suits.[37] He also responded to questions about whether lawyers (*wakīls*) could accept payment for representing clients in "false" (*jhūṭhī*) cases.[38] Detached from formal court proceedings, muftis fulfilled other legal needs that not only challenged the courts' apparent separation of substance and procedure but also blurred the categories of cases.

Concerns over court fines, lawyers' fees, and stamped paper were not exclusive to one type of case or another. Instead, they mixed elements of religious personal law and secular public law. They also marked a departure from the earlier types of questions court muftis received. If native law officers in the first half of the nineteenth century responded primarily to matters of substance and only passively to questions of procedure, by the second half of the nineteenth century, muftis routinely engaged with questions that crossed these flimsy divisions. Here, the emphasis was less on guiding the courts toward the right interpretation and more on helping Muslims pursue the right course of action, and such advice routinely spilled over from courtroom litigation to guidance for settling disputes out of court. In the absence of formal shariʿa courts or other venues for dispute resolution, muftis employed fatwas to advise litigants inside and outside the courtroom.

Negotiating Out-of-Court Options

Consider the following contest over the cancellation of a sale. After the seller agreed to buy a house for Rs. 12,500, he paid Rs. 1,000 as an advance, and the parties drew up an agreement on stamp paper. The agreement stipulated that the buyer would complete the purchase and pay the remaining Rs. 11,500 after the current renters moved out and he took control of the property. They would then record the sale with the government registrar.[39] Both parties agreed, and the seller gave "notice" (*nōṭis*) to his renters. Once the renters emptied the upper portion (*bālāʾī ḥiṣṣa*) of the house, the seller handed over the key. In the meantime, however, the buyer's circumstances had changed, business had declined, and he could no longer make good on his purchase. The buyer wanted to terminate the sale, but the seller was hesitant.[40] He had already evicted his tenants and forfeited their rental income. Simply terminating the sale was not an option, even if the buyer offered to forgo his advance or to treat the remaining portion of the purchase price as a loan. The seller proposed a public auction (conducted according to government rules) to recover the remaining portion, but if the auction was not successful, the buyer might still be on the hook to pay the remaining amount if the seller took him to court. A court decree might help the seller recover his costs, but could he demand more than the baseline purchase price (to account for his trouble and expenses, say)? Going to court was an unpredictable option and the buyer increasingly resisted this prospect, urging the seller simply to settle the matter privately by taking some amount from him (*kōʾī miqdār mujh sē lē lō*). Could the mufti suggest a reasonable amount?

It is clear from the fatwa seeker's lengthy narrative that the unresolved dispute was plaguing him, yet aside from making a few references to the permissibility or impermissibility of accepting various sums through courtroom settlements, it is not clear what aid the seller thought the mufti might be able to provide. Unlike other mustaftis, he did not include a copy of the original sale contract, nor did he refer to specific legal categories or concepts that might apply. The mufti's possible role only seems to have appeared *after* the buyer recommended a private settlement (*muṣālaḥat*). Could the mufti mediate such an arrangement? If so, what amount would be reasonable? If the seller could not recover the full amount, could he treat the remaining expense as damages? Would damages also include future lost rent if the house remained vacant? In closing, the seller asked the mufti to consider an appropriate settlement amount and then added, in the final line, that the seller was a Muslim and the buyer was a non-Muslim (*kāfir*).[41]

Before offering his advice, Mufti Muḥammad Kifāyatullāh walked the seller through parts of the legal process. He outlined the terms that made an original sale contract valid and those that would render it null and void (*fāsid*). Specifying a closing date for the sale and transfer was key; a contract without a date would be invalid. If the seller failed to transfer the property by the closing date, the buyer could renege, or the two could agree to extend the sale. Once the parties inspected the original terms of the sale and determined that the seller was not at fault, Kifyatullah offered the parties several options. The seller could cancel the agreement and return the buyer's advance. He could auction the property and subsequently demand the difference between the auction price and the agreed-on sale price from the buyer. Alternatively, the two could make another agreement releasing the buyer from the sale contract in exchange for a specified sum, provided they treat the cancellation (*iqāla*) of the sale contract and settlement payment as separate transactions.[42] That way, they could get out of the original agreement without any (Islamic) legal recriminations (*sharʿī ilzām*).[43] Stepping in as an unofficial arbitrator, the mufti walked the disputants through a possible resolution and brought together his knowledge of the colonial legal system with his training in Islamic jurisprudence to outline the legal paths the seller might pursue.

Guiding ordinary individuals through legal matters that extended beyond the scope of personal law was thus part of the mufti's day-to-day activities. In February 1936 Hāfiẓ Ṣabīḥ-ud-Dīn directed a question about the termination of a commercial partnership—and the relationship between an investor and his agent—to the mufti.[44] The matter went back to the previous century when "Zayd" and his partners founded a successful business named "Zayd and Company." The first generation of partners passed away, but the business continued, growing in size and reputation such that the company's name became synonymous with "credibility and dignity" (*baṛī sākh wa ʿizzat*).[45] Along the way, one of the partners opened a new branch under the supervision of an agent, "Bakr." Bakr worked at this branch for some time until the Zayd and Co. investor became dissatisfied and decided to terminate the agent-investor relationship.

The dissolution of Bakr's partnership was straightforward: The parties consulted an arbitrator (*s̤ālis̤*) who told Bakr to hand over the accounts and account books (*ḥisāb kitāb*) and explain them to the investor.[46] Bakr complied, but in exchange, he had a few demands of his own, the most pressing of which was his desire to continue using the company's name, Zayd and Co., for his own enterprise. The arbitrator struggled with the trademark question. The investor argued that the company name was integral to the business's success, that it had been part of the company's identity for the last hundred years, and that confusion would ensue if two companies operated under that name. The postal service would struggle to separate one Zayd and Co.'s mail from the other, and customers would have no way of knowing with whom they were working. If the arbitrator allowed both outfits to use the same name, the public would understandably assume that the two were related. How else could they explain two men, neither named Zayd, operating businesses under the name Zayd and Co.? Furthermore, the investor argued, the company's name was its property, so it, too, should revert to the investor upon the agent's termination.

Dissolving the partnership engaged several areas of law, each with deep roots and robust precedents in Islamic and Anglo-Indian jurisprudence, but in the eyes of the colonial state, the mufti had little reason to settle this dispute. Trademark did not fall under Muslim personal law, and even though "partnerships" had a robust history in Islamic jurisprudence, colonial law had substantially reconfigured everything from trade relations, to government charters, to contracts such that a judge hearing this case would have little reason to refer to Islamic law. Yet the parties' decision to call on an arbitrator (and willingness to follow his recommendations) signaled their desire to find an amicable solution that fit with shariʿa. Reaching out to Kifayatullah was simply the next step in that process, even if the mufti's advice remained unenforceable.[47] The unconventional nature of the request was not lost on Kifayatullah. He prefaced his remarks by admitting that his knowledge was limited. Unlike the arbitrator, who heard both sides, he had only partial access to Bakr's demands. Nonetheless, he confirmed the arbitrator's assessment that the agent was responsible for preparing, returning, and explaining the accounts to the investor, even if he considered it his *sharʿī ḥaqq* (shariʿa right) to use the Zayd and Co. name. Moving from the law of partnerships to the name's status, Kifayatullah then explained that in merchant culture (*ʿurf-i tujjār*), a "firm's name holds a special status and stature" (*firm kā nām aik k̲h̲āṣṣ ḥaiṣīyat aur darja rakhtā hai*). This firm had indeed garnered considerable prestige after years of reliable and trustworthy work (*diyānat dārī sē kām karnē kī wajē sē*), but Bakr's contributions were minimal and came after the name had already risen to prominence. As a result, he had no right to continue using the name Zayd and Co., even if, in any other context, he would have been permitted to do so. To justify his response, Kifayatullah cited a well-known hadith ("Man should not preach his brother's sermon") and offered several examples drawn from it.[48]

Rather than engage with the nuances of contracts, partnerships, or trademarks, Kifayatullah grounded his answer not in commercial law but in moral principles. If using the Zayd and Co. name, a name he might rightfully use in another context, would cause someone else harm (in this case the original Zayd and Co. firm), then Bakr should refrain from doing so. Rather than referring the disputants to court, or probing the partnership agreement for terms and conditions, Kifayatullah offered a response that was more fitting with what was morally just than what was permissible within the letter of the law. *Sharʿī ḥaqq* or no, the name belonged to the investors, and Bakr should return it to them, untarnished, upon the dissolution of the partnership. Had the parties gone to court, it is unclear which way the pendulum would have swung. Contemporary case law suggests that the courts would have reached a similar conclusion, recognizing the investors' claims to the company name, but looking at the big picture, the mufti gave a response that neither side could dispute.[49]

Topics like commercial law, trademarks, and corporate reputations did not belong to the mufti's putative domain of personal, religious, or ritual matters, but the mufti nonetheless had an answer to offer—one that followed the broader contours of informal legal consultation that offset the effects of formal legal pluralism in South Asia. By reasoning analogically from a hadith, the mufti moved the dispute away from the technicalities of commercial contracts and trading partnerships back into the realm of religion and ethics. While Islamic legal experts had no authority over the former, they could freely advise parties on the latter. Thus by responding to an impending legal dispute in broadly ethical terms, the mufti could settle the dispute without talking about "the law" and without crossing the boundaries that separated personal or religious cases from public or secular ones. Scholars should not dismiss this move. At a time when appeals to religion overlapped with anticolonial activism, rhetoric was a powerful tool, and subtle reframing extended the mufti's authority while minimizing its encroachment into the domains of colonial law.

Rather than separating legal life into personal, religious, and commercial categories, fatwa requests engaged with elements of substantive law and legal procedure that crossed these categories. Asking about court fines and stamp fees, they probed the legality of taking legal action. Calling on muftis to consider contracts, sales, commercial partnerships, and trademarks, they looked beyond the limits of personal law into the morality and ethics of colonial capitalism. Debating the pros and cons of accepting the court's decree or arriving at a private settlement, they tested the limits of adjudication and proved the colonial court's determination of legal categories to be a legal fiction. Indeed, as countless other examples relate, questions about managing mosques and *waqfs* (endowments) were tied up in concerns over taxes, debts, court decrees, banking infrastructure, and salary payments.[50] Questions about marriage were caught up in concerns over registration and verification and affected by new colonial measures like the Child Marriage Restraint (Sharda) Act (1929).[51] Pilgrimage and overseas trade—the former tied to personal law (ritual) and the latter to commercial law—were both affected by new laws relating to passports and the photographs they required.[52] In other words, the inquiries that ordinary Muslims sent to muftis reflected concerns over the effects of colonial law on religious life and the insertion of religious life into colonial law. What is more, as muftis responded to these inquiries, it became increasingly clear that neither legal world could operate independently of the other. The two grew closer together, rather than further apart, as ordinary Muslims volleyed questions over substance and procedure across and between multiple legal fora, from courtrooms to councils, jurists to lawyers. Maryam Bi's inquiry was no exception in this regard.

Sifting through Substance and Procedure

The legal question at the heart of Maryam Bi's matter—the question of what to do given her husband's ongoing absence—had already, ostensibly, been answered, not by jurists alone but through legislation as well. For decades, concerns about divorce had prompted juristic and legislative interventions into Muslim personal law.[53] By the 1930s, however, it was apparent that the existing judicial and administrative options did not meet Muslim women's needs. Women struggled, as Maryam Bi's account suggests, to secure a divorce or judicial separation, even when they met the relevant criteria under Islamic law. The Dissolution of Muslim Marriages Act (DMMA) of 1939 was the latest attempt to enshrine existing interpretations of those criteria in legislation.[54]

Emanating from the combined efforts of Indian legislators, Muslim social reformers, and Islamic jurists, the DMMA enumerated nine situations that would entitle a married Muslim woman to obtain a "decree for the dissolution of her marriage" from a judge.[55] Maryam Bi's case, in which "the whereabouts of her husband have not been known," was the first of these situations. The act stipulated that after a period of four years, she would be eligible for a judicial divorce.[56] Other circumstances included a husband's failure to pay maintenance (after two years of which women were eligible for divorce); his being sentenced to serve a term in jail for seven or more years; his failure to perform marital obligations for three years; impotence continuing from the time of marriage; insanity or venereal disease; a minor's decision to renounce her marriage upon reaching the age of maturity (provided the marriage was not consummated); evidence of spousal cruelty, defined in bodily, emotional, and material terms;[57] or any other reason recognized in the Qur'an.[58] By recognizing the validity of divorce for each of these situations, the act made it clear that neither wives nor judges should tolerate neglect, abuse, cruelty, or mistreatment in marriage but discouraged women from leaving Islam to escape an abusive relationship by forbidding apostasy or conversion as grounds for nullification.[59] Following its introduction, the act received public praise and recognition for extending and confirming Muslim women's legal rights to divorce and for embracing the spirit of collaborative law reform, but it did not alleviate the legal obstacles women faced.[60] The act was well intentioned in theory but overlooked important practical details.[61]

Fatwas provide some evidence of the procedural problems surrounding Muslim women's access to divorce in the years leading up to (and following) the DMMA. In August 1936 Kifayatullah fielded a series of questions from Muḥammad Ḥayāt Ṣāḥib in Pratapgarh (now in Uttar Pradesh) regarding the marriage of a young girl named Zahīr-un-Nisāʾ. A dozen or so years ago, when she was seven years old, Zahir-un-Nisa was pledged to marry ʿAzīz Muḥammad, who was nine years old at the time.[62] A short while later, the young girl's "husband" left town and went abroad (to "pardēs"; foreign country). For a couple of years, Zahir-un-Nisa and her family received updates from the boy and knew he was doing well. For the last eight years, however, the family had heard nothing. Much like Maryam Bi, they had received no letters, no news, and no indication about the boy's wish to remain married or not. The girl was now twenty and needed to move out of her natal home, but without her husband, where would she go?[63]

The legal remedy was straightforward: Owing to the husband's prolonged absence, a Muslim judge could annul the marriage and the girl could contract a second one after the requisite waiting period (*ʿiddat*, typically four months and ten days in this instance). A quick visit to the local magistrate should solve the problem, Kifayatullah suggested.[64] Relaying the situation to the dar-ul-ifta at Deoband, Muhammad Hayat explained that this theoretically straightforward solution was practically complicated by the absence of a Muslim judge (*Musalmān ḥākim*) in his district. Additionally, if the family were to pursue this matter in court, they would have to place advertisements in the local paper asking for information about the boy's whereabouts. These advertisements (costing upwards of twenty-five rupees) extended beyond the family's means. There must be other options.

"If there is no Muslim judge," Masʿūd Aḥmad, the naʾib mufti at Deoband replied, "or if it is difficult to bring the case before the court due to insolvency or parsimony, a handful of pious Muslims can form a council, or *panchāyat*, of which one of the members should be a trustworthy [*muʿtabar*] and upstanding [*mustanad*] scholar [*ʿālim*]. These individuals can then take the place of the qazi and perform his functions."[65] Inviting local Muslims to form a panchayat (a council like the one referenced in chapter 7) gave Muhammad Hayat a do-it-yourself solution. The community could fill in for the Muslim judge. The young mufti cited Ashraf ʿAli Thanwi's texts on the question of women's rights to divorce, *Al-Hīlat al-Nājizah li'l-Ḥalīlat al-ʿĀjiza*, which he published in 1931, and *Al-Marqūmāt li'l Manẕūmāt*, to support his answer.[66]

The reply provided Muhammad Hayat with little comfort. Anxious to see Zahir-un-Nisa's situation resolved, he again wrote to Kifayatullah, this time citing and summarizing the response from Deoband. Waiting one more year for a reliable scholar to investigate the young woman's case before granting a nullification was too long, he complained. Was there no other way? Muhammad Hayat's misreading (or misrepresentation) of the response from Deoband angered Kifayatullah, who seized on the misreading and admonished Muhammad Hayat for thinking that a single scholar could perform the role of a panchayat. The fatwa from Deoband had instructed him to form a council (*jamāʿat*) to take the judge's place to nullify the marriage (*faskẖ-i nikāḥ*). At least one member of the council needed to be a reliable scholar (*kam az kam aik muʿtabar ʿālim bhī hō*), but on his own, a single scholar's declaration was insufficient, Kifayatullah clarified. Throwing up his hands, the mufti concluded by frustratedly asking how forming a panchayat could be as difficult as going to court and proclaiming that he could do no more to help Muhammad Hayat.[67]

This series of exchanges highlights two important issues surrounding the everyday practicalities of Muslim personal law in British India. First, both muftis' responses show that the legal content of the question—that is, the question of whether Zahir-un-Nisa was eligible for a judicial nullification (and eventual remarriage)—was virtually irrelevant. Aside from Maʾsud Ahmad's references to Thanwi's texts, neither mufti engaged with questions related to the length or nature of the absence; eight years (the approximate length of the husband's absence) was more than enough to qualify for a nullification.[68] Second, the exchange clearly reveals that the local courts—charged with the task of adjudicating Muslim personal law cases—were incapable of addressing Muhammad Hayat's or Zahir-un-Nisa's concerns. At the same time, neither mufti was willing to grant Muhammad Hayat outright permission to consider the marriage nullified. Instead, they both insisted on following the proper procedure of establishing a council and letting the council hear—and investigate—the complaint, and they refused to do this work for the fatwa seeker. The relevant solution here lay not in forming the requisite council but in advising ordinary Muslims how to orchestrate their own legal solutions. In other words, they laid out the mustafti's legal path.

On paper, the DMMA shifted the authority for granting judicial separations from the community to the courts, but questions of access remained, and need for the mufti's input and intercession continued. Substantive legislative interventions did not, in practical terms, resolve the question of what women like Maryam Bi or Zahir-un-Nisa should do when their husbands were missing. Jurisdictional uncertainties and procedural obstacles continued to affect how litigants approached and resolved legal disputes, contributing to the proliferation, rather than limitation, of the legal paths they followed. Thus, even when the answer to a legal question was clear (or had been clarified through legislation), procedural conflicts remained, as Maryam Bi's experience in Hyderabad further illustrates.

In his role as mufti, Kifayatullah shied away from getting directly involved in individuals' legal disputes, referring them to the courts or to local councils instead. Embracing its demi-official status, the dar-ul-ifta in princely Hyderabad took a different approach. Accordingly, the assistant who handled Maryam Bi's complaint opened her file with an "Office Note" (*kaifiyat*) outlining the situation. "Ordinarily" (*ʿām ṯaur par*), he began, the power to dissolve a marriage and grant a wife permission to remarry lay with the qazi, but Maryam Bi's petition reflected new circumstances (*jadīd ṣūrat*). It was unclear whether the old procedures were still relevant. The authority to grant a judicial separation lay with the guardian of shariʿa (*k͟hādim-i sharʿī*), who was, in his mind, the chief qazi (*qāẓī-ul-quẓāt*) of the office (*daftar*) of the Ṣadārat-ul-ʿĀliya (Noble Secretariat), but it was unclear to him whether the qazi still had this authority. Echoing concerns that routinely surfaced in British India, the assistant suggested that changes in the political landscape might have remade the legal landscape, too. He would need to investigate and concluded his memo by suggesting that, if given permission, he would perform the necessary investigation by bringing together the petitioner (*dar-k͟hwāst-guẕāra*) and witnesses, whose testimony was necessary to prove the husband's disappearance before granting a separation. In addition to granting him permission to question witnesses, the assistant's supervisor also demanded additional research into the legal question from "the perspective of shariʿa" (*sharʿī nuqṯa-i naẕr*).[69] After all, the dar-ul-ifta could only respond to new circumstances if it understood the question fully. Proceeding along two tracks, the assistant and his colleagues thus gathered evidence from witnesses and conducted their own research.

The research unfolded as follows: On the next page, the assistant compiled and summarized relevant passages from key works of Hanafi jurisprudence, including excerpts from multiple volumes of the *Radd al-Muḥtār* (a well-known work of Hanafi *fiqh* [jurisprudence] frequently cited in the British courts) and a contemporary printing of the *Wāqiʿāt al-Muftain* (*Occurrences of the Muftis*). Reviewing the information, he then noted that a woman was eligible for remarriage following her husband's death. If proof of his death was not available, then witnesses could fill in the gaps. In other words, the research seemed to suggest that by testifying that the husband was dead (not simply missing), witnesses could provide the evidence the jurist needed to nullify the marriage and grant the woman permission to remarry.[70] The assistant thus proceeded to gather testimony from witnesses.

After her initial visit, Maryam Bi returned to the dar-ul-ifta with two witnesses. The first witness, Laʿl K̲h̲ān, began his testimony by stating that he had known Maryam Bi and her husband, Amīn Ṣāḥib, for more than two years and that they were "distant relatives" (*dūr kē rishtē*). He then reported that during the Razakars' conflict, Amin Sahib had gone missing. Since then, Maryam Bi had struggled to survive. Laʿl Khan's heart told him that Amin Sahib was dead, but he had no proof. Laʿl Khan listened as his statement was read back to him and certified its accuracy by placing his thumbprint on the page.[71] The next witness, Jalāl Ṣāḥib, provided similar testimony. He began by stating that he had known Maryam Bi for four years and that he also knew her husband. (They all came from the same village.) Jalal Sahib further testified that Amin Sahib was part of the Razakars and had been captured during the police action (*pōlīs akshan*). He had been missing since then. They had traveled to places like Nizamabad and Burhan (Bodhan) to look for him. They even inquired after him at the local jails (*jail k̲h̲āna-jāt*) but had not found him. "My opinion," Jalal Sahib offered, is that "he is not alive and has been killed" (*voh zinda nahīn̲; mār diyā gayā hai*). Jalal Sahib confirmed that the recorded testimony was accurate and then signed his name at the bottom.[72] Both witnesses thus confirmed that Amin Sahib was missing, presumed dead.

Finally, Maryam Bi gave her own statement. "My husband's name is Amin Sahib," she began. "We are residents of Bhakar in Nandair [Nanḍēḍ] District" (now in Maharashtra). She then explained that her husband had been missing (*g̲h̲āʾib*) for the last two years, that he had been a Razakar, and that he had been missing since the *ḥamla* (attack). She and her husband were agriculturalists, and her father, who was blind, no longer had the ability (*sakat*) to care for her. She wanted to contract a second marriage. Like the other witnesses, Maryam Bi listened to the recorded statement and signed the document with her thumbprint.[73] It would appear that the assistant had the evidence he needed to decide Maryam Bi's case: Two upright individuals—Laʿl Khan and Jalal Sahib—had testified not only that Amin Sahib was missing and had been missing since the time of the Razakars' action but also that they had searched for him and had not found him or any trace of him. They both presumed he was dead. Maryam Bi's testimony further added that she had been without marital support since her husband's disappearance and that she was struggling. The dar-ul-ifta was her last hope.

As the dar-ul-ifta investigated the case, Maryam Bi's request ran into two obstacles. First, even though two witnesses testified to her husband's involvement in and subsequent disappearance following the police action, neither could testify to his death. They did not see him die, nor had they found his body. During their testimony, they came close by swearing and affirming that they "thought" or felt "in [their] heart[s]" that he was dead, but suspicion was not the same as proof. Ordinarily, when women approached a qazi to perform or record a second marriage, they would bring witnesses to testify to their eligibility. These witnesses, as marriage registers from Meerut suggest, would testify that the former husband (*sābiq shauhar*) was dead and that the woman had not contracted a second marriage since his death.[74] Maryam Bi's witnesses could not make this claim; they assumed Amin Sahib was dead but did not know for sure.

Second, without sufficient proof, Maryam Bi's case hinged on her timeline. Witness testimony made it clear that Amin Sahib had been missing for at most "two, two and a half" years.[75] Two years is a long time to wait for a missing husband to return, but unfortunately, two years was not long enough to nullify a marriage under the rules relating to absentee husbands. In British India, the DMMA standardized the length of time married women had to wait to four years. In princely Hyderabad, a similar intervention came by way of a *farmān* (decree), issued by the *ṣadr-us-ṣudūr* (chief ecclesiastical officer) in 1920 CE (1339 AH), which amended the state's penal code (the *Taʿzīrāt-i Āṣafiya*) to make four years the length of time that women had to wait in these cases.[76] Maryam Bi was still short of the four-year waiting period, but the dar-ul-ifta seemed willing to make exceptions.

When Afsar Begum, a woman whose husband had been missing for "one, two, or three years," according to her count, came to the dar-ul-ifta a few days after Maryam Bi to complain about her missing husband, the office granted her permission to remarry. Like Maryam Bi, Afsar Begum's husband was also *mafqūd-ul-k̲h̲abar* and had been missing for no more than three years. Unlike Maryam Bi, however, Afsar Begum had recently learned that her husband had immigrated to Pakistan, leaving her behind in Hyderabad.[77] This detail thus shifted Afsar Begum's case into another legal category; he was no longer absent but was instead willfully neglectful. Failing to pay maintenance for over two and a half years (even if Afsar Begum's initial math was a bit fuzzy) was sufficient grounds for divorce. The dar-ul-ifta thus provided her with the necessary permission to contract a second marriage.

Despite her best efforts to claim lack of maintenance, Maryam Bi could not persuade the dar-ul-ifta to treat her case like Afsar Begum's. Before issuing an opinion, the dar-ul-ifta sent one additional inquiry to the city qazi, asking him for input on the situation. Disappointing though it was, his response was clear: because Maryam Bi's husband had been involved with the Razakars and had gone missing during the police action, her case fit the textbook definition of *mafqūd-ul-k̲h̲abar*, for which "four years . . . is a requirement" (*chār sāl . . . sharṯ hai*). There was no way around it. Despite Maryam Bi's creative calculations, not even two years had passed between the end of the police action in Hyderabad in September 1948 and her petition to the dar-ul-ifta in March 1950. "Until at least four years had passed, [the qazi] would not agree to grant her permission to remarry" (*jab tak chār sāl guz̲ar jāʾin̲, ʿaqd-i s̤ānī kī ijāzat kē ham majāz nahīn̲ hai*).[78] She would need to wait an additional two years (or find her husband's dead body) before receiving permission to remarry.

The dar-ul-ifta balked at the qazi's response. Internal memos suggest that employees found his response to be "cursory" (*sarsarī*), incomplete, and insensitive to Maryam Bi's current circumstances, yet the dar-ul-ifta lacked the judicial authority to override the city qazi's opinion and could not act against his advice. In June 1950, the office closed the file on Maryam Bi and her missing husband, and shortly thereafter, the office closed, leaving little archival trace of its activities and personnel after 1950. Although her case closed without a favorable resolution (and without an official fatwa to boot!), Maryam Bi was one of hundreds of women who approached the dar-ul-ifta with questions about the status of their marriages. These women (and their male relatives and supporters) sought assistance from the office to secure permission to remarry; to escape poverty, destitution, or an unnatural dependence on their parents; and to navigate the multiple fora that dotted the legal landscape in colonial and postcolonial South Asia. Some of these women (like Afsar Begum) found easy solutions to their problems; others, like Maryam Bi, were told to wait; and some, like Zahir-un-Nisa, were told to try other options first. Going to the dar-ul-ifta was thus one of many legal paths ordinary individuals could follow when trying to resolve their legal disputes in British India and postcolonial South Asia.

Conclusion: The State, the "Law," and the Limits of Flexible Fora

For petitioners like Maryam Bi, going to the dar-ul-ifta was about more than finding the right answer to a legal question. It was about seeking assistance when times were tough and calling on Islamic legal experts to provide that assistance. To that end, many of the questions muftis received—and many of the answers they wrote—referred to problems that were common, questions that were settled, and answers that had already been determined through research and deliberation. Maryam Bi was hardly the first woman to bring a *mafqūd-ul-k̲h̲abar* case to the dar-ul-ifta. Jurists had engaged with the permutations of this question and its implications for centuries, and Maryam Bi's situation fit the paradigmatic, textbook case. Furthermore, in British India and in princely Hyderabad, the absent-husband question had already been scrutinized, and scholars, legislators, and jurists had already decided to accept a shorter, four-year waiting period. Yet despite its paradigmatic features, and despite prior substantive interventions, Maryam Bi's situation frustrated and agitated the dar-ul-ifta's employees, who desperately wanted to intervene on her behalf. They conducted research, gathered testimony, and (out of obligation) consulted the city qazi, who rejected their efforts to find a flexible solution. Despite this disappointing outcome, the dar-ul-ifta's engagement with Maryam Bi's already-answered legal issue shows how muftis and nonstate legal experts worked as advisers and counselors as ordinary individuals struggled to resolve their legal conflicts. These exchanges, inquiries, investigations, and consultations thus contributed to the making of everyday Islamic law and outlined the multiple paths and possibilities that individuals could pursue to resolve legal disputes.

For Maryam Bi, the solution was simple: she needed permission to remarry, but her path to remarriage was complicated by the circumstances. The Razakars' action in 1948 caused her husband's disappearance and left her without the means to prove his death. Was he missing? Absolutely. What he dead? Presumably. Witnesses tried to provide the necessary proof, but their testimony was insufficient. No one had seen Amin Sahib die; therefore, according to the city qazi, he was still missing and she would have to wait. The dar-ul-ifta attempted to intervene, but it could not overturn the qazi's determination. Whether Maryam Bi returned to Hyderabad two years later or simply made do with a makeshift solution is anyone's guess.

Across South Asia, dar-ul-iftas like the Sadarat-ul-ʿAliya's in Hyderabad or Kifayatullah's at the Madrasa Aminiya in Delhi worked with and on behalf of their petitioners and fatwa seekers to find reasonable solutions to their legal troubles, in light of the shariʿa and in line with state law. They wrote legal opinions based on the information mustaftis provided and outlined next steps for fatwa seekers to follow. When they could not investigate a situation or access both sides in a conflict, they inserted caveats into their answers and framed their advice in hypotheticals.[79] Kifayatullah, for instance, did not know what Bakr demanded in response to the arbitrator's decision about dividing Zayd and Co.'s assets, so he set aside those possibilities when addressing the trademark issue. Similarly, without access to the original sale agreement between the Muslim seller and non-Muslim buyer, the mufti explained the details that would make the original agreement void, before offering advice on the seller's next steps. A court would have demanded the original deed, read its terms without considering the buyer's or the seller's intent, and issued a summary judgment in relation to the facts of the case. (The court also would have demanded filing fees and court costs.) Kifayatullah's response was more cautious, hesitant to lay blame on one side or the other, reticent to make demands against one party or the other, but he weighed several possibilities and urged the parties to arrive at a compromise. These exchanges between muftis and mustaftis neither fit neatly into histories of Islamic law nor do they have a place in histories of colonial law. Instead, they moved across and between types of law and legal systems, as individuals drew on the resources, structures, and legal knowledge accessible and available to them.

Complaining about the problems they encountered or the dissatisfaction they faced when going to court proved productive for many fatwa seekers, who turned the complexities of formal litigation into opportunities to rethink the solution they wanted by pursuing their disputes through informal channels. Responding to these complaints, muftis acknowledged the authority of the state to regulate and govern certain aspects of everyday life—through its laws and law courts—but also offered alternative paths disputants might follow to resolve their disputes in accordance with Islamic aims and expectations. Following these alternative paths lays bare some of the conflicts that arise when legal history ignores the social side of law's intersections with society. Fatwas are by no means perfect sources for tracing the social life of law—they rarely recount what happens after the fatwa's receipt, and their narrators are in most cases of questionable impartiality—but they do represent a relatively untapped source for learning not what a scholar said or what answer he gave but how ordinary individuals called on him to tackle their problems. As such, their production, circulation, and consumption reveal the multiple shades of legal pluralism that continue to color postcolonial South Asia.

Conclusion

The Limits of Legal Possibilities

Maryam Bi's experience provides a fitting place to end because it not only shows how the possibilities for Islamic legal practice continued after Independence and Partition but also reveals the limits of legal pluralism. While for many, the dar-ul-ifta offered new possibilities—the possibility of finding a reasonable solution, the possibility of having a mufti reclassify the question, the possibility of having a nonstate institution offer assistance—uncertainty also surrounded Islamic legal practitioners and the institutes they ran. Even if the mufti determined that a written contract was not necessary to forgive a dower debt, the court might decide it was. Even if the dar-ul-ifta called witnesses to testify to a husband's disappearance, the local qazi might refuse to treat the case as one involving maintenance and insist on a longer waiting period. And even if the courts had the ultimate authority to decide questions of property, trademarks, and commercial law, disputants might still prefer to take the case to another venue for an alternative interpretation. Whether the advice they received would satisfy both parties; whether it would produce a lasting, legal change; and whether that decision would stand if subsequently tested in court were the risks that many legal actors accepted as they explored their options and pursued the legal paths and possibilities that remained open to them. Uncertainty and ambiguity lay on the obverse of the possibility and plurality coin.

In postcolonial South Asia, the legacies of colonial legal change have been mixed. On the one hand, British rule brought disparate social, cultural, and religious traditions under a shared legal umbrella that persists today. Not only did the Indian Penal Code, the Indian Contract Act, and the Acts of Civil and Criminal Procedure entirely remake law and legal procedure, but these codes—and the legal infrastructures they engendered—continued largely unchanged and unchallenged after independence.[1] Specific acts like the Kazis' Act, the Muslim Personal Law (Shariat) Application Act, and the Dissolution of Muslim Marriages Act also continued.[2] These and other statutory interventions further remade the legal landscape. On the other hand, colonial law left many questions unanswered, and those questions continue to define debates over law, society, and the state across South Asia today, especially (though not exclusively) in the domain of personal, family law.

Today, the threads of this debate play out among Islamic scholars, ordinary Muslims, state representatives, and nonstate actors. In India, religious personal law sits uncomfortably alongside the constitution's claims to secularism and promises of equality.[3] For some communities and for some types of cases, legislative interventions and statutory reforms remain an option; for other groups and other issues, asserting community autonomy and demanding noninterference offer necessary safeguards and protections against majoritarian dominance and cultural hegemony.[4] Muftis, qazis, the courts they hold, and the institutes they direct remain pawns and players in these contests, treading a treacherous line between meeting the needs of the communities they serve and overstepping the bounds of their nonstate, nonjudicial authority.[5] With each turn in national politics, new allies, new enemies, new perspectives, and new possibilities emerge, shaping the reception of their work and reinterpreting its meaning—symbolically and practically.

For some Muslims, legislative reform and statutory intervention remain a possibility, both to restore shariʿa to its rightful place at the heart of Muslim life and to "modernize" Islamic law within the secular nation-state. Imperfect though its implementation may be, colonial-era legislation (like the Shariat Application Act and the Dissolution of Muslim Marriages Act) provides a model to follow, but doing so in the present requires doing more than simply introducing new proposals: it requires recognizing the collaborative, cooperative, and nationalist origins of those earlier measures.[6] For others, the path to a better Muslim life lies not in statutory enactments and legislative proposals but in religious autonomy and exemptions from secular state law granted under Clause 2 of the Shariat Application Act (1937) and Articles 25 and 26 of the Indian Constitution (1950). Recognizing religion as an area of exemption from state regulation provides room for nonstate Islamic legal actors to maneuver,[7] but by opening the door for their own maneuvers, they also offer a point of entry for others to enter the arena. ʿAbd-ul-Awwal Jaunpuri's concerns about the uneducated interventions of "half-maulvis" remain pertinent as individuals, institutions, and government agencies navigate the tensions between central authority and regional autonomy, national unity and cultural diversity, secular identity and religious plurality.

In Pakistan and Bangladesh (after 1971), similar interests operate as proposals circulate through state-sponsored Islamic law reforms, official shariʿa councils, and nonstate Islamic institutions. Pakistan's constitution, for instance, dictates that shariʿa remain the source of law, but this status has not eliminated ensuing conflicts over whose interpretation of shariʿa applies to which cases. From above, the Council of Islamic Ideology (established in 1962) ensures that the laws of Pakistan are not repugnant to Islam while, from below, Islamists and secularists push back against the legitimacy of the state's one-size-fits-all brand of Islam. Furthermore, the rearticulation of Islamic legal prescriptions through legislative mechanisms like the Hudud Ordinance of 1979 suggests that legislation and shariʿa are mutually dependent—the one reinforcing the other. Sharʿi governance requires legislative enactments, and legislative enactments require sharʿi justifications. In the domain of everyday Islamic law, the Council of Islamic Ideology and nonstate religious bodies continue responding to new issues and novel legal questions as they arise, and the state continues to implement laws following the scholarly opinions and consensuses they produce. Neither operates independently of the other; they remain coconstitutive.

In addition to contests over whether and to what extent Islamic legal reform is possible through the state or must remain autonomous from the state, two additional views deserve mention here. The first is a view that embraces the *maqāṣid*, the larger aims or goals of shariʿa, as part of (and in addition to) the modern law project and reinvigorates ideas about Muslim governance and law with more expansive understandings of public good (*maṣlaḥa*) and public law (*siyāsa*).[8] Focusing on the big picture, rather than the finer points, this approach to shariʿa-minded living reframes renewed efforts to live in accordance with God's law along another set of axes. Morals and ethics (*ak͟hlāq* and *ādāb*), which evoke the *maqāṣid* in spirit, have a lengthy history among South Asia's Muslims and have found a new importance within South Asia's diaspora communities.[9] Likewise, in India, Pakistan, Bangladesh, and the South Asian diaspora, there have also been renewed efforts to reform Islamic legal practice by strengthening its administration through state bureaucracies, offices, and institutions. The model *nikāḥ-nāma* (marriage contract) campaign is one example of these efforts that aims to solve the problems tied to men's and women's different rights and responsibilities in marriage by providing them with a model marriage agreement.[10] A properly executed contract, the supporters of this second view argue, will improve relations between husbands and wives, using an Islamic legal instrument (the *nikāḥ-nāma*) to enforce and inscribe the couple's wishes.[11] (The written marriage contract also provides safeguards and protections that come into play if the relationship sours.)[12] These efforts resonate with and reflect earlier marriage registration campaigns, again hinging on the efficacy and authority of the legal document and its connection to the couple's everyday reality.

Regardless of how the scales tip in these debates, the everyday Islamic law that emerged in British India remains alive and well today. Fatwa institutes continue to do quick business, answering questions, handling disputes, and offering advice. The authority of their fatwas is still contested; their legal status remains in dispute; and their influence in everyday Muslim life remains open to debate. While for some, the muftis who write fatwas for local institutes, for newspapers, or on the internet are, in the words of ʿAbd-ul-Awwal, "half-maulvis"—in it only for the money, fame, or prestige—for others, the learned opinions these respected scholars produce offer relevant and important advice that not only shapes their understanding of Islam but also frames their understanding of what it means to be a Muslim in the world today. Likewise, courts continue to make rulings on matters pertaining to personal law, and members of the community—and the broader public—continue to agree (or disagree) and accept (or refute) their decisions to varying degrees, depending on the judge and the judgment. Litigants continue to shop for fora, to take their questions to multiple muftis and multiple venues, and to consult outside experts when looking for a slightly different or a slightly better answer to their questions.

British rule did not invent these practices, but it did give birth to the spaces, contexts, and conditions that came to define them. Despite earlier antecedents across Asia, imperial rule accelerated their presence in the public sphere and exacerbated the contest between religious laws and the laws of the land in ways that were unprecedented—and unpredictable. Print and new communications technologies contributed to the speed and extent to which discourses of law circulated, and with those circulations, knowledge about, investment in, and concern over the law also grew. In this context, colonial modernity and legal modernity went hand in hand, and everyday Islamic law emerged as the by-product of the two. Imperialism and the so-called jural colonization of the Muslim world did not fix or settle the sticky questions that boggled the minds of British lawyers, judges, and administrators in the eighteenth, nineteenth, and twentieth centuries, nor did it produce definitive answers. Yet it did produce a new type of legal awareness and give voice to new forms of legal articulation. Written in letters, scribbled on postcards, transmitted through telegraphs, and typed on clumsy Urdu typewriters, everyday Islamic law found new voices, new venues, and new forums as it competed with, engaged in contests over, and challenged the hegemony of the Anglo-Indian legal system. And although these quotidian debates pushed the benchmarks of substantive legal change forward, they left unanswered the cutting questions that remain unresolved today. As everyday Islamic law continues to inhabit the multiple spaces and multivocal forms that it developed throughout the colonial period, it continues to define and to contribute to the making of law, state, and society in modern South Asia.

Acknowledgments

According to a hadith, all scholarly effort receives a reward. She who performs *ijtihād* (independent reasoning) to the best of her ability but errs will receive one reward. She who performs *ijtihād* and is right will receive a double reward. This book is the result of my efforts to understand how Islamic legal pluralism was produced through the colonial encounter in British India, but it also emerged from the guidance, input, suggestions, recommendations, assistance, and challenges I received from others along the way. The answer I've produced might not earn me a double reward, but those who supported the project deserve additional credit.

From the beginning, I have been grateful for the funding agencies and programs that continue to support and sustain deep scholarly engagement in the humanities and social sciences. The Mellon Foundation, the American Council of Learned Societies, the Fulbright-Nehru Student Program, the Social Science Research Council's International Dissertation Research Fellowship Program, the American Institute of Pakistan Studies, the American Institute of Indian Studies, and the Foreign Language and Area Studies Fellowship Program have all contributed to this project. In today's fast-paced world, funding for prolonged, sustained, archival research enriches scholarship and society. I thank these programs for their past support and hope they will continue to support new research.

I also thank the many institutions that have housed and hosted me as this book has evolved. At the University of Chicago, I thank friends and colleagues in South Asian Languages and Civilizations, the History Department, and the Divinity School, including Muzaffar Alam, Dipesh Chakrabarty, Iza Hussin (now at Cambridge), Emily Lynn Osborn, and Ulrike Stark.

At the University of Wisconsin–Madison, I thank Megan Massino and the Mellon Postdoctoral Fellows Program, Mitra Sharafi and the South Asia Legal Studies Working Group, Lalita du Perron (now at Stanford) and the Center for South Asia, Andrew Amstutz, Maura Capps, and the rest of my wonderful colleagues in the Center for the Humanities, the Institute for Research in the Humanities, and the Legal Studies Program.

At Dartmouth College, I thank the Society of Fellows, the Department of History, the Asian Societies, Cultures, and Languages Program, and the Bodas Family Academic Programming Fund. I thank Mona Domosh, M. Cecilia Gaposchkin, Allen Hockley, and Laura McDaniel for supporting my work. I thank Pamela Kyle Crossley, Douglas E. Haynes, A. Kevin Reinhart, and members of the South Asian Studies Collective for taking time to read and comment on the manuscript. Rohit De, Brannon D. Ingram, and Kimberly M. Welch participated in a manuscript workshop and offered tremendously helpful advice. I thank them for their generosity—and curiosity. Jonathan W. Chipman deserves special thanks for making the maps to accompany the text.

At the University of North Carolina Press, I thank Carl W. Ernst, Andreina Fernandez, Bruce B. Lawrence, Elaine Maisner, and the anonymous reviewers who ushered this project through the publishing process.

Advice, feedback, and support have come in many sizes and shapes over the last few years. I thank the supportive community of the American Society for Legal History; the Wallace Johnson Program for First Book Authors and especially Reuel Schiller, who led our inaugural cohort; Sarah Barringer Gordon for her always enthusiastic support; and Mitch Fraas for his generous reading of early drafts. I also thank Trina Hogg and Wesley Chaney for being excellent readers. Nicholas Abbott, Benjamin B. Cohen, Laura F. Edwards, Mahmood Kooria, Jaclyn Michael, Durba Mitra, James Pickett, Raha Rafii, Kalyani Ramnath, Paolo Sartori, Mitra Sharafi, Julia Stephens, and others have generously read parts of the book, invited me to present my work, and graciously responded to my requests for advice. Nandini Chatterjee, Mariam Sheibani, Samira Sheikh, and Mytheli Sreenivas also deserve credit for the comments they provided as discussants and readers. Whether they know it already, their comments helped me hone my arguments, big and small.

A project like this would not be possible without tireless, unending support from the archivists, librarians, scholars, and students who made accessible the records, registers, and unpublished writings I consulted for this study. In India, I benefited from the generosity and patience of archivists at the National Archives of India, the Maharashtra State Archives, the Andhra Pradesh (now Telangana) State Archives, the Salar Jung Museum and Library, the Oriental Manuscript Library and Research Institute, the Uttar Pradesh State Archives (Allahabad and Lucknow branches), the Lucknow University Library, and the Shibli Library at the Dar-ul-ʿUlum Nadwat-ul-ʿUlama. I am particularly grateful for the staff and attendants at the *dār-ul-iftāʾs* (fatwa institutes) I visited at Nadwa, Jamiʿa Nizamiya, and the Madrasa Aminiya who took time to answer my questions. This book is a testament to their willingness to welcome foreigners into their offices and institutes. I also thank Qazi Zainus Sajidin for granting me permission to include images from his family's records in chapter 6. The British Library remains a treasure trove for historians working on imperial and global history. I thank everyone in the Asia, Pacific and Africa Reading Room, as well as friends and colleagues in the United Kingdom who make doing research in London such a treat. In the United States, I have benefited greatly from the robust collections of Urdu- and Persian-language materials housed at the University of Chicago's Regenstein Library and the Memorial Library at the University of Wisconsin–Madison. Research librarians J. Wendel Cox, James Nye, and Laura Ring have all assisted me with their diligent, patient efforts to acquire sources. Finishing this book during the COVID-19 pandemic also made me especially grateful for the librarians at Dartmouth (who worked to fulfill my last-minute interlibrary-loan requests) and at the Center for Research Libraries (who went above and beyond to digitize sources for me).

Finally, I thank my family for cheering me across the finish line and Nick for his unwavering support.

Glossary

ʿadālat court
ʿādat custom, habit, usage, practice
anjuman society, organization, company, assembly

dār-ul-iftāʾ fatwa institute, institute for issuing fatwas (legal opinions)
dār-ul-qaẓā qazi's court; place of judgment
dār-ul-ʿulūm educational institution; abode of knowledge
dīwānī ʿadālat civil (revenue) court

farmān (royal) order, decree
faskḫ dissolution, marital dissolution
Faṣlī, Fasli calendar based around the harvest (*faṣl*), used in Hyderabad with the Persian (solar) months
fatwa (pl. *fatāwá*) legal opinion; opinion written by a mufti; answer to a legal question; response to an *istiftāʾ*
faujdārī ʿadālat criminal court
fiqh jurisprudence, Islamic jurisprudence

ḥadīth, *ḥadīṣ* tradition or saying of the Prophet
Ḥanafī one of the four schools of Sunni jurisprudence, predominant in South Asia; named for Abū Ḥanīfa (d. 767 CE)
Ḥanbalī one of the four schools of Sunni jurisprudence; named for Aḥmad ibn Ḥanbal (d. 855 CE)
ḥaqq right, truth, obligation, duty, due (sometimes meaning "fee")
hiba gift
ḥukm (*ḥukm-nāma*) order, command, decree, decision

ʿiddat waiting period (for divorcee or widow) during which remarriage is unlawful
iftāʾ legal inquiry; legal consultation; asking a (legal) question; practice of giving legal advice
ijmāʿ consensus; agreement within the community; one of the sources of law
imām prayer leader
indirāj-kunanda lit. entry-doer; one who records entries in a marriage register
iqrār, *iqrār-nāma* statement, legal statement, affidavit
istiftāʾ fatwa question, fatwa request

jā'iz/nā-jā'iz permissible/impermissible
jalsa, ijlās council, meeting; marriage ceremony
jalsa-yi 'ām public meeting; public gathering
jawāb answer (as in *suwāl-jawāb*; question and answer); reply

k̲h̲ul' female-initiated divorce, termination of marriage

madad-i ma'āsh grant-in-aid, subsistence grant
madrasa school, university, academy
mafqūd-ul-k̲h̲abar absent; absent without information; away without notification
mahr marriage portion, dower, amount paid from husband to wife at time of marriage (*mahr-i mu'ajjal*; immediate *mahr*) or later (*mahr-i mu'ajjal*; deferred *mahr*)
majmū'a collection, compilation
Mālikī one of the four schools of Sunni jurisprudence; named for Imām Mālik ibn Anas (d. 795 CE)
maulawī, maulvī a learned man; scholar of Islam; member of the *'ulamā'*
maẕhab (pl. *maẕāhib*) religion; school of jurisprudence
muftī scholar of law; one who writes fatwas
munshī scribe
mustaftī one who presents an *istiftā'* (fatwa question), fatwa seeker

nā'ib deputy, assistant
nā'ib qāẓī assistant qazi
-nāma lit. letter; suffix attached to different types of documents (e.g., *ṯalāq-nāma*, *wakālat-nāma*)
nikāḥ marriage
nikāḥ-k̲h̲ẉān marriage reader
nikāḥ-nāma marriage contract; also *'aqd-i nikāḥ*
niẓām order, system, arrangement; one who governs or administers order
niẓāmat rule, administration, government
niẓāmat 'adālat appellate court

panchāyat council, usually consisting of five (*pānch*) members
panḍit scholar, Hindu scholar; here: scholar of Hindu law
pargana district

qānūn law (usually in the sense of statutory or state law)
qāẓī judge, Islamic judge, *sharī'a*-court judge
Qur'ān revealed text; holy book of Islam

rūpiya, rupee monetary unit (Rs., ₹); equivalent to 16 *ānna*; equivalent to 192 *pie*

ṣadr chief, principle
ṣadr 'adālat chief/supreme court

sanad certificate of appointment
Shāfiʿī one of the four schools of Sunni jurisprudence; named for Muḥammad ibn Idrīs al-Shāfiʿī (d. 820 CE)
sharʿī (adj.) legal, just, related to divine law
sharīʿa lit. the way, the path; law of God; divine guidance
sharʿ-i sharīf divine way, divine law, "holy *sharīʿa*"
Shīʿa (Shīʿī), Shiʿism one who belongs to the Shīʿatu ʿAlī (Party of ʿAli); a branch of Islam
suʾāl, suwāl question
sunna practice, habit, custom; way; manner of acting; ways of the Prophet
Sunni (Sunnī) one who follows the sunna; a branch of Islam

ṭalāq divorce, male-initiated divorce
talfīq drawing from other schools to make law

ʿulamāʾ group of scholars (pl. of *ʿālim*: scholar, learned person); scholarly community
ʿurf custom

wakālat-nāma power of attorney; deed of representation
wakīl agent, representative, attorney
walī guardian, patron, protector; also, governor, magistrate
waqf (pl. *auqāf*) endowment, bequest
waṭan residence, dwelling, homeland, nation

zamīndār landholder, revenue collector, Mughal official
ẓilaʿ district

Notes

Abbreviations Used in Notes

AIR	All India Reporter
AIR (All)	All India Reporter, Allahabad Series
AIR (Bom)	All India Reporter, Bombay Series
AP/TSA	Andhra Pradesh / Telangana State Archives
BL	British Library
B.	Indian Law Reports, Bombay Series
B. & C.	Barnewall and Cresswell's King's Bench Reports
Bom HCR	Bombay High Court Reports
Bom LR	Bombay Law Reports
BTJC	*Bombay Times and Journal of Commerce*
CSSH	*Comparative Studies in Society and History*
DMMA	Dissolution of Muslim Marriages Act, 1939
FHL-MMR	Family History Library, Muslim Marriage Records
IESHR	*Indian Economic and Social History Review*
Ind Cas	Indian Cases
IOR	India Office Records (Asia, Pacific and Africa Collection, British Library)
ILR	Indian Law Reports
ILR (All)	Indian Law Reports, Allahabad Series
ILR (Cal)	Indian Law Reports, Calcutta Series
ILS	*Islamic Law and Society*
IR	Indian Reports
JDP	Judicial Department Proceedings
LHR	*Law and History Review*
LSR	*Law and Society Review*
Mad	Madras
MAS	*Modern Asian Studies*
MSA	Maharashtra State Archives
NAI	National Archives of India
Rs.	rupees
SDA	sadr diwani ʿadalat
Sel. Rep. (N)	Select Reports, New Series
Term Rep.	Durnford and East's Term Reports in the Court of King's Bench
TOI	*Times of India*

UPSA	Uttar Pradesh State Archives
UPSA-All.	Uttar Pradesh State Archives—Allahabad Regional Archives

Note on Translation and Transliteration

1. Steingass, *Comprehensive Persian-English Dictionary.*

2. For an extended discussion of orthographic standardization, see Tony K. Stewart, *Witness to Marvels*, xxv–xxx.

Introduction

1. "True to Islamic Traditions," *Bombay Chronicle*, August 16, 1931.

2. Kifāyatullāh, *Kifāyat-ul-Muftī*, 9:245.

3. A fatwa on working as a photographer appeared in *Al-Jamᶜīyat* on June 18, 1927, and another on photography on November 6, 1927. They were reprinted in Kifayatullah, *Kifāyat-ul-Muftī*, 9:245. In 1940, the mufti subsequently upheld his earlier position that making images "by hand or by any other means" was "strictly forbidden" (*hargiz nā-jā'iz*) but noted that when required by law (*sak͟ht ẓarūrī yā qānūnī majbūrī kē waqt*), photographs were permissible (e.g., for passports). Kifāyatullāh, *Kifāyat-ul-Muftī*, 9:244.

4. "Ḥawādiṣ wa Aḥkām," *Al-Jamᶜīyat*, October 13, 1931; also in Kifāyatullāh, *Kifāyat-ul-Muftī*, 9:245–46.

5. The paper also announces the return to Delhi on October 11 of Kifayatullah, the Jamᶜiyat's president (*ṣadr*), and Aḥmad Saᶜīd, its secretary (*nāẓim*). "Ḥawādiṣ wa Aḥkām."

6. On the influences of print and the public sphere, see Gelvin and Green, *Global Muslims*; Green, *Bombay Islam*; Orsini, *Hindi Public Sphere*; Robb, *Print and the Urdu Public*; and Stark, *Empire of Books.*

7. Partha Chatterjee lays out this conundrum in *Nation and Its Fragments*, 10.

8. Certeau, *Practice of Everyday Life*, xviii–xix.

9. Merry, *Getting Justice*, 2–3. See also Sarat, "'Law Is All Over'"; and Sarat and Felstiner, "Lawyers and Legal Consciousness."

10. For the distinction between legal consciousness and legal culture, see Silbey, "Legal Culture." For a critical reflection on "legal consciousness" as a concept, see Silbey, "After Legal Consciousness."

11. Merry, *Getting Justice*, 5.

12. On legal uncertainty, see Merry, "Colonial Law." See also Ellickson, *Order without Law*; and Sarat, "'Law Is All Over.'"

13. Ewick, "Law and Everyday Life," 469. See also Felstiner, Abel, and Sarat, "Emergence and Transformation."

14. For colonial histories, see Benton, "Historical Perspectives"; Benton, *Law and Colonial Cultures*; Benton and Ross, *Legal Pluralism and Empires*; Nandini Chatterjee, *Making of Indian Secularism*; Menski, *Comparative Law*; Merry, *Colonizing Hawai'i*; Merry, "Colonial Law"; Mommsen and Moor, *European Expansion and Law*; and Sharafi, *Law and Identity.* For postcolonial effects, see Benda-Beckmann,

"Forum Shopping"; Mastura, "Legal Pluralism"; Newbigin, *Hindu Family*; Shahar, "Legal Pluralism"; Solanki, *Adjudication*; Subramanian, *Nation and Family*; and Williams, *Postcolonial Politics*.

15. On the family law exception, see Halley and Rittich, "Critical Directions." On other communities, see Adcock, *Limits of Tolerance*; Nandini Chatterjee, *Making of Indian Secularism*; Purohit, *Aga Khan Case*; and Sharafi, *Law and Identity*.

16. See interlude I for a further elaboration of this point; and Stephens, *Governing Islam*, 11–14.

17. For introductions to these more recent projects, see Hallaq, *Sharīʿa*, 443–99; and Vikør, *Between God*, 222–79. For further discussion, see Layish, "Transformation of the Sharīʿa"; Layish, "Adaptation"; Peters, "From Jurists' Law"; and Welchman, "Islamic Law."

18. For some critiques, see Hallaq, *Impossible State*; and Quraishi-Landes, "Sharia Problem."

19. See also Yngvesson's reflections on "popular legal culture" in "Inventing Law."

20. Ewick, "Law and Everyday Life," 470.

21. In part, my narrative moves away from the *habitus* of Pierre Bourdieu toward an engagement with Certeau's "strategies and tactics." Where the former operates as "second nature," the latter focuses on ordinary individuals as law's consumers. Certeau, *Practice of Everyday Life*, 58–59 (on Bourdieu); 34–39 (on "strategies and tactics").

22. While the history of secularism is not the focus here, I draw from recent contributions to the study of secularism to complicate and challenge this (assumed) bifurcation. For further elaborations, see Agrama, *Questioning Secularism*; Asad, *Formations of the Secular*; Saba Mahmood, *Religious Difference*; Joan Wallach Scott, *Politics of the Veil*, 90–123; and Taylor, *Secular Age*.

23. See also Redding, *Secular Need*, 32–55, on "Muslim and mundane."

24. The ubiquity of these everyday forms shows up, for instance, in Mufti, "Grand Mufti of Google."

25. For debates in other contexts, see, e.g., Agrama, *Questioning Secularism*; Bowen, *On British Islam*; Hussin, *Politics of Islamic Law*; Lemons, *Divorcing Traditions*; Peletz, *Islamic Modern*.

26. On documentation in British India, see, e.g., Bellenoit, *Formation*; Heath, "Bureaucracy, Power and Violence"; Kalpagam, *Rule by Numbers*; Ogborn, *Indian Ink*; and Bhavani Raman, *Document Raj*. See also Crooks and Parsons, *Empires and Bureaucracy*; and Findley, *Bureaucratic Reform*.

27. On precolonial scribal cultures, see Muzaffar Alam and Subrahmanyam, "Making of a Munshi"; Muzaffar Alam and Subrahmanyam, *Writing the Mughal World*; Blake, "Patrimonial-Bureaucratic Empire"; Kumkum Chatterjee, "Scribal Elites"; Kinra, "Master and Munshī"; and Kinra, *Writing Self, Writing Empire*.

28. In other words, they imagined an Islamic legal community. See Benedict R. O'G. Anderson, *Imagined Communities*.

29. See chapter 4 for further elaboration of these points.

30. On these institutions, see, e.g., Barbara D. Metcalf, *Islamic Revival*; Barbara D. Metcalf, "Madrasa at Deoband"; Lelyveld, *Aligarh's First Generation*; and Robinson, *'Ulama of Farangi Mahall*. Barbara D. Metcalf compares these institutions

and their educational models in *Islamic Revival*, chapter 8, "Further Alternatives," 315–47. Founded in 1891, the Nadwa anjuman held its first meeting in Kanpur in 1894.

31. See chapters 3 and 4 for further discussion of these examples.

32. See chapters 5 and 6, respectively.

33. While *daftar-k̲h̲āna* (record house) is a more precise term for an office or archive, in Hindi-Urdu usage today, *daftar* means "office" on its own.

34. For an introduction, see Tyan and Káldy-Nagy, "Ḳāḍī"; and Esposito, "Shariah Courts," in *Oxford Dictionary of Islam*.

35. Vikør, *Between God*, 182–83.

36. Agrama draws attention to this tension by emphasizing the "suspicion" with which litigants receive judgments from the personal status courts in Egypt. See Agrama, "Ethics, Tradition, Authority."

37. Frankfurter's reference appears in *Terminiello v. Chicago*; Intisar A. Rabb discusses some of these examples in the context of "negative citation" in "Against Kadijustiz." See also Rosen, "Equity and Discretion"; and Powers, "Kadijustiz or Qāḍī-Justice?"

38. Vikør, *Between God*, 170–73.

39. For examples, see Gerber, *State, Society, and Law* (esp. chap. 2); Peirce, *Morality Tales*; and Masud, Peters, and Powers, *Dispensing Justice in Islam*.

40. See, e.g., Hallaq, "'Qāḍī's Dīwān (*Sijill*)'"; Barbara D. Metcalf, "Ibn Battuta," 271–78; and Peirce, *Morality Tales*.

41. See, e.g., Fluehr-Lobban, *Islamic Law and Society*; Jeppie, Moosa, and Roberts, *Muslim Family Law*; Rosen, *Anthropology of Justice*; Rosen, *Justice of Islam*; Starr and Collier, *History and Power*; Thurston, "Muslim Politics and Shariʿa." For minority-Muslim contexts, see, e.g., Bowen, *On British Islam*; Emon, "Islamic Law"; Lemons, *Divorcing Traditions*; Redding, *Secular Need*; and Vatuk, *Marriage and Its Discontents*.

42. The following discussion of the mufti's office draws on Tyan and Walsh, "Fatwā"; Vikør, *Between God*, 140–53; and, for South Asia, Aḥmad, *Janūbī Eshiyā*.

43. The five categories of rules are *wājib/farẓ* (required/obligatory), *mandūb* (recommended), *mubāḥ* (neutral), *makrūh* (repulsive), and *ḥarām* (forbidden). Vikør, *Between God*, 36–37.

44. See chapter 4; and Halevi, *Modern Things on Trial*, among others.

45. Gary Bunt's work, for instance, explores the nuances of Islamic authority online. See, e.g., Bunt, *Hashtag Islam*; Bunt, *iMuslims*; Bunt, *Islam in the Digital Age*; Bunt, *Virtually Islamic*; and Jon W. Anderson, "Wiring Up."

46. See, e.g., Bowen, *On British Islam*; Bowen, *Why the French*; Emon, "Islamic Law"; and Jackson, "Islamic Law."

47. According to a recent Pew Research Center report, the majority (60 percent) of the world's Muslims live in the Asia-Pacific region. Pakistan is expected to pass Indonesia as the country with the largest Muslim population by 2030. India will likely pass both countries by 2050. Pew Research Center Forum on Religion and Public Life, *Future*.

48. Hallaq rejects the idea that fatwas were detached from practical concerns. I suggest, however, that qazis/judges learned to settle routine disputes without the

mufti's input and tended to call on muftis for more complicated cases. On the mechanisms of inquiry and adjudication, see Vikør, *Between God*, 143–47; Hallaq, "From *Fatwās* to *Furuʿ*," 31–38; and Messick, *Sharīʿa Scripts*, for further discussion of the relationship between the "library" and "archive" of Islamic law.

49. For scholars like Hallaq, shariʿa and the modern state are fundamentally incompatible. See Hallaq, *Impossible State*.

50. The collection from Bharuch is available at the National Archives of India. The collection from Meerut is available through the Family History Library run by the Church of Jesus Christ of Latter-Day Saints.

51. See chapter 5.

52. Here, I follow the law-and-society tradition. See, e.g., Ewick, "Law and Everyday Life"; Moore, "Law and Social Change"; and Sarat and Kearns, *Law in Everyday Life*.

53. Merry, *Getting Justice*, 2–4. Writings on "rural law" are also useful here. See, e.g., Edwards, *People and Their Peace*; and Prifogle, "Winks, Whispers."

54. See chapter 7.

55. On these justices, see, e.g., Guenther, "Syed Mahmood"; Nandini Chatterjee, "Law, Culture and History"; and Hussin, *Politics of Islamic Law*, 184–90.

56. On multiplicities and hybridities, see, e.g., Berman, "New Legal Pluralism"; Berman, *Global Legal Pluralism*.

57. See Hussin, *Politics of Islamic Law*, 68–75, for a reading of this treaty alongside jurisdictional formations.

58. BL, IOR/L/PJ/7/6711: The Kazi's Bill.

59. See, e.g., Hussin, *Politics of Islamic Law*, 59; Lemons, *Divorcing Traditions*, 8–16; Stephens, *Governing Islam*, 25, 167–73; and Williams, *Postcolonial Politics*, 6–7. Sharafi also uses 1772 to start her chronology in *Law and Identity*.

60. Mantena, *Alibis of Empire*. See also Partha Chatterjee, *Nation and Its Fragments*, 32–34.

61. Stephens, however, looks at this act in relation to economics in *Governing Islam*, 167–73.

62. For a recent reappraisal of precolonial pluralism, see Farhat Hasan, "Law as Contested Communication"; along with Nandini Chatterjee, "Reflections on Religious Difference."

63. See interlude I for a further articulation of these concepts.

64. See interlude III.

65. "Muftis" (native law officers) appointed to serve as expounders of law in the Company courts are the exception here. See chaps. 1 and 3 for further discussion of this role.

Interlude I

1. Morley provides background and analysis of the plan in *Administration of Justice*, 44–48. He also notes that "although the constitution of the Courts was shortly afterwards completely altered, many of the rules which it contained were, and are still, preserved in the Bengal Code of Regulations" (45).

2. The plan applied only to Bengal, but as a framework for understanding the history of law and religion on the subcontinent, its reach has been much wider.

3. "A Plan for the Administration of Justice, Extracted from the Proceedings of the Committee of Circuit, 15th August 1772," appendix B in Forrest, *Selections from the State*, 290–99. Travers suggests that this passage was the result of Hastings's communications with Muhammad Reza Khan. See Travers, *Ideology and Empire*, 119–23; also cited in Stephens, *Governing Islam*, 25n10. Both Travers and Stephens situate the Hastings plan within the context of the Company's late eighteenth-century administration and in relation to later discussions on the origins of personal law in British India.

4. Travers, *Ideology and Empire*, 104.

5. "Plan," 290, clauses I–III.

6. "Plan," 290–91.

7. "Plan," 292.

8. "Plan," 292.

9. "Plan," 292–93.

10. "Plan," 292.

11. "Plan," 294–95.

12. "Plan," 294. On fiscal and judicial interests, see also Travers, *Ideology and Empire*, 118.

13. "Plan," 297–98.

14. Bernard S. Cohn reads the plan as an outline for British rule in South Asia: "In Hastings' plan the theory was clear: Indians should be governed by Indian principles, particularly in relation to law. . . . India had an ancient constitution which was expressed in what came to be thought of as two codes, one Hindu and the other Muslim." Cohn, *Colonialism*, 26–27.

15. Divide and rule (*divide et impera*) has a long history, though it is often associated with later phases of British rule on the subcontinent. See, e.g., Neil Stewart, "Divide and Rule."

16. Hussin, *Politics of Islamic Law*, 70–71, 138–39.

17. For a discussion of the plan in relation to personal law, see Stephens, *Governing Islam*, 30.

18. Stephens, 30.

19. Bernard S. Cohn, *Colonialism*, 27 (and his references at 27n33).

20. For a recent consideration of the plan's contributions to whitewashing legal diversity, see Hussin, *Politics of Islamic Law*, 70. On the construction of a uniform "Muslim" category, see Morgenstein Fuerst, *Indian Muslim Minorities*.

21. See Hobsbawm and Ranger, *Invention of Tradition*, for a more comprehensive discussion of these ideas.

22. Rudolph and Rudolph, "Barristers and Brahmans," 33–35.

23. On the history of "Hindu law" and its transformation across the colonial period, see Davis, "Law and 'Law Books'"; Derrett, "Administration of Hindu Law"; Derrett, *Religion, Law*; Mallampalli, "Escaping the Grip"; Menski, *Hindu Law*; and Newbigin, "Codification of Personal Law," among others.

24. More recent scholarship has pushed back against this narrative, though the tension between historical precedents and normative frameworks still shapes scholarship. On precolonial normative orders, see Muzaffar Alam, *Languages of Political Islam*. For an example of the latter problem, see Kugle, "Framed, Blamed and Renamed."

25. Cohn describes the quest for law codes in these terms. Bernard S. Cohn, *Colonialism*, 29. Iza Hussin, by contrast, emphasizes the relevance and importance of Islamic law's precolonial accretions, accumulations, and adaptations. See Hussin, *Politics of Islamic Law*, 141–43.

26. Ahmed, *What Is Islam?* For additional contributions to this perspective from anthropology and religious studies, see, e.g., Asad, "Idea of an Anthropology"; Geertz, *Islam Observed*; Geertz, *Local Knowledge*; and Reinhart, *Lived Islam.*

27. See, e.g., Hallaq, *Introduction to Islamic Law*, 85–89; and Hallaq *Sharīʿa*, 376–77, for a summary of this view.

28. Esposito and DeLong-Bas estimate that the Qurʾan "does contain about eighty verses that address strictly legal matters, but [compared with biblical books such as Leviticus or Deuteronomy] the Quran is not a law book." *Shariah*, 36. Vikør comes up with a different calculation, writing that of the "6,200 verses in the Koran, . . . some 350 are considered to be relevant for the law." *Between God*, 33.

29. This source derives from the prophetic expression "My community will not agree on an error," but scholars call on *ijmāʿ* as a source of law in varying ways. See Vikør, *Between God*, 73–88.

30. Shīʿa Muslims draw on other sources, including the example of ʿAli and the Imams. Esposito and DeLong-Bas, *Shariah*, 36–37. Vikør includes additional differences; see *Between God*, 129–39.

31. Benton, *Law and Colonial Cultures*, 13–15. Griffiths outlines these concerns in "What Is Legal Pluralism?," 7. Sullivan's characterization of the competing aims of disestablishment and the protection of religious freedom is also relevant here. See Sullivan, *Impossibility of Religious Freedom.*

32. See, e.g., Nandini Chatterjee, "English Law"; Sharafi, *Law and Identity*; Mallampalli, "Meet the Abrahams"; and Mallampalli, *Race, Religion, and Law*, among others.

Chapter 1

1. Persian/Urdu: *qāẓī*; Arabic: *qāḍī*. The simplest translation for this term is "Islamic judge," but this definition hardly captures the term's many meanings.

2. This ancient city (mentioned by Herodotus) was for centuries a bustling port town on the Narmada River. Today, the Sardar Sarovar Dam constrains much of the river's flow, and Bharuch's prominence as a port has declined.

3. A report from 1864 suggests that Nur-ud-Din received Rs. 786 annually. MSA, JDP, 1864, Vol. 6, No. 207: "General Statement shewing [*sic*] the lands and emoluments now enjoyed by the Cazees in the Several Districts of the Bombay Presidency."

4. Female qazis have become a possibility only recently. See, e.g., Yesha Kotak, "Mumbai Couple Gets Woman Qazi to Solemnise Wedding," *Hindustan Times*, January 28, 2019; Mohta, "Rise of Female"; and Erika Cohn, *Judge*. For normative descriptions, see Tyan and Káldy-Nagy, "Ḳāḍī"; and Vikør, *Between God*, 168–84.

5. Arguments came from local Muslims and from British administrators. See also Jalal, *Self and Sovereignty*, 141–53.

6. Law served imperialism in other contexts, too. See, e.g., Benton, *Search for Sovereignty*; Benton, *Law and Colonial Cultures*; Herzog, *Frontiers of Possession*; Yannakakis, *Art of Being In-Between*; and Yannakakis, "'Indios Ladinos.'"

7. On the "company-state," see Stern, *Company-State*. My discussion of qazis draws from literature on legal intermediaries: Aguirre, "Tinterillos, Indians"; Lawrance, Osborn, and Roberts, *Intermediaries, Interpreters, and Clerks*; Osborn, "'Circle of Iron'"; Ramsay, "Scriveners and Notaries"; Sharafi, "New History"; Yannakakis, *Art of Being In-Between*; and Yannakakis, "'Indios Ladinos.'"

8. Patterns were similar with other officeholders. To date, much of the scholarship has focused on landholders (*zamīndārs*) and the transformation from "status" to "contract." See Bernard S. Cohn, "From Indian Status"; and Dirks, "From Little King."

9. Records from Bombay use the spelling *cazee*. Later records tend to use *kazí* or *kazi*.

10. One memorandum advocated their appointment to district courts, explaining "that in Civil as well as Criminal cases which come before the Zillah Courts . . . it is necessary, that both the Court and the public should feel satisfied with the exposition of the Law on references to the Officers appointed to propound it, . . . they felt that there was not sufficient security for a just[,] unbiased and careful exposition and . . . they considered it essentially necessary to insure a faithful and punctual discharge of duties of such high importance to the interests of the community, that the establishment of two each . . . should be every where maintained." BL, IOR/F/4/768/20878, Appointment of Mahomedan & Hindoo Law Officers to the Several Courts, "Extract, Judicial Letter from Bombay, Dated the 15th January 1822."

11. According to one report, the qazi and mufti in the city of Surat were "also Law Officers of that Court, and give their opinion when called upon, but receive no Salaries, the regular public fees of their Office being deemed sufficient." BL, IOR /F/4/768/20878, Appointment.

12. Vikør, *Between God*, 171–72.

13. Nur-ud-Din Husain's family received appointments under the Mughals and the successor Nawabs of Bharuch. Other qazis in the presidency referred to appointments granted under the Maratha Peshwas. Two of the families I discuss here trace their lineages back to the Prophet's family. Nur-ud-Din Husain's family in Bharuch descended through Husain, son of ʿAli. Zain-ul-ʿĀbidīn's family in Meerut descended through Abu Bakr.

14. The inverse was also true: Judge William Richardson recommended the nearby "Molvee of the Adawlut" to fill a vacancy in the office of qazi in Nawapur, for example. MSA, JDP, 1856, Vol. 13: No. 956 of 1856: Khandeish—Nawapoor, Cazee appointment of.

15. Most qazis did not receive a salary from the Company, but their time in office counted toward government pension requirements. See NAI, Financial Department, Pensions and Gratuities, November 1864, Nos. 330–332 (A).

16. See chapter 3.

17. Qazi Shaikh Ahmad was examined by a committee that included British officials, the court maulvi, and the court shastri, suggesting that native law officers outranked community qazis. MSA, JDP, 1859, Vol. 14: "The Humble Petition of Cazee Shaikh Ahmed."

18. This was also the period in which the Company was actively commissioning the translation and publication of these texts. On the translation and transmission of copies of *The Hidaya* to the Court of Directors in London, see BL, IOR/H/205: Translation of the Medaya [*sic*—Hidaya]; IOR/H/207: Hedaya or Mahomedan Law; and IOR/F/4/128/2391: Edward Colebrooke's proposals for remedying alleged defects in the Muhammadan Criminal Law. Stephens examines the development of Muslim personal law over time in *Governing Islam*. See also Fraas, "Readers, Scribes, and Collectors," on law books. For critiques of colonial translations, see, e.g., Bernard S. Cohn, "Command of Language"; and Hallaq, *Sharīʿa*, 376.

19. Recent scholarship has drawn attention to the qazi's multiple roles, but more work remains. See, e.g., Nandini Chatterjee, *Negotiating Mughal Law*; and Farhat Hasan, *State and Locality*. Grewal's earlier work is also illuminating. See Grewal, "Qazi in the Pargana"; and Grewal, *In the By-lanes*.

20. See, e.g., Nur-ud-Din's complaints about changes in this practice later in this chapter and in chapter 3.

21. Many acted as "Cazee and Khuteeb"—that is, qazi and *k̲h̲āṭib/k̲h̲āṭīb* (preacher or sermon-reader). See, e.g., MSA, JDP, 1833, Vol. 6/271: "Substance of a petition from Cazee Ahmed son of Cazee Khuteeb of Rajapoor Talooka . . . arrived 22nd February 1833"; MSA, JDP, 1837, Vol. 11/205: "Substance of a Petition from Cazee Mohummud Sufdarr . . . 1st July 1837"; and BL, IOR/F/4/1238/51468: "Riot in the Mosque at Mangalore and dismissal of the Cazee."

22. Reading marriages and granting divorces were central to later debates (see chapter 3); the status of minors was important for gifts; the issue of appointing trustees was key for debates over endowments. See also Carroll, "Definition and Interpretation"; Abbasi, "*Sharīʾa*"; and chapter 7 for further discussion.

23. Chapter 2 explores these alternative forms of "employment" in more detail. Quoting the *Ain-i Akbari*, Muzaffar Alam lists the following categories of *madad-i maʿāsh* recipients: "(i) scholars, who were 'seekers after truth and renounced the world,' (ii) persons who 'eschewed the urge for greater gain and chose a life of seclusion and self-abnegation,' (iii) the destitute and the poor 'who were incapacitated to earn their livelihood,' and (iv) 'persons of noble lineage, who ignorantly deemed it below their dignity to take to any employment.'" Alam, *Crisis of Empire*, 112. Candidates for the qazi's office often accused their rival's supporters of being indebted—and therefore beholden—to him.

24. The corrupt qazi is a common trope in Persian *ḥikāyāt* (tales) and *laṭāʾif* (jokes) literature. Kuka's compilation of Persian jokes and tales includes no fewer

than sixteen humorous stories involving qazis and several witticisms. In many, the qazi is corrupt or bumbling, ignorant of the law. See Kuka, *Wit and Humor.*

25. Muzaffar Alam, *Crisis of Empire*, 112–20.

26. Travers, *Ideology and Empire*, 137. I address this process in more detail in chapter 2.

27. Departure from the qazi's core functions also added to this mockery.

28. See Travers, *Ideology and Empire*, 105; and Bernard S. Cohn, *Colonialism*.

29. Travers, *Ideology and Empire*, 126–32.

30. My reading of localized legal practice and imperial expansion draws on Edwards, *People and Their Peace*.

31. Company efforts to separate courtroom qazis (qua native law officers) from community qazis were imperfect at best; individuals routinely moved from one position to another.

32. On utilitarians, liberalism, and empire, see Pitts, *Turn to Empire*; Kartik Kalyan Raman, "Utilitarianism"; Eric Stokes, *English Utilitarians and India*; and Thomas, "Liberalism and Utilitarianism." See also Edwards on "localized law" in *People and Their Peace*, 64–99.

33. Previous regimes also accommodated religio-legal difference, so pluralism was not the Company's invention. For recent examinations of precolonial legal culture, see Nandini Chatterjee, *Negotiating Mughal Law*; Nandini Chatterjee, "Reflections on Religious Difference"; and Guha, "Qazi."

34. Forrest, *Selections from the State*, 283.

35. Forrest, 283.

36. Giunchi, "Reinvention of '*Sharīʿa*'," 1126–27.

37. BL, IOR/V/8/16, *Regulations passed by the Governor General in Council of Bengal, with an Index and Glossary, Vol. I, containing the regulations passed in the years 1793, 1794, and 1795*.

38. Travers, *Ideology and Empire*, 35.

39. Historians have shown that notaries, clerks, and record-keepers are instrumental to the workings of law. See, e.g., Hardwick, *Practice of Patriarchy*; Burns, "Notaries, Truth, and Consequences"; Burns, *Into the Archive*; Merwick, *Death of a Notary*; Nussdorfer, *Brokers of Public Trust*; and Ramsay, "Scriveners and Notaries."

40. Government of India, *Regulations*, 162.

41. Government of India, 163.

42. The governor in council for the Bombay Presidency introduced the first regulations in 1799, with Regulation V for the appointment of native law officers arriving the following year. Regulation X of 1815 was the first statute relating to community qazis. The "Bombay Code" replaced these earlier regulations in 1827.

43. BL, IOR/Z/P/3150, Index, Bombay Judicial Consultations, 1816.

44. BL, IOR/Z/P/152, Index, Bombay Judicial Consultations, 1818. Officeholders and dignitaries received honorary shawls (*k̲h̲ilʿats*), robes, and hats as compensation for and recognition of their service and esteem. See Stillmann, "K̲h̲ilʿa," generally; Loomba, "Of Gifts"; and Pinch, "Same Difference."

45. BL, IOR/Z/P/3155, Index, Bombay Judicial Consultations, 1821.

46. BL, IOR/Z/P/3156, Index, Bombay Judicial Consultations, 1822.

47. BL, IOR/Z/P/3160, Index, Bombay Judicial Consultations, 1826.

48. BL, IOR/V/8/24, The First Twenty-Six Bombay Regulations of 1827; also available in House of Commons, Parliamentary Papers, 1829, Vol. 23, Paper No. 201, "Regulations passed by the Governments of *Bengal, Fort St. George,* and *Bombay,* 1827."

49. BL, IOR/V/8/24, First Twenty-Six Bombay Regulations.

50. Even beyond British India, these issues generally belong to family law. See Halley and Rittich, "Critical Directions"; and Sezgin, *Human Rights.*

51. Precolonial qazis heard disputes across communities. See Nandini Chatterjee, *Negotiating Mughal Law*; Grewal, "Qazi in the Pargana"; Guha, "Qazi"; Ibn Hasan, *Central Structure*; and Farhat Hasan, *State and Locality.*

52. Lemons, *Divorcing Traditions*; Redding, *Secular Need*; Solanki, *Adjudication.*

53. In 1864 the judicial department finally managed to compile an (almost) comprehensive list of compensation for the Bombay Presidency's qazis. The list, which abounded with overlapping jurisdictions and incomplete information, resulted from nearly four decades of effort. MSA, JDP, 1864, Vol. 6, No. 207: "General Statement." See also chapter 2 of this book.

54. Recent scholarship on legal pluralism today all but ignores the early nineteenth century. See, e.g., Lemons, *Divorcing Traditions,* 8–12; and Redding, *Secular Need,* 33–34.

55. Nur-ud-Din Husain's great-grandfather Zain-ul-ʿĀbidīn is the first family member to appear in these records. For a family tree, see Lhost, "Writing Law," 260.

56. MSA, JDP, 1842, Vol. 21/798: No. 307 of 1842: "Translation of an Arzee [petition] from Cazy Syed [Zainul] Abid deen of Broach . . . received 27th September 1804 C.E." The East India Company held onto the city of Bharuch until 1783, when they handed it over to Mahadaji Sindhia.

57. MSA, JDP, 1842, Vol. 21/798: No. 307 of 1842: "The humble petition of Syed Ahmudhoosun Quazee of the Court of Broach Adalat."

58. MSA, JDP, Vol. 21/798: Letter from Prendergast, February 6, 1805.

59. MSA, JDP, 1841, Vol 21/711: "Substance of a petition from the Cazee of Broach Syud Ahmed Hoosane . . . received 16th November 1841."

60. According to one later account, Sayyid Murtaza became qazi in 1819 (1235 AH). Company records are sparse for this period, but his first Company sanad is dated January 1822. Husain, "Kājīonā Insāf . . . [Part 3]," 133.

61. Company records show that Zain-ul-ʿAbidin received this stipend as "a life interest" for his position and his pledge to "uphold [it] with respectability." The stipend ceased upon his death, but "a moiety was however revived in favor of a widow and child he left [ʿAbbās ʿAlī?] and the remainder was granted to the Son who became Qazee." The family relates that Sayyid Murtaza received half of the monthly allowance upon his father's death, and the remaining half went to Zain-ul-ʿAbidin's "concubine." MSA, JDP, 1833, Vol. 6/271: "Substance of a petition from Kazee Syud Ahmed Hoossain of Broach . . . Received 5th March 1833"; and "Notes" on it.

62. MSA, JDP, 1831, Vol. 3/217: Letter to J. P. Willoughby, February 28, 1831.

63. His earlier sanad was granted under Regulation X of 1815.

64. The monthly allowance was designed to supplement the qazi's meager income and to move the office away from its dependence on hereditary entitlements and stipendiary grants.

65. Sayyid Ahmad's sanad has the date January 3, 1832. MSA, JDP, 1849, Vol. 25: Cancelled Sanad of Suyud Ahmed Hoossein.

66. MSA, JDP, 1837, Vol. 11/405: Judicial Department Letter, No. 31 of 1836.

67. MSA, JDP, 1836, Vol. 10/363: Letter No. 345 to the Adjutant General of the Army, March 4, 1836. The final note reads, "This matter having gone by, I think things may be allowed to take their course and these papers may be recorded," which I interpret to mean the governor thought it best to let the matter be, without taking any further action in response to the request. When the matter surfaced again in 1842, the judge at Surat noted that he formally ended these ceremonial practices in conformity with "the directions of Government" in October 1841. MSA, JDP, 1842, Vol. 21/798: Letter No. 72, February 16, 1842.

68. MSA, JDP, 1839, Vol. 20/547: "Humble Petition of Kauzee Ahmed Hossein of Broach."

69. "Humble Petition of Kauzee Ahmed Hossein." He would also send his assistant to the homes of women in seclusion to verify these details before accepting documents presented to him ex parte, and he further confirmed that those appointed to represent individual interests were of age and were not insane—confirmations that relied on his familiarity with the community and his commitment to due diligence. Farhat Hasan also suggests that qazis took an interest in protecting women's claims. See Farhat Hasan, *State and Locality*, esp. chap. 4, "Women, kin and shariʿa."

70. MSA, JDP, 1839, Vol. 20/547: Petition from Mahomed Hossein oodeen Wulud Mahommed Sabh, February 28, 1839.

71. MSA, JDP, 1839, Vol. 20/547: Petition from Shaikh Surfoodeen Shaikh Rahimtoolah, August 10, 1839. (After first accessing this volume in 2013, it was unavailable when I returned to the archives in 2015, leaving me to rely on the index and brief summaries for these items.)

72. MSA, JDP, 1839, Vol. 20/547: Letter to the Judge of Poona, No. 870 of 1838.

73. Letter to the Judge of Poona.

74. I refer here to the Stamp Act's role in precipitating the American Revolution. For a recent appraisal, see Hutchins, *Community without Consent*.

75. According to his father, Nur-ud-Din was twenty-seven years old in 1848. MSA, JDP, 1848, Vol. 21/1392: "Translation of a Petition from Syed Ahmed Hussain Cazee of Broach . . . dated 8th October 1848."

76. "Translation of a Petition."

77. MSA, JDP, 1848, No. 21/1392: Letter from W. C. Andrews, Judge, Court of Adawlut, Surat, November 18, 1848.

78. MSA, JDP, 1849, Vol. 25: Letter No. 973 dated April 16; No. 1749 dated May 5, 1849.

79. For a discussion of how Company officials limited the qazi's practice, see Lhost, "Writing Law"; and chapters 2 and 3 of the present book.

80. For more on the documents they produced, see Lhost, "Writing Law."

81. Articles about the meetings of these organizations refer to the "Kazi of Bharuch" as an esteemed participant but rarely identify the qazi by name, leaving one to guess, at times, whether the "Kazi" was Nur-ud-Din's son, grandson, or another relative.

82. I thank Andrew Amstutz for sharing information about the publication of this manuscript with me.

83. MSA, JDP, 1847, Vol. 21/1284: "Translation of a Memorial from Syud Hyat Ullah Khan Cauzee and Khuteeb of Poona."

84. MSA, JDP, 1847, Vol. 21/1284: Captain Morse's Letter, No. 29, February 12, 1847 [J. R., or possibly Thomas Robert Morse]; "Certificate from Thomas Ellis, Asst. Supt. of Bazars"; and "Translation of Gen'l Smith's Hookoom Nama."

85. "Translation of Gen'l Smith's."

86. "Translation of Gen'l Smith's"; MSA, JDP, 1859, Vol. 14: Petition from the Residents of Poona and Kerkee [Khadki] Camps, October 11, 1859.

87. MSA, JDP, 1847, Vol. 21/1284: Letter to the Adjutant General of the Army, Bombay, February 17, 1847; and Letter to the Secretary of Government in the Judicial Dept., May 21, 1847.

88. MSA, JDP, 1848, Vol. 21/1392: No. 194 of 1848, Ahmed wd. Mahomed Issuff Naib Cazee investigated.

89. The file includes depositions from Sakina, the wife of Karim Bakhsh; Lalkhan [Laʿl Khān], a *ṣūbadār*; Shaik̲h̲ Raḥīm, a *jamaʿdār*; Richard Jones Edgerly, lieutenant adjutant; Shaikh Ali, a sepoy; and Shaik̲h̲ Mak̲h̲dūm, a *ḥawāldār* of the Twenty-Ninth Regiment. MSA, JDP, 1848, 21/1392: Translations of Deposition Nos. 1–7, from October 2 to 7, 1847.

90. MSA, JDP, 1848, Vol. 21/1392: "Translation of defence given by Cauzee Ahmed Wuld Mohomet Isuf of the Poonah and Kurkee Cantonment."

91. MSA, JDP, 1848, Vol. 21/1392: Judicial Consultations, Nos. 1613/28, March 4, 1848; 3153/61, May 1, 1848; and 6489/6507, September 6, 1848.

92. MSA, JDP, 1855, Vol. 20: Letter from Keays to the SDA [Sadr Diwani ʿAdalat], No. 659, dated 5 July 1855.

93. MSA, JDP, 1855, Vol. 20: Resolution No. 5070 of 1855, 26 Nov. to Registrar S[adr] A[dalat].

94. MSA, JDP, 1859, Vol. 14: "Substance of a petition from Shaikh Allaoodeen Ahmud Wullud Shaikh Ahmud Kazee of the Sudr Adawlut and 21 other Mussalmands. . . . dated the 22nd August [1859]."

95. MSA, JDP, 1859, Vol. 14: "The Humble Petition of Cazee Shaikh Ahmed Vulud Shaikh Mohamed Esooof, inhabitant of Poonah Cantonment."

96. "Humble Petition of Cazee Shaikh Ahmed." Other petitions cited these figures as well. See MSA, JDP, 1859, Vol. 14: Petition from the "undersigned Mohammedans[,] inhabitants of Poona and Kerkee Camps"; and "Substance of a petition from Shaikh Allaoodeen Ahmud."

97. MSA, JDP, 1859, Vol. 14: "Substance of a Petition from Shaikh Allaoodeen Ahmud." The petitioners claimed that the committee members "gave him a very easy examination such as those given to young boys . . . [and] that he was not fit

for the office of kazee, that he had no knowledge at all of Arabic and Persian, and that he knew a little Oordoo [Urdu]."

98. "Substance of a Petition."

99. MSA, JDP, 1859, Vol. 14: Petition from the undersigned Mohammedans.

100. MSA, JDP, 1859, Vol. 14: No. 1424 of 1859, Bombay Sudr Adawlut, September 3, 1859.

101. Hidayatoolah Khan received his deceased father's position as qazi for the city of Pune.

102. For further discussion of elections, vote tallies, and public favor, see chapters 2 and 3.

103. Dalvī, *Bamba'ī maiṉ Urdū*, 82. Some doubt surrounds this date: Dalvī gives 1189 AH (1775–76) as the year of his birth. During a deposition in 1861, Yusuf Moorghay gave his age as eighty-eight years, which would put the year of his birth around 1773–74.

104. MSA, JDP, 1837, Vol. 11/405: Memorandum by W. H. Wathen, Esqr., May 27, 1837.

105. Memorandum by W. H. Wathen. (Using Hindustani transcribed in the Latin alphabet as code is an amusing but not unreasonable idea. Company officials' diaries are filled with scribbles, notes, inscriptions, and tracings in multiple scripts.)

106. BL, IOR/F/4/895/2329: Extract from a Political Letter from Bombay, February 6, 1823. (Yusuf Moorghay refers to supporting multiple families, at least one each in Bombay and Hyderabad.)

107. Memorandum by W. H. Wathen.

108. BL, IOR/F/4/1265/50902: Reduction in the establishment of the Native Agent at Hyderabad in Sind. After Yusuf Moorghay, the Company reduced the native agent's budget from Rs. 520 to Rs. 100 per month, suggesting that Yusuf Moorghay's compensation was quite lavish.

109. MSA, JDP, 1837, Vol. 11/405: "Substance of a Petition from Rabiah Beebee . . . Dated 27th Zilhajeh or 4th April."

110. MSA, JDP, 1837, Vol. 11/405: "Statement respectfully submitted by Mahomed Yoosoof Moorgay . . . in respect to the Petition of Rabia Bebee, the widow of his late Brother Mahomed Yoonoos Moorgay."

111. "Statement respectfully submitted."

112. MSA, JDP, 1837, Vol. 11/405: "Substance of a petition from the Moosulman Inhabitants of the Island of Bombay . . . Dated 7th Ziihuj (15th March) and received 27th March 1837."

113. MSA, JDP, 1837, Vol. 11/405: "Substance of a Petition of the Mussulman Inhabitants of Bombay . . . dated 23rd Zihuj (31 March) and received 7th April 1837" and "Substance of a Petition from Hossainoodeen . . . received April 1837."

114. Memorandum by W. H. Wathen. There was some doubt about which school of jurisprudence Yusuf Moorghay represented, but he was almost certainly Sunni. According to one account, Sayyid Ahmed Barelvi (1786–1831) appointed him as "Khalifa" of Bombay, and before his death, Moorghay composed a three-hundred-page prose-poem, called *Zain-ul-Majālis*, dedicated to Sayyid ʿAbd al-Qadir Jilani (d. 1166 CE), a Hanbali Sunni Muslim preacher and mystic.

115. The signatories represented Bombay's prominent families, including M. A. Rogay, who later held the position of vice-president of the Anjuman-i Islam of Bombay (founded in 1874 by Justice Badruddin Tyabji, a Sulaimani Bohra), under the leadership of Kamruddin Tyabji, the justice's elder brother. The translation does not include the original list of signatures, only a handful of names, followed by a reference to "upwards of 575 signatures."

116. MSA, JDP, 1837, Vol. 11/405: "Substance of a Petition from Rabiah Beebee . . . Dated 27th Zilhajeh or 4th April."

117. MSA, JDP, 1837, Vol. 11/405: Letter to W. H. Wathen . . . in the Persian Department.

118. MSA, JDP, 1837, Vol. 11/405: "Statement of Mahomed Yoosoof Saheb bin Mahhomed Hoossain Moorgay, Cazee of Bombay, dated Second day of Rubee-ul-avul, corresponding with 6 June 1837."

Chapter 2

1. MSA, JDP, 1850, Vol. 19: "Petition submitted by Gayasoodeen Mooftee of the Ahmednuggur Adawlut," August 20, 1850. See chapter 1 for further discussion of this regulation. Gayasoodeen's biography is sparse. In 1844 he applied to be mufti for the Bombay Sadr Diwani ʿAdalat, but the position was filled before his petition arrived. MSA, JDP, 1844, Vol. 24/973: "Substance of a Petition from Giasoodeen Mooftee to the Hon'ble the Governor in Council, dated 17 and received 22 April 1844."

2. "Petition submitted by Gayasoodeen Mooftee."

3. "Petition submitted by Gayasoodeen Mooftee." (One could also add Konkani, Kannada/Canarese, and Telugu to this list.)

4. "Petition submitted by Gayasoodeen Mooftee."

5. Drawing from the *Jān-i Bombāʾī* (*Soul of Bombay*, 1816), Green describes Bombay's Muslims as "Arabs and Turks, Iranis and Turanis, Sindis and Hindis, Kabulis and Qandaharis, Punjabis and Lahoris, Kashmiris and Multanis, Madrasis and Malabaris, Gujaratis and Dakanis, Baghdadis and Basrawis, Mascatis and Konkanis"—or what he terms "the full medley of Muslims from Bombay's vast maritime marketplace." Green, *Bombay Islam*, 4. Sectarian differences became a thornier issue in later periods. See Jalal, *Self and Sovereignty*, 149.

6. On the adoption of separate laws for some communities and not for others, including those among Cutchee Memons and Khojas, see Sharafi, *Law and Identity*, 121, 127–40. Pleas for greater pluralism came through legislative petitioning (see, e.g., UPSA, Judicial [Civil] Department Proceedings, Box 16, File No. 804B, 1896: Bill to render it permissive to the members of the Memon Community to declare themselves subject to Muhammadan Law) and through litigation (see Purohit, *Aga Khan Case*).

7. "Petition submitted by Gayasoodeen Mooftee."

8. See, e.g., MSA, JDP, 1850, Vol. 19: Letter from W. E. Frere, No. 1139 of 1850.

9. MSA, JDP, 1850, Vol. 19: Letter No. 3489, September 23, 1850. Company policy on hereditary offices was inconsistent. Two years later, an official in Khandesh expressed the opposite: "On a Kazee dying, his heir, if well qualified, should be

selected to succeed to the vacated office, in preference to anyone else not belonging to the family of the deceased." MSA, JDP, 1853, Vol. 20: Letter from A. Elphinstone, Esq., August 21, 1852.

10. MSA, JDP, 1864, Vol. 6: No. 214, "General Statement shewing [*sic*] the lands and emoluments now enjoyed by the Cazees in the several Districts of the Bombay Presidency."

11. Wuttan (*waṯan*) here refers to the hereditary (home)lands assigned to officeholders. *Waṯandārs* are possessors of *waṯans*. Under the Mughals, *waṯan-jāgīrs* were *jāgīrs* (land grants) assigned to *manṣabdārs* (officers) in their home districts. By the nineteenth century, the term *waṯan* had become almost interchangeable with other types of land grants, including *inʿāms* ("financial subsidies and presents") and *madad-i maʿāsh* grants (grants-in-aid, subsistence grants). On Mughal *waṯans*, see Habib, *Agrarian System*, 302, 579. On *waṯans* and *inʿāms* under the British, see Sturman, *Government of Social Life*, 52–68. On *madad-i maʿāsh* grants, see Muzaffar Alam, *Crisis of Empire*, 112–20.

12. *Qazipan* roughly translates to "qaziship," the condition or state of being a qazi. The term is a compound of the Arabic *qāẓī* and the Sanskritic suffix/affix *-pan* (the state or condition of being the object to which it is attached). The English suffixes "-hood," "-ship," and "-ness" are rough equivalents. Platts, *Dictionary of Urdu*, 269.

13. MSA, JDP, 1833, Vol. 6/271: Letter to J. H. Pelly, Esq., Acting Judge, Tannah, No. 42, February 11, 1833.

14. After Hasan ʿAli, the qazi of Surat, passed away, the acting judge sought recommendations for the vacancy. After receiving several self-nominations, the judge consulted the local *jamāʿat* (community organization) to find a suitable replacement. MSA, JDP, 1837, Vol. 11/405: No. 655 of 1837, Cazees, Surat, Death of late Husen Ulee Reported.

15. Similarly, when Muhammad ʿAli, the qazi at Dhandhoka, passed away, the judge at Ahmedabad recommended that the qazi's son take the position, and the government approved. MSA, JDP, 1837, Vol. 11/405: No. 118 of 1837, Cazees, Death of [Mahomed Ally].

16. Cazees, Surat, Death of late Husen Ulee Reported.

17. See, e.g., correspondence surrounding the appointments of Abdool Ruhim for Vijayadrug and Fakeer Mahomed of Gogo in MSA, JDP, 1837, Vol. 11/405.

18. The British Library holds sample qazi sanads from earlier periods. See, e.g., OMS/OR 11697 and OMS/OR 11699.

19. House of Commons, Parliamentary Papers, 1829, Vol. 23, Paper No. 201, "Regulations passed by the Governments of *Bengal, Fort St. George,* and *Bombay* in the Year 1827," 302. The language of the sanad was intentionally vague.

20. The text varied slightly across sanads. The text here follows Ummeermeea Fujjoomeea's canceled sanad. MSA, JDP, 1853, Vol. 20: No. 923 of 1853, "Ahmedabad: Umeermeea Fujjoomeea, Sunnud Cancelled."

21. MSA, JDP, 1832, Vol. 4/247: "Substance of a petition from the Undersigned principal Moosulmans under the Jurisdiction of Kazee Shumsoodeen Wullud Kazee Moohummud inhabitants of Kurdee . . . 25 June 1832."

22. MSA, JDP, 1832, Vol. 4/427: "Substance of a petition from the undersigned [principal] Musulmans of Hurnee . . . 19 June 1832"; and Shaw's letter, August 14, 1832.

23. MSA, JDP, 1832, Vol. 4/427: Notes on Shaw's letter, August 14, 1832.

24. MSA, JDP, 1832, Vol. 4/427: "Substance of a petition from Kazee Shaboodeen Wullud Kazee Adam Hukeem . . . 9 July 1832."

25. MSA, JDP, 1832, Vol. 4/247: "Substance of a petition from Kazee Inoosbin Kazee Ahmed . . . 7 July 1832."

26. MSA, JDP, 1836, Vol. 10/363: "The Petition from Cauzy Muhammed Sufdur." The loose application of this policy led to the introduction of "new rules" in 1850. See MSA, JDP, 1850, Vol. 19: Rules respecting the qualifications of qazis.

27. "Petition from Cauzy Muhammed Sufdur."

28. The writing is unclear here. I take Nicholas Abbott's suggestion of "Khwas," as in *ḵẖawāṣṣ*, meaning ministers, grandees, nobles, or distinguished persons. Platts, *Dictionary of Urdu*, 495.

29. MSA, JDP, 1836, Vol. 10/363: "A list of Sunnuds."

30. MSA, JDP, 1836, Vol. 10/363: No. 381 of 1836, Bombay Sudr Foujdaree Udalut to J. P. Willoughby, Secretary to the Government in the Judicial Department, Bombay, September 19,1836.

31. MSA, JDP, 1836, Vol. 10/363: Judicial Consultation No. 42, September 19, 1836.

32. MSA, JDP, 1836, Vol. 10/363: Minute by the Right Hon'ble the Governor Subscribed to by the Board.

33. MSA, JDP, 1837, Vol. 11/405: No. 5 of 1837, from the Poona, Court of Udalat to the Chief Secretary to Government, Bombay, April 11, 1837. The petitioner "Shaik Ally" (son of Shaikh Fukee Camel) was not the same "Shaikh ʿAli" (son of Mahomed Hoosain) later appointed as Hyatoolakhan's naʾib.

34. Qazis sometimes used *ḥaqq* to refer to their claim to the office, but Shaik Ally's usage here refers to the fee families would pay to the qazi as his due, or *ḥaqq*, for performing a ceremony. MSA, JDP, 1837, Vol. 11/405: "Translation of a representation of Shaik Ally Wullud Shaik Fukee Camel . . . 29 March 1837."

35. In 1842 petitioners accused Qazi Lootfoodeen [Luṭf-ud-Dīn] at Ahmednagar of impropriety. The complaints against him included "exact[ing] a fee of two hundred Rupees for affixing his seal to deeds, for which he [also] took a bond in writing." The qazi's fee was exorbitant, but formal disciplinary charges could not be brought against him because he had never received adequate guidance. Judge Hutt learned while investigating that "no Table of Fees . . . was ever laid down for the guidance of Lootfoodeen . . . nor was any Table of Fees whatever ever delivered for the same purpose to that officer." MSA, JDP, 1842, Vol. 21/798: Letter from Hutt, April 1, 1842; Letter from Birdwood, July 26, 1842.

36. Fees for first marriages were between two and three rupees. (See chapter 3 for further discussion of fees.)

37. MSA, JDP, 1837, Vol. 11/405: "Memorandum" from J. P. Willoughby, April 25, 1837. The exact circumstances remain murky. In his defense, Muhammad Safdar

sent petitions to the judge at Pune (now lost) and to the governor in council at Bombay in which he claimed that he had been suspended from office and therefore could not perform the ceremonies, but Judge Bell clarified that the qazi was not suspended but had "virtually suspended himself" by refusing to work. MSA, JDP, 1837, Vol. 11/405: "Humble Petition of Kazee Mahomed Sufdur"; No. 23 of 1837 to the Secretary to Government, Bombay from the Poona, Court of Udalut, May 31, 1837; and "Report" from Hutt, August 14, 1837.

38. MSA, JDP, 1837, Vol. 11/405: Minute by the Right Hon'ble the Governor Subscribed to by the Board, September 2, 1837.

39. Judge Bell asked both qazis to submit their papers in December 1837, but it was Ramadan and Hyatoolakhan could not submit his on time. Hyatoolakhan received permission to have a "confidential Agent" carry the documents "to prevent their being lost or mislaid." MSA, JDP, 1837, Vol. 11/405: Humble petition of Cawjee Syed Haya Toolla Khan, December 11, 1837; and MSA, JDP, 1838, Vol. 14/458: Memorandum, January 25, 1838.

40. Before Hyatoolakhan submitted any of his documents, Muhammad Safdar wrote to declare them forgeries and "requested that they might be called for in the original and examined by a committee comprised of the Government Moonshee, the Cazee and Moolvee." Memorandum, January 25, 1838.

41. Hyatoolakhan's documentation was extensive. Unlike Muhammad Safdar, who presented several sanads belonging to his family members, Hyatoolakhan presented evidence that came primarily from the 1820s and 1830s, when the two were feuding over land. See MSA, JDP, 1838, Vol. 14/458: Letter from Kennedy, Oriental Translator to Government, to Willoughby, February 21, 1838.

42. MSA, JDP, 1840, Vol. 21/621: "Humble petition of Cazee Mahamad Sufdar, January 9, 1840." (I have amended some parts of the translated petition for clarity.)

43. MSA, JDP, 1840, Vol. 21/621: Memorandum, passed February 26, 1840.

44. MSA, JDP, 1843, Vol. 23/876: From John Warden, Judge at Pune, to the Register of the Sudder Court, Bombay, April 6, 1843. (To guard against reprobation, Warden quotes earlier government memos and correspondence, which I omit here for clarity.) The Company refused to appoint Muhammad Safdar's son as his replacement and in 1845 finally granted Hyatoolakhan a sanad naming him as qazi for Pune. MSA, JDP, 1844, Vol. 24/973: No. 344: Mahomed Hyder, Praying for Cazeeship of Poona; and 1845, Vol. 18: No. 697: Syud Huyatoolla Khan . . . Sunnud.

45. See Lhost, "Writing Law," 261–62.

46. An 1836 memorandum on "examinations" suggests that committees with a European officer, a native judge, the judge's "sheristedar," a "mamlutdar," and a "respectable and intelligent native gentleman, not in the Company's service," administered exams. To pass, candidates were expected (1) "to read such papers [as] Petitions, and proceedings in Criminal & Civil suits . . . and the Printed book of Government Regulations with tolerable fluency"; (2) "to be able to take down in writing in a good plain hand any depositions or examinations of witnesses, and any orders, and judgments that may be passed"; (3) "to answer questions on some of the most prominently useful points of the general Regulations"; and (4) to be "of respectable character." MSA, JDP, 1836, Vol. 19/372: "Rules for Committee."

47. MSA, JDP, 1853, Vol. 20: Letter from A. W. Jones, Esq., No. 71, February 26, 1853.

48. MSA, JDP, 1885, Vol. 21: "The Humble petition of Cazee Abdurrahman."

49. On Hindustani, see the later discussion.

50. MSA, JDP, 1850, Vol. 19: "Substance of a Petition from Moojrodin Wullud Nooroodin . . . dated 15 and received 24 August 1849."

51. Knowledge of these languages alone did not imply legal knowledge. On the "vernacularization" of Islamic law on the subcontinent, see Nandini Chatterjee, *Negotiating Mughal Law*, among others.

52. MSA, JDP, 1845, Vol. 18: Letter from R. D. Luard, No. 109, January 29, 1845.

53. Hindustani might not be the obvious regional vernacular for the Konkan, but it is not surprising to find a spoken dialect loosely classified as "Hindustani" in the region, especially given the history of transregional trade along the coast. Lelyveld, "Colonial Knowledge"; Lelyveld, "Fate of Hindustani"; Majeed, "'Jargon of Indostan.'"

54. See, e.g., the petition from Qazi ʿAbd-ur-Raḥmān, August 3, 1845, and discussions surrounding the qazi's office in Anjanwel and Severndroog from 1860, in which the judges reflected that the Shafiʿi candidate "ha[d] read none of the great Law books of the Mahomedans and experienced some difficulty in explaining the portion of the Hidaya given him to read." (The *Hidaya* is influential in the Hanafi school.) The Hanafi qazi passed a "tolerable examination and . . . may be recommended for a Sunnud conferring him as Kazee in the Hunfee sect of the Unjunwell and Sooverndoorg Talookas, except in such villages as have other persons appointed to them." MSA, JDP, 1855, Vol. 21: No. 512, "Appointment of Cazee for Certain Villages in Ratnagherry"; and MSA, JDP, 1860, Vol. 17: No. 129, "Absorption of the cazayut at Unjunwell and Sooverndroog."

55. For a discussion of the *Hidaya* in the context of Anglo-Muslim law, see Hallaq, *Sharīʿa*, 373–76; and Stephens, *Governing Islam*, 27, 31–32.

56. This transition is the subject of chapter 4.

57. On law books and knowledge of the law, see, e.g., Stephens, *Governing Islam*, 72–73, 117–18; Fraas, "Readers, Scribes, and Collectors"; and Kolsky, *Colonial Justice*, 117. For comparison, see Zhang, *Circulating the Code*. On popular publishing and reading publics, see also Orsini, *Hindi Public Sphere*; Robb, *Print*; J. Barton Scott and Ingram, "What Is a Public?"; and Stark, *Empire of Books*.

58. Later, petitions for the reintroduction of the qazi's office quoted specific passages and listed specific books. The "Statement of Objects and Reasons" for the "Bill for the appointment of Persons to the Office of Kazi" explicitly referred to the "powers and duties" of the qazi from Book XX of the *Hidaya*, and the Anjuman-i Panjab quoted from it to support its position. Furthermore, the "Memorial of Maulavi Muhammad Sidik and others" specifically mentioned the "*Hedáya*," "*Shah Wakaya*," "*Dúrúl Mikhtár*," "*Fatawa-e-Alamgíri*, &c." as the "Muhammadan law books" qazis should know. Such specificity did not appear in petitions from this earlier period when Company officials themselves lamented the dearth of law books available to them. BL, IOR/L/PJ/6/15, File 803: Bill for the appointment of persons to the office of Kazi; and IOR/L/PJ/6/17, File 954: Anjuman-i Panjab

Proceedings on Papers relative to the Bill for appointment of persons to the office of Kází.

59. MSA, JDP, 1850, Vol. 19: Frere's letter to Larken, No. 1139, July 16, 1850 (referring to Budihal, Karnataka).

60. Frere's letter to Larken.

61. MSA, JDP, 1849, Vol 25: Letter from J. W. Woodcock, Senior Assistant Judge, Khandesh Court of Adawlut, April 30, 1849; Judge Bazett's remarks in MSA, JDP, 1850, Vol. 19: Khandesh Circuit Court, Letter No. 11 of 1849, December 14, 1849.

62. Letter from J. W. Woodcock.

63. Letter from J. W. Woodcock.

64. Khandesh Circuit Court, Letter No. 11 of 1849. Hoossain Beebee was the widow of Qazi Muttoo Mia; Chandabee was the widow of Qazi Muhammad Aʿzam. Hoossain Beebee wanted her son-in-law, Ghulam ʿAli, to take the position of deputy.

65. MSA, JDP, 1850, Vol. 19: Minute, February 23, 1850.

66. MSA, JDP, 1850, Vol. 19: Letter to the Secretary to Government, No. 1196, April 20, 1850.

67. Letter to the Secretary to Government.

68. After Hoossain Beebee's husband's death, Mr. Hodges, then first assistant collector of Khandesh, allowed her brother-in-law, Muhammad Aʿzam (Chandabee's husband), to take over as qazi. When he passed away in 1845, her son-in-law served as deputy until Woodcock's selection, ʿAbd-ur-Rahman, stepped in. MSA, JDP, 1850, Vol. 19: Khandesh Circuit Court, Letter No. 11 of 1849, December 14, 1849.

69. The parcel of land was approximately 600 *bīghas*, valued at 1,157 rupees, 9 *annas*, and 9 *pie*. The annual amount of rent was just over five hundred rupees, which, when combined with cultivation yields, amounted to over one thousand rupees annually. The loss of that income would have been a tremendous blow.

70. MSA, JDP, 1850, Vol. 19: Minute, September, 24 1850. The question here revolved around whether the lands assigned to qazis fell under the Hereditary Offices Act, Act XI of 1843. Government opinion on the matter was split.

71. MSA, JDP, 1850, Vol. 19: Letter No. 5969, October 9, 1850.

72. MSA, JDP, 1853, Vol. 20: Letter No. 152, April 4, 1851.

73. MSA, JDP, 1853, Vol. 20: Letter No. 1435, April 8, 1853. This recommendation arose in part because Chandabee claimed that only 100 bighas of the 600 or so bighas the women claimed were attached to the qazi's service. Other qazis also had their land grants reviewed by the Inam Commissioner around this time. See, e.g., MSA, JDP, 1853, Vol. 20: No. 720, Relative to the Claim of Cazee Amroodin; 1854, Vol. 12: No. 145, Cazees, Alienated Service Land; 1859, Vol. 14: No. 59, Cazees, Sholapoor; and 1861, Vol. 7: No. 731, Cazees, Poonah, Certain Appointments. The government established the Inam Commission to investigate (and reclaim) lands held under rent- and tax-free title. For reports on the commission, see BL, IOR/V/23/256, *Narrative of the Bombay Inam Commission and Supplementary Settlements*; BL, IOR/V/26/312/7, *A Brief Report on the entire operations of the inam commission from its commencement*; and Knight, *Inam Commission Unmasked*. On

the effects, see Jegatheesan, "Inam Settlement"; Preston, *Devs of Cincvad*; Rabitoy, "Sovereignty"; and Sturman, *Government of Social Life*, 56–69.

74. Attempts to rationalize these appointments appear in proposals to transfer individuals and to rearrange qazis' jurisdictions. See, e.g., Arthur St. John Richardson's proposed rearrangement in the Khadesh district, MSA, JDP, 1857, Vol. 18: No. 827, Cazees of Dhoolia; the transfer of the village Poontambee to the jurisdiction of the qazi of Patoda, MSA, JDP, 1855, Vol. 20: No. 531, Ahmednugger; and subsequent proposals in MSA, JDP, 1858, Vol. 12: No. 64, Judicial Department 1858: Cazees, Khandeish, Certain Appointments.

75. Qazis periodically applied for transfer back to their home districts. In 1840 Syud Nizamoodeen wullud Syud Boorhamodeen "pray[ed]" to be transferred to Ankleshwar. MSA, JDP, 1840, Vol. 21/621: No. 445 of 1840, Cazees of Broach. Later, Sayyid Mir Sahib applied to be transferred back to his home territory, where his family resided and the income for the qazi's office was higher. MSA, JDP, 1855, Vol. 20: "The humble petition of Syud Meersaheb Cazee of Ranpoor Pergunnah Dhundooka, Zillah Ahmedabad," July 19, 1854.

76. See, e.g., Muhammad Safdar's story and MSA, JDP, 1860, Vol. 17: No. 258, Dharwar Cazees, Mahomed Essoob wd. Mahomeed Dawood, Application for the Cazaet of Bankapoor. The hereditary claimant here received eighteen months to qualify for the examination.

77. On petitioning in South Asia, see De and Travers, "Petitioning and Political Cultures" (along with the other contributions to their special issue); Bhavani Raman, *Document Raj*; and more broadly, Ben-Bassat, *Petitioning the Sultan*; van Voss, *Petitions in Social History*; Zaret, *Origins of Democratic Culture*; and Yannakakis, *Art of Being In-Between*.

78. MSA, JDP, 1845, Vol. 18: No. 204, Poona auxiliary Horse and the Military Cantonment at Seroor; MSA, JDP, 1841, Vol. 21/711: No. 554, Rutnagherry, Cazee Mahomed . . . prays that persons residing within his jurisdiction may be restricted from having their marriages performed by a Cazee of different district.

79. MSA, JDP, 1850, Vol. 19: No. 18, Jooneer, Cazee Mahomed Asslum, complaint of the interference with his duties.

80. I take this phrase from Benton and Ford, *Rage for Order*, 6–7.

81. Muhammad Safdar was nonsuited by the native commissioner at Pune, and the appeal was also rejected. MSA, JDP, 1837, Vol. 6/271: "Humble petition of Kazee Seyud Hyat oolla Khan of Poona," n.d. The land had been split equally among the two officeholders by order of the Peshwa's chief minister (*dīwān*) around 1808.

82. BL, IOR/V/22/551, Roodrageer Gosavee, deceased, and his Disciple and Heir Vishwaeshwurgeer [Appellant] v. Kazee Hyutoolakhan wulud Kazee Mahomed Tukeeka [Respondent], in *Reports of the Selected Cases Decided by the Sudder Dewanee Adawlut, Bombay*, 95–98.

83. See, e.g., Dattatraya Vishwanath Sulakhe v. The Secretary of State for India (1949) 51 Bom LR 133; Sattappa Gurusattappa Hukeri v. Mahomedsaheb Appalal Kazi (1935) 136 Ind Cas 305; and Baba Kakaji Shet Shimpi v. Nasaruddin Valad Aminuddin Qazi and Another (1893) 18 B. 103. See also Suehiro, "Office of the Qazi."

84. BL, IOR/Z/P/3166: Index to the Bombay Judicial Proceedings, 1832.

85. MSA, JDP, 1833, Vol. 6/271: Letter to J. H. Pelly, Esq., Acting Judge, Tannah, No. 42, February 11, 1833.

86. MSA, JDP, 1838, Vol. 14/458: Letter to the Secretary to Government, Bombay from Shaw[?], Conkun Court of Adawlut, December 5, 1837.

87. See, e.g., MSA, JDP, 1838, Vol. 14/458: "Humble Petition of Cazee Hoossein son of Cazee Kootboodeen," March 7, 1838; Letter No. 767 to Cazee Hoossain Kootboodeen, Bombay, April 20, 1838.

88. MSA, JDP, 1838, Vol. 14/458: Letter to the Secretary to Government, December 5, 1837.

89. Sharafi, *Law and Identity*, 235.

90. MSA, JDP, 1838, Vol. 14/458: "Humble Petition of the undersigned Moosoolman Inhabitants of Cusba Tannah," January 8, 1838.

91. Regulation XXVI of 1827 authorized district judges to address issues of misconduct. The principal amin apparently did not think he ranked high enough to settle the dispute, and the court qazi felt there was no valid basis for the complaint in Islamic jurisprudence.

92. MSA, JDP, 1838, Vol. 14/458: Letter from the Konkun, Court of Adawlut, January 12, 1838.

93. On the courts' "objective" status, see Sharafi, *Law and Identity*, 258.

94. Details of the investigation appear in MSA, JDP, 1842, Vol. 22/799: No. 22 of 1842, Cazees, Rutnagherry, Misconduct of the Kazee Abdool Kurreem.

95. Failure to provide maintenance for one's wife can be grounds for divorce in some schools of jurisprudence. (See chapters 4 and 8 for a more detailed discussion of this issue.)

96. If the family knows where he is and he sends financial support, the wife cannot make legitimate claims of absenteeism (*mafqūd-ul-k̲h̲abarī*) or of failure to provide maintenance.

97. The Muhammadan law officers from the sadr ʿadalat of Bombay and the district (*ẕillaʿ*) courts at Ahmednagar, Sholapur, Pune, Tannah, and Surat provided answers to the seven questions.

98. MSA, JDP, 1842, Vol. 22/799: "Humble Petition of Kajee Abdool Cureem bin Abdool Khan."

99. While the Hanafi school is predominant in South Asia, the Shafiʿi school has a strong presence along India's western coast, owing to long-standing trade connections. The city of Bombay had followers of all four Sunni schools, and several Shiʿi schools, but the biggest factions within the community consisted of Shafiʿis and Hanafis.

100. Muhammad Ibrahim v. Gulam Ahmed et al., Suit No. 49 of 1863, 239–40; on guardianship and *maẕhab*, see also Vikør, *Between God*, 301.

101. "Complaints against the Cazee of Bombay," *BTJC*, July 6, 1859.

102. "Writ of Habeas Corpus," *BTJC*, June 8, 1859.

103. Her father, husband, and cousin battled it out in court until 1863 at least.

104. See "Complaints against the Cazee."

105. The newspaper refers to a petition dated March 2, 1859, but the petition was not submitted to government until May 11. It was returned for failure to follow

proper rules and finally accepted on May 28. "Editor's Room: Note," *BTJC*, July 6, 1859.

106. "The Cazee vs. the Mahomedans of Bombay," *BTJC*, March 12, 1859.

107. "Complaints against the Cazee."

108. "Complaints against the Cazee."

109. "Editorial," *BTJC*, June 29, 1859.

110. Assessors combined the outside knowledge of an expert witness with the evaluative prerogative of a jury. At the end of their commission, assessors would write an opinion that the judge could either accept or reject, in total or in part.

111. "The Cazee Trial," *BTJC*, August 24, 1859 (emphasis added).

112. "Acquittal of the Cazee of Bombay," *BTJC*, November 9, 1859.

113. The assessors explicitly referred to changing venues, if the inquest were to follow Islamic legal procedure.

114. "The Cazee of Bombay," *BTJC*, October 22, 1859; "Acquittal of the Cazee."

115. "Acquittal of the Cazee." (See chapter 3 for discussion of the civil suit.)

116. "Acquittal of the Cazee."

117. "Acquittal of the Cazee."

118. "The Mahomedans and Their Cazee," *BTJC*, November 12, 1859.

119. The *Times* referred to the faction opposing Yusuf Moorghay as "persons of the Concanee sect . . . and for the most part of the lowest order of their community." "Acquittal of the Cazee."

120. Early Company reports identify Yusuf Moorghay as a Hanafi, but other accounts, including the civil suit surrounding Khuteeza Bebee's marriage, suggest he was Shafiʿi. (It would not have been uncommon, though, for him to be familiar with multiple schools.)

121. The dispute over Khuteeza Bebee's marriage led to a protracted civil suit, though many of the participants later reconciled and together supported the city's leading Muslim organizations.

122. Publics played an important role in colonial policy. See Ingram, "Crises of the Public"; Orsini, "What Did They Mean?"; Orsini, *Hindi Public Sphere*; J. Barton Scott and Ingram, "What Is a Public?"; and Charu Singh, "Science and Its Publics." For other contexts, see Eickelman and Anderson, *New Media*; and Salvatore and Eickelman, *Public Islam*.

Chapter 3

1. See chapter 1.

2. Yusuf Moorghay was appointed in 1837; during trial, he stated his age as eighty-eight. "Supreme Court—Plea Side (the Rival Cazees)," *Bombay Times and Standard*, March 12, 1861. He may have been closer to eighty-six.

3. MSA, JDP, 1859, Vol. 14: No. 906, Proposal of the Home Gov't for the abolition of the office of Cazee.

4. See, e.g., Tahir Mahmood, *Muslim Personal Law*, 63–65. For a recent reappraisal, see Redding, *Secular Need*, 67–69.

5. Michael R. Anderson, "Islamic Law"; Michael R. Anderson, "Legal Scholarship"; Hallaq, *Sharīʿa*, 377; Kugle, "Framed, Blamed and Renamed"; Stephens, *Governing Islam*; Strawson, "Islamic Law."

6. On the ascendance of Anglo-Indian "justice," see Fisch, *Cheap Lives*; and Singha, *Despotism of Law.*

7. Nandini Chatterjee provides a succinct analysis of the way one Muslim judge worked from within the Anglo-Indian legal system to shape legal interpretation in "Law, Culture and History." See also Sharafi, "New History."

8. The effects of Act XI of 1864 varied not only across officeholders but also across regions. Jalal, *Self and Sovereignty*, 145.

9. See also debates over *waqf*s (endowments) in, e.g., Abbasi, "*Sharīʾa*"; and Kozlowski, *Muslim Endowments.*

10. Following Sharafi, Chatterjee treats these lawyers and judges as "native anthropologists" whose insider perspectives gave them greater authority when addressing outsider audiences. Nandini Chatterjee, "Law, Culture and History," 46. See also chapter 7.

11. Interest in protecting "vulnerable" Muslim women was a consistent feature of colonialist and imperialist interventions. See Hussin, *Politics of Islamic Law*, 134–37.

12. In a related civil suit, *Muhammad Ibrahim bin Muhammad Sayad Parkar (Plaintiff) v. Gulam Ahmed bin Muahmmad Sayad Roghe and Muhammad Sayad bin Muhammad Ibrahim Roghe (Defendants)*, the court described the "Kázi of Bombay" (Yusuf Moorghay) as "of the Sháfi sect." Suit No. 49 of 1863, Bombay Original Civil Jurisdiction, 239. When Moorghay was appointed in 1837, judicial department officials listed him as a Sunni but did not mention his school. The *Gazetteer of Bombay City and Island* mentions Moorghay within the section on "Konkani Muslims," which seems to suggest he was Shafiʿi. Edwardes, *Gazetteer of Bombay City*, 1:254, 261. See also chapter 1.

13. Elsewhere, I have documented Sayyid Ahmad Husain's complaints against the Company's interference with his collection of fees on *vakālat-* and *mukẖtār-nāmas* (deeds of representation; powers of attorney), but he was not the only qazi to present complaints of this kind. See chapter 1; and Lhost, "Writing Law."

14. The most successful effort appeared in 1844, when the government compiled data comparing incomes in 1843 with those in 1833, revealing a decrease in the qazis' incomes across most of the districts surveyed. MSA, JDP, 1844, Vol. 25/947: "Statement of the allowances of Cazees and other Mahomedan Officers."

15. MSA, JDP, 1864, Vol. 6: S. No. 207 under "Information required by the Govt of India regarding the lands and emoluments enjoyed by [qazis]."

16. See Lhost, "Writing Law," for additional details on fees. Discussion of Qazi Nur-ud-Din Husain's records also appears in chapter 6.

17. Yusuf Moorghay's accounts revealed an "aggregate . . . income from fees and gratuities" of Rs. 3,917-8-0 and Rs. 3,778-12-0 for the previous years. His income dropped to Rs. 1,440 for the year following Ahmadshah's interference. Muhammad Yussub v. Sayad Ahmed (1861) Bom HCR 1 Appendix xviii–xlii (1862–65) at xli. (This case uses an unconventional citation because the Bombay Supreme Court

became the Bombay High Court in 1862, and the case was not reported until after the change.)

18. *Muhammad Yussub*, Bom HCR 1 at xxxviii.

19. "Supreme Court—Plea Side."

20. The qazi of Hansot produced a similar table for his fees in 1834. He collected Rs. 2-2 for each "Neeka [*nikāḥ*; marriage]" for local ("kusbatee [*qaṣbatī*]") Muslims; Rs. 3-0 for *nikāhs* among Pinjara Kunbis; Rs. 2-2 for releasing the bride's dower (*mahr*); and Rs. 3-2 for performing second marriages for Hindus, along with collecting fees on shops, crops and sundry goods, and other rents. MSA, JDP, 1834, Vol. 6/296: "Memorandum of the fees levied by the Kauzee of Hunsote."

21. *Muhammad Yussub*, Bom HCR 1 at xxxvii. Yusuf Moorghay likely inherited the registers from his predecessor.

22. *Muhammad Yussub*, Bom HCR 1 at xxxvii.

23. "Supreme Court—Plea Side"; *Muhammad Yussub*, Bom HCR 1 at xxxviii.

24. The court considered two sets of legal ideas. The first related to the issue of "disturbance of a franchise," for which the court drew parallels between the qazi's office and "the franchise of holding a court, of keeping a fair or market, of taking [a] toll &c., or . . . any other species of franchise whatsoever." The second issue revolved around the qazi's involvement in marriages and divorces, for which the court determined that "the entry [of marriage] in the Kázi's books is the best, the safest, and the most enduring medium of proof," and as it was for marriage, "so it is of divorce." *Muhammad Yussub*, Bom HCR 1 at xix, xxvii.

25. *Muhammad Yussub*, Bom HCR 1 at xxxvii. Other precedents included Peter v. Kendal 6 B & C. 703; and Boyter v. Dodsworth 6 Term Rep. 681.

26. *Muhammad Yussub*, Bom HCR 1 at xxx.

27. MSA, JDP, 1859, Vol. 14: Letter from Charles Wood to Viscount Canning, August 31, 1859.

28. MSA, JDP, 1864, Vol. 22: Abolition of Hindoo and Mahomedan Law Officers (Comments submitted to the Honorable Board, October 14, 1862); WBSA, JDP, June 1861: Kazis, Letter from H. U. Browne to Seton-Karr, May 2, 1861.

29. Charles Wood to Viscount Canning.

30. WBSA, JDP, April 1861: Kazis, No. 193, Letter from E. Jackson to the Sec'y to the Gov't of Bengal, February 28, 1861.

31. MSA, JDP, 1860, Vol. 17: Minute by Judge H. T. Raikes, July 5, 1859.

32. Both registration acts were later repealed by Act XVI of 1864, "An Act to Provide for the Registration of Assurances." See Whitley Stokes, "First Appendix," in *Anglo-Indian Codes*, 1008. On the nuances of Anglo-Indian registration law, see Jagannāthaprasāda, *Manual of Registration*.

33. WBSA, JDP, April 1861: Kazis, No. 193, Letter from E. Jackson to the Sec'y to the Gov't of Bengal, February 28, 1861.

34. MSA, JDP, 1860, Vol. 17: Minute by G. Loch, August 10, 1859.

35. MSA, JDP, 1860, Vol. 17: Minute by Raikes.

36. MSA, JDP, 1859, Vol. 14: Extract from G. F. Edmonton, Register of the Court of Sudder Dewanny Adawlut, North-Western Provinces, Allahabad, October 9, 1843,

reproduced in Secretary of State Charles Wood's letter to Governor General Canning, August 31, 1859.

37. Extract from G. F. Edmonton.

38. MSA, JDP, 1860, Vol. 17: No. 6063, From Lushington; Minute by Raikes.

39. From Lushington.

40. From Lushington.

41. MSA, JDP, 1865, Vol. 22: Extract from a letter from the Acting Registrar of the Suder Adawlut, July 31, 1862.

42. Several of the judges who supported the abolition of qazis advocated the continuation of native law officers as expounders of law. Drawing on the minutes from various judges, A. W. Russell, register of the sadr diwani ʿadalat in Bengal, confirmed that the court did not want to see the court qazi position terminated but suggested that his title might be changed "to one denoting his real functions, the exposition of Mahomedan Law." MSA, JDP, 1860, Vol. 17: From A. W. Russell, No. 1138, August 1859; and MSA, JDP, 1859, Vol. 14: No. 35 from Charles Wood, August 31, 1859.

43. MSA, JDP, 1865, Vol. 22: No. 475 and No. 26 of 1864/65: Hindoo & Mahomedan Law Officers.

44. Extract from . . . the Acting Registrar.

45. See, e.g., MSA, JDP, 1860, Vol. 17: Lushington's remarks to the Secretary to the Government of India, October 18, 1859, and the accompanying minute by Samuels.

46. See, e.g., Lushington's remarks; and the minutes by Samuels (August 4, 1859) and G. Loch (August 10, 1859).

47. MSA, JDP, 1860, Vol. 17: Lushington to the Secretary to the Government of India, Home, November 23, 1859 in MSA, JDP, 1860, vol. 17.

48. Extract from . . . the Acting Registrar.

49. Extract from . . . the Acting Registrar.

50. MSA, JDP, 1865, Vol. 22: "The Humble Petition of Mohomed Abdoola wd. Ghulam Husain," August 17, 1862.

51. WBSA, JDP, February 1863, Law Officers: Resolution by the Hon'ble Lt-Gov of Bengal, No. 1869. The resolution refers to the "CPC coming into operation" on this date, which may mean act XXV of 1861.

52. WBSA, JDP, June 1864, Vol. 70, Nos. 1–11: Abolishing [the] office of Hindu Law Officer.

53. Act No. XI of 1864 in *Collection of the Acts,* [45]. When the bill was up for debate, advocates argued that the act "would be a mere repealing enactment, and would erase some twenty-five Regulations and Acts in whole in or part from the Statute Book." It was designed to decrease government involvement that developed after they "found Cazis existing in every City, Town, and Pergunnah," when "all that [their] earlier legislators sought to do was to define generally what the duties of Cazes were, and to provide that persons of character . . . should be appointed to those offices." See Abstract of the Proceedings of the Council of Governor-General of India assembled for the purpose of making Laws and Regulations under the provisions of the act of Parliament 24 and 25 Vic. C. 67 under "Hindoo and Mahomedan Law Officers' Bill" in MSA, JDP, 1865, Vol. 22: Hindu and Muslim Law Officers.

54. Schedule attached to Act No. XI of 1864, *Collection of the Acts*, [45–51].

55. The act did not address all of the regulations relating to qazis and law officers in the Bombay Presidency, so the government there subsequently passed legislation repealing those additional acts.

56. Clause II, Act No. XI of 1864, *Collection of the Acts*, [45].

57. On these earlier moves, see Travers, *Ideology and Empire*.

58. WBSA, JDP, September 1862, Law Officers: Memorandum from C. J. Mackenzie, Esq., Magistrate at Midnapore, No. 174, August 15, 1862. See also WBSA, JDP, February 1863: Law Officers.

59. MSA, JDP, 1865, Vol. 22: "The Humble Petition of Mohomed Abdoola wd. Ghulam Husain," August 17, 1862.

60. MSA, JDP, 1866, Vol. 6: Cazees. Bombay, death of Mahomed Yoosoof Moorgay. When a dispute arose over Muhammad Husain's successor in 1878, the court recognized that "Kazi Mahomed Husain Murgay, however, assumed the office, and was generally accepted by the community as Kazi of Bombay. No difficulty occurred in his lifetime." Advocate-General of Bombay (Plaintiff) v. Moulvi Abdul Kadir Jitaker and Others (Defendants), (1894) 18 B. 401, 415.

61. It was Lieutenant-Colonel F. M. Birch, officiating commissioner and superintendent, Delhi Division, who remarked on the "consternation" felt after Act XI of 1864's introduction. BL, IOR/L/PJ/6/17, File 954: Papers relative to the Bill for appointment of persons to the office of Kází, Letter No. 661, Delhi, March 24, 1880.

62. *Muhammad Yussub*, Bom HCR 1 at xxx. The *Hidaya* was a thirteenth-century compendium of Hanafi jurisprudence that became the source par excellence for British interpretations of Islamic law. For a reference to it in legislative debates, see, e.g., "Statement of Objects and Reasons," in BL, IOR/L/PJ/6/7, File 340: Bill for appointment of persons to the office of Kazi.

63. Jalal says complaints arose as early as 1865. Jalal, *Self and Sovereignty*, 148–49.

64. See Sharafi, *Law and Identity*, for Parsi law, esp. chap. 2, "Making Law"; and Nandini Chatterjee, "Universality in Difference," in *Making of Indian Secularism*, for Christian law.

65. NAI, Home, Judicial, June 1877, Nos. 361–66 (A): Registration of Muslim Marriages.

66. NAI, Home, Judicial, January 1876, Nos. 88–91: Bill to provide for the Voluntary Registration of Mahomedan Marriages and Divorces, H. L. Dampier, "Statement of Objects and Reasons," November 29, 1873.

67. Dampier, "Statement of Objects."

68. Officials regurgitated several key phrases throughout these debates. The "looseness of the marriage tie" was one of them; "machinery of registration" was another. See, e.g., NAI, Home, Judicial, December 1879, Nos. 185–89: Letter from C. G. Master (May 24, 1879); Dampier, "Statement of Objects"; and UPSA, Judicial (Civil) Dept. Proceedings, Sl. No. 10, Box No. 6B, File No. 245B.

69. Bill to provide for the Voluntary Registration.

70. NAI, Home, Judicial, February 1876, Nos. 42–81 (A): Right of Govt to Appoint Kazis.

71. NAI, Home, Judicial, June 1877, Nos. 361–66 (A): Registration of Muslim Marriages.

72. MSA, JDP, 1879, Vol. 91: Letter from M. A. Rogay, September 25, 1879. After the death of Yusuf Moorghay's successor in 1878, the Muslim community in Bombay feuded over his successor, leading to at least one legal dispute involving the attorney general of Bombay. Inquiries related to this dispute may have motivated Rogay's investigation, rather than the legislative discussions taking place at this time.

73. MSA, JDP, 1879, Vol. 91: Report No. 5562. Later, the government concluded that there was no information available on the third point, regarding the confiscation of lands, but it supplied cursory answers to points two and four.

74. NAI, Home, Judicial, December 1879, Nos. 185–89, Re-establishment of the office of Kazis in the Madras Presidency: Letter from C. G. Master, May 24, 1879.

75. NAI, Home, Judicial, December 1879, Nos. 185–89, Re-establishment of the office of Kazis in the Madras Presidency: Letter to the Right Honourable Vicount Cranbrook, Secretary of State for India, from the Home, Revenue and Agricultural Department, Judicial, No. 31, December 19, 1879. Also quoted in BL, IOR/L/PJ/6/2, File 76. They cite the role of Act XI of 1864 (an imperial act) as the source of the problem and the idea that only the imperial sovereign (not a district or provincial official) could appoint a qazi as their evidence.

76. BL, IOR/L/PJ/6/2, File 76: Re-establishment of office of Kazi for registration of Muslim marriages in Madras Presidency, "A Bill for Continuing the Office of Kazi among the Mahomedans."

77. NAI, Home, Judicial, December 1879, Nos. 185–89 (A): Proposal made by the Government of Madras to re-establish the Office of Kazi in the Madras Presidency: Letter from C. B[ernard], July 2, 1879.

78. For another telling of this act's history, see Lhost, "From Documents." ʿAbd-ul-Luteef describes the contents of his speech in appendix A, attached to UPSA, Judicial (Civil) Department Proceedings, Sl. No. 10, Box No. 6B, File No. 245B, Legislation to provide for the registration of certain domestic events in the Muhammadan and Hindu families. Along with H. L. Dampier and V. H. Schalch, ʿAdb-ul-Luteef contributed to the revised Bengal Act I of 1876. (See "Amended Bill to Provide for the Voluntary Registration of Mahomedan Marriages and Divorces.") A summary of Sayyid Ahmad's feelings appears in C. Bernard's comments on the draft proposal from Madras, July 2, 1879. NAI, Home, Judicial, December 1879, Nos. 185–89 (A): Proposal made by the Government of Madras to re-establish the Office of Kazi in the Madras Presidency; and NAI, Legislative Department, August 1880, Nos. 17–87 (A): The Kazi's Act.

79. BL, IOR/L/PJ/6/7, File 340: Bill for appointment of persons to office of Kazi: "Statement of Objects and Reasons."

80. "Statement of Objects and Reasons."

81. See, e.g., commentary in NAI, Home, Judicial, December 1879, Nos. 185–89: Re-establishment of the office of Kazis in the Madras Presidency; and BL, IOR/L/PJ/6/13, File 675: The Bill for the appointment of persons to the office of Kazi.

82. Jalal notes that interest in "restoring the office of qazi found support among educated Muslims cutting across regions and ideological divisions." Jalal, *Self and Sovereignty*, 148.

83. MSA, JDP, 1859, Vol. 14: Letter from Sir Charles Wood, Secretary of State for India, August 31, 1859.

84. "Anjuman-i Panjab Proceedings in connection with the Proposed Bill for the Appointment of Persons to the Office of Kazi," in BL, IOR/L/PJ/6/17, File 954, Papers relative to the Bill for appointment of persons to the office of Kází.

85. See, e.g., comments from the *Koh-i Nur* (March 13), the *Aftab-i Panjab* (March 12), and other papers summarized in UPSA, *Selections from the Vernacular Newspapers*, Vol. 13.

86. UPSA, Judicial (Civil) Department Proceedings, Sl. No. 10, Box No. 6B, File No. 245B, Legislation to provide for the registration of certain domestic events in the Muhammadan and Hindu families.

87. See, e.g., BL, IOR/L/PJ/6/15, File 803: The Bill for the appointment of persons to the office of Kazi, No. 157, From Mohideen Sheriff Khan Bahadur, Honorary Surgeon Triplicane Dispensary; and Nawab ʿAbd-ul-Luteef's minute in UPSA, Judicial (Civil) Department Proceedings, Sl. No. 10, Box No. 6B, File No. 245B, Legislation to provide for the registration of certain domestic events in the Muhammadan and Hindu families.

88. See Morgenstein Fuerst, *Indian Muslim Minorities*, esp. chap. 2, "Suspect Subjects," 49–85.

89. NAI, Home, Judicial, Nos. 233–44: Memorandum from C. G. W. Macpherson, Esq., Under-Secretary to the Gov't of Bombay, Judicial Dept., July 11, 1881.

90. In outlining these questions, the legal remembrancer added that "the lawfulness of extending the Act to any place and the expediency of so doing are, of course, entirely separate questions." Investigating the two issues mentioned earlier would help determine the "expediency" of extending the act, regardless of its lawfulness. BL, IOR/P/1796: Bombay Judicial Proceedings, 1881: Remembrancer of Legal Affairs, No. 144, January 31, 1881. The summary report appears in NAI, Home, Judicial, Nos. 233–44: Macpherson's memorandum, July 11, 1881.

91. Macpherson's memorandum.

92. MSA, *Bombay Government Gazette*, May 4, 1882, 320–26. A handwritten copy of the list, with the qazis' names in English, Devanagari, and Perso-Arabic scripts, appears in MSA, JDP, 1882, Vol. 45.

93. MSA, JDP, 1882, Vol. 45, includes a list of errata.

94. See, e.g., Nos. 7 and 8, Kazi Muhmmad Sharifuddin valad Kazi Muhammad Abdul Latif and Kazi Maulvi Sirajuddin valad Haji Kazi Maulvi Muhmmad Bahuddin, who were each appointed to the "whole táluka" of Sangamner. *Bombay Government Gazette*, May 4, 1882, 320.

95. See, e.g., No. 12, Kazi Muhammad Sharifuddin valad Kazi Muhammad Abdul Latif, who received one village, "Shiregaon." *Bombay Government Gazette*, May 4, 1882, 320. It is unclear whether this is the same Sharifuddin as at No. 22.

96. See, e.g., No. 22, Kazi Muhammad Sharifuddin valad Kazi Muhammad Abdul Latif, whose entry includes ninety-five villages; and No. 57, Kazi Muhammad

Samshuddin [*sic*] valad Kazi Muhammad Nuruddin, whose entry lists eighty-eight villages. *Bombay Government Gazette*, May 4, 1882, 321, 325–26.

97. For an example of the district-level management of qazis, see the discussion of Allahabad later. There are references to qazis in judicial department proceedings volumes for 1893, 1894, and 1895, at which point the paper trail becomes too thin to follow.

98. NAI, Home, Judicial, Nos. 233–44: C. G. Master to the Officiating Secretary to the Government of India, No. 1172, June 13, 1881.

99. They reported, for instance, that "the Act is approved by the Mahomedan community generally," that "these appointments appear to have met with the approval of the Mahomedan population generally," that "no complaints have been received of the working of the Act," that "the Mahomedan community have generally appreciated the advantages resulting from its operation," that "the Mahomedan gentlemen who have been consulted on the subject are unanimously of opinion that the Act has met with the general approval of the Mahomedan community," and that "these Kazis have given satisfaction and that the institution of the office under an Act of the Legislature is popular with the Mahomedan community." NAI, Home, Judicial, June 1882, No. 77A (B), Kazi Act, XII of 1880: Letter from J. Sturrock, April 19, 1882; L. R. Burrows, April 22, 1882; Letter from W. S. Foster, March 10, 1882; and Letter from J. G. Horsfall, April 1, 1882.

100. The district magistrate at South Canara mentioned difficulties "settling the local jurisdiction of the various nominees," though "no complaints have been received on the working of the Act." The magistrate at Chingleput District mentioned learning that one of the qazis appointed in the district "does his work by deputy," which "appear[ed] to be contrary to the intention of the" act. The district magistrate at Coimbatore reported "factions" between "the old and the new Kazi," which he thought government might avoid by "refrain[ing] from making any official appointment in the future." NAI, Home, Judicial, June 1882, No. 77A (B), Kazi Act, XII of 1880: Letter from J. Sturrock, April 19, 1882; Letter from J. F. Price, February 21, 1882; Letter from A. J. Stuart, January 21, 1882.

101. NAI, Home, Judicial, June 1882, No. 77A (B): Letter from N. A. Roupell, February 11, 1882.

102. NAI, Home, Judicial, June 1882, No. 77A (B): Letter from W. S. Whiteside, February 12, 1882.

103. NAI, Home, Judicial, June 1882, No. 77A (B): Letter from Cruickshank, February 2, 1882.

104. NAI, Home, Judicial, June 1882, No. 77A (B): Letter from A. J. Stuart, January 21, 1882; and H. St. A. Goodrich, February 7, 1882 (on existing arrangements and factions); Letters from H. J. Stokes, February 15, 1882; and H. G. Turner, March 11, 1882 (on government orders and gazette notifications).

105. See, e.g., petitions in UPSA-All., Bundle No. 184, File No. 12, Box No. 256, S. No. 6: Appointment of Umrao Ali, Qazi of Farrukhabad; Bundle No. 198, Box No. 276, S. No. 13, File No. 10: Appointment of Qazis, Cawnpore, 1884 (Judicial); and Bundle No. 258, Box No. 352, S. No. 6, File No. 14: Appt. of Kazi of Mouzah Ratkala.

106. See, e.g., vernacular petitions in Appointment of Umrao Ali.

107. See, e.g., UPSA-All., Commissioner of Faizabad, Bundle No. 28, S. No. 25: Judicial (Civil) Dept. letter No. 1174 of 1883, Allahabad November 29, 1883; No. 160 from the Deputy Commissioner at Rae Bareli, January 25, 1884.

108. UPSA-All., Commissioner's Office Allahabad Records, Bundle No. 285, S. No. 4, File No. 275, "Kaziship of Fatehpur District."

109. UPSA-All., Commissioner of Allahabad, Bundle 241, Box No. 328, S. 12, File 6, Appointment of Kazis, 1905: Letter from Fisher, Collector at Etawa, January 13, 1886; Bundle 254, Box No. 346, Serial No. 4, File No. 100, Kaziship Allahabad: Letter from F. W. Porter to A. J. Lawrence in response to No. 2862/90 of April 27, 1885, and No. 4122/90 of June 12, 1885.

110. UPSA-All., Bundle No. 258, Box No. 352, Serial No. 6, File No. 14, Appointment of Kazi of Mouzah Ratkala: S. 27, Reports on the petitions of ʿAbd-ul-Kayum and Kamruddin. Kamruddin was forty-six years old, while ʿAbd-ul-Kayum was only twenty-two, and Nicholls trusted the older candidate more.

111. In a similar vein, the proceedings submitted by the Anjuman-i Panjab included a list of students engaged in special law classes at the Oriental College in Lahore that included the father's profession. Some of the students descended from hereditary qazi families; others had fathers who were scribes, police inspectors, merchants, teachers, zamindars, and tahsildars. See BL, IOR/L/PJ/6/17, File 954, Anjuman-i Panjab Proceedings, Appendix I-B: 7–8.

112. ʿAbd-ul-Luteef, Sayyid Ameer Husain, and Diler Jung were some of its members. NAI, Home, Judicial, August 1881, Nos. 233–44: "Report of the Committee Appointed by His Honor the Lieutenant-Governor to Consider and Report Upon the Registration of Mahomedan Marriages and Divorces in Bengal" (hereafter "Report").

113. "Report," 8.

114. "Report," 8.

115. "Report," 9–10.

116. "Report," 10. While the committee proposed amendments to the act, it does not appear that any changes were legislated until 1932, with the Bengal Muhammadan Marriages and Divorces Registration (Amendment) Act, 1932 (Bengal Act VI of 1932).

117. The typed file mislabels the office as "Kali," which was likely an error in transcription from the original handwritten documents.

118. Part IV (General) included generic information about the terms, meanings, and extent of the ordinance. NAI, Home, Judicial, August 1881, Nos. 233–44: Report on Ordinance No. 5 of 1880, An Ordinance to provide for the registration of Marriages and Divorces among Mahomedans . . . by T. Braddell, Esq., Attorney General, Straits Settlements, Singapore, August 31, 1880. See also Napier, "Introduction to the Study"; and Yahaya, *Fluid Jurisdictions*, 43–46.

119. On law's travels from British India to the Straits Settlements, see Yahaya, *Fluid Jurisdictions*.

120. "An Ordinance to Amend the Law Relating to the Matrimonial Rights of Married Persons with regard to Property and the Law of Inheritance," Cap. 57 (June 29, 1877).

121. See chapter 6; and Lhost, "From Documents."

122. Comments on the "Bombay Bill regarding the Prevention of Gambling," for instance, suggested that terms related to gambling must be clearly defined, or the law would sweep up all "Hindus from the Himalaya mountains to Ceylon," owing to shared activities. NAI, Home, Judicial, January 1888, Nos. 43–46 (B): Bombay Bill Regarding prevention of gambling.

123. Regulations like these tied the administration of marriage to other forms of colonial surveillance, often overlapping with policies aimed at curbing "criminality." See, e.g., Major, "State and Criminal Tribes"; Singha, "Punished by Surveillance"; and Yang, "Introduction."

124. Ordinance to Define the Law Relating to Mohammedan Marriages in the Colony of Sierra Leone and to Provide for Giving Proof of Such Marriages (No. 20 of 1905), Section 3.

125. Gold Coast Colony, Ordinance No. 21 of 1907, An Ordinance to Provide for Registration of Marriages and Divorces among Muhammadans, Section 14.

126. Sierra Leone, Section 9; Gold Coast, Section 10; Straits Ordinance, Part III. See also Sharafi, *Law and Identity*, 127–29, for legislation regarding intestate Parsis.

127. See, e.g., the work of Bishara, *Sea of Debt*; Hussin, *Politics of Islamic Law*; Mawani, *Across Oceans of Law*; and Mawani and Hussin, "Travels of Law."

Interlude II

1. She would not, however, become "Empress of India" until later.

2. The queen appointed her "beloved Cousin and Councillor, Charles John Viscount Canning" to be the first "Viceroy and Governor-General." "Proclamation of Queen Victoria on the 1st day of November 1858."

3. Thomas R. Metcalf, *Ideologies of the Raj*, 28–42. The names and structure of the courts also changed.

4. Metcalf, 43.

5. See Morgenstein Fuerst, *Indian Muslim Minorities*, for a further discussion of the Uprising's role in shaping these views.

6. "Proclamation of Queen Victoria on the 1st day of November 1858."

7. See, e.g., Ingram's remarks on this practice within Deoband. Ingram, *Revival from Below*, 31–32.

8. See chapter 3 for further discussion of this dynamic.

9. See Stephens, *Governing Islam*.

10. More recently, scholarship on secularism in India suggests that these negotiations are still in progress. See, e.g., Gould, "Contesting Secularism"; Lemons, *Divorcing Traditions*; and Redding, *Secular Need*.

11. See, e.g., Asif, *Loss of Hindustan*, 13–14; and Hussin, *Politics of Islamic Law*, 115–20.

12. Stephens, *Governing Islam*, 57–85, 105–31.

13. The Muslim Personal Law (Shariat) Application Act resulted from anxieties over the widespread influence of "custom" in the adjudication of personal law disputes. See interlude III.

14. Exceptions include scholarship in secularism studies (e.g., Asad, *Formations of the Secular*; and Saba Mahmood, *Religious Difference*) and criticisms of the modern state more broadly (e.g., Hallaq, *Impossible State*).

Chapter 4

1. ʿAbd-ul-Ḥayy, *Majmūʿa-ul-Fatāwá* (1889), 2:13–15. "Ūn par kufr jārī karnā jā'iz hai yā nahīn̲?" he asks.

2. Amir Khan's address is the Madrasa Muḥammadiya in Haliyāl.

3. See Robinson, *'Ulama of Farangi Mahall*, along with Barbara D. Metcalf's reflections on the family's earlier roles in *Islamic Revival*, 30–34.

4. Thomas Macaulay's introduction to the 1837 draft of the Indian Penal Code mentions problems arising from "very different provisions" existing across the three presidencies, for instance. Macaulay et al., *Indian Penal Code*, ix.

5. Mantena, *Alibis of Empire*.

6. See, e.g., Guenther, "Colonial Court"; and Hussin, *Politics of Islamic Law*, 96, 238–44; along with debates over blasphemy and apostasy in Zaman, *Ulama in Contemporary Islam*, 29–31; and Stephens, *Governing Islam*, 153–54.

7. For another perspective on these questions, see Lhost, "To Flower and Fructify," 54–57. For broader reflections within the field of Islamic studies, see Ahmed, *What Is Islam?*; and Reinhart, *Lived Islam*.

8. Metcalf, *Islamic Revival*, 65–67.

9. Michael R. Anderson, "Islamic Law"; Hallaq, *Introduction to Islamic Law*, 85–89; Giunchi, "Reinvention of 'Sharīʿa'," 1125–30; Hussin, *Politics of Islamic Law*, 85; Kugle, "Framed, Blamed, and Renamed"; Stephens, *Governing Islam*; and Derrett, "Administration of Hindu Law," for the Hindu case.

10. Hussin, *Politics of Islamic Law*, 147. See also chapter 7.

11. On steam and print, see Gelvin and Green, *Global Muslims*.

12. For another take on these debates, see, e.g., Tareen, *Defending Muḥammad in Modernity*.

13. Bunt, *iMuslims*; Bunt, *Islam in the Digital Age*; Bunt, *Virtually Islamic*; and cooke and Lawrence, *Muslim Networks*.

14. El Shamsy, *Rediscovering the Islamic Classics*; Robinson, "Technology and Religious Change."

15. Institutions certainly aided the expansion of Islamic discourses. On Deoband, see Ingram, *Revival from Below*; and Barbara D. Metcalf, *Islamic Revival*.

16. Although many take the 1772 Hastings Plan as the point of origin for these categories (see interlude I), Stephens demonstrates that the content of Muslim personal law changed over time. See Stephens, "Forging Secular Legal Governance," in *Governing Islam*, 22–56.

17. For statistics on the number of muftis trained and fatwas issued by Deoband, see Barbara D. Metcalf, *Islamic Revival*, 110–11.

18. On the growth of these institutions, see, e.g., Arshad Alam, "Enemy Within"; Ingram, *Revival from Below*; Barbara D. Metcalf, "Madrasa at Deoband"; and Zaman, "Religious Education."

19. For representative accounts, see Hallaq, "From *Fatwās* to *Furūʿ*"; Hallaq, "Was the Gate?"; and Masud, Messick, and Powers, *Islamic Legal Interpretation*.

20. Hallaq, "From *Fatwās* to *Furūʿ*," 29. Messick also considers the tension between theory and practice in *Sharīʿa Scripts*.

21. Schacht, *Introduction to Islamic Law*, 75, cited in Hallaq, "From *Fatwās* to *Furūʿ*," 30.

22. For Islamic law as textual practice, see Messick, *Sharīʿa Scripts*; and Messick, *Calligraphic State*.

23. Messick, *Sharīʿa Scripts*.

24. Messick, *Sharīʿa Scripts*, 172.

25. In the Ottoman context, historians have been able to work with extant collections to produce informative social histories, yet even with the robust Ottoman legal archive, writing the social history of legal discourse is difficult. For a further elaboration of these obstacles, see Messick, *Sharīʿa Scripts*.

26. See Messick, "Mufti."

27. Hallaq, "From *Fatwās* to *Furūʿ*."

28. Hallaq demonstrates this process using a case study from twelfth-century Cordoba in "Murder in Cordoba."

29. For a bottom-up history of religious revival, see Ingram, *Revival from Below*.

30. On Bahadur Shah Zafar's trial, see Hussin, *Politics of Islamic Law*, 115–20.

31. The broader implications of this debate play out in the exchange between W. W. Hunter and Sayyid Ahmad Khan. See Hunter, *Indian Musalmans*; *Syed Ahmed Bahadoor, C.S.I.*; Morgenstein Fuerst, *Indian Muslim Minorities*; and Ghose, "Islamic Law."

32. In other words, governmentality of the modern state. See Foucault, "Governmentality"; David Scott, "Colonial Governmentality"; and Hallaq, *Impossible State*, esp. 156–67.

33. David Scott, "Colonial Governmentality," 193; Partha Chatterjee, "Colonial State," in *The Nation and Its Fragments*, 14, quoted in Scott, 194.

34. On "Anglo-Muhammadan" law and its relation to "British perceptions of governance," see Hallaq, *Sharīʿa*, 377–79.

35. See, more broadly, Asad, *Formations of the Secular*; Durkheim, *Elementary Forms*; and Saba Mahmood, *Religious Difference*.

36. See Stephens on *lex loci* in *Governing Islam*, 40–51. Mujīb Aḥmad echoes this point in his history of the fatwa, saying, "The Islamic *shariʿa* always held pride of place as the basis for government law [*sarkārī qānūn*], regardless of who was in power." Aḥmad, *Janūbī Eshiyā*, 35.

37. Hallaq, *Impossible State*, 167. Here I depart from Hallaq's general assessment, which he refers to elsewhere as "jural colonization," to highlight the vibrancy of Islamic legal discourse in this period. Hallaq, *Sharīʿa*, 371–95.

38. Asad, "Idea of an Anthropology." See also Anjum, "Islam."

39. The following account draws on handbooks for muftis, personal observation, and ethnographic research. Some manuals caution muftis not to accept questions directly from women or children, but even though evidence of intermediaries

appears in the archives, there are plenty of instances in which women approached the mufti directly.

40. Manṣūr, *Ādāb-i Fatwá Nawīsī*, 14.

41. Mufti Kifayatullah's collection came from three sets of records: his notebooks at the Madrasa Aminiya, where he ran the dar-ul-ifta, papers found in his home, and the fatwas he published in *Al-Jamʿīyat*.

42. Sulaiman Manṣūrpūrī accounts for this possibility in his guidebook for muftis, *Fatwá Nawīsī Kē Rahnumā Uṣūl*, 123.

43. Hallaq, "From *Fatwās* to *Furūʿ*," 36n40.

44. Handbooks for muftis emphasize clarity and comprehension. Kifayatullah, for instance, mostly conducted his business in Urdu but would respond to istiftas submitted in Persian and Arabic in those languages. He also employed more Arabic terminology, more citations, and longer quotations when responding to a maulvi's question than when responding to a nonscholar's request. I discuss one of his Persian fatwas in Lhost, "Of Horizontal Exchanges."

45. If the original page does not provide adequate room, the mufti can copy the question and the answer onto a fresh page. Manṣūrpūrī, *Fatwá Nawīsī kē Rahnumā Uṣūl*, 122. Messick notes that muftis in Yemen typically write their answers in the space above the original question. Messick, *Calligraphic State*, 234.

46. Institutions like Deoband and Nadwa made the records from their fatwa institutes accessible through publication, often privileging the answers over the historical context of the questions, updating and amending questions as necessary. Other institutes, such as the Jamiʿa Nizamiya in Hyderabad, published collections at the beginning of the twentieth century but have not published much since then. They have, however, produced dozens of meticulous fatwa registers that await scholarly attention. Ḥafīẓ-ur-Raḥmān Wāṣif, the disciple who edited and compiled Kifayatullah's fatwas, refers to the practice of disciples copying the fatwas of their teachers as standard practice but at the same time suggests that the four complete and one incomplete registers he found among Kifayatullah's records at the Madrasa Aminiya in Delhi were only a partial record of the fatwas Kifayatullah wrote. The first register begins in 1913 and the final one ends in 1944, which only includes the middle decades of Kifayatullah's career. Wāṣif, "Dībācha," 8–9.

47. See, e.g., NAI, Oriental Records, Acquired Documents, No. 2150, Fatwa issued by Shaikh̲ Maḥmūd.

48. When I visited in 2013, the dar-ul-ifta at Dar-ul-ʿUlum Nadwat-ul-ʿUlama in Lucknow used a multifunction printer-copier to photocopy the fatwas they produced before returning the original page with the answer to the fatwa seeker. The Jāmiʿa Niẓāmiya in Hyderabad uses registers to record its questions and answers, though it will provide official fatwas (for a small fee) to individuals who seek answers in relation to court cases. On the relationship between muftis and judges, see, e.g., Gerber, *State, Society, and Law*; Powers, *Law, Society, and Culture*; and Messick, *Sharīʿa Scripts*, 169–70. For contemporary practices, see also Lemons, *Divorcing Traditions*.

49. Mujīb Aḥmad suggests that even for muftis whose records survive, written archives do not include the thousands more they gave orally. Aḥmad, *Janūbī Eshiyā*,

46. Wāṣif describes the process of collecting fatwas from these private collections when compiling *Kifāyat-ul-Muftī*, and Messick notes the complications arising from the scattered nature of shariʿa discourse. See Wāṣif, "Dībācha"; and Messick, *Sharīʿa Scripts*, 163. On the fear of losing fatwas, see also Hallaq, "From *Fatwās* to *Furuʿ*," 42n68.

50. For an introduction to this genre in South Asia, see Masud, "*Ādāb al-Muftī*."

51. Manṣūr, *Ādāb-i Fatwá Nawīsī*, 15.

52. Manṣūr, 15.

53. Today, muftis receive requests and provide answers using all forms of media: digital, electronic, and mobile. See Bunt, *Islam in the Digital Age*, esp. 124–34.

54. On the growth of commercial printing, see Anindita Ghosh, *Power in Print*; Orsini, *Print and Pleasure*; and Stark, *Empire of Books*.

55. On print and Islamic learning, see Ingram, "Portable Madrasa"; and Robinson, "Technology and Religious Change." On Arabic-language publishing more broadly, see Atiyeh, "Book"; Mahdi, "From the Manuscript Age"; Pedersen, *Arabic Book*; and Proudfoot, "Mass Producing Houri's Moles."

56. See the introduction for an example.

57. Scholarship on South Asia often focuses on Sunni-Shiʿi sectarianism or Hindu-Muslim communalism, but other forms of factionalism were also present and were often contested in the courts of law. See, e.g., Mushirul Hasan, "Traditional Rites"; Ilahi, "Sectarian Violence"; and Ziad, "Mufti 'Iwāz."

58. ʿAbd-ul-Ḥayy, *Majmūʿa-ul-Fatāwá* (1887), 2:467. Several undated fatwas follow this one, though.

59. ʿAbd-ul-Ḥayy, (1887), 1:46–54. *Jihād* (struggle; struggle for Allah) has several degrees of meaning.

60. ʿAbd-ul-Ḥayy, (1887), 1:2–3.

61. Robinson, *ʿUlama of Farangi Mahall*, 36–37, 124–26. Named for Niẓām-ud-Dīn al-Sihālawī, of Farangi Mahall, the dars-i nizami was a method of instruction popular in South Asia's Islamic institutions.

62. Maulvī Imdād ʿAli, for instance, quoted ʿAbd-ul-Hayy in opposition to Sir Sayyid's efforts to found the Muhammadan Anglo-Oriental College at Aligarh (now Aligarh Muslim University) even though the fatwa supported Sir Sayyid's efforts—albeit with the caveats and critiques that Imdād ʿAlī emphasized. Robinson, *ʿUlama of Farangi Mahall*, 123n35.

63. For his opinions on *taqlīd*, see ʿAbd-ul-Ḥayy, *Majmūʿa-ul-Fatāwá* (1889), 1:24–32. For his position on history, see Robinson, *ʿUlama of Farangi Mahall*, 122–23.

64. See, e.g., the earlier discussion about compiling the *Kifāyat-ul-Muftī* later.

65. ʿAbd-ul-Ḥayy, *Majmūʿa-ul-Fatāwá* (1889), 1:429.

66. The intermediary edition published in 1911 CE (1330 AH) used chapters but did not refer to itself as an Urdu translation. Unfortunately, whatever these editions gained from the chapters in terms of ease of access, they lost by way of the cramped arrangement of the text on the page. Rather than using line breaks and white space to help the reader locate the beginning of each chapter, later editions from 1911 CE and 1926 CE turned the fatwas into a continuous stream of text, allowing questions to begin in the middle of the line, one leading directly into the next.

67. Wāṣif acknowledges that many of the mufti's fatwas were lost before the establishment of robust record-keeping practices at the madrasa. To aid his compilation, he printed advertisements in newspapers asking individuals to send the fatwas they received from Kifayatullah for inclusion in the collection. He received many submissions but only included those fatwas written in the mufti's hand. Wāṣif, "Dībācha," 1:9.

68. ʿAbd-ul-Ḥayy, *Majmūʿa-ul-Fatāwá* (1926), 2:145–312.

69. ʿAbd-ul-Ḥayy, 2:199, 202.

70. Marc Galanter evaluates modern legal systems according to two sets of criteria: the modernization of rules and the modernization of institutions. Galanter, "Modernization of Law."

71. On the codification of "general Indian law" after 1860, see, e.g., Menski, "Uniform Civil Code Debate," 222–24. On codification and the penal code, see, e.g., Macaulay et al., *Indian Penal Code*; Chan, Wright, and Yeo, *Codification*; and Mawani and Hussin, "Travels of Law."

72. See Hallaq, *Sharīʿa*, 367–70.

73. For comparison, see Layish, "Transformation of the *Sharīʿa*."

74. On the relationship between theory and practice, see Hallaq, "Considerations on the Function"; and Hallaq, "Legal Theory," in *Sharīʿa*, 72–124. He expands many of these points in Hallaq, *Origins and Evolution*, particularly chap. 6, 122–49.

75. Hallaq, *Sharīʿa*, 84–87.

76. Hallaq refers to it as "dialectical." Hallaq, *Sharīʿa*, 78–83. Darnton's "communications circuit" is also a useful model to consider. Darnton, "What Is the History?,"67.

77. Messick, "Fatwā: Process and Function"; and Messick, "Fatwā, Modern."

78. Vikør, *Between God*, 149. The spelling and pronunciation of these stand-in names differ slightly across languages and contexts. Compare to Messick, *Sharīʿa Scripts*, 171–72.

79. Messick describes how *fulān* operates in relation to theoretical ("library") and applied ("archival") texts in *Shariʿa Scripts*, 22–24.

80. Not only does normative literature highlight the importance of responding to inheritance questions accurately, but samples from extant fatwa files (see chapter 5) also reveal the extensive use of personal names.

81. See Vikør, *Between God*, 73–88, e.g., on *ijmāʿ* [consensus] and social sanction.

82. Fatwa seekers often concluded their questions with statements like "taʿmīl karē̱n" (I will implement) or "pāband hōgā" (I will follow) to show their respect for the mufti's decision.

83. Two observations support this argument. First, marriage, divorce, inheritance, and other categories of "personal law" remained central topics within fatwa literature, despite the courts' involvement with them. Second, other legal topics—e.g., sales, mortgages, contracts, even *ḥadd* crimes—remained part of the mufti's canon. Few were content to let the courts interpret these issues autonomously, even if the colonial state claimed authority over them. Questions on these and other topics advised Muslims on how to live in accordance with both legal

systems—Islamic and British. See, by contrast, Barbara D. Metcalf, *Islamic Revival*, 147–48.

84. Hallaq, "From *Fatwās* to *Furūʿ*," 44–54.

85. These classifications originate from my reading of late colonial fatwa literature, but scholars have observed similar practices elsewhere, including instances of the "collective fatwa." See Esposito and DeLong-Bas, *Shariah*, 40–42, on the 2004 Amman message.

86. Ṭōnkī, *Majmūʿa-yi Fatāwá-yi Ṣābriya*. Most answers received eight or nine affirmations.

87. One of the anjuman's goals was, in fact, to overcome sectarian disputation by authoring fatwas collectively, rather than independently. Rather than facilitating sectarian and factional rivalries and adding to the "pamphlet wars" Barbara Metcalf cites among the Deobandi, Barelvi, and other ʿulama, the anjuman wanted to reduce infighting.

88. ʿAbd-ul-Ḥayy, *Majmūʿa-ul-Fatāwá* (1887), 1:7.

89. Barbara D. Metcalf, *Islamic Revival*, 145. On demand for a dar-ul-ifta at Deoband, see Robinson, "Strategies of Authority," 7; Rizvi, *Tārīḵẖ*, 186, 202; and Rizvi, *History*, 1:143, 156.

90. The lithographed reproduction of the qazi's seal on printed registers in chapter 6 is another example.

91. Vikør, *Between God*, 142.

92. BL, IOR/L/PJ/6/924, File 774: Fatwa or judicial opinion regarding the duties and obligations of Muhammedans towards the British in India.

93. Bamford, *Histories of the Non-co-operation*, appendix G, "Translation of a Pamphlet Entitled 'Mutafiqa Fatwa,'" 251–55. I thank Jim Jaffe for drawing my attention to this reference. See also Jaffe, "Gandhi," 1346.

94. See Ricci, *Islam Translated*, for additional commentary on the relationship between questions, answers, and novel situations.

95. For a look at newness and legal innovation, see Halevi, *Modern Things on Trial*.

96. In other words, repetition allows *tajrīd* (abstraction) and *talḵẖīṣ* (abridgment) to render explanation and explication unnecessary; the rule stands on its own.

97. Revision is also part of repetition. See, e.g., Masud, "Apostasy and Judicial Separation."

98. Naẕīr Ḥusain, *Fatāwá Naẕīriya*, 1:638. The mustafti uses the verb *mānnā* for "to believe."

99. Naẕīr Ḥusain, 1:639.

100. Naẕīr Ḥusain, 1:640.

101. By which he means *Al-Durr Al-Muḵẖtār*. Elsewhere in these answers, he refers to "Kanz" (*Kanz al- daqā'iq*), "Hidaya" (*Al-Hidāya*), and "other books of *fiqh*" (*wa-g̱ẖaira kutub-i fiqh*). Naẕīr Ḥusain, 1:639.

102. Naẕīr Ḥusain, 1:639–40.

103. Naẕīr Ḥusain, 1:639.

104. ʿUṣmānī, *ʿAzīz-ul-Fatāwá*, 372–73. For a brief biography, see Idrawi, *Taẕkira-yi Mashāhīr-i Hind*, 197–98.

105. Kifāyatullāh, *Kifāyat-ul-Muftī*, 4:197–98.

106. Kifāyatullāh, 4:198.

107. See, e.g., Kifāyatullāh, 4:203–4, 205–7, 209–10 (on the telephone), and 210–11 (on the radio).

108. For further elaboration of these processes, see Hallaq, *Introduction*, 10–11, 22–27; Hallaq, *Authority, Continuity, and Change*, 133–46; and Hallaq, "From *Fatwās* to *Furūʿ*," among others.

109. Urdu novelist and civil servant Nazir Ahmad was critical of the role "tricks" played in the courts of law and drew a distinction between the ethics of shariʿa and the maneuvers of litigation. Lhost, "To Flower and Fructify," 48.

110. Hallaq, *Sharīʿa*, 72–87; Hallaq, "Considerations on the Function," 681–85.

111. Who can practice *ijtihād* (and to what extent) is a matter of debate. See Hallaq, *Sharīʿa*, 110–13; Stephens, *Governing Islam*, 108–31; and Zaman, "Evolving Conceptions of *Ijtihād*."

112. The term *talfīq* comes from the root *la-fa-qa*, "to invent, fabricate, or concoct." Accordingly, *talfīq* is not without its critics, who condemn the practice as *bidʿat*, or heretical innovation. For a further elaboration, see Krawietz, "Cut and Paste." Though he does not mention *talfīq* by name, Muhammad Khalid Masud describes Ashraf ʿAli Thanwi's correspondence with Maliki jurists in the Middle East to expand women's access to divorce in British India. See Masud, "Apostasy and Judicial Separation."

113. Even within the Hanafi school there is some variation in interpretation. Syed Ameer Ali, whose interpretation receives more attention later, says that Abu Hanifa required 120 years, while two of his prominent disciples argued for 90 or 70. Alternatively, some jurists argue that the waiting period should be relative to the life-span of the abandoned wife's husband's companions. As soon as his companions have passed away, she may seek a judicial separation and receive permission to remarry. Masud says that a case from the first half of the nineteenth century required an abandoned woman to wait fifty years according to the Hanafi interpretation. By the beginning of the twentieth century, however, none of the muftis I surveyed advocated this position. Despite these changes in interpretation, however, there was still concern about women renouncing Islam to escape unpleasant marriages.

114. The waiting period is technically three to five years, but the median (four) seems to be universal among jurists. Masud, "Apostasy and Judicial Separation," 202.

115. De, "Mumtaz Bibi's Broken Heart"; Fareeha Khan, "Traditionalist Approaches"; and Masud, "Apostasy and Judicial Separation."

116. For histories of the act, see De, "Mumtaz Bibi's Broken Heart"; and Zaman, *Ashraf ʿAli Thanawi*. For a description of the research process, see Masud, "Apostasy and Judicial Separation."

117. See, e.g., Kifāyatullāh, *Kifāyat-ul-Muftī*, 6:106.

118. Ali, *Personal Law*, 384n. At the time of his book's publication, Syed Ameer Ali was a member of the faculty of law at Calcutta University, former member of the legislative council of Bengal, and presidency magistrate.

119. Ali, 385.

120. Perhaps a pseudonym?

121. Kifāyatullāh, *Kifāyat-ul-Muftī*, 4:83–84.

122. ʿAbd-ul-Ḥayy, *Majmūʿa-ul-Fatāwá* (1926), 1:368. Buzurg provides the volume and page number in his question, which match this printing of ʿAbd-ul-Hayy's *Majmūʿa*.

123. Kifāyatullāh, *Kifāyat-ul-Muftī*, 4:71–107.

Chapter 5

1. Jaunpūrī, *Mufīd-ul-Muftī*, 2. The Qurʾan and Sunna are two of the four principal sources of Islamic law, from which scholars draw, with the aid of analogy (*qiyās*) and consensus (*ijmāʿ*), to answer legal questions. See also Vikør, *Between God*, 31–88; and Hallaq, *Sharīʿa*, 74–83. On the office of the mufti specifically, see Masud, "*Ādāb al-Muftī*"; and Masud, Messick, and Powers, "Muftīs, Fatwas, and Islamic Legal Interpretation," (along with the other contributions to that volume).

2. On these institutions, see Ingram, *Revival from Below*; Barbara D. Metcalf, *Islamic Revival*; Riaz, *Faithful Education*; Sikand, *Bastions of Believers*; and Zaman, "Religious Education."

3. Mufti Kifayatullah was, for instance, in communication with Muslims from across the subcontinent—and from elsewhere in the British Empire, too.

4. See chapter 4 for ʿAbd-ul-Hayy's introduction.

5. ʿAbd-ul-Awwal lists sixty great living scholars (*maujūda akābir ʿulamāʾ*), noting that their presence brought pride to the present age ("jinkē wujūd sē is chaudhwīn ṣadī kō bahut baṛa fak̲h̲r ḥāṣil hai"). Jaunpūrī, *Mufīd-ul-Muftī*, 145. The list appears on 145–48.

6. See chapter 4.

7. Here I depart from Barbara D. Metcalf's assessment that muftis did not attend to matters of court procedure. Metcalf, *Islamic Revival*, 148.

8. See, e.g., Tareen, *Defending Muḥammad in Modernity*.

9. Here I draw from scholarship on secularism and religious freedom. See, e.g., Agrama, *Questioning Secularism*; Asad, *Formations of the Secular*; Saba Mahmood, *Religious Difference*; and Sullivan, *Impossibility of Religious Freedom*.

10. Sally Engle Merry offers a similar account of legal authority in Hawaii; see her *Colonizing Hawai'i*, esp. introduction and chap. 1. Princely state rulers also contributed to Islamic institutions in British India.

11. Muttalib, *Administration of Justice*, i; K̲h̲ān, *Tārīk̲h̲-i ʿAdālat-i Āṣafī*, 26.

12. Zaman, *Ulama in Contemporary Islam*, 27.

13. On Hyderabad's history as an independent state, see, e.g., Briggs, *Nizam*; Faruqui, "At Empire's End"; Yusuf Husain Khan, *First Nizām*; and Leonard, "Hyderabad Political System."

14. Ashraf, *Guide to Persian*, 43.

15. Guidebooks to the archive mention over 3,000 files. I accessed 1,200 of these, primarily from the years 1947–50 (1357–60 Fasli), while working at the archive in 2013. My reading of "the file" as object and process draws from Hull, "File"; Hull,

Government of Paper; Kafka, "Demon of Writing"; Kafka, *Demon of Writing*; Latour, *Making of Law*; and Vismann, *Files*.

16. I have calculated this rate using the files that remain and the limited set of dates they cover.

17. The process at most working dar-ul-iftas today involves either receiving a written fatwa question or helping visitors transcribe their requests into writing, reviewing and researching the question, writing an answer on the same piece of paper, making a record of the question and the answer in the dar-ul-ifta's register, and returning the original question and answer to the fatwa seeker. Electronic media have revised but have not entirely remade these procedures.

18. He assigned number one to Muhammad ʿAbd-ul-Khalīl ʿUṣmānī in July 1933, thirty years after he first began to write fatwas. The numbering system was not perfect. Occasionally, Kifayatullah mistakenly assigned a new number to a mustafti who had already received a number. At the same time, he also had unnumbered correspondents whose questions were preserved in other records. Kifāyatullāh, *Kifāyat-ul-Muftī*.

19. I am grateful to the staff at the dar-ul-ifta for allowing me to look at their registers.

20. See, e.g., *Fatāwá-yi ʿAdālat*.

21. Ṭōnkī, *Majmūʿa-yi Fatāwá-yi Ṣābriya*. See also figure 4.1.

22. As chapter 4 explained, not all fatwas were written or recorded. Many individuals continued to request fatwas orally, for which little trace remains.

23. British bureaucrats followed similar protocols. See, e.g., Master, *Diaries of Streynsham Master*; along with Moir, "Kaghazi Raj"; Ogborn, *Indian Ink*, esp. 67–103; Bhavani Raman, *Document Raj*; and Saumarez Smith, *Rule by Records*, for further discussion of these protocols. On similar types of legal paperwork, see Bishara, "Paper Routes."

24. The original would have been mailed or delivered to the fatwa seeker. Files that include originals reflect an incomplete transmission.

25. As the discussion that follows reveals, petitioners' legal consciousness was an important part of the process. See Gallagher, "Mobilizing the Law"; Lobel, "Paradox of Extralegal Activism"; Merry, *Getting Justice*; Sarat and Felstiner, "Lawyers and Legal Consciousness"; Silbey, "Legal Culture"; Silbey, "After Legal Consciousness"; Young, "Everyone Knows the Game."

26. My reading of these representations—and the dar-ul-ifta's response to them—draws from science studies, particularly Latour's analysis of how "paper forms" produce knowledge. See Latour, *Science in Action*, 234–46; and Latour, *Making of Law*.

27. On the role of petitions, see Bhavani Raman, *Document Raj*; and the introduction to the special issue of *Modern Asian Studies* on petitioning, De and Travers, "Petitioning and Political Cultures."

28. AP/TSA, Fatwa No. 149/1, 3 Mihr 1358 F, "Taqsīm-i matrūka, Shāh Ḵẖwāja Ḥabīb-ud-Dīn Ṣāḥib." The petitioner makes a clear attempt to use elevated language, adding the Persian plural ending *-jāt* to the word fatwa (*fatwá*), which he writes with a *chōṭī hē* (thereby necessitating the use of the *-jāt* plural ending, in his mind). Arabic uses a broken plural, *fatāwá*.

29. AP/TSA, Fatwa No. 95/5, 10 Tir 1358 F, "Darkẖwāst-i Ṣālim bin Nāṣir Ṣāḥib, Mutafarriq."

30. AP/TSA, Fatwa No. 5/4, 9 Azar 1356 F, "Mutafarriq, Muḥammad Kalīm-ud-Dīn Ṣāhib"; and No. 7/5, 14 Azar 1356 F, "Darkẖwāst-i Shujāᶜ-ud-Dīn, dar bāra-yi ṭalāq."

31. AP/TSA, Fatwa No. 91/5, 10 Tir 1358 F, "Darkẖwāst-i Sayyid Makẖdūm Kẖān, masʾala-yi ᶜaqd-i ṣānī."

32. Such expectations are not unlike those that accompany other forms of advice seeking, and several scholars have compared the practice of seeking and receiving fatwas to the procedures for producing responsa in Jewish (and other) legal traditions. See, e.g., Furber, "Reducing the Role"; and for comparison, Davis, "Responsa in Hindu Law." I extend this comparison further and place the fatwa, as a genre of legal advice, alongside other forms of advice that use the newspaper, radio, and television, like those found in the *New York Times*' "The Ethicist" column, the nationally syndicated "Dear Abby" column (and its franchises), the Catholic "More2Life" radio program, or the popular sex advice column and podcast "Savage Love."

33. In this context, "family law" disputes sit at the intersection of public and private life; between the areas of behavior governed by the state and those governed by personal and interpersonal relations; and between the domains relating to religion and those relating to formal (state) law.

34. My analysis of lay legal interpretation draws from work on legal consciousness, which Merry defines in relation to "commonsense" understandings, "habitual action[s]," and experiences that reveal law's contradictions. Merry, *Getting Justice*, 5.

35. Hallaq, "From *Fatwās* to *Furūᶜ*," 33. On ᶜAmrū/ᶜAmr, see Steingass, *Dictionary*, 867.

36. On the mufti's changing role, see Ingram, *Revival from Below*, 47–48; Kozlowski, "Modern Indian Mufti"; Barbara D. Metcalf, *Islamic Revival*, 49–50; and Zaman, *Ulama in Contemporary Islam*, 25. The mufti's position was changing elsewhere, too. For the nineteenth and early twentieth centuries, see Gerber, *State, Society, and Law*, esp. chap. 3; and Skovgaard-Petersen, *Defining Islam*. For more recent periods, see Agrama, "Ethics, Tradition, Authority"; Agrama, "Law Courts"; Messick, *Calligraphic State*; and Messick, "Mufti."

37. Masud describes the mufti's role as focused on the interpretive aspects of the process, while the qazi's work revolved around context and investigation. Muftis at the dar-ul-ifta in Hyderabad engaged in both types of activities. Masud, "*Ādāb al-Muftī*."

38. "Hinda" is the generic name for women; "Zayd" is the male equivalent. See chapter 4 for further discussion.

39. AP/TSA, Fatwa No. 34/5, 5 Bahman 1359 F, "Mutafarriq, adā-yi mahr, Sayyid Ḥaidar Riẓvī Ṣāḥib."

40. Hyderabad State's official calendar combined the Mughal Fasli calendar (which begins around July and is tied to the harvest) and the Persian (solar) calendar. Thus, the first month of the Hyderabadi Fasli calendar was Āẕar, the ninth month of the Persian calendar.

41. AP/TSA, Fatwa No. 34/5, 5 Bahman 1359 F.

42. AP/TSA, Fatwa No. 34/5, 5 Bahman 1359 F.

43. AP/TSA, Fatwa No. 31 (38/1), 1357 F.

44. AP/TSA, Fatwa No. 31 (38/1), 1357 F.

45. He later sent a third postcard to say the correct number was nine years. His knowledge was imprecise, but Ghulam Ahmad Khan knew that Amina Bi had passed away after her father.

46. AP/TSA, Fatwa No. 95/5, 10 Tir 1358 F, "Darḵẖwāst-i Ṣālim bin Nāṣir Ṣāḥib, Mutafarriq."

47. AP/TSA, Fatwa No. 95/5, 10 Tir 1358 F. It was not uncommon for women to have close relationships with a dewar, particularly if he was unmarried. The man in question here, though perhaps not actually the wife's dewar, nonetheless occupied that position. In some families, the unmarried dewar would be expected to marry his sister-in-law in the unfortunate circumstance of his brother's death. Writing on the family in India, David Mandelbaum notes that "among some groups there is a joking relationship and a special bond of affection and intimacy between a woman and her husband's youngest brother." Mandelbaum, "Family in India," 131n17. Incidentally, this fatwa question reached the dar-ul-ifta in the same year Mandelbaum published this article.

48. AP/TSA, Fatwa No. 95/5, 10 Tir 1358 F.

49. AP/TSA, Fatwa No. 95/5, 10 Tir 1358 F.

50. AP/TSA, Fatwa No. 95/5, 10 Tir 1358 F.

51. Mukharji, "Handwriting Analysis"; Bhavani Raman, "Duplicity of Paper"; Bhavani Raman, "Duplicity and Evidence," in *Document Raj*, 137–60.

52. See Hallaq, *Sharīʿa*, 87–92; and Messick, "Indexing the Self."

53. AP/TSA, Fatwa No. 60 (71/5), 1950 CE.

54. See, e.g., the section on *taḥrīrī ṭalāq* (written divorce) in Kifāyatullāh, *Kifāyat-ul-Muftī*, 6:227–36.

55. AP/TSA, Fatwa No. 60 (71/5), 1950 CE, 3a.

56. AP/TSA, Fatwa No. 60 (71/5), 1950 CE, 3a.

57. Islamic law recognizes a distinction between custody/care and guardianship. The father remains guardian and provides financial support, but the mother (or mother's family) provides care and emotional support for young children up to the age of seven or, in some cases, nine.

58. AP/TSA, Fatwa No. 45/5, 1356 F, "Jaʿfar ʿAlī Ṣāḥib, ṭalāq-nāma wa ḵẖulʿ-nāma."

59. For a rich description of the vexed pasts—and presents—of stamp paper in India, see Shrimoyee Nandini Ghosh, "'Not Worth the Paper.'"

60. AP/TSA, Fatwa No. 45/5, 1356 F. Juristic preference for reconciliation and marital continuity meant that mitigating factors like anger or drunkenness would invalidate a divorce decree.

61. AP/TSA, Fatwa No. 45/5, 1356 F. The waiting period provides an opportunity to determine whether the woman is pregnant with her former or deceased husband's child. In cases of divorce, the husband continues to provide for his wife during this period.

62. Triple talaq, or *ṭalāq-i bā'in*, as the petitioner refers to it here, speeds up this process but is considered reprehensible by many jurists and has been the cause of considerable controversy in India and elsewhere. For further elaboration, see Khurshid, *Triple Talaq*; and Vikør, *Between God*, 309–10.

63. AP/TSA, Fatwa No. 7/5, 1356 F, "Darḵẖwāst-i Shujāʿ-ud-Dīn Ṣāḥib dar bāra-yi ṭalāq." Shujaʿ-ud-Din included additional mitigating circumstances in his follow-up reply, but the mufti ignored these additional details and gave preference to the written document. AP/TSA, Fatwa No. 8/5, 1355 F [1356 F], "Darḵẖwāst-i Shujāʿ-ud-Dīn Ṣāḥib dar bāra-yi ṭalāq."

64. In other words, he wrote *fatwa* as فتوح not as فتوی; and *fasḵẖ* as فسق not as فسخ. Not all dar-ul-iftas were as forgiving. Katherine Lemons opens her work on muftis in contemporary India with a story about the rejection of an improperly written request. Lemons, *Divorcing Traditions*, 1.

65. AP/TSA, Fatwa No. 15/5, 19 Azar 1356 F, "Mutafarriq, Fasḵẖ-i nikāḥ."

66. See, e.g., the introduction.

67. See also Hallaq on the "new patriarchy" of personal status law in *Sharīʿa*, 450–59. Aspects of gendered justice play out in other fora as well. See Sharafi's writings on "chivalric imperialism" in "Semi-autonomous Judge"; and Merry's reference to women in lower courts in *Getting Justice*, 4. On law, justice, and access more broadly, see Baxi, "'State's Emissary'"; Galanter, "Why the 'Haves'"; and Jacquot and Vitale, "Law as Weapon."

68. AP/TSA, Fatwa No. 37/1, 6 Farwardin 1358 F, "Taqsīm-i matrūka, G̱ẖulām Muḥammad Ḵẖān Ṣāḥib." Registration, more than anything, sparked the Waqf Board's interest in his property.

69. The Religious Affairs Department oversaw endowments from its inception in 1884 CE (1294 Fasli), but it was not until the department formalized its procedures for the management of waqfs with measures like the Hyderabad Endowments Regulation of 1940 CE (1349 Fasli) that the government took a more active role in supervising and managing properties. These regulations were later modified under the government of India's Central Wakfs Act of 1954 and the subsequent Wakf Act of 1995. On the role of the Religious Affairs Department's involvement in managing waqfs, see AP/TSA, Report on the Administration of HEH the Nizam's Dominions, for the year 1347 F. I use the terms "waqf" and "endowment" interchangeably here since the Religious Affairs Department managed Hindu as well as Muslim endowments, suggesting a more general use of the term.

70. AP/TSA, Fatwa No. 37/1, 6 Farwardin 1358 F.

71. On the definition of waqfs, see Heffening, "Waḳf."

72. For the history of waqfs in British India, see, e.g., Abbasi, "*Sharīʿa*"; Abbasi, "Islamic Law"; Beverley, "Property"; Kozlowski, *Muslim Endowments*; Anantdeep Singh, "Zamindars"; Anantdeep Singh, "Women, Wealth, and Law"; and Stephens, *Governing Islam*, 168–69. For contemporary measures in Central and Southeast Asia, see McChesney, *Waqf in Central Asia*; and Yahaya, *Fluid Jurisdictions*.

73. For a further elaboration of this point, see Messick, *Calligraphic State*, 227–30; and Lhost, "From Documents," 1015.

74. AP/TSA, Fatwa No. 169/5, 17 Aban 1358 F, "Mutafarriq, Ruqaiya Bī Sāḥiba."

75. On the introduction of this act, see De, "Mumtaz Bibi's Broken Heart." Chapters 7 and 8 address the laws relating to marital dissolutions in British India and princely Hyderabad in more detail.

76. AP/TSA, Fatwa No. 169/5, 17 Aban 1358 F.

77. AP/TSA, Fatwa No. 169/5, 17 Aban 1358 F.

78. AP/TSA, Fatwa No. 169/5, 17 Aban 1358 F.

79. It was further limited by the traditional division of labor between the investigative work of the qazi's court and the legal principle-oriented work of the mufti.

Chapter 6

1. FHL-MMR, Microfilm 1356702, Vol. 97: Announcement, September 25, 1925. The 1901 census counted 118,129 individuals living in Meerut (including the cantonment). Muslims accounted for 50,317 people, or 42.5 percent of the population. *Statistical Abstract*, 4.

2. See chapter 3.

3. Studies of marriage in other contexts also reveal this confluence of law, family, and property. See, e.g., Hartog, *Man and Wife*; Howell, *Marriage Exchange*; and Rapoport, *Marriage, Money and Divorce*, among others.

4. See chapter 3 for an example.

5. These snippets appear in fatwa files, court cases, and administrative discourse.

6. In thinking about the expansiveness of marriage as a legal status, I draw on Edwards, "'Marriage Covenant'"; and Perrone, "'Back into the Days,'" among others.

7. He also founded and ran a madrasa. S. Raju, "North India's First Mosque Going Strong after 999 Years," *Hindustan Times*, June 8, 2018.

8. A family tree appears at the beginning of FHL-MMR, Microfilm 1307221. (Members of the family use the surname Siddiqui and the toponym Meeruṭhī.) Rizvi, however, notes that the family's connection to the qazi's office in Meerut dates to Muhammad bin Tughluq (r. 1325–51 CE). Rizvi, *History of the Dar al-Ulum*, 115.

9. FHL-MMR, Microfilm 1356702, Vol. 98.

10. FHL-MMR, Microfilm 1356702, Vol. 98, "Iʿlān" [Announcement], October 12[?], 1915. The announcement is only visible because the ink bled through the page and remained visible on the backside after microfilming.

11. "Iʿlān."

12. See, e.g., Waṣī-ud-Dīn's petition in UPSA-All., Bundle No. 198, Box No. 276, Sl. 13, File No. 10: Appointment of Qazis, Cawnpore, 1884 (Judicial). See chapter 3 for further discussion of these petitions.

13. FHL-MMR, Microfilm 1307226, "Important Announcement regarding the order of the Tahsildar of Meerut," September 24, 1925.

14. On the relationship between narrative documents and registers, see Lhost, "Writing Law," 265–69.

15. FHL-MMR, Microfilm 1307221, Vol. 4, Inʿam Allah Khan's Statement, February 3, 1910.

16. FHL-MMR, Microfilm 1307222, Vol. 15 [1], Entry dated January 31, 1910. The note, dated February 4, 1910, explained that after investigation (*taḥqīq*), it became known (*maʿlūm hūʾā*) that the couple's marriage (*nikāḥ*) was impermissible (*nā-jāʾiz*) and had been nullified. It also referred to the production of two *iqrār-nāmas* (legal statements) related to the incident.

17. Inʿam Allah Khan's Statement.

18. Although Act XII of 1880 did not provide specific guidelines, other regulations relating to Muslim marriage registration gave individuals a week or more to have their marriages recorded.

19. Inʿam Allah Khan's Statement.

20. FHL-MMR, Microfilm 1307221, Vol. 4, Nathe's Statement, February 3, 1910.

21. FHL-MMR, Microfilm 1307222, Vol. 15 [1], Entry dated January 31, 1910.

22. See the discussion of "model *nikāḥ-nāmas*" in the conclusion and Redding, *Secular Need*, esp. chapters 4 and 5; and Redding, "Secularism."

23. See also Qazi Yusuf Moorghay's discussion of his assistants in chapter 3.

24. Zain-ul-ʿAbidin (1910–91), who facilitated the microfilming of the Meerut qazi records in the late 1970s, taught history at Jamia Millia in Delhi, wrote articles for newspapers, and held prominent positions at Deoband. His name appears on the cover of the registers from this period but he did not read or record individual marriages.

25. The practice of having qazis and nikah-khwans use the same registers to record marriages continued during Bashir-ud-Din's lifetime, but under his successor, Zain-ul-ʿAbidin, each naʾib appears to have had his own registers, which the head qazi then collected and preserved.

26. FHL-MMR, Microfilm 1307222, Vol. 4.

27. This volume is particularly large; later volumes included twenty, fifty, and sometimes one hundred entries.

28. Similar approaches to marriage registration also operated in princely Hyderabad and Imperial Russia. For Hyderabad, see AP/TSA, Report on the Administration of H.E.H. The Nizam's Dominions for the years 1332 F and 1334 F. For Russia, see Garipova, "Married or Not Married?"

29. Fatwa questions suggest that couples continued to produce nikah-namas in British India, though evidence of them in other archives is fleeting.

30. Fāʾiq, "Qabāla-yi nikāḥ," in *Inshāʾ-yi Fāʾiq*, 28. See also Esposito, "Family Law," in *Oxford Dictionary of Islam*.

31. Additional images of these registers appear in Lhost, "From Documents." ʿAbd-ul-Bari was also involved in the 1857 Uprising—and arrested afterward. Rizvi, *History of the Dar al-Ulum*, 115; Raju, "North India's Mosque."

32. FHL-MMR, Microfilm 1307221, Vol. 2 (September 1881 to December 1884), Entries 230–34.

33. Entries 230–34.

34. FHL-MMR, Microfilm 1307221, Vol. 2, Entries 235–39. While *musammāt*, drawn from the Arabic root *a-s-m* (*ism*; name), literally means "so-called," or the one who is named, in British Indian usage, the term often appeared before a woman's name like the title "Ms." or "Mrs."

35. See chapter 3 for further discussion of these acts.

36. See chapter 3 for further discussion of this case.

37. Qazis in Bulandshahr also kept registers. See Lhost, "From Documents," 1028–31.

38. See chapter 1 as well as Lhost, "Writing Law."

39. These records are preserved on microfilm at the National Archives of India.

40. The Meerut records from this collection continue to the 1980s.

41. NAI, Microfilm No. 851, Sr. No. 40, Entry 18, October 17, 1869.

42. NAI, Microfilm No. 851, Sr. No. 40.

43. For records produced in Bharuch, scripts included Gujarati, Persian (written in *nastaʿlīq*), and Arabic (written in *naskẖ*). Later records from places like Meerut and Bulandshahr included signatures in Hindi (*devanāgarī*), Urdu (*nastaʿlīq*), and English, alongside the finger- and thumb-tip impressions that stood in for signatures. On bilingual legal documents, see Nandini Chatterjee, *Negotiating Mughal Law.*

44. NAI, Microfilm No. 851, Sr. No. 40, Entry 25.

45. NAI, Microfilm No. 851, Sr. No. 40, Entries 23, 24, 25, 26, 30.

46. As of August 28, 2020, the amount is roughly equivalent to $1,538.46 (USD). Today, websites provide Muslims with approximate values in today's currency, along with descriptions of the various terms. See "Zakâh Nisâb and Mahr Prices—Daily Updates," WellWishers, accessed August 30, 2020, https://wellwishers.org.uk/tools/zakah-nisab-and-mahr-prices-daily-updates.

47. This practice, which often appeared in written documents as "hiba biʾl-ʿiwaẓ" or "a gift in exchange for [*mahr*]," confounded colonial judges and led to several high court decisions debating the status of dower as gift (in exchange for marriage).

48. See Stephens for further discussion of family wealth and property in relation to marriage and mahr in *Governing Islam*, 57–85.

49. NAI, Microfilm No. 851, Sr. No. 40, Entry 22.

50. NAI, Microfilm No. 851, Sr. No. 40, Entry 13.

51. On the contested histories of identity documents in South Asia, see, e.g., Brinham, "'Genocide Cards'"; Chowdhury, "Picture-Thinking," in *Paradoxes of the Popular*, 31–62; Singha, "Great War"; Sriraman, *In Pursuit of Proof*; and Rao and Nair, "Aadhaar" along with other essays in the special issue they coedited. For elsewhere, see Igo, *Known Citizen*; Ragas, "Beyond Big Brother"; and Thompson, "'Não há Nada.'"

52. See, e.g., FHL-MMR, Microfilm 1356702, Vol. 98.

53. See chapter 3.

54. See, e.g., FHL-MMR, Microfilm 1307224, Vol. 47.

55. On the *waraq/waraqa* as legal document, see Bishara, *Sea of Debt*, 100–104.

56. See, e.g., FHL-MMR, Microfilm 1356706, Vol. 143 [114].

57. FHL-MMR, Microfilm 1356771, Vol. 7, Entry 6. Nūr Bakẖsh was the nikahkhwan. At this time (1968), "U.P." refers to the Indian state of Uttar Pradesh. Note that Zain-ul-ʿAbidin also refers to the completion of his *fāẓil* degree (roughly equivalent to a bachelor's) in Islamic studies.

58. FHL-MMR, Microfilm 1356771, Vol. 7, Entry 6.

59. The name of the nikah-khwan appears on the front of these registers, suggesting that individual registrars were responsible for recording marriages and then depositing the records with the chief qazi.

60. FHL-MMR, Microfilm 1307224, Vol. 47, Entry 90.

61. FHL-MMR, Microfilm 1356706, Vol. 143 [114], Entry 4.

62. FHL-MMR, Microfilm 1356706, Vol. 143 [114], Entry 6.

63. Not all canceled or incomplete entries included explanatory notes, but the fact that registrars crossed out these pages suggests that the presence or appearance of incomplete entries concerned them.

64. FHL-MMR, Microfilm 1356704, Vol. 119, Entry 50.

65. FHL-MMR, Microfilm 1356706, Vol. 143 [114], Entry 17.

66. On the history of fingerprinting, see Sengoopta, *Imprint of the Raj*.

67. The administrative summary from 1334 F reports, "The system of affixing thumb impressions in *Sihajat* (marriage registers) was introduced and the Naibs were trained for the purpose in the Anthropometry Branch of the office of the Director-General of District Police." AP/TSA, Report on the Administration of H.E.H. the Nizam's Dominions, for the year 1334 Fasli (1924 CE).

68. See, e.g., FHL-MMR, Microfilm 1356706, Vol. 143 [114], Entries 15, 16, 18, 24.

69. Again, most marriage statutes allowed couples to register their marriages within a certain period *after* the ceremony.

70. Carroll, "*Talaq-i-Tafwid*."

71. ʿUṣmānī, *ʿAzīz-ul-Fatāwá*, 508.

72. ʿUṣmānī, 504–5.

73. Similar cases abound in fatwa collections. In one, a husband divorced his wife and signed a divorce decree in front of witnesses. He later went to court, claiming his father-in-law (*k͟husur*) forced him to make the divorce and that he wanted to get back together with his wife. The mufti validated the divorce decree. In another, the husband sent a divorce decree in the mail. One witness signed the letter and another (a *ḥāfiẓ*) stated that the word *ṭalāq* appeared in it, even though the letter had been destroyed (*miṭā hūʾā*). With only one witness, the divorce decree was not valid, the mufti relayed. ʿUṣmānī, 475–76.

74. FHL-MMR, Microfilm 1307224, Vol. 48 [2], Entry 23.

75. FHL-MMR, Microfilm 1307224, Vol. 48 [2], Entry 24.

76. FHL-MMR, Microfilm 1356704, Vol. 121 [98], Entry 53. This tactic was common. Having women speak from seclusion (*parda*) allowed them to participate in the legal process while at the same time respecting their privacy. Unlike the registration of births and deaths, for which third parties reported to the registrar in fulfillment of the registration requirements, marriages required individuals to transgress the boundary between a private ceremony and a public event. Qazis accommodated varying degrees of privacy and seclusion by allowing women to speak from "behind *parda*" and by recording marriages for which women were not present.

77. FHL-MMR, Microfilm 1356704, Vol. 120, Entry 67.

78. Men did not face similar scrutiny, since they could have more than one wife.

79. Many of the copies of these documents, especially divorce decrees, were inserted into or written on the back of the register entry. Unfortunately, the microfilm

operator skipped these pages when preserving the records, though evidence of their contents is sometimes visible through the page.

80. FHL-MMR, Microfilm 1356704, Vol. 120 [96], Entry 72.

81. FHL-MMR, Microfilm 1356704, Vol. 120 [96], Entry 64.

82. FHL-MMR, Microfilm 1356704, Vol. 120 [96], Entry 38.

83. FHL-MMR, Microfilm 1356704, Vol. 120 [96], Entry 35.

84. The statement refers to *jahīz*, which typically means "dowry," or property given by the bride to the groom's family. However, the exchange clearly goes from the husband to his wife ("Shāh Jahān nē . . . musammāt kē pās diyā"), suggesting that the term *jahīz* here refers to mahr. Some of the details are missing for this entry, including the bride's full name ("Ḵẖātūn" means lady, though sometimes it functions as a given name), leading me to guess that the couple went to the marriage registrar to record the property exchange after having already been married for a while. FHL-MMR, Microfilm 1356704, Vol. 119, Entry 42.

85. FHL-MMR, Microfilm 1356704, Vol. 120, Entry 23.

86. One judgment made clear the court's skepticism toward the marriage registers: "An entry of the amount in the Qazi's register is also a rarity; and even where such an entry exists, it is not always safe to accept it with implicit confidence. When a controversy arises as to the amount of dower, the place of documents is, in [a] great many cases, sought to be supplied by a mass of oral evidence. At times, it becomes extremely difficult for a Court of law to disentangle the truth from the conflicting statements of witnesses, many of whom are not generally free from the taint of partiality or prejudice." Mohammad Zahur Ahsan And Ors. v. Mt. Maimuna And Ors., AIR 1929 All 142. In another instance, the judgment stated a clear preference for witness testimony over the qazi's records: "The learned Subordinate Judge has disbelieved all this evidence on the ground that the Qazi's register does not show that one-half was fixed as the prompt dower. This may be true, but we have no reason to say that all these respectable witnesses chose to tell untruths for the sake of their sister who was bound to recover, in any case, a substantial proportion from the defendant as her prompt dower." Mt. Maimuna Begam v. Sharafat Ullah Khan, AIR 1931 All 403.

87. Reported cases from the high courts are a poor indication of the registers' legal value. Stamps found within the extant registers marking them as "exhibits" suggest that they routinely appeared as evidence in the lower courts. For an example of a case in which the wife successfully called on information from the marriage register to assert her property rights, see Jaitunbi Fatrubhai v. Fatrubhai Kasambhai and Ors., AIR 1948 Bom 114.

88. The government appointed qazis but allowed those qazis to then appoint their own assistants. The qazis in Meerut—on whom this chapter focuses—employed dozens of assistants who compiled their registers independently and then brought them to the head qazi for safekeeping.

Interlude III

1. "Application of Personal Law to Muslims. No Statute to Be Affected," *TOI*, September 17, 1937. There was little specificity in the use of the term "custom" here,

and whether it referred to ʿ*urf* or ʿ*ādat*. For earlier debates about custom and the limitations of Muslim personal law in Punjab, see Jalal, *Self and Sovereignty*, 149–53. Writing several decades later, Tahir Mahmood remarked that in Muslim-majority states like Malaysia and Indonesia, "adat law (customs and usages having the force of law though repugnant to the classical law of Islam) . . . is well known" and India had "never been much different" with respect to the "sharp cleavage between legal theory and social practices prevailing among many sections of the Muslims." Mahmood, "Indian Muslims—Their Life and Law," *TOI*, December 25, 1977.

2. "Muslim Personal Law. Objects of the New Bill," *TOI*, April 2, 1937.

3. "Muslim Personal Law."

4. The use of "custom" (meaning variably ʿ*urf*, ʿ*addat*, *rawāj*, etc.) was particularly problematic in Punjab. Gilmartin, "Customary Law and *Shariat*"; Jalal, *Self and Sovereignty*, 151–52; Sharma, "Custom, Law"; Stephens, *Governing Islam*, 169. For a look at customary law in action, see Chaudhary, *Justice in Practice*; and Saumarez Smith, *Rule by Records*. For compilations of customary law from Punjab, see Ellis, *Notes on Punjab Custom*; Tupper, *Punjab Customary Law*; and Qureshi and Anand, *Punjab Custom*.

5. Stephens describes the act as "one of several legislative interventions . . . that sought to reform the colonial administration of religious law." *Governing Islam*, 168.

6. The Parsi Divorce Bill passed on April 18, 1936, at the same meeting in which H. M. Abdullah "moved consideration of the Muslim Personal Law (Shariat) Application Bill." Several of these other measures were also under discussion at the time. "Repeal of Repressive Laws Urged in Assembly," *TOI*, April 18, 1936.

7. The laws of succession, inheritance, and endowments (*waqfs*) were points of contention. See Jalal, *Self and Sovereignty*, 151; Purohit, *Aga Khan Case*, 22–25; and Stephens, *Governing Islam*, 168–69.

8. "Application of Personal Law."

9. "Application of 'Shariat' Law for Benefit of Women," *TOI*, September 10, 1937.

10. "Application of Personal Law."

11. "Women's Share in Property. Muslim Personal Law," *TOI*, September 10, 1937.

12. State-appointed boards would, of course, run the risk of producing factionalized, regional interpretations (perhaps resembling "custom"), too.

13. "SHARIAT BILL. Muslim M. L. A.'s to Move Agreed Amendments," *TOI*, September 8, 1937.

14. Muslim Personal Law (Shariat) Application Act, Clause 2; and Stephens, *Governing Islam*, 171.

15. Stephens, *Governing Islam*, 171.

16. Stephens, 171.

17. Jalal mentions the introduction of "*qazi fazl* and *qazi alim* qualifying tests" (roughly equivalent to a BA and a diploma, respectively) in the 1870s, for instance. Jalal, *Self and Sovereignty*, 149. On the Imarat-i Shariah, see Papiya Ghosh, "Muttahidah Qaumiyat"; and Papiya Ghosh, "Community, Questions."

18. Stephens, *Governing Islam*, 172.

19. See, e.g., discussions of anxiety over religious adjudication in Bowen, *On British Islam*; Emon, "Islamic Law"; and Quraishi-Landes and Syeed, "No Altars."

Chapter 7

1. The term *ʿamal-dārī* may be variously translated as "administration," "authority," "government," "jurisdiction," or "limits of jurisdiction." As the crux of the question revolves around the limits of the qazi's jurisdiction under the administration, jurisdiction, or authority of the British government, I have translated the term as "jurisdiction" here and as "administration" later, to highlight the term's multiple meanings and to capture the idea of layered or overlapping jurisdictions.

2. Kifāyatullāh, *Kifāyat-ul-Muftī*, 2:210–11.

3. Perhaps a reference to Ab-ud-Raʾūf Danāpūrī (1874–1948)?

4. On panchayats in British India, see Jaffe, *Ironies of Colonial Governance*; Jaffe, "Layering Law upon Custom"; Jaffe, "Constructing Corruption"; and Shodhan, "East India Company's Conquest."

5. *Ṣadāqat*, October 2, 1916, quoted in Kifāyatullāh, *Kifāyat-ul-Muftī*, 2:211. See Platts, *Dictionary of Urdu*, 725, on the *sharīʿa/sharʿīya* spelling.

6. I have identified at least six questions related to local councils and four on the responsibilities or status of the qazi in Kifayatullah's collection.

7. For recent discussion of these jurisdictional debates, see Redding, *Secular Need*; Redding, "Secularism"; and Vatuk, "Extra-judicial *Khulʿ* Divorce."

8. See, e.g., Agnes, "His and Hers"; Papiya Ghosh, "Muttahidah Qaumiyat"; Lemons, *Divorcing Traditions*; Redding, *Secular Need*; and Vatuk, *Marriage and Its Discontents*, among others.

9. Ingram, *Revival from Below*; Masud, "Apostasy and Judicial Separation"; Barbara D. Metcalf, "Madrasa at Deoband." See, more broadly, Müller and Steiner, "Bureaucratisation of Islam"; Peletz, *Islamic Modern*; and Sezgin and Künkler, "Regulation of 'Religion.'"

10. Stephens, *Governing Islam*, 82. See also Radhika Singha, *Despotism of Law*, 140–45; and Fisch, *Cheap Lives*, on the intersections of criminal and personal law.

11. Kifāyatullāh, *Kifāyat-ul-Muftī*, 2:211.

12. Kifāyatullāh, 2:211. Historically, early qazis acted as arbitrators. Vikør, *Between God*, 168.

13. Today, India's *dār-ul-qaẓās* (qazi courts) embrace this interpretation. Redding, *Secular Need*, 69–71.

14. On the history of Deoband, see Barbara D. Metcalf, *Islamic Revival*; and more recently, Ingram, *Revival from Below*.

15. Wāṣif, "Dībācha," in Kifāyatullāh, *Kifāyat-ul-Muftī*, 1:6–13.

16. Aḥmad, *Janūbī Eshiyā*.

17. Wāṣif, *Muftī-yi Aʿẓam kī Yād*.

18. Ingram, *Revival from Below*, 48–49.

19. Minault, "Women, Legal Reform," 7. Thanwi originally published the fatwa in 1913. It was revised and republished as *Al-Hīlat al-Nājizah liʾl-Ḥalīlat al-ʿĀjiza*

(*Successful Legal Device for the Helpless Wife*) in 1931. For more on this issue, see Masud, "Apostasy and Judicial Separation," and Zaman, *Ulama in Contemporary Islam*, 29–30.

20. Kifāyatullāh, *Kifāyat-ul-Muftī*, 2:210–40.

21. See Sharafi, "Marital Patchwork."

22. The government of India required individuals to compose legal documents on stamped paper and to register their deeds with local registrars. The ubiquity of stamp paper and the pervasiveness of stamp-paper requirements meant that individuals started to include stamps on all kinds of legal documents—registered and unregistered. On the social life of stamp paper, see Shrimoyee Nandini Ghosh, "'Not Worth the Paper.'"

23. Ṭōnkī, *Majmūʿa-yi Fatāwá-yi Ṣābriya*, 76–79. The full text of this statement is not available, but Muhammad Shah likely conceived of his statement as a form of delegated divorce. See Carroll, "*Talaq-i-Tafwid*."

24. Islamic courts do not have formalized mechanisms for appeal or judicial review, but that does not mean there were no hierarchies of authority. In British (and princely) India, disputes between or among local muftis often migrated to those I refer to as the "mufti's mufti" for resolution. In addition to the practice among litigants of sourcing multiple answers to a single question, nested hierarchies of authority also existed among muftis, with urban institutes assuming more authority than rural ones and well-known muftis receiving requests to answer unresolvable contests or disputes. For more on appeals in Islam, see Powers, "On Judicial Review."

25. In the anjuman's typical fashion, the fatwa included additional attestations of approval from Qazi Zafar-ud-Din Ahmad (teacher at the local Arabic School), Ghulam Rasul (teacher at the Madrasa Hamidia), Muhammad Hasan (another teacher at the Madrasa Hamidia), Ghulam Ahmad (teacher at the Madrasa Naʿimia), Muhammad Ismaʿil (teacher at the Madrasa Rahimia), Ahmad ʿAli (teacher at Islamia College), Qazi Nur-ul-Hasan (assistant at the Anjuman-i Mustashar-ul-ʿUlama), and Muhammad ʿAlam (teacher at the Madrasa Hamidia).

26. Alan Guenther provides a detailed history of Syed Mahmood's [Sayyid Maḥmūd's] career and influence on the development of Anglo-Indian and Muslim personal law in British India. See Guenther, "Syed Mahmood"; Guenther, "Colonial Court"; and Guenther, "Justice Mahmood."

27. These references not only demonstrated Syed Mahmood's facility as a justice working between two textual worlds but also expanded the material on which later judges could draw for their decisions. Guenther, "Syed Mahmood," 303.

28. Guenther, "Syed Mahmood," 5.

29. Jafri Begam v. Amir Muhammad Khan (1885) ILR 7 All 822, 826.

30. Guenther, "Syed Mahmood," 3.

31. *Jafri Begam*, ILR 7 All at 826.

32. Ali, *Al-Qur'ān*, 74–75.

33. *Al-Sirajiyyah* was translated for the British East India Company by William Jones in the late eighteenth century and served as a point of reference for high court judges throughout the nineteenth and into the twentieth century. References

to it appear in several cases: Nimai Chand Addya v. Golam Hossein (1910) ILR 37 Cal 179; Shankar Lal and Anr. v. Mohammad Ismail and Anr. (1930) AIR 1930 All 552; Aminabi Mahmulal Patil v. Abasaheb Mirasaheb Patil (1931) 33 Bom LR 469; and T. Ravi & Anr v. B. Chinna Narasimha & Ors. Etc., March 21, 2017.

34. *Jafri Begam*, ILR 7 All at 827.

35. *Jafri Begam*, ILR 7 All at 823.

36. *Jafri Begam*, ILR 7 All at 825. Note that the full bench also amended the original question.

37. *Jafri Begam*, ILR 7 All at 826.

38. *Jafri Begam*, ILR 7 All at 827.

39. *Jafri Begam*, ILR 7 All at 826.

40. *Jafri Begam*, ILR 7 All at 832, 833, 834, 838, 839, 841.

41. *Jafri Begam*, ILR 7 All at 841.

42. *Jafri Begam*, ILR 7 All at 844 (emphasis in original). Justice Mahmood ties Islamic legal procedure to the context of its origins, adding, "There were, of course, reasons arising from the exigencies of life (such as the difficulty of communication and travelling) which induced Muhammadan jurists in the middle ages to frame rules of procedure in many essentials different from those which regulate the procedure of our Courts. But those conditions of life no longer exits [*sic*]: the law of British India has framed its own rules of procedure." (844)

43. This approach to separating substance from procedure became more common in the modern period. See Vikør, *Between God*, 225–28.

44. "Procedural justice" is a robust field of law-and-society scholarship. Recent contributions include Solum, "Procedural Justice"; Hollander-Blumoff and Tyler, "Procedural Justice"; Worden and McLean, *Mirage of Police Reform*; McLean, "Ethnic Identity, Procedural Justice"; and Tyler, "What Is Procedural Justice?" For comparative analysis, see, e.g., Sun et al., "Procedural Justice, Legitimacy"; and for gender-based analysis, see, e.g., Baker and Gau, "Female Offenders' Perceptions."

45. *Jafri Begam*, ILR 7 All at 847.

46. *Jafri Begam*, ILR 7 All at 830.

47. Syed Ameer Ali and Syed Mahmood both grew up in elite, North Indian Muslim families and were part of the Aligarh Movement. Badruddin Tyabji was a member of the Sulaimani Bohra Muslim community, a branch of Shiʿī Ismāʿilī Islam. See Beverley, "Property, Authority"; and Kozlowski, "Judges and Lawyers," in *Muslim Endowments and Society*.

48. See Moosa Adam Patel v. Ismail Moosa (1909) 12 Bom LR 169. Beaman was not the only justice to struggle with the concept of *hiba biʾl ʿiwaẓ*. The term frequently came into question in marriage and divorce cases in which the husband pledged or promised his wife property "in lieu of" (or, as some rendered it, "in consideration of") her mahr. Nor were Beaman's contributions confined to Muslim personal law; he also played a role in the adjudication of disputes among Parsis. See Sharafi, *Law and Identity*, 33–34.

49. Beaman did not set the record straight on this debate; it continued after this decision, so although he wanted to make a substantive contribution to the understanding of these concepts, even he could not write the definitive answer.

50. *Moosa Adam Patel* 12 Bom LR 169.

51. Ramzan Mistri and Ors. v. Haji Zahur Hossein (1913) 18 Ind Cas 241, 242.

52. Bhutnath Dey and Anr. v. Ahmed Hosain and Ors (1885) ILR 11 Cal 417; Narain Das v. Kazi Abdur Rahim Mutawalli (1920) 58 Ind Cas 705; Zafar Husain v. Ummat-ur-Rahman (1919) 49 Ind Cas 256; Anjuman Islamia Represented by Zahur Uddin v. Latafat Ali and Ors (1949) AIR 1950 All 109; Ajaz Hossain Jafri v. Altaf Hossain and Ors. (1928) AIR 1928 Cal 651; Mohammad Ali Khan v. Ahmad Ali Khan and Ors. (1945) AIR 1945 All 261; Fakhrunnessa Begam alias Badshah Begam v. The District Judge of the 24 Pargunnas (1920) 56 Ind Cas 475; Ambalavana Thambiran v. Vageesam Pillai and Ors (1929) IR 1930 Mad 226; Mohsenuddin Ahammad v. Khabiruddin Ahmed and Ors (1920) 57 Ind Cas 945.

53. Srimutty Jamila Khatun v. Abdul Jalil Meah and Anr. (1918) 49 Ind Cas 799.

54. Mohiuddin Chowdhury v. Aminuddin Chowdhury and Ors. (1922) 72 Ind Cas 930, 931. He notes explicitly that this case is "clearly distinguishable" from *Srimutty Jamila Khatun.*

55. *Mohiuddin Chowdhury*, 72 Ind Cas at 931. He further contends that interested parties "may or may not themselves have a remedy . . . by way of suit under Section 92 of the Code or otherwise." (931)

56. In Re: Halima Khatun v. Unknown (1910) ILR 37 Cal 870.

57. *In Re: Halima Khatun*, ILR 37 Cal 870. Acts XXVII and XXVIII of 1866, respectively.

58. *In Re: Halima Khatun*, ILR 37 Cal at 875.

59. *Mohiuddin Chowdhury*, 72 Ind Cas at 931.

60. The role of the Privy Council was not negligible when it came to deciding personal law cases. See, e.g., De, "Mumtaz Bibi's Broken Heart"; Stephens, *Governing Islam*, 57; and Sharafi, *Law and Identity*, 77.

61. Kifāyatullāh, *Kifāyat-ul-Muftī*, 2:223. He qualifies these as "*ṭalāq, nikāḥ, mīrāṣ, wag̱haira.*" Not all muftis accepted this view. Zaman, *Ulama in Contemporary Islam*, 204n50.

62. Zaman suggests that the ʿulama were, at least in some instances, willing to accept "a judge who was not versed in the Shariʿa but not one who was not a Muslim." Zaman, *Ulama in Contemporary Islam*, 205n53.

63. Kifāyatullāh, *Kifāyat-ul-Muftī*, 2:214.

64. Kifāyatullāh, 2:217. ("Qāẓī muqarrar karnē kā iḵẖtiyār bādshāh aur imām kō hai.")

65. Kifāyatullāh, 2:217.

66. Accepting community-appointed qazis would, no doubt, undermine the ʿulama's demands for qazi appointments. See Zaman, *Ulama in Contemporary Islam*, 27–29.

67. Kifāyatullāh, *Kifāyat-ul-Muftī*, 2:223.

68. Agrama notes a similar dynamic in Egypt, relative to its "shariʿa courts" and nonjudicial dar-ul-iftas. Agrama, "Ethics, Tradition, Authority"; Agrama, *Questioning Secularism*, 109–22.

69. Here I follow a "social scientific" view of legal pluralism, borrowing also from Moore's idea of the "semi-autonomous social field." See Griffiths, "What Is Legal Pluralism?"; Merry, "Legal Pluralism," 871; and Moore, "Law and Social Change."

70. Kifāyatullāh, *Kifāyat-ul-Muftī*, 8:75–76.

71. Unfortunately, I have not been able to find the case in the printed judgments.

72. Kifāyatullāh, *Kifāyat-ul-Muftī*, 8:105.

73. Kifāyatullāh, 8:105–6.

74. Kifāyatullāh, 8:97, 103, etc. Interest, in these cases, tends to originate in government banks. In questions about taking interest directly from another individual, Kifayatullah cautions against it. See, e.g., Kifāyatullāh, 8:99.

75. The Qur'an provides specific punishments for the five *ḥudūd* crimes. On British attitudes toward Islamic punishments, see Fisch, *Cheap Lives*.

76. Kifāyatullāh, *Kifāyat-ul-Muftī*, 2:173–74. It was unusual for individuals to ask questions about criminal activity. The British East India Company assumed responsibility for punishing most criminal activity in the first half of the nineteenth century, and by the time the Indian Penal Code took effect in 1862, Muslim personal law had no connection with Anglo-Indian criminal law, save for the bizarre classification of adultery as a crime that could only be prosecuted by the victim, not by the state.

77. Kifāyatullāh, 2:173–74. The question further asks whether the person can serve as imam before the family is compensated. The assistant mufti answers that one should not pray behind the one who committed the murder until he gives compensation to the family, asks for forgiveness, and repents.

78. Kifāyatullāh, 2:174.

79. See Hallaq, *Sharīʿa*, 378–79.

80. Jurists cautioned petitioners against agreeing to dower amounts outside their means but emphasized the validity of the debt nonetheless.

81. The Indian Contract Act (1872), for instance, specified that "agreements made in consideration of marriage" were subject to the same requirements as other instruments. Stamp duties on deeds of gift and dower were chargeable at the same rate as deeds of settlement, which followed the rates for bonds. See Donogh, *Stamp Law*, 176.

82. Kifāyatullāh, *Kifāyat-ul-Muftī*, 5:114–15.

83. Kifāyatullāh, 5:116.

84. Kifāyatullāh, 5:116.

Chapter 8

1. See also Merry's reflections on turning to the court as a "last resort" in *Getting Justice*, 3.

2. AP/TSA, Fatwa No. 79/5, March 16, 1950, "ʿAqd-i s̤ānī, Maryam Bī bint-i Muḥammad bin ʿAlī."

3. For a brief history of this institution, see chapter 5.

4. Kozlowski, "Loyalty, Locality."

5. Owing to the use of the thumbprint at the bottom of the page, I suspect that Maryam Bi was illiterate and either narrated her account to someone at home before traveling to Hyderabad or did so upon her arrival. Today, scribes sit outside courtrooms and inside madrasas to aid petitioners in the completion of their

paperwork. See, e.g., "In a Corner Outside a Courtroom, Typing for Decades," *Indian Express,* December 15, 2017; and Lemons, *Divorcing Traditions,* 125–26.

6. These are formulaic ways to begin a fatwa question. For further discussion of the *istiftāʾ* (fatwa question), see Masud, "Significance of *Istiftāʾ*"; and chapter 4 of this book.

7. AP/TSA, Fatwa No. 79/5, March 16, 1950.

8. AP/TSA, Fatwa No. 79/5, March 16, 1950. I read Maryam Bi's use of the term *muhājirīn* as a reference to the migrants of the partition.

9. The two-state partition of India and Pakistan was one of several proposals. See Purushotham, "Federating the Raj."

10. On partition and the princely states, see Copland, "Princely States." For other perspectives, see Nair, *Changing Homelands;* and Zamindar, *Long Partition,* among others.

11. "100 Armed Razakars Attack Village. Houses Broken Open & Valuables Removed," *Sunday News of India,* June 20, 1948.

12. "Indian Enclaves in Hyderabad. Essential Supplies under Escort," *Sunday News of India,* June 20, 1948.

13. "Border Clashes with Razakars" and "Madras Express Escapes Attack," *TOI,* August 7, 1947.

14. See interlude III.

15. Ghosh, "'Not Worth the Paper.'"

16. On everyday engagements with economic arguments under the Indian Constitution, see De, *People's Constitution.*

17. For accounts that use trauma as a framework for understanding partition, see, e.g., Coombs, "Partition Narratives"; Dasgupta, "Remembering the Bengal Partition"; Mushirul Hasan, "Partition"; and Mubarki, "Violence, Victimhood and Trauma."

18. Petitioners employed a variety of expressions to convey this sentiment—"according to shariʿa" (*sharīʿā kē muṭābiq*), wondering whether something "is permissible in shariʿa" (*sharīʿān̠ jāʾiz hai*), asking for the "shariʿa commands" (*sharʿī aḥkām*), and so on.

19. In the chapter on marriage (*nikāḥ*), for instance, many petitioners referred to the Child Marriage Restraint (Sharda) Act of 1929 and its effects on the marriage of minors. See, e.g., Kifāyatullāh, *Kifāyat-ul-Muftī,* 6:33.

20. Petitioners and muftis made clear distinctions between *qānūn* (law), meaning the statutes and regulations of British India, and shariʿa, as a separate category of religious guidance. They further distinguished between government *ḥukms* (orders, commands) and the commands of Allah, demonstrating a robust understanding of state law as separate from religious law, despite the overlap in their use of these terms.

21. On the separation of family status from the market and economic governance, see Birla, *Stages of Capital;* Stephens, *Governing Islam;* and Sturman, *Government of Social Life,* among others.

22. Kifāyatullāh, *Kifāyat-ul-Muftī,* 8:63.

23. Naẕīr Ḥusain, *Fatāwá-yi Naẕīriya*, 2:35. The question cites part of Qurʾan verse 5:44.

24. For examples, see Kifāyatullāh, *Kifāyat-ul-Muftī*, 8:53; Naẕīr Ḥusain, *Fatāwá-yi Naẕīriya*, 2:37–43; and Shafīʿ, *Imdād-ul-Muftain*, 454, 662–65.

25. Naẕīr Ḥusain, *Fatāwá-yi Naẕīriya*, 2:55.

26. By comparison, see Agrama, *Questioning Secularism*; Asad, *Formations of the Secular*; and Sullivan, *Impossibility of Religious Freedom*.

27. Some scholars refer to nonstate solutions as "extralegal," implying that they are beyond or outside the law. I prefer "nonstate," as it reflects the procedural and doctrinal legality of these options while acknowledging their unofficial origins.

28. Kifāyatullāh, *Kifāyat-ul-Muftī*, 8:22, 24, 33.

29. Kifāyatullāh, 8:23, 43.

30. Kifāyatullāh, 8:30–31.

31. Gholam Nubby Chowdry v. Gour Kishore Rai (1811) 1 Sel. Rep. 469, 475 (N).

32. Kulb Ali Hoosein v. Syf Ali (1814) 2 Sel. Rep. 139, 141 (N). Justice Ghose, writing his concurring opinion for *Bikani Mia* (1892), cites this case, along with several others from this era, as part of his deliberations. See Bikani Mia (Defendant No. 1) v. Shuk Lal Poddar and Another (Plaintiffs) (1893) ILR 20 Cal 116, 188.

33. Ranee Buksh Beebee v. Nadir Beebee (1820) 3 Sel. Rep. 79 (N). The question put to the mufti and the mufti's response appear on 80–82.

34. See also Hallaq, *Sharīʿa*, 220–11, citing Hanna, *State and Its Servants*.

35. ʿAbd-ul-Ḥayy, *Majmūʿa-yi Fatāwá* (1964), 356–57.

36. ʿAbd-ul-Ḥayy, 358.

37. Shafīʿ, *Imdād-ul-Muftain*, 652.

38. Shafīʿ, 667. The mufti replied that working as a lawyer was okay but that representing clients who made false claims was not acceptable and the money received for such work was "illegal" (*ḥarām*).

39. Kifāyatullāh, *Kifāyat-ul-Muftī*, 8:33.

40. Kifāyatullāh, 8:34.

41. Kifāyatullāh, 8:34–35. The religious identity of the buyer is unclear here. Mustaftis typically referred to Christians as *kāfirs* and used "Hindu" or another, more specific, term to refer to members of other religious communities.

42. To make this arrangement legitimate, the mufti suggested that the buyer offer to pay the seller a specified amount as a debt (*qarẓ*), then the seller could release the buyer from the sale agreement and return the advance (which he would be obligated to do legally), after which the seller would pay the debt (here in the same amount) to end their dealings with each other.

43. Kifāyatullāh, 8:36.

44. Kifāyatullāh, 8:115–18.

45. Kifāyatullāh, 8:116.

46. Kifāyatullāh, 8:116.

47. Ṣabīḥ-ud-Dīn gives the town of Meerut, not quite fifty miles from Delhi, as his address. Kifāyatullāh, 8:117.

48. Kifāyatullāh, 8:118.

49. The question of reputation was central to many trademark disputes in British India. See, e.g., The Swadeshi Mills Co. v. Juggi Lal, Kamlapat Cotton (1926) AIR 1927 All 81; A. J. Von Wulfing v. D. H. Jivandas and Co. (1924) AIR 1926 Bom 200; and Thomas Bear and Sons (India) v. Prayag Narain (1934) AIR 1935 All 7.

50. See, e.g., Kifāyatullāh, *Kifāyat-ul-Muftī*, 7:43, 56–57, 63, 65–66.

51. See, e.g., Kifāyatullāh, 6:23, 28–29, 33.

52. See, e.g., Kifāyatullāh, 9:244–46.

53. Legislative interventions came from measures like the Kazis' Act of 1880, the Muslim Personal Law (Shariat) Application Act of 1937, and the Dissolution of Muslim Marriages Act of 1939. On judicial interventions through *mahr,* see Sharafi, "Semi-autonomous Judge." On juristic debates, see Masud, "Apostasy and Judicial Separation"; Fareeha Khan, "Traditionalist Approaches"; and Zaman, *Ulama in Contemporary Islam.*

54. On the debates surrounding this act, see De, "Mumtaz Bibi's Broken Heart."

55. DMMA, 1939, 2(i–ix).

56. DMMA, 2(i).

57. The act defines six forms of cruelty: habitual assault or making life miserable in other ways; frequenting prostitutes or having extramarital affairs (i.e., "associat[ing] with women of evil repute or lead[ing] an infamous life"); attempting or forcing his wife to live an immoral life; taking a woman's property or preventing her from exercising her legal rights over property; obstructing his wife's religious observance or practice; and having more than one wife and not treating them equally.

58. DMMA, 2(ii–ix).

59. On the apostasy question see Fareeha Khan, "Traditionalist Approaches"; and Masud, "Apostasy and Judicial Separation."

60. In fact, the legislation overlooked some key concerns like providing Muslim judges to grant divorces. Zaman, *Ulama in Contemporary Islam*, 30–31.

61. Subsequent contests over divorce and maintenance reflect these tensions as well. See Carroll, "Shah Bano"; Zoya Hasan and Menon, *Unequal Citizens*; Lemons, *Divorcing Traditions*; Redding, *Secular Need*; Vatuk, *Marriage and Its Discontents*; and the Muslim Women (Protection of Rights on Divorce) Act 1986.

62. The text refers to the arrangement as a "nikāḥ," but an engagement (after which the children would continue to live separately) is more likely. The narrator's timeline is a bit confused. He refers to ʿAziz Muhammad's departure ten years ago, adding that news arrived for two years after his departure and that no news has arrived for the last eight years. However, he refers to Zahir-un-Nisa's age as "sāt sāl" (seven years) at the time of the marriage and "bīs sāl" (twenty years) at the time of his writing. Either he has misstated the number of years ʿAziz Muhammad has been away, has used the expression "a few days" (*kuchh din*) to refer to a longer length of time between the betrothal and the boy's departure, or has misstated Zahir-un-Nisa's present age. None of these inconsistencies, however, affected the substance of the case. Kifāyatullāh, *Kifāyat-ul-Muftī*, 6:104.

63. Kifāyatullāh, 6:104. For another engagement with this question, see Vatuk, *Marriage and Its Discontents*, 1–28.

64. Kifāyatullāh, 6:104. Kifayatullah's first response is all of twenty words.

65. Kifāyatullāh, 6:105.

66. Kifāyatullāh, 6:105.

67. Kifāyatullāh, 6:105–6. See also Stephens, *Governing Islam*, 76–85.

68. The length of time necessary to declare one's husband *mafqūd-ul-k̲h̲abar* varied for the different schools of law. I discuss some of these calculations in relation to substantive change in chapter 4.

69. AP/TSA, Fatwa No. 79/5, March 16, 1950, [3a].

70. AP/TSA, Fatwa No. 79/5, March 16, 1950, [3a–b].

71. AP/TSA, Fatwa No. 79/5, March 16, 1950, [4b].

72. AP/TSA, Fatwa No. 79/5, March 16, 1950, [5b].

73. AP/TSA, Fatwa No. 79/5, March 16, 1950, [6b].

74. See, e.g., FHL-MMR, Reel 1356704, Vol. 22, Entry 63, November 3, 1933.

75. AP/TSA, Fatwa No. 79/5, March 16, 1950, [2a].

76. Originally, that section (Section 421) of the Hyderabad penal code stipulated that the courts could grant a woman permission to remarry (*ʿaqd-i ṣānī*) after her husband was missing (*mafqūd-ul-k̲h̲abar*) for more than seven years. The sadr's *farmān* changed this duration to four years, explaining that four years was "in the shariʿa" (*sharʿ-yi sharīf main̲*) and seven years was in the penal code but that it was "appropriate" (*munāsib*) to amend the penal code to bring it in line with *sharīʿa*. AP/TSA, Mixed Farmans, Daftar-i Peshkārī, No. 132, 20 Ramadan 1339 AH.

77. AP/TSA, Fatwa No. 81/5 of 1950, March 24, 1950, "Afsar Begam, *ʿaqd-i ṣānī*."

78. AP/TSA, Fatwa No. 79/5, March 16, 1950, [9a].

79. Indeed, Hallaq cites specific strategies muftis would use when they suspected misrepresentation. See Hallaq, "From *Fatwās* to *Furūʿ*," 38n47.

Conclusion

1. See, e.g., debates about the colonial origins of censorship, blasphemy, and sedition laws in Kaur, "Specters of Macaulay"; and Nandakumar, "Why India Should Repeal."

2. Redding, *Secular Need*, 46–47.

3. The literature here is vast and growing. For representative examples, see Badran, *Feminism in Islam*; Das Acevedo, "Secularism"; Dutta, "From Accommodation"; Hussain, "Shariat Courts"; Larson, *Religion and Personal Law*; Lemons, "Sharia Courts"; Newbigin, "Codification of Personal Law"; Parashar, "Religious Personal Laws"; Redding, "Secularism"; Rudolph and Rudolph, "Living with Difference"; Vatuk, "Islamic Feminism in India"; and Vatuk, "Moving the Courts."

4. Menski suggests that uniformity in civil law has been achieved through diversity in religious law reforms. Menski, "Uniform Civil Code Debate."

5. See, e.g., Vishwa Lochan Madan's public interest litigation petition in Vishwa Lochan Madan v. Union of India, 1995 AIR 1531 (SC), discussed in Redding, *Secular Need*, 56–78. Disputes over the legality of fatwas also belong to this category. See, e.g., Kanchan Gupta, "Should India Tolerate Fatwas?," *DNA*, January 18, 2018, https://www.dnaindia.com/analysis/column-should-india-tolerate-fatwas-257

3665; Jain, "After Villagers Issue Fatwa"; "India's Supreme Court Sets Rules for Sharia Courts," *Dawn*, July 7, 2014, https://www.dawn.com/news/1117667; and Samanwaya Rautray, "SC Stays Uttarakhand HC Order Banning Religious Outfits from Issuing Fatwas," *Economic Times*, October 13, 2018.

6. Debates over "triple talaq" are exemplary here. For reflections on the political context of recent legislation in India, see Siddiqui, "Triple Divorce."

7. The All-India Muslim Personal Law Board highlighted these constitutional and legislative provisions in response to a public interest litigation petition challenging the legality of their dispute resolution practices. See Redding, *Secular Need*, 65–71.

8. Elsewhere, I have written on Urdu novelist Nazir Ahmad's advocacy for these ideas. See Lhost, "To Flower and Fructify." For additional reflections on these approaches, see, e.g., Jackson, "Islamic Reform"; Massoud and Moore, "Shariʿa Consciousness"; Quraishi-Landes, "Sharia Problem"; and Quraishi-Landes, "Muslim Vote."

9. See, e.g., Muzaffar Alam, "Guiding the Ruler"; and Muzaffar Alam, *Languages of Political Islam*.

10. M. H. Lakdawala, "'Model *Nikahnama*'," *Milli Gazette*, October 16–31, 2004; Mandhani, "Triple Talaq"; Suneetha, "Muslim Women"; Tschalaer, *Muslim Women's Quest*, 104–41; Mohammed Wajihuddin, "All India Muslim Personal Law Board Mum on Model Nikahnama," *Economic Times*, February 12, 2018. While the matter is still under debate in India, multiple websites advise brides in Pakistan on how to read their contracts and what to look for in them (e.g., Chagani, "Read This"; Khan and Khan, "Women's Rights"), and for Bangladesh, downloadable forms are available online. See also Quraishi and Vogel, *Islamic Marriage Contract*.

11. Tschalaer, *Muslim Women's Quest*, 107–11.

12. Tschalaer, 118–33.

Bibliography

Archival Collections

Allahabad, India

Uttar Pradesh State Archives—Allahabad Regional Archives (UPSA-All.)

Commissioner of Faizabad's Records

Commissioner's Office, Allahabad Records

Delhi, India

National Archives of India (NAI)

Financial Department

Home Department, Judicial Branch

Legislative Department

Oriental Records Department, Microfilms from Broach (Bharuch)

Hyderabad, India

Andhra Pradesh (now Telangana) State Archives (AP/TSA)

Ecclesiastical Department, Fatwas

Mixed Farmans, Daftar-i Peshkari

Reports on the Administration of HEH the Nizam's Dominions

Kolkata, India

West Bengal State Archives, Judicial Department Proceedings (WBSA-JDP)

London, United Kingdom

British Library (BL), Asia, Pacific and Africa Collections

India Office Records (IOR)

IOR/F/4 Board of Control, Board Collections

IOR/H Home, Miscellaneous Series

IOR/L/PJ/9 Public and Judicial, Departmental Papers

IOR/P Proceedings

IOR/V Official Publications

IOR/Z Index

IOR/Z/P Index to the Proceedings

Oriental Manuscripts (OMS)

Vernacular Tracts (VT)

Lucknow, India

Uttar Pradesh State Archives (UPSA)

Judicial (Civil) Department Proceedings

Selections from the Vernacular Newspapers

Mumbai, India
Maharashtra State Archives (MSA)
Bombay Government Gazette
Judicial Department Proceedings (JDP)
Salt Lake City, Utah, United States
Family History Library, Muslim Marriage Records (FHL-MMR)

Periodicals

Bombay Chronicle
Bombay Times and Journal of Commerce (*BTJC*)
Economic Times
Hindustan Times
Indian Express
Al-Jamʿīyat
Sunday News of India
Times of India (*TOI*)

Published Materials

Abbasi, Zubair. "Islamic Law and Social Change: An Insight into the Making of Anglo-Muhammadan Law." *Journal of Islamic Studies* 25, no. 3 (September 2014): 325–49.
——. "*Sharīʿa* under the English Legal System in British India: Awqāf (Endowments) in the Making of Anglo-Muhammadan Law." PhD diss., Oxford University, 2013.
ʿAbd-ul-Ḥayy Farangī Maḥallī. *Majmūʿa-ul-Fatāwá*. Edited by Wazīr ʿAlī Tajāwuz Allāh. 2 vols. Lucknow: Maṯbaʿ Shaukat-e Islām, 1889/90 CE (1307 AH).
——. *Majmūʿa-ul-Fatāwá*. Edited by Muḥammad Maʿshūq ʿAlī. 2 vols. Lucknow: Maṯbaʿ-ul-ʿAlawī, 1887/88 CE (1305 AH).
——. *Majmūʿa-ul-Fatāwá, Tarjuma-yi Urdū*. Edited by Muḥammad Qamr-ud-Dīn. Kanpur: Maṯbaʿ-yi Qaumī, 1926 CE (1345 AH).
——. *Majmūʿa-yi Fatāwá-yi ʿAbd-ul-Ḥayy, Urdū, Kāmil Mabūb*. Translated and edited by Ḵhurshīd ʿĀlam. Karachi: Qurʾan Mahal, 1964.
Adcock, C. S. *The Limits of Tolerance: Indian Secularism and the Politics of Religious Freedom*. New York: Oxford University Press, 2013.
Agnes, Flavia. "His and Hers." *Economic and Political Weekly* 47, no. 17 (2012): 10–12.
Agrama, Hussein Ali. "Ethics, Tradition, Authority: Toward an Anthropology of the Fatwa." *American Ethnologist* 37, no. 1 (February 1, 2010): 2–18.
——. "Law Courts and Fatwa Councils in Modern Egypt: An Ethnography of Islamic Legal Practice." PhD diss., Johns Hopkins University, 2005.
——. *Questioning Secularism: Islam, Sovereignty, and the Rule of Law in Modern Egypt*. Chicago: University of Chicago Press, 2012.

Aguirre, Carlos. "Tinterillos, Indians, and the State: Towards a History of Legal Intermediaries in Post-independence Peru." In *One Law for All? Western Models and Local Practices in (Post-) Imperial Contexts*, edited by Stefan B. Kirmse, 119–51. New York: Campus Verlag, 2012.
Aḥmad, Mujīb. *Janūbī Eshiyā ke Urdū Majmūʿa hā-yi Fatāwá: Unīsviṉ aur Bīsviṉ Ṣadī ʿĪsvī*. Islamabad: Nīshnal Buk Fāʾūnḍīshan, 2011.
Ahmed, Shahab. *What Is Islam? The Importance of Being Islamic*. Princeton, NJ: Princeton University Press, 2015.
Alam, Arshad. "The Enemy Within: Madrasa and Muslim Identity in North India." *MAS* 42, nos. 2–3 (2008): 605–27.
Alam, Muzaffar. *The Crisis of Empire in Mughal North India: Awadh and the Punjab, 1707–48*. 2nd ed. 1986; Delhi: Oxford University Press, 2013.
———. "Guiding the Ruler and Prince." In *Islam in South Asia in Practice*, edited by Barbara D. Metcalf, 279–92. Princeton, NJ: Princeton University Press, 2009.
———. *The Languages of Political Islam in India, c. 1200–1800*. Delhi: Permanent Black, 2004.
Alam, Muzaffar, and Sanjay Subrahmanyam. "The Making of a Munshi." *Comparative Studies of South Asia, Africa and the Middle East* 24, no. 2 (January 1, 2004): 61–72.
———. *Writing the Mughal World: Studies on Culture and Politics*. New York: Columbia University Press, 2012.
Ali, Ahmed. *Al-Qurʾān: A Contemporary Translation*. Princeton, NJ: Princeton University Press, 2001.
Anderson, Benedict R. O'G. *Imagined Communities: Reflections on the Origin and Spread of Nationalism*. Rev. ed. 1983; London: Verso, 1991.
Anderson, Jon W. "Wiring Up: The Internet Difference for Muslim Networks." In *Muslim Networks from Hajj to Hip Hop*, edited by miriam cooke and Bruce B. Lawrence, 252–63. Chapel Hill: University of North Carolina Press, 2005.
Anderson, Michael R. "Islamic Law and the Colonial Encounter in British India." In *Institutions and Ideologies: A SOAS South Asia Reader*, edited by David Arnold and Peter Robb, 165–85. London: Curzon, 1993.
———. "Legal Scholarship and the Politics of Islam in British India." In *Perspectives on Islamic Law, Justice, and Society*, edited by R. S. Khare, 65–91. Lanham, MD: Rowman and Littlefield, 1999.
Anjum, Ovamir. "Islam as a Discursive Tradition: Talal Asad and His Interlocutors." *Comparative Studies of South Asia, Africa and the Middle East* 27, no. 3 (2007): 656–72.
Asad, Talal. *Formations of the Secular: Christianity, Islam, Modernity*. Stanford, CA: Stanford University Press, 2003.
———. "The Idea of an Anthropology of Islam." *Qui Parle* 17, no. 2 (2009): 1–30.
Ashraf, Syed Dawood, ed. *A Guide to Persian and Urdu Records Preserved in Andhra Pradesh State Archives and Research Institute*. [Hyderabad]: Andhra Pradesh State Archives and Research Institute, 1993.

Asif, Manan Ahmed. *The Loss of Hindustan: The Invention of India*. Cambridge, MA: Harvard University Press, 2020.

Atiyeh, George N. "The Book in the Modern Arab World: The Cases of Lebanon and Egypt." In *The Book in the Islamic World: The Written Word and Communication in the Middle East*, edited by George N. Atiyeh, 233–53. New York: State University of New York Press, 1995.

Badran, Margot. *Feminism in Islam: Secular and Religious Convergences*. Oxford: Oneworld, 2009.

Baker, Thomas, and Jacinta M. Gau. "Female Offenders' Perceptions of Police Procedural Justice and Their Obligation to Obey the Law." *Crime and Delinquency* 64, no. 6 (2018): 758–81.

Bamford, P. C. *Histories of the Non-co-operation and Khilafat Movements*. Delhi: Deep, 1974.

Baxi, Upendra. "'The State's Emissary': The Place of Law in Subaltern Studies." In *Subaltern Studies VII: Writings on South Asian History and Society*, edited by Partha Chatterjee and Gyanendra Pandey, 247–64. Delhi: Oxford University Press, 1992.

Bellenoit, Hayden J. *The Formation of the Colonial State in India: Scribes, Power and Taxes, 1760–1860*. New York: Routledge, 2017.

Ben-Bassat, Yuval. *Petitioning the Sultan: Protests and Justice in Late Ottoman Palestine, 1865–1908*. London: I. B. Tauris, 2013.

Benda-Beckmann, Keebet von. "Forum Shopping and Shopping Forums: Dispute Processing in a Minangkabau Village in West Sumatra." *Journal of Legal Pluralism and Unofficial Law* 13, no. 19 (January 1, 1981): 117–59.

Benton, Lauren. "Historical Perspectives on Legal Pluralism." *Hague Journal on the Rule of Law* 3, no. 1 (2011): 57–69.

———. *Law and Colonial Cultures: Legal Regimes in World History, 1400–1900*. New York: Cambridge University Press, 2002.

———. *A Search for Sovereignty: Law and Geography in European Empires, 1400–1900*. New York: Cambridge University Press, 2010.

Benton, Lauren A., and Lisa Ford. *Rage for Order: The British Empire and the Origins of International Law, 1800–1850*. Cambridge, MA: Harvard University Press, 2016.

Benton, Lauren A., and Richard Jeffrey Ross, eds. *Legal Pluralism and Empires, 1500–1850*. New York: New York University Press, 2013.

Berman, Paul Schiff. *Global Legal Pluralism: A Jurisprudence of Law beyond Borders*. Cambridge, UK: Cambridge University Press, 2012.

———. "The New Legal Pluralism." *Annual Review of Law and Social Science* 5, no. 1 (December 1, 2009): 225–42.

Beverley, Eric Lewis. "Property, Authority and Personal Law: Waqf in Colonial South Asia." *South Asia Research* 31, no. 2 (July 1, 2011): 155–82.

Birla, Ritu. *Stages of Capital: Law, Culture, and Market Governance in Late Colonial India*. Durham, NC: Duke University Press, 2009.

Bishara, Fahad Ahmad. "Paper Routes: Inscribing Islamic Law across the Nineteenth-Century Western Indian Ocean." *LHR* 32, no. 4 (November 2014): 797–820.

———. *A Sea of Debt: Law and Economic Life in the Western Indian Ocean, 1780–1950.* New York: Cambridge University Press, 2017.

Blake, Stephen P. "The Patrimonial-Bureaucratic Empire of the Mughals." *Journal of Asian Studies* 39, no. 1 (1979): 77–94.

Bowen, John R. *On British Islam: Religion, Law, and Everyday Practice in Shariʿa Councils.* Princeton Studies in Muslim Politics. Princeton, NJ: Princeton University Press, 2016.

———. *Why the French Don't Like Headscarves: Islam, the State, and Public Space.* Princeton, NJ: Princeton University Press, 2008.

Briggs, Henry George. *The Nizam, His History and Relations with the British Government.* London: B. Quaritch, 1861.

Brinham, Natalie. "'Genocide Cards': Rohingya Refugees on Why They Risked Their Lives to Refuse ID Cards." OpenDemocracy, October 21, 2018. https://www.opendemocracy.net/en/genocide-cards-why-rohingya-refugees-are-resisting-id-cards/.

Bunt, Gary R. *Hashtag Islam: How Cyber-Islamic Environments Are Transforming Religious Authority.* Chapel Hill: University of North Carolina Press, 2018.

———. *iMuslims: Rewiring the House of Islam.* Islamic Civilization and Muslim Networks. Chapel Hill: University of North Carolina Press, 2009.

———. *Islam in the Digital Age: E-Jihad, Online Fatwas and Cyber Islamic Environments.* Sterling, VA: Pluto, 2003.

———. *Virtually Islamic: Computer-Mediated Communication and Cyber Islamic Environments.* Religion, Culture and Society. Oxford: Oxford University Press, 2000.

Burns, Kathryn. *Into the Archive: Writing and Power in Colonial Peru.* Durham, NC: Duke University Press, 2010.

———. "Notaries, Truth, and Consequences." *American Historical Review* 110, no. 2 (April 1, 2005): 350–79.

Carroll, Lucy. "Definition and Interpretation of Muslim Law in South Asia: The Case of Gifts to Minors." *ILS* 1, no. 1 (1994): 83–115.

———. "Shah Bano, The Muslim Women (Protection of Rights on Divorce) Act and Muslim Women's Right to Nataa: Bangladesh Shows Way out of Imbroglio." *Journal of the Indian Law Institute* 39, no. 1 (1997): 83–95.

———. "*Talaq-i-Tafwid* and Stipulations in a Muslim Marriage Contract: Important Means of Protecting the Position of the South Asian Muslim Wife." *MAS* 16, no. 2 (1982): 277–309.

Certeau, Michel de. *The Practice of Everyday Life.* Translated by Steven F. Rendall. Berkeley: University of California Press, 1984.

Chagani, Anum Rehman. "Read This before You Sign Your Nikah Nama." Images, April 5, 2018. https://images.dawn.com/news/1178937.

Chan, Wing-Cheong, Barry Wright, and Stanley Yeo, eds. *Codification, Macaulay and the Indian Penal Code: The Legacies and Modern Challenges of Criminal Law Reform.* Farnham, UK: Ashgate, 2001.

Chatterjee, Kumkum. "Scribal Elites in Sultanate and Mughal Bengal." *IESHR* 47, no. 4 (2010): 445–472.

Chatterjee, Nandini. "English Law, Brahmo Marriage, and the Problem of Religious Difference: Civil Marriage Laws in Britain and India." *CSSH* 52, no. 3 (2010): 524–52.
———. "Law, Culture and History: Amir Ali's Interpretation of Islamic Law." In *Legal Histories of the British Empire: Laws, Engagements and Legacies*, edited by Shaunnagh Dorsett and John McLaren, 45–57. Abingdon, UK: Routledge, 2014.
———. *The Making of Indian Secularism: Empire, Law and Christianity, 1830–1960*. New York: Palgrave Macmillan, 2011.
———. *Negotiating Mughal Law: A Family of Landlords across Three Indian Empires*. Cambridge: Cambridge University Press, 2020.
———. "Reflections on Religious Difference and Permissive Inclusion in Mughal Law." *Journal of Law and Religion* 29, no. 3 (2014): 396–415.
Chatterjee, Partha. *The Nation and Its Fragments: Colonial and Postcolonial Histories*. Princeton, NJ: Princeton University Press, 1993.
Chaudhary, Muhammad Azam. *Justice in Practice: Legal Ethnography of a Pakistani Punjabi Village*. New York: Oxford University Press, 1999.
Chowdhury, Nusrat Sabina. *Paradoxes of the Popular: Crowd Politics in Bangladesh*. Stanford, CA: Stanford University Press, 2019.
Cohn, Bernard S. *Colonialism and Its Forms of Knowledge: The British in India*. Princeton, NJ: Princeton University Press, 1996.
———. "The Command of Language and the Language of Command." In *Subaltern Studies IV: Writings on South Asian History and Society*, edited by Ranajit Guha, 276–329. Delhi: Oxford University Press, 1985.
———. "From Indian Status to British Contract." *Journal of Economic History* 21, no. 4 (1961): 613–28.
Cohn, Erika, dir. *The Judge*. [Los Angeles]: Idle Wild Films, 2017. https://www.thejudgefilm.com.
A Collection of the Acts Passed by the Governor General of India in Council in the Year 1864. Calcutta: C. T. Cutter, Military Orphan Press, 1865.
cooke, miriam, and Bruce B. Lawrence, eds. *Muslim Networks from Hajj to Hip Hop*. Islamic Civilization and Muslim Networks. Chapel Hill: University of North Carolina Press, 2005.
Coombs, Catherine. "Partition Narratives: Displaced Trauma and Culpability among British Civil Servants in 1940s Punjab." *MAS* 45, no. 1 (January 2011): 201–24.
Copland, Ian. "The Princely States, the Muslim League, and the Partition of India in 1947." *International History Review* 13, no. 1 (1991): 38–69.
Crooks, Peter, and Timothy Parsons, eds. *Empires and Bureaucracy in World History: From Late Antiquity to the Twentieth Century*. Cambridge: Cambridge University Press, 2016.
Dalvī, Maimūnah. *Bamba'ī maiṉ Urdū*. New Delhi: Maktab-i Jāmiʿa, 1970.
Darnton, Robert. "What Is the History of Books?" *Daedalus* 111, no. 3 (Summer 1982): 65–83.

Das Acevedo, Deepa. "Secularism in the Indian Context." *Law and Social Inquiry* 38, no. 1 (2013): 138–67.
Dasgupta, Shumona. "Remembering the Bengal Partition: Trauma and the 'Slow Violence' of Refugee Existence." *South Asian Review* 36, no. 3 (December 1, 2015): 51–64.
Davis, Donald R. "Law and 'Law Books' in the Hindu Tradition." *German Law Journal* 9, no. 3 (March 2008): 309–25.
———. "Responsa in Hindu Law: Consultation and Lawmaking in Medieval India." *Oxford Journal of Law and Religion* 3, no. 1. (2014): 57–75.
De, Rohit. "Mumtaz Bibi's Broken Heart: The Many Lives of the Dissolution of Muslim Marriages Act." *IESHR* 46, no. 1 (2009): 105–30.
———. *A People's Constitution: The Everyday Life of Law in the Indian Republic.* Princeton, NJ: Princeton University Press, 2018.
De, Rohit, and Robert Travers. "Petitioning and Political Cultures in South Asia: Introduction." *MAS* 53, no. 1 (January 2019): 1–20.
Derrett, J. Duncan M. "The Administration of Hindu Law by the British." *CSSH* 4, no. 1 (November 1961): 10–52.
———. *Religion, Law, and the State in India.* New York: Free Press, 1968.
Dirks, Nicholas B. "From Little King to Landlord: Property, Law, and the Gift under the Madras Permanent Settlement." *CSSH* 28, no. 2 (1986): 307–33.
Donogh, Walter R. *The Stamp Law of British India as Constituted by the Indian Stamp Act (No. 1 of 1879); Rulings and Circular Orders of the High Courts; Notifications, Resolutions, Rules and Orders by the Government of India and by the Various Local Governments and Also Schedules of All the Stamp Duties Chargeable on Instruments in India from the Earliest Date with Notes, Introductory Sketch, Tables, &c.* Calcutta: Thacker, Spink, 1886.
Durkheim, Émile. *The Elementary Forms of Religious Life.* New York: Free Press, 1995.
Dutta, Sagnik. "From Accommodation to Substantive Equality: Muslim Personal Law, Secular Law, and the Indian Constitution 1985–2015." *Asian Journal of Law and Society* 4, no. 1 (May 2017): 191–227.
Edwardes, S. M. *The Gazetteer of Bombay City and Island.* 3 vols. New Delhi: Cosmo, 1909.
Edwards, Laura F. "'The Marriage Covenant Is at the Foundation of All Our Rights': The Politics of Slave Marriages in North Carolina after Emancipation." *LHR* 14, no. 1 (April 1996): 81–124.
———. *The People and Their Peace: Legal Culture and the Transformation of Inequality in the Post-Revolutionary South.* Chapel Hill: University of North Carolina Press, 2009.
Eickelman, Dale F. and Jon W. Anderson, eds. *New Media in the Muslim World: The Emerging Public Sphere.* Bloomington, IN: Indiana University Press, 2003.
Ellickson, Robert C. *Order without Law: How Neighbors Settle Disputes.* Cambridge, MA: Harvard University Press, 1994.

Ellis, Thomas Peter. *Notes on Punjab Custom*. Lahore: Civil and Military Gazette Press, 1921.

El Shamsy, Ahmed. *Rediscovering the Islamic Classics: How Editors and Print Culture Transformed an Intellectual Tradition*. Princeton, NJ: Princeton University Press, 2020.

Emon, Anver M. "Islamic Law and the Canadian Mosaic: Politics, Jurisprudence, and Multicultural Accommodation." *Canadian Bar Review* 87, no. 2 (2009): 391–425.

Esposito, John L. *The Oxford Dictionary of Islam*. New York: Oxford University Press, 2003.

Esposito, John L., and Natana J. DeLong-Bas. *Shariah: What Everyone Needs to Know*. New York: Oxford University Press, 2018.

Ewick, Patricia. "Law and Everyday Life." In *International Encyclopedia of the Social and Behavioral Sciences*, 2nd ed., edited by James D. Wright, 468–73. Oxford: Elsevier, 2015.

Fāʾiq, Muḥammad ibn G̱ẖulām Ḥusain. *Inshāʾ-yi Fāʾiq*. Kanpur: Naval Kishore, 1880.

Faruqui, Munis D. "At Empire's End: The Nizam, Hyderabad and Eighteenth-Century India." *MAS* 43, no. 1 (January 2009): 5–43.

Fatāwá-yi ʿAdālat-i Sharʿ Sharīf, Ṭōnk. 6 vols. Tonk, India: Maulānā Abūlkalām Āzād ʿArabik Parshiyan Risarch Insṭīṭiyūṭ Rājasthān, 2002.

Felstiner, William L. F., Richard L. Abel, and Austin Sarat. "The Emergence and Transformation of Disputes: Naming, Blaming, Claiming . . ." *LSR* 15, no. 3/4 (1980): 631–54.

Findley, Carter V. *Bureaucratic Reform in the Ottoman Empire: The Sublime Porte, 1789–1922*. Princeton, NJ: Princeton University Press, 1980.

Fisch, Jörg. *Cheap Lives and Dear Limbs: The British Transformation of the Bengal Criminal Law, 1769–1817*. Beiträge Zur Südasienforschung, Bd. 79. Wiesbaden, Germany: F. Steiner, 1983.

Fluehr-Lobban, Carolyn. *Islamic Law and Society in the Sudan*. Totowa, NJ: F. Cass, 1987.

Forrest, George, ed. *Selections from the State Papers of the Governors-General of India*. Vol. 2, *Warren Hastings*. Oxford: B. H. Blackwell, 1910.

Foucault, Michel. "Governmentality." In *The Foucault Effect: Studies in Governmentality, with Two Lectures by and an Interview with Michel Foucault*, edited by Graham Burchell, Colin Gordon, and Peter Miller, 87–104. Chicago: University of Chicago Press, 1991.

Fraas, Arthur Mitchell. "Readers, Scribes, and Collectors: The Dissemination of Legal Knowledge in Eighteenth-Century British South Asia." Unpublished paper, 2012. https://works.bepress.com/mitch_fraas/14/.

Furber, Musa. "Reducing the Role of Decision-Making Biases in Muslim Responsa." *Tabah Analytic Brief* 12, no. 2 (2012): 1–10.

Galanter, Marc. "The Modernization of Law." In *Modernization: The Dynamics of Growth*, edited by Myron Weiner, 153–65. New York: Basic Books, 1966.

———. "Why the 'Haves' Come out Ahead: Speculations on the Limits of Legal Change." *LSR* 9, no. 1 (1974): 95–160.

Gallagher, Mary E. "Mobilizing the Law in China: 'Informed Disenchantment' and the Development of Legal Consciousness." *LSR* 40, no. 4 (December 1, 2006): 783–816.

Garipova, Rozaliya. "Married or Not Married? On the Obligatory Registration of Muslim Marriages in Nineteenth-Century Russia." *ILS* 24, nos. 1–2 (2017): 112–41.

Geertz, Clifford. *Islam Observed: Religious Development in Morocco and Indonesia.* Chicago: University of Chicago Press, 1971.

———. *Local Knowledge: Further Essays in Interpretive Anthropology.* 3rd ed. New York: Basic Books, 2008.

Gelvin, James L., and Nile Green, eds. *Global Muslims in the Age of Steam and Print.* Berkeley: University of California Press, 2014.

Gerber, Haim. *State, Society, and Law in Islam: Ottoman Law in Comparative Perspective.* Albany: State University of New York Press, 1994.

Ghose, Rajarshi. "Islamic Law and Imperial Space: British India as 'Domain of Islam' circa 1803–1870." *Journal of Colonialism and Colonial History* 15, no. 1 (2014). https://doi.org/10.1353/cch.2014.0020.

Ghosh, Anindita. *Power in Print: Popular Publishing and the Politics of Language and Culture in a Colonial Society, 1778–1905.* New Delhi: Oxford University Press, 2006.

Ghosh, Papiya. "Community Questions and Bihar Politics, 1917–23." In *Community and Nation: Essays on Identity and Politics in Eastern India*, 11–33. New York: Oxford University Press, 2008.

———. "Muttahidah Qaumiyat in Aqalliat Bihar: The Imarat i Shariah, 1921–1947." *IESHR* 34, no. 1 (March 1, 1997): 1–20.

Ghosh, Shrimoyee Nandini. "'Not Worth the Paper It's Written On': Stamp Paper Documents and the Life of Law in India." *Contributions to Indian Sociology* 53, no. 1 (February 1, 2019): 19–45.

Gilmartin, David. "Customary Law and *Shariat* in British Punjab." In *Shariat and Ambiguity in South Asian Islam*, edited by Katherine P. Ewing, 43–62. Berkeley: University of California Press, 1988.

Giunchi, Elisa. "The Reinvention of 'Sharīʿa' Under the British Raj: In Search of Authenticity and Certainty." *The Journal of Asian Studies* 69, no. 4 (2010): 1119–42.

Gould, William. "Contesting Secularism in Colonial and Postcolonial North India between the 1930[s] and 1950s." *Contemporary South Asia* 14, no. 4 (December 2005): 481–94.

Government of India. *The Regulations of the Bengal Code in Force in September 1862.* Calcutta: Savielle and Cranenburgh, 1862.

Green, Nile. *Bombay Islam: The Religious Economy of the West Indian Ocean, 1840–1915.* New York: Cambridge University Press, 2011.

Grewal, J. S. *In the By-lanes of History: Some Persian Documents from a Punjab Town.* Shimla, India: Indian Institute of Advanced Study, 1975.

———. "The Qazi in the Pargana." In *Studies in Local and Regional History*, edited by J. S. Grewal, 1–17. Amritsar, India: Guru Nanak University, 1974.

Griffiths, John. "What Is Legal Pluralism?" *Journal of Legal Pluralism and Unofficial Law* 18, no. 24 (January 1, 1986): 1–55.
Guenther, Alan M. "A Colonial Court Defines a Muslim." In *Islam in South Asia in Practice*, edited by Barbara D. Metcalf, 293–304. Princeton, NJ: Princeton University Press, 2009.
———. "Justice Mahmood and English Education in India." *South Asia Research* 31, no. 1 (February 1, 2011): 45–67.
———. "Syed Mahmood and the Transformation of Muslim Law in British India." PhD diss., McGill University, 2004.
Guha, Sumit. "The Qazi, the Dharmadhikari and the Judge: Political Authority and Legal Diversity in Pre-modern India." In *Law Addressing Diversity: Premodern Europe and India in Comparison (13th–18th Centuries)*, edited by Gijs Kruijtzer and Thomas Ertl, 97–115. Boston: Walter de Gruyter, 2017.
Habib, Irfan. *The Agrarian System of Mughal India, 1556–1707*. 2nd rev. ed. New Delhi: Oxford University Press, 1999.
Halevi, Leor. *Modern Things on Trial: Islam's Global and Material Reformation in the Age of Rida, 1865–1935*. New York: Columbia University Press, 2019.
Hallaq, Wael B. *Authority, Continuity, and Change in Islamic Law*. Cambridge: Cambridge University Press, 2001.
———. "Considerations on the Function and Character of Sunnī Legal Theory." *Journal of the American Oriental Society* 104, no. 4 (1984): 679–89.
———. "From *Fatwās* to *Furūʿ*: Growth and Change in Islamic Substantive Law." *ILS* 1, no. 1 (1994): 29–65.
———. *The Impossible State: Islam, Politics, and Modernity's Moral Predicament*. New York: Columbia University Press, 2013.
———. *An Introduction to Islamic Law*. New York: Cambridge University Press, 2009.
———. "Murder in Cordoba: Ijtihâd, Iftâʾ and the Evolution of Substantive Law in Medieval Islam." *Acta Orientalia* 55 (1994): 55–83.
———. *The Origins and Evolution of Islamic Law*. Themes in Islamic Law. Cambridge: Cambridge University Press, 2004.
———. "The 'Qāḍī's Dīwān (*Sijill*)' before the Ottomans." *Bulletin of the School of Oriental and African Studies* 61, no. 3 (January 1, 1998): 415–36.
———. *Sharīʿa: Theory, Practice, Transformations*. New York: Cambridge University Press, 2009.
———. "Was the Gate of Ijtihad Closed?" *International Journal of Middle East Studies* 16 (1984): 3–41.
Halley, Janet, and Kerry Rittich. "Critical Directions in Comparative Family Law: Genealogies and Contemporary Studies of Family Law Exceptionalism." *American Journal of Comparative Law* 58, no. 4 (2010): 753–75.
Hanna, Nelly, ed. *The State and Its Servants: Administration in Egypt from Ottoman Times to the Present*. Cairo, Egypt: American University in Cairo Press, 1995.
Hardwick, Julie. *The Practice of Patriarchy: Gender and the Politics of Household Authority in Early Modern France*. University Park: Pennsylvania State University Press, 1998.

Hartog, Hendrik. *Man and Wife in America: A History.* Cambridge, MA: Harvard University Press, 1999.
Hasan, Farhat. "Law as Contested Communication: Literacy, Performativity and the Legal Order in the Mughal Empire." *Oxford Journal of Law and Religion* 8, no. 2 (June 1, 2019): 396–413.
——. *State and Locality in Mughal India: Power Relations in Western India, c. 1572–1730.* Cambridge: Cambridge University Press, 2004.
Hasan, Mushirul, "Partition: The Human Cost." *History Today* 47, no. 9 (1997): 47–53.
——. "Traditional Rites and Contested Meanings: Sectarian Strife in Colonial Lucknow." *Economic and Political Weekly* 31, no. 9 (March 2, 1996): 543–50.
Hasan, Zoya, and Ritu Menon. *Unequal Citizens: A Study of Muslim Women in India.* New Delhi: Oxford University Press, 2004.
Heath, Deanna. "Bureaucracy, Power and Violence in Colonial India: The Role of Indian Subalterns." In *Empires and Bureaucracy in World History: From Late Antiquity to the Twentieth Century,* edited by Peter Crooks and Timothy Parsons, 364–90. Cambridge: Cambridge University Press, 2016.
Heffening, W. "Waḳf." In *Encyclopaedia of Islam, First Edition (1913–1936),* edited M. Th. Houtsma, T.W. Arnold, R. Basset, and R. Hartmann. Leiden: Brill, 2012. http://dx.doi.org/10.1163/2214-871X_ei1_COM_0214.
Herzog, Tamar. *Frontiers of Possession: Spain and Portugal in Europe and the Americas.* Cambridge, MA: Harvard University Press, 2015.
Hobsbawm, Eric, and Terence Ranger, eds. *The Invention of Tradition.* New York: Cambridge University Press, 1983.
Hollander-Blumoff, Rebecca, and Tom R. Tyler. "Procedural Justice and the Rule of Law: Fostering Legitimacy in Alternative Dispute Resolution." *Journal of Dispute Resolution* 2011, no. 1 (2011): 1–19.
House of Commons, Parliamentary Papers. *Accounts and Papers in Seven Volumes: (6) Papers Relating to East India Affairs: Viz. Regulations Passed by the Governments of Bengal, Fort St. George, and Bombay in the Year 1827 (Presented in Pursuance of Act 53 Geo. III c. 155, Sec. 66).* Vol. 23. Session February 5–June 24, 1829. London: House of Commons, 1829.
Howell, Martha C. *The Marriage Exchange: Property, Social Place, and Gender in Cities of the Low Countries, 1300–1550.* Chicago: University of Chicago Press, 2009.
Hull, Matthew S. "The File: Agency, Authority, and Autography in an Islamabad Bureaucracy." *Language and Communication,* 23, nos. 3–4 (2003): 287–314.
——. *Government of Paper: The Materiality of Bureaucracy in Urban Pakistan.* Berkeley: University of California Press, 2012.
Hunter, William Wilson. *The Indian Musalmans: Are They Bound in Conscience to Rebel against the Queen?* London: Trübner, 1871.
Husain, Shrī Kājī Saiyid Nuruddīn. "Kājīonā Insāf Par Uḍtī Najar [Part 3]." *Shri Forbes Gujarati Sabha Traimasik* 13, no. 4 (1948): 129–49.
Hussain, Sabiha. "Shariat Courts and the Question of Women's Rights in India." *Pakistan Journal of Women's Studies* 14, no. 2 (December 2007): 73–102.
Hussin, Iza R. *The Politics of Islamic Law: Local Elites, Colonial Authority, and the Making of the Muslim State.* Chicago: University of Chicago Press, 2016.

Hutchins, Zachary McLeod, ed. *Community without Consent: New Perspectives on the Stamp Act*. Hanover, NH: Dartmouth College Press, 2016.

Ibn Hasan. *The Central Structure of the Mughal Empire and Its Practical Working up to the Year 1657*. New York: Oxford University Press, H. Milford, 1936.

Idrawi [Adrawī], Asīr. *Taẕkira-yi Mashāhīr-i Hind: Kārwān-i Rafta*. Deoband, India: Dar-ul-Muʾlifīn, 1994.

Igo, Sarah E. *The Known Citizen: A History of Privacy in Modern America*. Cambridge, MA: Harvard University Press, 2018.

Ilahi, Shereen. "Sectarian Violence and the British Raj: The Muharram Riots of Lucknow." *India Review* 6, no. 3 (August 13, 2007): 184–208.

Ingram, Brannon D. "Crises of the Public in Muslim India: Critiquing 'Custom' at Aligarh and Deoband." *South Asia: Journal of South Asian Studies* 38, no. 3 (July 3, 2015): 403–18.

———. "The Portable Madrasa: Print, Publics, and the Authority of the Deobandi ʿUlama." *MAS* 48, no. 4 (2014): 845–71.

———. *Revival from Below: The Deoband Movement and Global Islam*. Berkeley: University of California Press, 2018.

Jackson, Sherman A. "Islamic Law, Muslims and American Politics." *ILS* 22, no. 3 (2015): 253–91.

———. "Islamic Reform Between Islamic Law and the Nation-State." In *The Oxford Handbook of Islam and Politics*, edited by John L. Esposito and Emad El-Din Shahin. New York: Oxford University Press, 2013. https://doi.org/10.1093/oxfordhb/9780195395891.013.0039.

Jacquot, Sophie and Tommaso Vitale. "Law as Weapon of the Weak? A Comparative Analysis of Legal Mobilization by Roma Women's Groups at the European Level." *Journal of European Public Policy* 21, no. 4 (587–604).

Jaffe, James. "Constructing Corruption: Narratives of Panchayat Justice under British Rule during the Early Nineteenth Century." *Naveiñ Reet: Nordic Journal of Law and Social Research*, no. 2 (December 1, 2011): 63–78.

———. "Gandhi, Lawyers, and the Courts' Boycott during the Non-cooperation Movement." *MAS* 51, no. 5 (September 2017): 1340–68.

———. *The Ironies of Colonial Governance: Law, Custom, and Justice in Colonial India*. New York: Cambridge University Press, 2015.

———. "Layering Law upon Custom: The British in Colonial West India." *FIU Law Review* 10, no. 1 (January 1, 2014): 85–110.

Jagannāthaprasāda. *A Manual of Registration Law, with Comprehensive Notes and Rulings*. Calcutta: S. K. Lahiri, 1897.

Jain, Akanksha. "After Villagers Issue Fatwa to Extern Minor Rape Victim's Family, U'khand HC Bans Religious Bodies & Panchayats from Issuing Such Diktats." LiveLaw.in, August 31, 2018. https://www.livelaw.in/after-villagers-issue-fatwa-to-extern-minor-rape-victims-family-ukhand-hc-bans-religious-bodies-panchayats-from-issuing-such-diktats-read-order/.

Jalal, Ayesha. *Self and Sovereignty: Individual and Community in South Asian Islam since 1850*. London: Routledge, 2005.

Jaunpūrī, ʿAbd-ul-Awwal. *Mufīd-ul-Muftī*. Lucknow: Āsī Prēs, 1908 CE (1326 AH).

Jegatheesan, P. "Inam Settlement in the Madras Presidency during [the] 19th Century." *Proceedings of the Indian History Congress* 45 (1984): 552–58.
Jeppie, Shamil, Ebrahim Moosa, and Richard L. Roberts, eds. *Muslim Family Law in Sub-Saharan Africa: Colonial Legacies and Post-colonial Challenges*. Amsterdam: Amsterdam University Press, 2010.
Kafka, Ben. "The Demon of Writing: Paperwork, Public Safety, and the Reign of Terror." *Representations* 98, no. 1 (2007): 1–24.
———. *The Demon of Writing: Powers and Failures of Paperwork*. New York: Zone Books, 2012.
Kalpagam, U. *Rule by Numbers: Governmentality in Colonial India*. Lanham, MD: Lexington Books, 2014.
Kaur, Raminder. "Specters of Macaulay: Blasphemy, the Indian Penal Code, and Pakistan's Postcolonial Predicament." In *Censorship in South Asia: Cultural Regulation from Sedition to Seduction*, edited by William Mazzarella, 175–205. Bloomington, IN: Indiana University Press, 2009.
Khan, Fareeha. "Traditionalist Approaches to Shariʿah Reform: Mawlana Ashraf ʿAli Thanawi's Fatwa on Women's Right to Divorce." PhD diss., University of Michigan, 2008.
Khan, Hooria Hayat and Azmeh Khan. "Women's Rights and the Nikah Nama in Pakistan." Lahore, Pakistan: Center for Economic Research in Pakistan, April 2019. https://www.cerp.org.pk/updata/files/files/41_20200504004625.pdf
K̲h̲ān, Mīr Basīṭ ʿAlī. *Tārīk̲h̲-i ʿAdālat-i Āṣafī*. Hyderabad: Shams-ul-Islām Prēs, 1937.
Khan, Yusuf Husain. *The First Nizām. The Life and Times of Nizāmu'l-Mulk Āsaf Jāh I*. 2nd ed. Bombay: Asia Publishing House, 1963.
Khurshid, Salman. *Triple Talaq: Examining Faith*. New Delhi: Oxford University Press, 2018.
Kifāyatullāh, Muftī Muḥammad. *Kifāyat-ul-Muftī: Yaʿnī Muftī-yi Aʿẓam Maulānā Kifāyatullāh kī Fatāwá*. 9 vols. Edited by Ḥafīẓ-ur-Raḥmān Wāṣif. Delhi: Kōh-i Nūr Prēs, 1971–77.
Kinra, Rajeev. "Master and Munshī: A Brahman Secretary's Guide to Mughal Governance." *IESHR* 47, no. 4 (October 1, 2010): 527–61.
———. *Writing Self, Writing Empire: Chandar Bhan Brahman and the Cultural World of the Indo-Persian State Secretary*. Berkeley: University of California Press, 2015.
Knight, Robert. *The Inam Commission Unmasked*. London: Effingham Wilson, 1859.
Kolsky, Elizabeth. *Colonial Justice in British India: White Violence and the Rule of Law*. New York: Cambridge University Press, 2010.
Kozlowski, Gregory C. "Loyalty, Locality and Authority in Several Opinions (Fatāwā) Delivered by the Muftī of the Jamiʿah Niẕāmiyyah Madrasah, Hyderabad, India." *MAS* 29, no. 4 (October 1, 1995): 893–927.
———. "A Modern Indian Mufti." In *Islamic Legal Interpretation: Muftis and Their Fatwás*, edited by Muhammad Khalid Masud, Brinkley Morris Messick, and David Stephan Powers, 242–50. Cambridge, MA: Harvard University Press, 1996.

———. *Muslim Endowments and Society in British India*. Cambridge: Cambridge University Press, 1985.
Krawietz, Birgit. "Cut and Paste in Legal Rules: Designing Islamic Norms with Talfiq." *Die Welt Des Islams* 42, no. 1 (2002): 3–40.
Kugle, Scott Alan. "Framed, Blamed and Renamed: The Recasting of Islamic Jurisprudence in Colonial South Asia." *MAS* 35, no. 2 (May 1, 2001): 257–313.
Kuka, Mehrjibhai Nosherwanji. *The Wit and Humor of the Persians*. Bombay: Education Society Steam Press, 1894.
Larson, Gerald James, ed. *Religion and Personal Law in Secular India: A Call to Judgment*. Bloomington, IN: Indiana University Press, 2001.
Latour, Bruno. *The Making of Law: An Ethnography of the Conseil d'Etat*. Cambridge, UK: Polity, 2010.
———. *Science in Action: How to Follow Scientists and Engineers through Society*. Cambridge, MA: Harvard University Press, 1987.
Lawrance, Benjamin N., Emily Lynn Osborn, and Richard L. Roberts, eds. *Intermediaries, Interpreters, and Clerks: African Employees in the Making of Colonial Africa*. Madison: University of Wisconsin Press, 2006.
Layish, Aharon. "Adaptation of a Jurists' Law to Modern Times in an Alien Environment: The Case of the Shari'a in Israel." *Die Welt Des Islams* 46, no. 2 (2006): 168–225.
———. "The Transformation of the *Sharīʿa* from Jurists' Law to Statutory Law in the Contemporary Muslim World." *Die Welt Des Islams* 44, no. 1 (2004): 85–113.
Lelyveld, David. *Aligarh's First Generation: Muslim Solidarity in British India*. Princeton, NJ: Princeton University Press, 1977.
———. "Colonial Knowledge and the Fate of Hindustani." *CSSH* 35, no. 4 (1993): 665–82.
———. "The Fate of Hindustani: Colonial Knowledge and the Project of a National Language." In *Orientalism and the Postcolonial Predicament: Perspectives on South Asia*, edited by Carol Appadurai Breckenridge and Peter van der Veer, 189–214. Philadelphia: University of Pennsylvania Press, 1993.
Lemons, Katherine. *Divorcing Traditions: Islamic Marriage Law and the Making of Indian Secularism*. Ithaca, NY: Cornell University Press, 2019.
———. "Sharia Courts and Muslim Personal Law in India: Intersecting Legal Regimes." *LSR* 52, no. 3 (2018): 603–29.
Leonard, Karen. "The Hyderabad Political System and Its Participants." *Journal of Asian Studies* 30, no. 3 (May 1971): 569–82.
Lhost, Elizabeth. "From Documents to Data Points: Marriage Registration and the Politics of Record-Keeping in British India (1880–1950)." *Journal of the Economic and Social History of the Orient* 62, no. 5–6 (November 12, 2019): 998–1045.
———. "Of Horizontal Exchanges and Inter-Islamic Inquiries." *Comparative Studies of South Asia, Africa and the Middle East* 41, no. 2 (August 1, 2021): 257–61.
———. "To Flower and Fructify: Rational Religion and the Seeds of Islam in Nazir Ahmad's (1830–1912) Late-Career Religious Non-fiction." *Journal of Islamic Studies* 31, no. 1 (January 1, 2020): 31–69.

———. “Writing Law at the Edge of Empire: Evidence from the Qazis of Bharuch (1799–1864).” *Itinerario* 42, no. 2 (August 2018): 256–78.
Lobel, Orly. “The Paradox of Extralegal Activism: Critical Legal Consciousness and Transformative Politics.” *Harvard Law Review* 120, no. 4 (2007): 937–88.
Loomba, Ania. “Of Gifts, Ambassadors, and Copy-Cats: Diplomacy, Exchange and Difference in Early Modern India.” In *Emissaries in Early Modern Literature and Culture: Mediation, Transmission, Traffic, 1550–1700*, edited by Brinda Charry and Gitanjali Shahani, 41–76. New York: Routledge, 2016.
Macaulay, T. B., G. W. Anderson, F. Millett, and J. M. Macleod. *The Indian Penal Code, as Originally Framed in 1837*. Madras: Higginbotham, 1888.
Mahdi, Muhsin. “From the Manuscript Age to the Age of Printed Books.” In *The Book in the Islamic World: The Written Word and Communication in the Middle East*, edited by George N. Atiyeh, 1–15. New York: State University of New York Press, 1995.
Mahmood, Saba. *Religious Difference in a Secular Age: A Minority Report*. Princeton, NJ: Princeton University Press, 2016.
Mahmood, Tahir. *Muslim Personal Law: Role of the State in the Subcontinent*. Delhi: Vikas Publishing House, 1977.
Majeed, Javed. “‘The Jargon of Indostan’: An Exploration of Jargon in Urdu and East India Company English.” In *Languages and Jargons: Contributions to a Social History of Language*, edited by Peter Burke, 182–205. Cambridge, UK: Polity, 1995.
Major, Andrew J. “State and Criminal Tribes in Colonial Punjab: Surveillance, Control and Reclamation of the ‘Dangerous Classes.’” *MAS* 33, no. 3 (1999): 657–88.
Mallampalli, Chandra. “Escaping the Grip of Personal Law in Colonial India: Proving Custom, Negotiating Hindu-ness.” *LHR* 28, no. 4 (November 2010): 1043–65.
———. “Meet the Abrahams: Colonial Law and a Mixed Race Family from Bellary, South India, 1810–63.” *MAS* 42, no. 5 (2008): 929–70.
———. *Race, Religion, and Law in Colonial India: Trials of an Interracial Family*. New York: Cambridge University Press, 2011.
Mandelbaum, David G. “The Family in India.” *Southwestern Journal of Anthropology* 4, no. 2 (1948): 123–39.
Mandhani, Apoorva. “Triple Talaq: Women’s Rights Activist Flavia Agnes Submits Model Nikahnama before SC.” LiveLaw.in, June 3, 2017. https://www.livelaw.in/triple-talaq-womens-rights-activist-flavia-agnes-submits-model-nikahnama-sc/.
Manṣūr, Abū Lubāba Shāh. *Ādāb-i Fatwá Nawīsī*. Ishāʿat-i 2. Karachi: Al-Saʿīd, 2009.
Manṣūrpūrī, Maulānā Muftī Muḥammad Sulaimān. *Fatwá Nawīsī kē Rahnumā Uṣūl*. Deoband, India: Kutub Ḵẖānah Naʿīmiya, 2006.
Mantena, Karuna. *Alibis of Empire: Henry Maine and the Ends of Liberal Imperialism*. Princeton, NJ: Princeton University Press, 2010.
Massoud, Mark Fathi, and Kathleen M. Moore. “Shariʿa Consciousness: Law and Lived Religion among California Muslims.” *Law and Social Inquiry* 45, no. 3 (August 2020): 787–817.

Master, Streynsham. *The Diaries of Streynsham Master, 1675–1680, and Other Contemporary Papers Relating Thereto.* Edited by Richard Carnac Temple. Indian Records Series. London: J. Murray, 1911.

Mastura, Michael O. "Legal Pluralism in the Philippines." *LSR* 28, no. 3 (1994): 461–75.

Masud, Muhammad Khalid. "*Ādāb al-Muftī*: The Muslim Understanding of Values, Characteristics, and Role of a *Muftī*." In *Moral Conduct and Authority: The Place of Adab in South Asian Islam*, edited by Barbara D. Metcalf, 125–45. Berkeley: University of California Press, 1984.

———. "Apostasy and Judicial Separation in British India." In *Islamic Legal Interpretation: Muftis and Their Fatwas*, edited by Muhammad Khalid Masud, Brinkley Morris Messick, and David Stephan Powers, 193–203. Cambridge, MA: Harvard University Press, 1996.

———. "The Significance of *Istiftā'* in the *Fatwā* Discourse." *Islamic Studies* 48, no. 3 (2009): 341–66.

Masud, Muhammad Khalid, Brinkley Morris Messick, and David Stephan Powers, eds. *Islamic Legal Interpretation: Muftis and Their Fatwas.* Cambridge, MA: Harvard University Press, 1996.

Masud, Muhammad Khalid, Rudolph Peters, and David Stephan Powers, eds. *Dispensing Justice in Islam: Qadis and Their Judgements.* Boston: Brill, 2006.

Mawani, Renisa. *Across Oceans of Law: The Komagata Maru and Jurisdiction in the Time of Empire.* Durham, NC: Duke University Press, 2018.

Mawani, Renisa, and Iza Hussin. "The Travels of Law: Indian Ocean Itineraries." *LHR* 32, no. 4 (November 2014): 733–47.

McChesney, R. D. *Waqf in Central Asia: Four Hundred Years in the History of a Muslim Shrine, 1480–1889.* Princeton, NJ: Princeton University Press, 2014.

McLean, Kyle. "Ethnic Identity, Procedural Justice, and Offending: Does Procedural Justice Work the Same for Everyone?" *Crime and Delinquency* 63, no. 10 (2017): 1314–36.

Menski, Werner. *Comparative Law in a Global Context: The Legal Systems of Asia and Africa.* New York: Cambridge University Press, 2006.

———. *Hindu Law: Beyond Tradition and Modernity.* New York: Oxford University Press, 2003.

———. "The Uniform Civil Code Debate in Indian Law: New Developments and Changing Agenda." *German Law Journal* 9, no. 3 (March 2008): 211–50.

Merry, Sally Engle. "Colonial Law and Its Uncertainties." *LHR* 28, no. 4 (November 2010): 1067–71.

———. *Colonizing Hawai'i: The Cultural Power of Law.* Princeton, NJ: Princeton University Press, 2000.

———. *Getting Justice and Getting Even: Legal Consciousness among Working-Class Americans.* Chicago: University of Chicago Press, 1990.

———. "Legal Pluralism." *LSR* 22, no. 5 (1988): 869–96.

Merwick, Donna. *Death of a Notary: Conquest and Change in Colonial New York.* Ithaca, NY: Cornell University Press, 2002.

Messick, Brinkley Morris. *The Calligraphic State: Textual Domination and History in a Muslim Society.* Berkeley: University of California Press, 1996.
———. "Fatwā, Modern." In *Encyclopaedia of Islam 3*, edited by Kate Fleet, Gudrun Krämer, Dennis Matringe, John Nawas, and Everett Rowson. Leiden: Brill, 2017. http://dx.doi.org/10.1163/1573-3912_ei3_COM_27049.
———. "Indexing the Self: Intent and Expression in Islamic Legal Acts." *ILS* 8, no. 2 (2001): 151–78.
———. "Fatwā: Process and Function." In *The Oxford Encyclopedia of the Modern Islamic World*, edited by John Esposito, 2:10–13. New York: Oxford University Press, 1995.
———. "The Mufti, the Text and the World: Legal Interpretation in Yemen." *Man*, n.s., 21, no. 1 (March 1, 1986): 102–19.
———. *Sharīʿa Scripts: A Historical Anthropology.* New York: Columbia University Press, 2018.
Metcalf, Barbara D. "Ibn Battuta as a Qadi in the Maldives." In *Islam in South Asia in Practice*, edited by Barbara D. Metcalf, 271–78. Princeton, NJ: Princeton University Press, 2009.
———. *Islamic Revival in British India: Deoband, 1860–1900.* Princeton, NJ: Princeton University Press, 1982.
———. "The Madrasa at Deoband: A Model for Religious Education in Modern India." *MAS* 12, no. 1 (January 1, 1978): 111–34.
Metcalf, Thomas R. *Ideologies of the Raj.* Cambridge: Cambridge University Press, 1994.
Minault, Gail. "Women, Legal Reform, and Muslim Identity." *Comparative Studies in South Asia, Africa, and the Middle East* 17, no. 2 (1997): 1–10.
Moir, Martin. "Kaghazi Raj: Notes on the Documentary Basis of Company Rule: 1783–1858." *Indo-British Review* 21, no. 2 (1983): 185–93.
Mommsen, Wolfgang J., and Jaap de Moor, eds. *European Expansion and Law: The Encounter of European and Indigenous Law in 19th- and 20th-Century Africa and Asia.* New York: Berg–St. Martin's, 1992.
Moore, Sally Falk. "Law and Social Change: The Semi-autonomous Social Field as an Appropriate Subject of Study." *LSR* 7, no. 4 (1973): 719–46.
Morgenstein Fuerst, Ilyse R. *Indian Muslim Minorities and the 1857 Rebellion: Religion, Rebels, and Jihad.* London: I. B. Tauris, 2017.
Morley, William H. *The Administration of Justice in British India; Its Past History and Present State: Comprising an Account of the Laws Peculiar to India.* London: Williams and Norgate, 1858.
Mubarki, Meraj Ahmed. "Violence, Victimhood and Trauma: Exploring the Partition Narratives of Bombay Cinema." *Visual Anthropology* 30, no. 1 (January 1, 2017): 45–64.
Mufti, Shahan. "The Grand Mufti of Google." *New York Times Magazine*, September 20, 2013.
Mukharji, Projit Bihari. "Handwriting Analysis as a Dynamic Artisanal Science: The Hardless Detective Dynasty and the Forensic Cultures of the British Raj." In *Global Forensic Cultures: Making Fact and Justice in the Modern Era*, edited

by Ian Burney and Christopher Hamlin, 86–111. Baltimore: Johns Hopkins University Press, 2019.
Müller, Dominik M., and Kerstin Steiner. "The Bureaucratisation of Islam in Southeast Asia: Transdisciplinary Perspectives." *Journal of Current Southeast Asian Affairs* 37, no. 1 (April 1, 2018): 3–26.
Muttalib, M. A. *Administration of Justice under the Nizams, 1724–1948*. [Hyderabad]: State Archives, Andhra Pradesh, 1988.
Nair, Neeti. *Changing Homelands: Hindu Politics and the Partition of India*. Cambridge, MA: Harvard University Press, 2011.
Nandakumar, Prathima. "Why India Should Repeal Sedition Law." *The Week*, June 4, 2021. https://www.theweek.in/news/india/2021/06/04/why-india-should-repeal-sedition-law.html.
Napier, W. "An Introduction to the Study of the Law Administered in the Colony of the Straits Settlements." *Malaya Law Review* 16, no. 1 (1974): 4–51.
Naẕīr Ḥusain, Sayyid Muḥammad. *Fatāwá Naẕīriya, Mabūb wa Mutarjam*. 2 vols. 4th ed. 1913. Delhi: Al-Kitāb International, 2007.
Newbigin, Eleanor. "The Codification of Personal Law and Secular Citizenship: Revisiting the History of Law Reform in Late Colonial India." *IESHR* 46, no. 1 (January 1, 2009): 83–104.
———. *The Hindu Family and the Emergence of Modern India: Law, Citizenship and Community*. New York: Cambridge University Press, 2013.
Nussdorfer, Laurie. *Brokers of Public Trust: Notaries in Early Modern Rome*. Baltimore: Johns Hopkins University Press, 2009.
Ogborn, Miles. *Indian Ink: Script and Print in the Making of the English East India Company*. Chicago: University of Chicago Press, 2007.
Orsini, Francesca. *The Hindi Public Sphere, 1920–1940: Language and Literature in the Age of Nationalism*. New Delhi: Oxford University Press, 2002.
———. *Print and Pleasure: Popular Literature and Entertaining Fictions in Colonial North India*. New Delhi: Permanent Black, 2009.
———. "What Did They Mean by 'Public'? Language, Literature and the Politics of Nationalism." *Economic and Political Weekly* 34, no. 7 (February 13, 1999): 409–16.
Osborn, Emily Lynn. "'Circle of Iron': African Colonial Employees and the Interpretation of Colonial Rule in French West Africa." *Journal of African History* 44, no. 1 (2003): 29–50.
Parashar, Archana. "Religious Personal Laws as Non-state Laws: Implications for Gender Justice." *Journal of Legal Pluralism and Unofficial Law* 45, no. 1 (March 1, 2013): 5–23.
Pedersen, Johannes. *The Arabic Book*. Princeton, NJ: Princeton University Press, 1984.
Peirce, Leslie. *Morality Tales: Law and Gender in the Ottoman Court of Aintab*. Berkeley: University of California Press, 2003.
Peletz, Michael G. *Islamic Modern: Religious Courts and Cultural Politics in Malaysia*. Princeton, NJ: Princeton University Press, 2002.

Perrone, Giuliana. "'Back into the Days of Slavery': Freedom, Citizenship, and the Black Family in the Reconstruction-Era Courtroom." *LHR* 37, no. 1 (February 2019): 125–61.
Peters, Rudolph. "From Jurists' Law to Statute Law or What Happens When the Shariʿa Is Codified." *Mediterranean Politics* 7, no. 3 (2002): 82–95.
Pew Research Center Forum on Religion and Public Life. *The Future of the Global Muslim Population*. Washington, DC: Pew Research Center, January 2011. https://www.pewforum.org/wp-content/uploads/sites/7/2011/01/Future GlobalMuslimPopulation-WebPDF-Feb10.pdf.
Pinch, William R. "Same Difference in India and Europe." *History and Theory* 38, no. 3 (October 1999): 389–407.
Pitts, Jennifer. *A Turn to Empire: The Rise of Imperial Liberalism in Britain and France*. Princeton, NJ: Princeton University Press, 2005.
Platts, John T. *A Dictionary of Urdu, Classical Hindi, and English*. London: W. H. Allen, 1884.
Powers, David S. "Kadijustiz or Qāḍī-Justice? A Paternity Dispute from Fourteenth-Century Morocco." *ILS* 1, no. 3 (1994): 332–66.
——. *Law, Society, and Culture in the Maghrib, 1300–1500*. New York: Cambridge University Press, 2002.
——. "On Judicial Review in Islamic Law." *LSR* 26, no. 2 (1992): 315–41.
Preston, Laurence W. *The Devs of Cincvad: A Lineage and the State in Maharashtra*. Cambridge: Cambridge University Press, 1989.
Prifogle, Emily A. "Winks, Whispers, and Prosecutorial Discretion in Rural Iowa, 1925–1928." *Annals of Iowa* 79, no. 3 (Summer 2020): 247–83.
Proudfoot, Ian. "Mass Producing Houri's Moles: Or Aesthetics and Choice of Technology in Early Muslim Book Publishing." In *Islam: Essays on Scripture, Thought and Society: A Festschrift in Honour of Anthony H. Johns*, edited by Peter G. Riddell and Tony Street, 161–84. Leiden: Brill, 1997.
Purohit, Teena. *The Aga Khan Case: Religion and Identity in Colonial India*. Cambridge, MA: Harvard University Press, 2012.
Purushotham, Sunil. "Federating the Raj: Hyderabad, Sovereign Kingship, and Partition." *MAS* 54, no. 1 (January 2020): 157–98.
Quraishi, Asifa, and Frank E. Vogel, eds. *The Islamic Marriage Contract: Case Studies in Islamic Family Law*. Cambridge, MA: Harvard University Press, 2009.
Quraishi-Landes, Asifa. "The Muslim Vote: Why It's Our Islamic Duty to Get Clean Water to Flint." *altmuslim* (blog), November 1, 2018. https://www.patheos.com/blogs/altmuslim/2018/11/the-muslim-vote-why-its-our-islamic-duty-to-get-clean-water-to-flint/.
——. "The Sharia Problem with Sharia Legislation." *Ohio Northern University Law Review* 41 (2015): 545–66.
Quraishi-Landes, Asifa, and Najeeba Syeed. "No Altars: A Survey of Islamic Family Law in the United States." In *Half of Faith: American Muslim Marriage and Divorce in the Twenty-First Century*, edited by Kecia Ali, 80–110. Boston: OpenBU, 2021.

Qureshi, Badr-ud-din, and Ram Lal Anand. *The Punjab Custom with Up-to-Date Case Law.* Lahore: University Book Agency, 1932.

Rabb, Intisar A. "Against Kadijustiz: On the Negative Citation of Foreign Law." *Suffolk University Law Review* 48 (2015): 343–77.

Rabitoy, Neil. "Sovereignty, Profits, and Social Change: The Development of British Administration in Western India, 1800–1820." PhD diss., University of Pennsylvania, 1972.

Ragas, Jose. "Beyond Big Brother: Turning ID Cards into Weapons of Citizenship." *Perspectives on History*, April 4, 2016.

Raman, Bhavani. *Document Raj: Writing and Scribes in Early Colonial South India.* Chicago: University of Chicago Press, 2012.

——. "The Duplicity of Paper: Counterfeit, Discretion, and Bureaucratic Authority in Early Colonial Madras." *CSSH* 54, no. 2 (2012): 229–50.

Raman, Kartik Kalyan. "Utilitarianism and the Criminal Law in Colonial India: A Study of the Practical Limits of Utilitarian Jurisprudence." *MAS* 28, no. 4 (1994): 739–91.

Ramsay, Nigel. "Scriveners and Notaries as Legal Intermediaries in Later Medieval England." In *Enterprise and Individuals in Fifteenth-Century England*, edited by Jennifer Kermode, 118–31. Wolfeboro Falls, NH: Alan Sutton, 1991.

Rao, Ursula and Vijayanka Nair. "Aadhaar: Governing with Biometrics." *South Asia: Journal of South Asian Studies* 42, no. 3 (2019): 469–481.

Rapoport, Yossef. *Marriage, Money and Divorce in Medieval Islamic Society.* Cambridge, UK: Cambridge University Press, 2005.

Redding, Jeffrey A. "Secularism, the Rule of Law, and 'Shariʿa Courts': An Ethnographic Examination of a Constitutional Controversy." *Saint Louis University Law Journal* 57, no. 2 (Winter 2013): 339–76.

——. *A Secular Need: Islamic Law and State Governance in Contemporary India.* Seattle: University of Washington Press, 2020.

Reinhart, A. Kevin. *Lived Islam: Colloquial Religion in a Cosmopolitan Tradition.* New York: Cambridge University Press, 2020.

Riaz, Ali. *Faithful Education: Madrassahs in South Asia.* New Brunswick, NJ: Rutgers University Press, 2008.

Ricci, Ronit. *Islam Translated: Literature, Conversion, and the Arabic Cosmopolis of South and Southeast Asia.* Chicago: University of Chicago Press, 2011.

Rizvi, Sayyid Mahboob. *History of the Dar al-Ulum, Deoband.* Deoband, India: Idāra-i Ihtimām, Dar al-ʿUlum, 1980.

——. *Tārīḵẖ-i Dār-ul-ʿUlūm-i Diyoband: Bar-saġẖīr kē Musalmānōṉ kā Sab sē Baṛā Dīnī Kār-nāma.* Vol. 1. Deoband, India: Idāra-i Ihtimām, Dar al-ʿUlum, 1977.

Robb, Megan Eaton. *Print and the Urdu Public: Muslims, Newspapers, and Urban Life in Colonial India.* New York: Oxford University Press, 2020.

Robinson, Francis. "Strategies of Authority in Muslim South Asia in the Nineteenth and Twentieth Centuries." *MAS* 47, no. 1 (2013): 1–21.

——. "Technology and Religious Change: Islam and the Impact of Print." *MAS* 27, no. 1 (February 1993): 229–51.

——. *The 'Ulama of Farangi Mahall and Islamic Culture in South Asia.* New Delhi: Permanent Black, 2001.
Rosen, Lawrence. *The Anthropology of Justice: Law as Culture in Islamic Society.* Lewis Henry Morgan Lectures, 1985. New York: Cambridge University Press, 1989.
——. "Equity and Discretion in a Modern Islamic Legal System." *LSR* 15, no. 2 (1980): 217–45.
——. *The Justice of Islam: Comparative Perspectives on Islamic Law and Society.* Oxford: Oxford University Press, 2000.
Rudolph, Lloyd I., and Susanne Hoeber Rudolph. "Barristers and Brahmans in India: Legal Cultures and Social Change." *CSSH* 8, no. 1 (October 1965): 24–49.
——. "Living with Difference in India: Legal Pluralism and Legal Universalism in Historical Context." In *Religion and Personal Law in Secular India: A Call to Judgment,* edited by Gerald James Larson, 36–65. Bloomington, IN: Indiana University Press, 2001.
Salvatore, Armando and Dale F. Eickelman, eds. *Public Islam and the Common Good.* Leiden: Brill, 2004.
Sarat, Austin. "'. . . The Law Is All Over': Power, Resistance and the Legal Consciousness of the Welfare Poor." *Yale Journal of Law and the Humanities* 2 (1990): 343–79.
Sarat, Austin, and William L. F. Felstiner. "Lawyers and Legal Consciousness: Law Talk in the Divorce Lawyer's Office." *Yale Law Journal* 98, no. 8 (1989): 1663–88.
Sarat, Austin, and Thomas R. Kearns, eds. *Law in Everyday Life.* Ann Arbor: University of Michigan Press, 1995.
Saumarez Smith, Richard. *Rule by Records: Land Registration and Village Custom in Early British Panjab.* Delhi: Oxford University Press, 1996.
Scott, David. "Colonial Governmentality." *Social Text,* no. 43 (1995): 191–220.
Scott, J. Barton, and Brannon D. Ingram. "What Is a Public? Notes from South Asia." *South Asia: Journal of South Asian Studies* 38, no. 8 (August 18, 2015): 357–70.
Scott, Joan Wallach. *The Politics of the Veil.* Princeton, NJ: Princeton University Press, 2007.
Sengoopta, Chandak. *Imprint of the Raj: How Fingerprinting Was Born in Colonial India.* London: Pan, 2003.
Sezgin, Yüksel. *Human Rights under State-Enforced Religious Family Laws in Israel, Egypt and India.* Cambridge, UK: Cambridge University Press, 2013.
Sezgin, Yüksel, and Mirjam Künkler. "Regulation of 'Religion' and the 'Religious': The Politics of Judicialization and Bureaucratization in India and Indonesia." *CSSH* 56, no. 2 (2014): 448–78.
Shafīʿ, Muḥammad. *Imdād-ul-Muftain,* Vol. 2 of *Fatāwá-yi Dār-ul-ʿUlūm Diyoband: Jild Duwum, Mabūb wa Mukammal.* Karachi: Dār-ul-Ishāʿat, 1976.
Shahar, Ido. "Legal Pluralism and the Study of Shariʿa Courts." *ILS* 15, no. 1 (2008): 112–41.
Sharafi, Mitra. *Law and Identity in Colonial South Asia: Parsi Legal Culture, 1772–1947.* New York: Cambridge University Press, 2014.

——. "The Marital Patchwork of Colonial South Asia: Forum Shopping from Britain to Baroda." *LHR* 28, no. 4 (November 2010): 979–1009.
——. "A New History of Colonial Lawyering: Likhovski and Legal Identities in the British Empire." *Law and Social Inquiry* 32, no. 4 (2007): 1059–94.
——. "The Semi-autonomous Judge in Colonial India: Chivalric Imperialism Meets Anglo-Islamic Dower and Divorce Law." *IESHR* 46, no. 1 (January 1, 2009): 57–81.
Sharma, Harish C. "Custom, Law and the Women in the Colonial Punjab." *Proceedings of the Indian History Congress* 62 (2001): 685–92.
Shodhan, Amrita. "The East India Company's Conquest of Assam, India, and 'Community' Justice: Panchayats/Mels in Translation." *Asian Journal of Law and Society* 2, no. 2 (November 2015): 357–77.
Siddiqui, Sohaira Z. "Triple Divorce and the Political Context of Islamic Law in India." *Journal of Islamic Law* 2, no. 1 (2021): 5–32.
Sikand, Yoginder. *Bastions of the Believers: Madrasas and Islamic Education in India*. Delhi: Penguin Books India, 2005.
Silbey, Susan S. "After Legal Consciousness." *Annual Review of Law and Social Science* 1, no. 1 (2005): 323–68.
——. "Legal Culture and Legal Consciousness." In *International Encyclopedia of the Social and Behavioral Sciences*, 2nd ed., edited by James D. Wright, 726–33. New York: Elsevier, 2015.
Singh, Anantdeep. "Women, Wealth, and Law: Anglo-Hindu and Anglo-Islamic Inheritance Law in British India." *South Asia: Journal of South Asian Studies* 40, no. 1 (2017): 40–53.
——. "Zamindars, Inheritance Law and the Spread of the Waqf in the United Provinces at the Turn of the Twentieth Century." *IESHR* 52, no. 4 (October 1, 2015): 501–32.
Singh, Charu. "Science and Its Publics in British India." In *The Routledge Handbook of Science and Empire*, edited by Andrew Gross, 218–27. London: Routledge, 2021.
Singha, Radhika. *A Despotism of Law: Crime and Justice in Early Colonial India*. New Delhi: Oxford University Press, 1998.
——. "The Great War and a 'Proper' Passport for the Colony: Border-Crossing in British India, c. 1882–1922." *IESHR* 50, no. 3 (2013): 289–315.
——. "Punished by Surveillance: Policing 'Dangerousness' in Colonial India, 1872–1918." *MAS* 49, no. 2 (March 2015): 241–69.
Skovgaard-Petersen, Jakob. *Defining Islam for the Egyptian State: Muftis and Fatwas of the Dār Al-Iftā*. Leiden: Brill, 1997.
Solanki, Gopika. *Adjudication in Religious Family Laws: Cultural Accommodation, Legal Pluralism, and Gender Equality in India*. New York: Cambridge University Press, 2011.
Solum, Lawrence. "Procedural Justice." *Southern California Law Review* 78, no. 18 (2004): 181–321.
Sriraman, Tarangini. *In Pursuit of Proof: A History of Identification Documents in India*. Delhi: Oxford University Press, 2018.

Stark, Ulrike. *An Empire of Books: The Naval Kishore Press and the Diffusion of the Printed Word in Colonial India*. Ranikhet, India: Permanent Black, 2007.
Starr, June, and Jane F. Collier, eds. *History and Power in the Study of Law: New Directions in Legal Anthropology*. Ithaca, NY: Cornell University Press, 1989.
Statistical Abstract Relating to British India from 1894–95 to 1903–04. Vol. 39. London: Her Majesty's Stationery Office, 1905.
Steingass, Francis Joseph. *A Comprehensive Persian-English Dictionary, Including the Arabic Words and Phrases to Be Met with in Persian Literature*. London: Routledge and K. Paul, 1892.
Stephens, Julia. *Governing Islam: Law, Empire, and Secularism in Modern South Asia*. New York: Cambridge University Press, 2018.
Stern, Philip J. *The Company-State: Corporate Sovereignty and the Early Modern Foundation of the British Empire in India*. New York: Oxford University Press, 2011.
Stewart, Neil. "Divide and Rule: British Policy in Indian History." *Science and Society* 15, no. 1 (1951): 49–57.
Stewart, Tony K. *Witness to Marvels: Sufism and Literary Imagination*. Oakland: University of California Press, 2019.
Stillmann, N. A. "K̲h̲ilʿa." In *Encyclopaedia of Islam*, 2nd ed., edited by P. Bearman, Th. Bianquis, C. E. Bosworth, E. van Donzel, and W. P. Heinrichs. Leiden: Brill, 2012. http://dx.doi.org/10.1163/1573-3912_islam_COM_0507.
Stokes, Eric. *The English Utilitarians and India*. Oxford: Clarendon, 1959.
Stokes, Whitley. *The Anglo-Indian Codes*. Vol. 2, *Adjective Law*. Oxford: Clarendon, 1887.
Strawson, John. "Islamic Law and English Texts." *Law and Critique* 6, no. 1 (1995): 21–38.
Sturman, Rachel. *The Government of Social Life in Colonial India: Liberalism, Religious Law, and Women's Rights*. New York: Cambridge University Press, 2012.
Subramanian, Narendra. *Nation and Family: Personal Law, Cultural Pluralism, and Gendered Citizenship in India*. Stanford, CA: Stanford University Press, 2014.
Suehiro, Akiko. "The Office of the Qazi in the Deccan: An Analysis of British Records." *Icfai University Journal of History and Culture* 2, no. 3 (2008): 77–88.
Sullivan, Winnifred Fallers. *The Impossibility of Religious Freedom*. Princeton, NJ: Princeton University Press, 2005.
Sun, Ivan Y., Yuning Wu, Rong Hu, and Ashley K. Farmer. "Procedural Justice, Legitimacy, and Public Cooperation with Police: Does Western Wisdom Hold in China?" *Journal of Research in Crime and Delinquency* 54, no. 4 (2017): 454–78.
Suneetha, A. "Muslim Women and Marriage Laws: Debating the Model Nikahnama." *Economic and Political Weekly* 47, no. 43 (2012): 40–48.
Syed Ahmed Bahadoor, C.S.I. on Dr. Hunter's "Our Indian Mussulmans—Are They Bound in Conscience to Rebel against the Queen?" Compiled by A Mahomedan. London: Henry S. King, 1872.
Tareen, SherAli K. *Defending Muḥammad in Modernity*. Notre Dame, IN: University of Notre Dame Press, 2020.

Taylor, Charles. *A Secular Age*. Cambridge, MA: Belknap Press, 2007.
Thomas, D. A. Lloyd. "Liberalism and Utilitarianism." *Ethics* 90, no. 3 (April 1, 1980): 319–34.
Thompson, Drew. "'Não Há Nada' ('There Is Nothing'): Absent Headshots and Identity Documents in Independent Mozambique." *Technology and Culture* 61, no. 2 (2020): S104–34.
Thurston, Alex. "Muslim Politics and Shari'a in Kano State, Northern Nigeria." *African Affairs* 114, no. 454 (2015): 28–51.
Ṭōnkī, Muftī Muḥammad ʿAbdullāh Ṣāḥib. *Majmūʿa-yi Fatāwá-yi Ṣābriya*. Lahore: Maṭbaʿ Faiẓī, 1907 CE (1325 AH).
Travers, Robert. *Ideology and Empire in Eighteenth Century India: The British in Bengal*. New York: Cambridge University Press, 2007.
Tschalaer, Mengia Hong. *Muslim Women's Quest for Justice: Gender, Law and Activism in India*. Cambridge, UK: Cambridge University Press, 2017.
Tupper, Charles Lewis. *Punjab Customary Law*. 5 vols. Calcutta: Office of the Superintendent of Government Printing, 1881.
Tyan, E., and Gy. Káldy-Nagy. "Ḳāḍī." In *Encyclopaedia of Islam, Second Edition*, edited by P. Bearman, Th. Bianquis, C. E. Bosworth, E. van Donzel, and W. P. Heinrichs. Leiden: Brill, 2012. http://dx.doi.org/10.1163/1573-3912_islam_COM_0410.
Tyan, E., and J. R. Walsh. "Fatwā." In *Encyclopaedia of Islam, Second Edition*, edited by P. Bearman, Th. Bianquis, C. E. Bosworth, E. van Donzel, and W. P. Heinrichs. Leiden: Brill, 2012. http://dx.doi.org/10.1163/1573-3912_islam_COM_0219.
Tyler, Tom R. "What Is Procedural Justice? Criteria Used by Citizens to Assess the Fairness of Legal Procedures." *LSR* 22, no. 1 (1988): 103–35.
ʿUṣmānī, ʿAzīz-ur-Raḥmān. *ʿAzīz-ul-Fatāwá*, Vol. 1 of *Fatāwá-yi Dār-ul-ʿUlūm Diyoband: Jild Awwal, Mabūb wa Mukammal*. Karachi: Dār-ul-Ishāʿat, 1976.
Van Voss, Lex Heerma, ed. *Petitions in Social History*. New York: Cambridge University Press, 2002.
Vatuk, Sylvia. "Extra-judicial *Khulʿ* Divorce in India's Muslim Personal Law." *ILS* 26, no. 1–2 (January 1, 2019): 111–48.
———. "Islamic Feminism in India: Indian Muslim Women Activists and the Reform of Muslim Personal Law." *MAS* 42, no. 2–3 (March 2008): 489–518.
———. *Marriage and Its Discontents: Women, Islam and the Law in India*. New Delhi: Kali for Women, 2017.
———. "Moving the Courts: Muslim Women and Personal Law." In *The Diversity of Muslim Women's Lives in India*, edited by Zoya Hasan and Ritu Menon, 18–58. New Brunswick, NJ: Rutgers University Press, 2005.
Vikør, Knut S. *Between God and the Sultan: A History of Islamic Law*. New York: Oxford University Press, 2006.
Vismann, Cornelia. *Files: Law and Media Technology*. Stanford, CA: Stanford University Press, 2008.
Wāṣif, Ḥafīẓ-ur-Raḥmān. "Dībācha." In Vol. 1, *Kifāyat-ul-Muftī: Yaʿnī Muftī-yi Aʿẓam Maulānā Kifāyatullāh kī Fatāwá*, edited by Ḥafīẓ-ur-Raḥmān Wāṣif, 6–13. Delhi: Kōh-i Nūr Prēs, 1971.

——. *Muftī-yi Aʿẓam kī Yād*. Delhi: Dilī Prinṭing Warks, 1967.
Welchman, Lynn. "Islamic Law: Stuck with the State?" In *Religion, Law and Tradition: Comparative Studies in Religious Law*, edited by Andrew Huxley, 61–83. London: Routledge, 2002.
Williams, Rina Verma. *Postcolonial Politics and Personal Laws: Colonial Legal Legacies and the Indian State*. New Delhi: Oxford University Press, 2006.
Worden, Robert E., and Sarah J. McLean. *Mirage of Police Reform: Procedural Justice and Police Legitimacy*. Oakland: University of California Press, 2017.
Yahaya, Nurfadzilah. *Fluid Jurisdictions: Colonial Law and Arabs in Southeast Asia*. Ithaca, NY: Cornell University Press, 2020.
Yang, Anand A. "Introduction: Issues and Themes in the Historical Study of Crime and Criminality: Passages to the Social History of British India." In *Crime and Criminality in British India*, edited by Anand A. Yang, 1–25. Tucson: University of Arizona, 1985.
Yannakakis, Yanna. *The Art of Being In-Between: Native Intermediaries, Indian Identity, and Local Rule in Colonial Oaxaca*. Durham, NC: Duke University Press, 2008.
——. "'Indios Ladinos': Indigenous Intermediaries and the Negotiation of Local Rule in Colonial Oaxaca, 1660–1769." PhD diss., University of Pennsylvania, 2003.
Yngvesson, Barbara. "Inventing Law in Local Settings: Rethinking Popular Legal Culture." *Yale Law Journal* 98, no. 8 (1989): 1689–709.
Young, Kathryne M. "Everyone Knows the Game: Legal Consciousness in the Hawaiian Cockfight." *LSR* 48, no. 3 (September 1, 2014): 499–530.
Zaman, Muhammad Qasim. *Ashraf ʿAli Thanawi: Islam in Modern South Asia*. Oxford: Oneworld, 2008.
——. "Evolving Conceptions of *Ijtihād* in Modern South Asia." *Islamic Studies* 49, no. 1 (2010): 5–36.
——. "Religious Education and the Rhetoric of Reform: The Madrasa in British India and Pakistan." *CSSH* 41, no. 2 (1999): 294–323.
——. *The Ulama in Contemporary Islam: Custodians of Change*. Princeton, NJ: Princeton University Press, 2010.
Zamindar, Vazira Fazila-Yacoobali. *The Long Partition and the Making of Modern South Asia: Refugees, Boundaries, Histories*. New York: Columbia University Press, 2007.
Zaret, David. *Origins of Democratic Culture: Printing, Petitions, and the Public Sphere in Early-Modern England*. Princeton, NJ: Princeton University Press, 2000.
Zhang, Ting. *Circulating the Code: Print Media and Legal Knowledge in Qing China*. Seattle: University of Washington Press, 2020.
Ziad, Waleed. "Mufti 'Iwāz and the 1816 'Disturbances at Bareilli': Inter-communal Moral Economy and Religious Authority in Rohilkhand." *Journal of Persianate Studies* 7, no. 2 (November 5, 2014): 189–218.

Index

decolonization, 15
decree (*farmān*), 34, 239
Deoband, dar-ul-ʿulum at 7, 129, 203, 204, 289n46; dar-ul-ifta at, 129, 185, 203, 228, 235–40, 289n46
dissent, 32–33, 37, 67, 113
Dissolution of Muslim Marriages Act (DMMA) of 1939, 17, 132, 161, 234–35, 237, 239, 245, 299n75, 312n57
divide-and-rule, 25, 260n15
divorce, 19, 205, 219, 234–36. *See also* fatwas (*fatāwá*); marriage; women; qazis; annulment or dissolution (*fasḵẖ*), 19, 158, 236; as category of personal law, 135, 193, 202, 85, 95–96, 97; delegated, 184–85; divorce decree (*ṭalāq-nāma*), 155–58, 175, 186–87, 188, 302n73, 302n79; fees for, 87; grounds for 161; judicial separation (*tafrīq*), 132, 161, 199, 215; male-initiated (*ṭalāq*), 152, 156, 158, 167; and muftis, 204; Parsi, 195; unilateral,105
dīwānī rights (rights to collect revenue), 15, 24–25, 34
doctrinal difference, 56, 75, 86, 116, 269n6. *See also* pamphlet wars; religious difference; sectarian differences
documentation. *See also* paperwork: copies of legal, 149, 153, 155–56, 178, 302n79; as expressions of legal knowledge, 148, 155, 157–58; forgery and authenticity, 155–56, 157–58; and interpretation, 160–62, 229–31; and language, 176, *177*; and law, 6, 160, 264n39, 297n51; marriage, 43, 166–72, *173*, 174–76, *177*, 178–79, 180, 181–89, 205, 300n16; and mustaftis, 142, 148, 155–63; post-independence, 225; and registration, 89, 94; and regulations, 43, 155–56; and seals, 35, 43, 74, 127, 129, 186, 189; and sharīʿa, 197; and stamps, 43, 60, 157, 169, 186, 189, 205, 208, 219, 225, 227, 229, 303n87, 306n22
dower (*mahr*). *See* marriage

Egypt, 258n36, 308n68
EIC (British East India Company). *See* Anglo-Indian legal system; appointments; colonial law; documentation; legal pluralism; petitions; religious legal pluralism; Specific Acts and Regulations
endowments (*waqf*), 35, 160–62, 228, 233, 298n69, 304n7
Enfield rifle cartridges, 110
English-language, 2, 60, 68, 180, 186, 207
equity jurisprudence, 211–12
everyday (concept), 2, 3–5, 8–9, 189. *See also* Certeau, Michel de
evidence. *See also* documentation; legal sources: from qazis and muftis, 228; from witnesses, 237–38; Islamic rules of, 218, 219, 239; uses of 210, 219

Family History Library, 259n50
family law, 4, 27–28, 201, 245, 296n33
Farangi Mahall. *See also* ʿAbd-ul-Hayy; and ʿAbd-ul-Hayy 7, 114, 123, 228; and dars-i nizami, 123, 290n61; ʿulama of 123
farmān (decree), 34, 239
Fatāwá-yi ʿĀlamgīrī, 68, 273n58
fatwa institute (*dār-ul-iftāʾ*). *See* specific institutes
fatwas (*fatāwá*), *141*, *143–45*. *See also* abstraction; documentation; marriage; mufti (*muftī*); paperwork; and affirmation, 127, 129–31, 292n85, 306n25; collections of, 11, 118–20, 122–25, 127, *128*, 129–30, 142, 164, 203–4, 289n41, 289n46, 291n83; and commerce, 229–33, 242, 311n42; and court fees, 228–29; and divorce, 156–57, 234–40, 297n60–n61, 298n62–n63, 302n73; and

Husain, Qazi (Ratnagiri), 62
Hussainoodeen (Ḥusain-ud-Dīn), 51
Hussin, Iza, 261n25
Hyatoolakhan (Ḥayāt Allāh Ḵẖān), 45–48, 63–66, 72–73, 272n39, n40–n41
Hyderabad State, 7, 11, 19, 64, 70, 124, 138–40, 149, 156, 159–161, 164, 183, 204, 223–24, 239
Hyderabad dar-ul-ifta, 7, 139–40, *141*, 142, *143–45*, 146–62, 163, 164, 208, 237, 242, 294n15. *See also* documentation; fatwas (*fatāwá*)
Hyderabad Endowments Regulation, 160

*iftā*ʾ (legal consultation), 9, 120, 122, 126, 136–37, 142, 146, 203
ijlās (also *jalsa*), 31, 37, 181, 185, 188
*ijmā*ʿ (consensus), 27–28, 261n29
ijtihād (reasoning), 27–28, 118, 131, 136
Imarat-i Shariah, 197
imperialism, 26–27. *See also* Anglo-Indian legal system; colonial law; Specific Acts and Regulations; effects of, 247; ideologies of, 25; and law, 104–5, 262n6; and policy, 102, 111; and qazis, 8, 32–33; and women, 278n11; and xenophobia, 27, 98
indentured labor, 104
Independence and Partition, 223–24, 240, 244
India, Republic of, 11, 246
Indian Constitution, 198, 225, 245
Indian Contract Act, 125, 208, 219, 244, 309n81
Indian Evidence Act, 125
Indian National Congress, 1–2, 195
Indian Penal Code, 110, 125, 202, 218, 224–25, 244, 287n4, 309n74
Indian soldiers, 110
Indian Trustees' Act (Act XXVII of 1866), 213
inheritance law, 52, 70–71, 207–14, 291n80, 304n7
Inoosbin (Yūnas bin) Ahmed (Qazi), 62–63
In Re: Halima Khatun v. Unknown, 213–14
Islamic jurisprudence (*fiqh*), 9. *See also specific schools of jurisprudence*: and appointments, 47; background on, 9, 12, 27, 118; and commerce, 231–32; and the courts, 83, 115, 211–12, 214–15, 276n91; and divorce, 161; and fatwas, 126, 135; and inheritance, 160, 207–209; and legislation, 27, 276n91; and muftis, 115, 117, 137–38, 146, 214, 220, 231
Islamic law. *See also* family law; legal pluralism; Muslim personal law; personal law; religious law; religious legal pluralism; religious personal law; sharīʿa: background on, 3–4, 8, 10–11, 13–15, 17–20, 41, 117, 119; control of, 5; and the courts, 20, 212, 216, 218, 220, 228, 232; and debate, 86, 113, 131, 133, 135; definition of, 3, 118; and documentation, 6, 155; interpreting, 118, 125, 201, 216, 281n62; and legislative intervention, 12, 29, 83–84, 93, 98, 197; modern, 5, 245–48; and nonstate participants, 2, 7, 9, 18–19, 106, 116–17, 140, 159, 164, 214, 218, 225–27, 241–42, 246–48; and ordinary people, 117, 225–27; precolonial, 261n25; and qazis, 11, 29, 85–86, 166, 169–70, 184; sources of, 211, 261n28, 294n1; and technology, 6; and women, 234
Islamic legal experts. *See* muftis (*muftīs*)
Islamic legal opinions. *See* fatwas (*fatāwá*)
Islamic legal publishing, 2–6, 12, 18, 85, 122–25, 138
Islamic scholars. *See* ʿulama
*istiftā*ʾ*s* (questions), 10, 136, 147

Jackson, E. (Judge), 89
Jafri Begam, 207–12, 221, 307n42

legal pluralism (cont.)
law: Anglo-Indian, 211; background on, 4, 13; and the courts, 85; and the EIC, 16, 26, 264n33; and fatwas, 233; and legislative intervention, 16–17, 26, 28–29, 84, 194, 197; limits of, 244; modern, 40, 80, 226, 243; precolonial, 259n62; and reform, 26, 56, 80; and scholarship, 265n54
legal procedure, 213–14; and problems with 235
legal substance. *See* substance and procedure
legislation. *See specific Acts and Regulations*
Legislative Council for the North-Western Provinces and Awadh, 207
lobbying, 74, 80, 84, 93, 98, 113. *See also* petitions
local council (*panchayat*; *ṣāliṣ*), 199–201, 235–36
local justice, 24–25, 28, 33
local law. *See also* local council: and arbitration, 232
Lootfoodeen, Qazi (Luṭf-ud-Dīn), 271n35
Lushington, E. H., 90

Macaulay, Thomas, 287n4
madad-i maʿāsh (subsistence grants), 35–36, 263n23
Madrasa ʿAin-ul-ʿIlm, 203
Madrasa ʿAliya Fatehpuri, 203
Madrasa Aminiya, 7, 142, 203–204, 242, 289n41, 289n46
Madrasa Dar-ul-ʿUlum Deoband. *See* Deoband
Madrasa Dar-ul-ʿUlum Nadwat-ul-ʿUlama. *See* Nadwat-ul-ʿUlama
Madrasa Jamiʿa Nizamiya. *See* Jamiʿa Nizamiya
madrasa networks, 117, 137, 203
Madras Code (1808): Regulation III of, 15; and changes to, 92
Madras government, 15; in relation to imperial legaislation, 94–96, 99
mafqūd-ul-k̲h̲abar (absentee husband), 132, 185, 188, 222, 239–41, 276n96, 313n68, 313n76
Mahimkur, Moohumud Syeed (Mahīmkar, Muḥammad Sayyid), 50–51
Mahmood, Syed (Judge), 199, 206–12, 214, 221, 306n26–n27, 307n42, 307n47
Mahmood, Tahir, 303n1
Mahometans, 26–27; *See also* Muslim; "A Plan for the Administration of Justice"
Majmūʿa-ul-Fatāwá (*Collection of Fatwas*), 116, 122–25, 127, 129, 133, 135, 290n66, 294n122
Majmūʿa-ul-Fatāwá-yi Ṣābriya, 127, *128*
Mak̲h̲zan-ush-Shuʿarā (*Treasury of Poets*), 44
Maliki school of jurisprudence, 132, 293n112
Manṣūrpūrī, Sulaimān, 289n42
Mantena, Karuna, 16
Maryam Bi, 222–25, 234–35, 237–38, 240–41, 244, 309n5
Markby, W. (Justice), 211–12, 214
marriage. *See also* divorce: and adultery, 24, 185, 202, 309n76; contract, 156, 161, 182, 222, 240, 246, 313n76; and dewar (*dēwar*), 152, 297n47; disputes, 75–79, 86, 148–53, 156–58, 161, 168–69, 199–200, 204–5, 218–20; dower (*mahr*), 91, 103, 150–51, 176, *177*, 178, 181–82, 187, 218, 301n46–n47, 303n84, 303n86, 309n80; fees, 86–87, 172, 271n36; and guardianship, 76, 86, 161, 172–73, *173*, 181; and Islamic law, 156–57, 297n57; and jurisdiction, 202; and the Kazis' Act, 85, 97, 165–70; legislation, 90–91, 93–98,

53–54; and Islamic jurisprudence, 220; and legislative intervention, 26–28, 73, 104–5, 193, 195, 197–98, 233, 260n3; modern, 19, 198, 247; and native law officers, 35; and ordinary people, 113, 116; and the Privy Council, 308n60; and the state, 4, 54, 90, 119, 187, 226–27; and textualism, 26–28, 81
The Personal Law of the Mahommedans (Syed Ameer Ali), 132
petitions. *See also* appointments; fatwas (*fatāwá);* lobbying: community, 84, 100; and income, 50; and the Kazis' Act, 99; and marriage, 77; and qazis, 13, 42–44, 47–53, 66, 72, 101, 282n72
physical offices (*daftars, dafātir*), 7. *See also specific institutes*
"A Plan for the Administration of Justice": background on the, 24–25, 260n2; and British imperialism, 25–28; as chronological marker, 15–16; Clause XXIII, 23; and dispute resolution, 28; interpretations of, 260n14, 261n31; and jural colonization, 27–28; legacy of, 28–29; and native law officers, 34–35; and political transformation, 194; and reference to religious groups (Mahometans, Gentoos), 23, 26–27; and religious legal pluralism, 17, 25–28, 37, 52, 197; and state administration, 28; and textualism, 27–28
postcolonial society, 4, 10–11, 33, 53, 80–81, 106, 112, 164, 225, 240–44
precolonial society, 6, 11, 14, 18, 27, 33, 37, 53, 202
print communications. *See* Islamic legal publishing; networks of exchange; technology
Privy Council in England, 88, 214, 308n60
procedure and substance. *See* substance and procedure
Prophet (Muḥammad), 8–9, 27–28, 118. *See also* sharīʿa
Provincial Court of Dewanee (*Mufaṣṣal Dīwānī ʿAdālat*), 24
Provincial Criminal Court (*Mufaṣṣal Faujdārī ʿAdālat*), 24
public sphere, 2, 85, 93, 115–16, 117, 119–20, 121, 129, 133, 135, 138, 247, 256n6, 277n122. *See also* technology
Pugh, L. P. E. (Justice), 213–14
Purkar, Muhammad Ibrahim, 76, 86

qazi court (*dār-ul-qaẓā*), 146, 203, 305n13
qazipan, 58, 270n12
qazis (*qāzīs*). *See also* appointments; dissent; documentation; marriage; Specific Acts and Regulations; Specific qazis: abolition of, 89–92, 95, 280n42; and adjudication, 38, 73–80, 83, 211–13, 215–16, 235, 240, 242, 262n11; and assistants (*na'ibs*), 87, 171, 175–76, *177*, 181, 185, 188, 303n88; and change, 54; community, 13, 34–35, 40, 84–85, 263n17, 264n31, 264n42; and competition, 54, 263n23; courtroom, 34–36, 264n31, 280n42; criticism of, 35, 105–6, 263n24, 264n27; definition of, 33, 261n1; and disputes, 114–15; and divorce, 167; education and examination of, 55–56, 59, 63, 69, 71274n36; and failure, 80; fees, 65, 86, *87*, 88, 175, 271n34, 278n14, 279n20, n35; and Hindus, 32; history of, 8, 14, 32, 258n36; and income, 25, 35–36, 39, 41–44, 50, 69–70, 74, 86, 263n15, 265n53, 266n64; and jurisdiction (*ʿamal-dārī*), 72, 85, 99, 146, 171, 199–203, 206, 275n74, 305n1; and land claims, 73, 101; and land grants (*waṭans*), 36, 54–55, 70–71, 270n11, 274n73; and marriage, 237; modern, 15, 224, 245; and muftis, 9–11, 240–42, 244; and the Muhammadan Marriages and Divorces Registration Act (Bengal Act I

qazis (*qāzīs*) (cont.)
of 1876), 94–96, 102–4, 282n78, 285n116; and religious noninterference, 28; restoring, 85, 96–97, 283n82; the role of, 8–9, 11, 14, 22, 28, 33–41, 44, 53, 62, 73, 85–86, 88–90, 94–97, 105, 165–68, 185, 200–202, 204, 263n21; and sectarian difference, 56, 75, 79, 86, 101, 132; transfers of, 71, 275n74, n75
qazi's office. See *dār-ul-qaẓā*
qiyās (analogy), 27–28
Queen's Proclamation of 1858, 15–17, 109–13, 194
Queen Victoria, 110, 286n1–n2
questions (*istiftāʾs*), 10, 136, 147, 164
Qurʾan (revealed text), 9, 26–28, 52, 121, 130, 149–51, 197, 207–8, 234, 261n28

Rabia Beebee (Rābiʿa Bībī), 50, 52
Raḥam Bībī, 204–5
Raikes, H. T. (Judge), 82, 89
Ramzan Mistri and Ors. v. Haji Zahur Hossein, 212
Razakars (Raẓākārs), 223–24, 238, 240
Razvi, Qasim, 224
reasoning (*ijtihad*), 27–28, 118, 131, 136
reform, 27–29, 37, 84–85, 101, 121–22, 138–39, 164, 170, 245–46, 313n4. *See also Specific Acts and Regulations*
registrars. *See* marriage
Regulation III of 1808 (Madras), 15–16, 89
Regulation XXVI of 1827 (Bombay), 15, 38–44, 58, 55, 60, *61*, 65, 75, 92, 276n91
Regulation XL of 1793 (Bengal), 38
Regulation XXXIX of 1793 (Bengal), 15–16, 38, 89
religion, definition of, 111–12, 117, 119, 226. *See also* secularism
Religious Affairs Department, 160–62, 298n69
religious difference, 15–16, 18, 28–29, 37, 54, 111–12, 115–16. *See also* doctrinal difference; pamphlet wars; sectarian differences
religious law. *See also* Hindu law; Islamic law; legal pluralism; Muslim personal law; personal law; religious legal pluralism; religious personal law: and British rule, 15–17, 165, 187, 222, 247; and community engagement, 47–48; and the courts, 115, 206, 214; and debates, 18, 117, 201; definition of, 28; and Hinduism, 26–27, 29; and legislation, 15–16, 23, 25–26, 28–29, 195, 198, 304n5; and marriage, 187–88; and nonstate solutions, 214, 310n20
religious legal pluralism, 16, 26, 28, 98, 111, 197, 264n33. *See also* Islamic law; legal pluralism; Muslim personal law; personal law; religious law; religious personal law
religious noninterference, 13, 28, 95, 97, 110–13, 197, 245
religious personal law: the application of, 54, 206; and the courts, 213, 221; and fatwas, 233; modern, 245; and "A Plan for the Administration of Justice," 26–28; and qazis, 189; and scholarship, 13, 113 (*See also* Islamic law; legal pluralism; Muslim personal law; personal law; religious law; religious legal pluralism); and the state, 13, 119, 189, 206, 227
Reports of the Selected Cases Decided by the Sudder Dewanee Adawlut for Bombay, 73
A Revised Edition of the Legislative Enactments of Ceylon, vol. 1, *103*, 105
Richardson, William (Judge), 214, 262n14
Riẓwī, Ḥaidar, 150–51
Robinson, Francis, 123
Rogay, Ghulam Ahmad, 76, 86
Rogay, M. A. (Muhammad Ali), 95, 269n115, 282n72
Roupell, N. A., 100

royal butchers (*sulṭānī qaṣṣāb*), 114–15
Russell, A. W., 280n42
Ruqaiya Bi, 161–62

Ṣadārat-ul-ʿĀliya (Noble Secretariat). *See* Hyderabad dar-ul-ifta
sadr amin (*ṣadr amīn*), 74–75
ṣadr dīwānī ʿadālat. See chief civil courts (*ṣadr dīwānī ʿadālat*)
ṣadr-uṣ-ṣudūr, 139–40, 239
ṣadr ʿadālat. See chief court (*ṣadr ʿadālat*)
Safdar, Muhammad, 63–67, 73, 271n28, 271n37, 272n44, 272nn40–41
Salar Jung I, 140
Salim bin Nasir (Ṣālim bin Nāṣir), 152–54
sanad (certificate of appointment), 30, 34, 42, 45, 58–59, *60–61,* 62, 79, 270n20. *See also* appointments
Sausse, Matthew (Chief Justice), 82, 88
Sayyid Ahmad. *See* Khan, Ahmad
Schacht, Joseph, 118
scholarship: and the everyday, 225; and factionalism, 290n57; and fatwas, 117, 125, 233, 292n85, 296n32; and the Hastings Plan, 25; and Hinduism, 26–27; law, 3, 26, 104, 113, 118, 208, 220, 261n24, 265n54, 294n1, 307n44, 311n27; and qazis, 8, 263n19; and secularism, 286n9, 287n13, 294n9; and technology, 121
schools of jurisprudence (*maẕāhib*). *See specific schools*
Shaikh Ahmad (Shaik̲h̲ Aḥmad), 263n17; background on, 30–31, 33, 53; and controversy, 45–48; petition of, 45–49, 72
sectarian differences, 48–49, 56, 74, 79, 114–15, 121, 196, 269n5, 290n57, 292n87. *See also* doctrinal difference; pamphlet wars; religious difference
secularism: and fatwas, 226–27, 229, 233; history of, 5, 257n22; and qazis, 33, 96, 98; and the Queen's Proclamation, 111–12; and reform, 120, 170, 245–46; and religious law, 4, 117, 119–20, 135, 189, 197–98, 201, 206; and scholarship, 257n22, 286n9, 287n13
Selections from the State Papers of the Governors-General of India (Forrest), 30
Shaboodeen (Shihāb-ud-Din), 62
Shafīʿ, Muḥammad (Mufti), 228–29
Shafiʿi school of jurisprudence, 9, 86, 132, 276n99
Shāh, Muḥammad, 204–6
Shah ʿAlam II (Emperor), 15
Shah Jahan Begum (Shāh Jahān Begum), 168–70, 174, 186
Shakespeare, William, 8
Shams-ud-Din, 62
Shariat Application Act. *See* Muslim Personal Law (Shariat) Application Act of 1937
sharīʿa. *See also* fatwas (*fatāwá*); muftis (*muftīs*); Prophet (Muhammad): application of, 15–17, 117, 194–96, 198, 218, 232, 310n20; courts (*ʿadalats*), 139, 142, 229; definition of, 3, 196; interpreting, 160, 197, 200–203, 246, 310n18; and Islamic legal discourse, 119–20, 288n37; and marriage, 150, 153, 200; and muftis, 9, 115; and qazis, 8, 202–3, 215; the role of, 119, 245–46, 288n36; and sanads, 60, *61,* 62; and the state, 4, 16, 27, 197–98, 242, 259n49
sharīʿat nishān (the emblem of shariʿa), 60, *61,* 62
sharīʿat panāh (the shelter of shariʿa), 60, *61,* 62
Shaster, 23, 26–27
shāstrīs, 34
Shaw, J. A., 58–59, 62–63, 66, 73–74
Shīʿa Islam, 101, 261n30, 276n99
Sierra Leone, 104
sign (*ʿalāmat*), 176, *177,* 178
Smith, Lionel, 45
Smith, Nicholas Hankey, 49–50

social history of law, 3, 5, 14, 113, 118–19, 133, 242, 288n25; and archives 11, 166; and chronology 16–18
South Africa, 104, 286n123
Sri Lanka, 11. *See also* Ceylon
stare decisis, 220. *See also* common law
Stephens, Julia, 196–97, 259n61, 260n3, 263n18, 287n16, 304n5
Story, Joseph, 211
Straight, Douglas, 209
Straits Settlements Ordinance (Ordinance No. 5 of 1880), 103–105, 285n118
subsistence grants (*madad-i maʿāsh*), 35–36, 294n1
substance and procedure: and the courts, 83, 155, 206, 210–11, 213–14, 219, 228–29, 307n42; and fatwas, 138, 155, 201, 220, 229; and marriage registration, 104; and Muslim personal law, 197, 201, 206, 210–11; and ordinary individuals, 20, 233–34; and procedural justice, 24–25, 211, 213, 307n44
Sufficiency of the Mufti (*Kifāyat-ul-Muftī*), 124, 203–4, 256n3, 290n46, 291n67, 305n6, 309n76
Sunna (the example of the Prophet Muhammad), 27–28, 121, 136, 149, 294n1
Sunni schools of jurisprudence, 27, 51, 75–76, 268n114, 276n99
Sutherland, James, 42

Tahir, Mahomed, 51
talfiq, 132, 293n112
talaq (*ṭalāq*). *See* divorce
taxes, 43–44, 216–17
Taylor on Evidence (Bacon), 88
technology. *See also* Islamic legal publishing: communications, 6, 116–17; and fatwas, 1–2, 7, 9–10, 120, 129–31, 152, 289n48, 290n53; and legal change, 1–3, 10, 18; and lithography, 121, *128*, 129, 133, 175, *180*, 292n90; print, 116, 121, 183, 189
testimony. *See also* documentation; evidence; 130,
textualism, 27–28, 68, 90, 97, 210–11. *See also* law books; Qurʾan (revealed text); Shaster
Thanwi, Ashraf ʿAli (Thānwī, Ashraf ʿAlī), 122, 204, 235–36, 293n112, 305n19. See also *Al-Ḥīlat al-Nājizah liʾl-Ḥalīlat al-ʿĀjiza*
The Administration of Justice in British India (Morley), 259n1
Tonki, ʿAbdullah, 205
Treasury of Poets *(Makhzan-ush-Shuʿarā)*, 44
Treaty of Allahabad, 15, 24
Treaty of Salbai, 41
Trinidad and Tobago, 104
trustee (*mutawalli*), 212–14
Trustees' and Mortgagees' Powers Act (Act XXVIII of 1866), 213
Tyabji, Badruddin, 212, 307n47

ʿ *ulama* (*ʿulamāʾ*, Islamic scholars), *xviii*, 7, 17, 121, 124, 200–201, 217, 223, 308n62, 308n66; and authority of, 216; and fatwas, 129–30, 132, 187; and law, 200–201. *See also specific institutions and scholars*
Uprising of 1857, 15, 85, 110, 119
Urdu language, 2, 123–24, *180*, 186
ʿUṣmānī, ʿAzīz-ur-Raḥmān, 130–31, 185

Waqf Board of the Religious Affairs Department, 160–62, 298n69
waqfs (endowments), 35, 160–62, 228, 233, 298n69, 304n7
Wāṣif, Ḥafīẓ-ur-Raḥmān, 124, 203–4, 289n46, 290n49, 291n67
Wathen, W. H., 268n105, 268n114
Weber, Max, 8
Willoughby, J.P., 42, 65

women: and colonial intervention, 85, 278n11; and access to law, and divorce, 75–76, 132, 160–61, 234, 236–40, 293n112; and fatwas, 159; and inheritance, 52, 71–72, 208; and the Kazis' Act of 1880, 85; and marriage, 43, 168–70, 173–74, 184–87, 202, 222–23, 314n10; and punishment, 46; and qazi appointments, 32, 69–72, 262n4; and sharīʿa, 195–96
Wood, Charles, 89
Woodcock, J. W., 69–71, 274n68
Young, Henry, 43–44
Yusuf, Muhammad (Yūsuf, Muḥammad), 122, 125

Zahir-un-Nisa (Zahīr-un-Nisāʾ), 235–37, 240–41
Zahur-ul-Hasan, 101
Zain-ul-ʿĀbidīn (Qazi of Bharuch), 41–42, 265n55
Zain-ul-ʿĀbidīn (Qazi of Meerut), 171, 181, 262n13, 265n55, 265n61, 300nn24–25, 301n57
zinā (adultery). *See* marriage

ISLAMIC CIVILIZATION AND MUSLIM NETWORKS

Elizabeth Lhost, *Everyday Islamic Law and the Making of Modern South Asia* (2022).

Scott Kugle, *Hajj to the Heart: Sufi Journeys across the Indian Ocean* (2021).

Michael Muhammad Knight, *Muhammad's Body: Baraka Networks and the Prophetic Assemblage* (2020).

Kelly A. Hammond, *China's Muslims and Japan's Empire: Centering Islam in World War II* (2020).

Zachary Valentine Wright, *Realizing Islam: The Tijaniyya in North Africa and the Eighteenth-Century Muslim World* (2020).

Alex Dika Seggerman, *Modernism on the Nile: Art in Egypt between the Islamic and the Contemporary* (2019).

Babak Rahimi and Peyman Eshaghi, *Muslim Pilgrimage in the Modern World* (2019).

Simon Wolfgang Fuchs, *In a Pure Muslim Land: Shiʿism between Pakistan and the Middle East* (2019).

Gary R. Bunt, *Hashtag Islam: How Cyber Islamic Environments Are Transforming Religious Authority* (2018).

Ahmad Dallal, *Islam without Europe: Traditions of Reform in Eighteenth-Century Islamic Thought* (2018).

Irfan Ahmad, *Religion as Critique: Islamic Critical Thinking from Mecca to the Marketplace* (2017).

Scott Kugle, *When Sun Meets Moon: Gender, Eros, and Ecstasy in Urdu Poetry* (2016).

Kishwar Rizvi, *The Transnational Mosque: Architecture, Historical Memory, and the Contemporary Middle East* (2015).

Ebrahim Moosa, *What Is a Madrasa?* (2015).

Bruce Lawrence, *Who Is Allah?* (2015).

Edward E. Curtis IV, *The Call of Bilal: Islam in the African Diaspora* (2014).

Sahar Amer, *What Is Veiling?* (2014).

Rudolph T. Ware III, *The Walking Qurʾan: Islamic Education, Embodied Knowledge, and History in West Africa* (2014).

Saʿdiyya Shaikh, *Sufi Narratives of Intimacy: Ibn ʿArabī, Gender, and Sexuality* (2012).

Karen G. Ruffle, *Gender, Sainthood, and Everyday Practice in South Asian Shiʿism* (2011).

Jonah Steinberg, *Ismaʿili Modern: Globalization and Identity in a Muslim Community* (2011).

Iftikhar Dadi, *Modernism and the Art of Muslim South Asia* (2010).

Gary R. Bunt, *iMuslims: Rewiring the House of Islam* (2009).

Fatemeh Keshavarz, *Jasmine and Stars: Reading More Than "Lolita" in Tehran* (2007).

Scott Kugle, *Sufis and Saints' Bodies: Mysticism, Corporeality, and Sacred Power in Islam* (2007).

Roxani Eleni Margariti, *Aden and the Indian Ocean Trade: 150 Years in the Life of a Medieval Arabian Port* (2007).

Sufia M. Uddin, *Constructing Bangladesh: Religion, Ethnicity, and Language in an Islamic Nation* (2006).

Omid Safi, *The Politics of Knowledge in Premodern Islam: Negotiating Ideology and Religious Inquiry* (2006).

Ebrahim Moosa, *Ghazālī and the Poetics of Imagination* (2005).

miriam cooke and Bruce B. Lawrence, eds., *Muslim Networks from Hajj to Hip Hop* (2005).

Carl W. Ernst, *Following Muhammad: Rethinking Islam in the Contemporary World* (2003).

CPSIA information can be obtained
at www.ICGtesting.com
Printed in the USA
LVHW110011210722
724041LV00007B/422

9 781469 668123

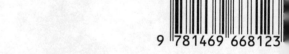